Prefaces to Shakespeare

Prefaces to
SHAKESPEARE

By Harley Granville-Barker

VOLUME II

Othello · Coriolanus
Romeo and Juliet
Julius Caesar
Love's Labour's Lost

PRINCETON, NEW JERSEY
PRINCETON UNIVERSITY PRESS

LCC 47-347
ISBN 0-691-01351-9 (paperback edition)
ISBN 0-691-06277-3 (hardcover edition)

First PRINCETON PAPERBACK printing, 1978

Publisher's Foreword

Because of the death of Harley Granville-Barker in Paris in August 1946, proof of this volume was not read by the author. The Preface to *Othello* was set from galley proof of the British edition, proofread by Mr. Granville-Barker before his death. The Preface to *Coriolanus* was set from the author's manuscript. The Prefaces to *Romeo and Juliet, Julius Cæsar* and *Love's Labour's Lost* are taken from the previously published British editions, with the exception of the analysis of the character of Cassius in *Julius Cæsar*, which the author reworked for this edition.

The manuscript of the Preface to *Coriolanus* was accompanied by the following note by Mr. Granville-Barker, dated March 1946:

"This Preface was first outlined in the form of lectures—the Alexander Lectures—given at University College, Toronto, in 1942. Let me thank Principal Wallace for his unbounded kindness to me on that occasion, his colleagues too. Professor Alexander himself was then still alive, and I found him among my audience; that also something not easily to be forgotten.

"For text I have used the (English) Arden edition, noting any departures from it and my reasons for them."

Contents

Contents

Prefaces to Shakespeare

Othello

SHAKESPEARE, as his habit was, took a ready-made story to work upon. It is as if, for a start, he feels a need to tie his exuberant imagination to something he can rank as fact. Cinthio's is a convincing story; its characters are clearly drawn, and it is, in its spare fashion, very well told. There was much to attract him in it: the romantic setting in Venice and Cyprus (he has never cared for commonplace backgrounds); the exotic figure of the Moor (of rarer stuff than Shylock), and the "Machiavellian" Ensign. It deals, moreover, with the degradation of love between man and woman, a subject in which about this time he was finding varied material, both for tragedy and for such so-called comedies as *Troilus and Cressida* and *Measure for Measure*. The story itself he by no means improves in the course of compressing it into drama; he omits, indeed, some of its most striking touches, and, towards its crux, so jeopardizes its very credibility that all his craftsman's skill is needed to save this from collapse. But he endows Cinthio's outlined characters with an extraordinary actuality and vitality; Desdemona and Emilia, Othello himself, Iago, Cassio, Roderigo and Bianca making a group in this respect unrivaled in the rest of his work. And he charges the sordid matter of his original with poetry to make it the high tragedy we know.

The Story and the Play

HE makes changes he could have avoided, but the purpose of them is clear. In the story Desdemona and the Moor—although she has married him against her parents' wish—have lived together in harmony and peace for some time. Shakespeare prefers an elopement for his starting point, since this gives an initial impetus to the action. He invents also the Cyprus war and its sudden crisis. Here is increased impetus, some evidence of Othello's soldiership, a background of notable event, and a pretext for transporting Desdemona to the isolation of a far island where she will be defenseless and he all-powerful. The Turks and their "mighty preparation" having served his purpose, he gets rid of them with a (dramatically) cynical ease. A "Third Gentleman's"

> News, lords! our wars are done.
> The desperate tempest hath so banged the Turks,
> That their designment halts. . . .

with Othello's as summary

> News, friends; our wars are done. The Turks are drowned. . . .

suffice. But it is not simply that he has no further use for them. They would be a positive hindrance to him now. For Iago must be set to work without more delay, and an Othello braced to action might prove intractable material. Jealousy thrives best in a stagnant soil.

The initial elopement must not be allowed to suggest a second tragedy of "violent delights" leading to "violent ends," for we are to have no such show of youthful folly. To prevent this the characters of Othello and Desdemona themselves are firmly outlined from the first; his austere dignity; the calm with which—mere girl that she is!—she faces the majestic Senate, confutes her father and wins her cause. And while Shakespeare cannot, without unduly slackening the play's action, produce the effect of the harmony and tranquillity of life in which the story discovers them, to replace this he sends them separately to Cyprus and, after bare escape with their lives—from the very tempest that so bangs the Turks, thus put to double use—reunites them in such an ecstasy of happiness that, cries Othello,

>   I fear,
> My soul hath her content so absolute,
> That not another comfort like to this
> Succeeds in unknown fate.

Among other changes, the Captain's wife disappears.[1] Three wives would be one too many. In her place—conjured out of a single phrase in the story concerning a courtesan he was about to visit—we have Bianca, whose frailty, with its affectations of virtue, is set both against Desdemona's innate chastity and Emilia's coarser honesty, the play's pattern of womanhood being thus varied and enlarged. And Bianca is put to appropriate use in the scene in which Othello, eavesdropping, takes what he hears of Cassio's light talk of her for further proof of Desdemona's guilt.

In the story the Ensign's wife ("a young, fair and virtuous lady; and being of Italian birth, she was much loved by Desdemona, who spent the greater part of every day with her"[2]) knows what is going forward, refuses all share in it, but dare not speak out for fear of him. For a combination of reasons Shakespeare cannot accept this. Such a theme demands elaboration and, elaborated, might prove engrossing, making the minor character the more interesting of the two. Nor could he well place an immobilized Emilia of this quality beside the passive Desdemona; he needs contrast here, not likeness. So he retains the intimacy, but changes the nature of it, makes them waiting-woman and mistress, and in every way contrasts them.[3] He contrasts his Emilia with Iago also; the growth of her loyal affection with his frigid treachery, her blindness to what is passing with his sharp wit.

To this end the episode of the handkerchief, as the story has it, is reshaped. The happy trait of the *"eccelentimente di mano,"* which lets the wicked Ensign himself filch the handkerchief from

---

[1] The Furness Variorum gives us five pages of footnotes upon Iago's description of Cassio in the first scene of the play as

a Florentine,
A fellow almost damned in a fair wife . . .

in face of the fact that Cassio, as it turns out, has no wife. But the explanation is surely simple enough. Shakespeare, when he wrote the line, meant to follow the story in this respect. Later, for good reasons, he changed his mind and gave Bianca to Cassio for a mistress instead, omitting, however, to alter the text of this first scene. And Cassio was "almost damned" because every fellow with a fair wife is, in Iago's estimation, a predestined cuckold.

[2] I quote, here and elsewhere, from the translation in the Furness Variorum.

[3] But Emilia is a waiting-gentlewoman. No rigid class-distinction is involved.

Desdemona's girdle, is sacrificed. Iago, instead, has, says Emilia,

> a hundred times
> Wooed me to steal it . . .

and, having at last picked it up, she gives it him and adds a covering lie to the fault. No more than this is left of the silent complicity of the story, though enough even so—coarse-grained as she is made, and for all Shakespeare's own dramatic *"eccelenti-mente di mano"*—to do some damage to Emilia's credit with us. The episode now serves as one more illustration of Iago's talent for using other hands to do his work for him. Roderigo, Cassio, Emilia, Bianca too; when he is in the vein they are his cat's-paws all. Not until, his affairs going awry, he gives Cassio that sword-slash in the dark, does he, we may remark, *do* one single thing himself. And even this, and even the subsequent stabbing of Roderigo, as will later appear, he bungles.

Again, the Captain in the story knows that the handkerchief he finds in his room is Desdemona's, and he attempts to return it to her; and, later, his wife is seen by the Moor at her window copying its embroidery, even as Bianca is asked to copy it. This goes well enough in a story. But clearly Cassio cannot be allowed to know. The play's close-knit action and its generalizing of location will make access to Desdemona seem easy, and his respect for her would never let him knowingly give her handkerchief to Bianca.

The Ensign's little daughter, whom Desdemona loves, is omitted. Iago as a fond father! Did Shakespeare feel that such a gem of irony might outshine the rest?

Roderigo is Shakespeare's invention. His gulling provides the shadow of an underplot, some comic relief—he makes a ridiculous counterpart to the nobler victim—and something more dramat-ically valuable than either. For, colorless himself, he is the mirror in which can be reflected an Iago that the stress of the main action will hardly let us see; cynically at his ease, ostentatiously base, yet meretricious even in this, and reckless too. Cinthio's Ensign—drawn like the rest in outline only, but firmly and precisely, without one false stroke—is patient, single-minded, veritably austere in his wickedness, and is victorious to the last, another story being needed to give him his deserts. But Iago must come by his within the compass of the play. And, for all his destructive cunning, here, from the beginning, is his own destruction implicit; in the cankering vanity, the innate malignity, crass appetite and mere itch to do evil, so vaingloriously displayed. It is in his coarse contempt for the "sick fool Roderigo" that his own fatal folly is visible from the first, and the more rapidly ripens.

The capital change, however, is that which converts the anonymous Moor into Othello, for with this it is that the whole brutal story is raised to the heights of tragedy. But, for all the gain, some loss is still involved. What, as Cinthio has it, could be better of its kind, after "the wicked Ensign" has resolved to wait patiently "until time and circumstance should open a path for him to engage in his foul project," than its unwitting opening by the Moor himself, who seeks and again and again questions the deprecatory villain, and waits in torture for the disclosure "which was to make him miserable to the end of his days," or than—while he is still convinced of her guilt—his demented grief for the murdered Desdemona and slowly gathering hatred of the man he had employed to murder her? But those lagging agonies, made so significant in the story—where also the very sparseness of the telling of them sets our imagination to work to fill the gaps— would provide too slack a mechanism altogether for Shakespeare's theater, with its primary need (in his eyes) for continuing and continuous action.

> Ay, that's the way;
> Dull not device by coldness and delay.

says Iago, when he has at last worked out his plan. And it is very much as if Shakespeare, with these dramatic drawbacks to the story in mind, were telling himself the same thing.

There is yet another capital difference between story and play. The story lacks all conflict. Cinthio's Moor is an ignorant, and— despite his bursts of rage—an unresisting victim throughout. The ignorance must be retained, or the plot, Iago's and the play's too, will collapse. Othello must be

> tenderly led by the nose
> As asses are.

By what replace, then, the conflict which in some sort seemingly all drama demands? Shakespeare gives us, between Iago and

Othello—as between Moor and Ensign Cinthio does not—and emphasizes from the first, radical and acute contrast of circumstance and character. In everything the two are opposed. Iago is a nobody and has his way to make, has an abundant conceit of himself and smarts under neglect; there, indeed, is the immediate spring of his villainy. Othello—while Cinthio's Moor was simply "*molto valoroso . . . per essere pio della persona*"—is of royal descent, although he has had the tactful modesty to conceal this so far from republican Venice. Again, while Desdemona in the story says to her husband, ". . . you Moors are of so hot a nature that every little trifle moves you to anger and revenge," Shakespeare gives us an Othello calm beneath Brabantio's threats and abuse, in the matter of Cassio's brawl of iron self-control, and against that he sets the gadfly Iago, impatient from the first to be stinging.[4]

The play is half through before the sting is planted, and the two characters have been developed meanwhile in no very close relation to each other. But when this becomes intimate, the contrast between them is progressively heightened until a species of conflict is created, not of action, since the story forbids that, but of the very essence of the men. And as this is distilled before us, ever more intensely—can two such elements in humanity, we are brought to asking, so opposed, peaceably partake for long one share of the world together? Is not conflict, victory and defeat innate and inevitable in what they *are*? For

> He has a daily beauty in his life
> That makes me ugly. . . .

That Iago says this, not of Othello, but of Cassio, says it incidentally, and that it somewhat belies, moreover, his diabolonian boastings, makes it none the less, but rather the more revealing. For of such intrinsic truths about themselves the most self-conscious men—and among these is Iago—will be the least

---

[4] One of the most remarkable things about Salvini's Othello—so I was told by William Poel, who saw and studied it—was the restraint in which he held himself until Iago's poison had begun to work in him. It made one think, said Poel, of a sleeping volcano. And when at last—and not till the play was half over—the passionate force in the man did begin to stir, the effect was terrific.

aware. Out they slip to pass unnoticed. And here is a better reason for his hatred of Othello—as we see it in action; and what Iago does is ever better evidence of the man than what he says— than all the vaunted "reasons" his intellectual vanity sets him seeking. His task demands a force beyond his braggart "wit." He finds this in the loosing of some need of his very being to reduce the nobility confronting him to baseness. He must, so instinct tells him, if he himself is to survive. Within a set arena great goodness and great wickedness cannot coexist for long; one must yield to the other, or the bounds of the arena be broken. There can be no compromise. Shakespeare gives us, then, in place of conflict of action, this conflict of being. The fortress of good, to which siege is laid, is defenselessly unaware of its own goodness, as true goodness is. We watch it falling, stone by stone.

But nobility must be brought even lower than the baseness which attacks it, if the triumph of evil is to be complete; and this dictates the culminating change from story to play. The Moor of the story stands callously by while the Ensign clubs Desdemona to death. That is horrible. But Othello is made to fall from his ideal heights to deeper damnation still, and to do the deed himself. How is this possible? Shakespeare sets himself the task—to which Iago's task inheres—of showing us, and convincingly, the process of the spiritual self-destruction which can make him capable of such a deed, to which his physical self-destruction after is the mere sequel. For, like all great tragedies, it is a tragedy of character. And it is epitomized at the end in the mockery of that one terrible paradox,

> O, thou Othello, that wert once so good, . . .
> What shall be said to thee?

That wert once so *good*!

> Why, anything;
> An honourable murderer, if you will. . . .

An honorable murderer! The soldier Othello saying it of himself. That was not within Cinthio's range.

The Shaping of the Play

Iᴛ has been often enough remarked that in the action of Othello there is, for Shakespeare, an unusually near approach to classic unity.[5] "Had the scene opened in Cyprus," says Johnson, "and the preceding incidents been occasionally related, there had been little wanting to a drama of the most exact and scrupulous regularity." But this (with due respect to Johnson) makes a misleading approach. There is no aiming at regularity and falling short of it. What unity there is—and it is very defective—is simply the outcome of an economy of treatment peculiar to the needs of the play. Unity of theme, that we have. As to unity of place; this is vaguely and implicitly established for several successive scenes within the bounds of Othello's residence. But Bianca and Roderigo—Bianca particularly—are most unlikely intruders there, where a while before Othello and Desdemona have been domestically disputing over the loss of the handkerchief. And time is given no unity of treatment at all; it is contracted and expanded like a concertina. For the play's opening and closing the time of the action is the time of its acting; and such an extent of "natural" time (so to call it) is unusual. But minutes stand for hours over the sighting, docking and discharging—with a storm raging, too!—of the three ships which have carried the characters to Cyprus; the entire night of Cassio's undoing passes uninterruptedly in the speaking space of four hundred lines: and we have, of course, Othello murdering Desdemona within twenty-four hours of the consummation of their marriage, when, if Shakespeare let us—or let Othello himself—pause to consider, she plainly *cannot* be guilty of adultery.[6]

Freedom with time is, of course, one of the recognized freedoms of Shakespeare's stage; he needs only to give his exercise of it the slightest dash of plausibility. But in the maturity of his art he learns how to draw dramatic profit from it. For this play's beginning he does not, as we have noted, contract time at all. Moreover, he allows seven hundred lines to the three first scenes

---

[5] *The Tempest*, however, makes a nearer one.

[6] Other explanations have been offered: one, that Othello is driven to suspect Desdemona of fornication with Cassio before her marriage. But this is frivolous.

when he could well have done their business in half the space or
less, could even, as Johnson suggests, have left it to be "occasionally
related" afterwards. The profit is made evident when later, by
contrast, we find him using contraction of time, and the heightening of tension so facilitated, to disguise the incongruities of the
action. He can do this more easily if he has already familiarized
us with the play's characters. And he has done that more easily
by presenting them to us in the unconstraint of uncontracted time,
asking us for no special effort of make-believe. Accepting what
they are, we shall the more readily accept what they do. It was
well, in particular, to make Iago familiarly lifelike. If his victims
are to believe in him, so, in another sense, must we. Hence the
profuse self-display to Roderigo. That there is as much lying as
truth in it is no matter. A man's lying, once we detect it, is as
eloquent of him as the truth.

The contraction of time for the arrival in Cyprus has its profitable dramatic purpose too. Shakespeare could have relegated the
business to hearsay. But the spectacular excitement, the suspense,
the ecstatic happiness of the reuniting of Othello and Desdemona,
give the action fresh stimulus and impetus and compensate for
the break in it occasioned by the voyage. Yet there must be no
dwelling upon this, which is still only prelude to the capital
events to come. For the same reason, the entire night of Cassio's
undoing passes with the uninterrupted speaking of four hundred
lines. It is no more than a sample of Iago's skill, so it must not
be lingered upon either. Amid the distracting variety of its
comings and goings we do not remark the contraction. As Iago
himself is let suggest to us:

> Pleasure and action make the hours seem short.

Then, upon the entrance of Cassio with his propitiatory *aubade*,
commences the sustained main stretch of the action, set to something more complex than a merely contracted, to a sort of ambiguous scheme of time, which is not only a profitable, but here,
for Shakespeare turning story into play, an almost necessary
device.[7] After which we have the long last scene set to "natural"

***

[7] To be examined more closely. See p. 24ff.

time, the play thus ending as it began. The swift-moving, close-packed action, fit product of Iago's ravening will, is over.

Enter Othello, and Desdemona in her bed.

—and, the dreadful deed done, all is done. And while the rest come and go about him:

Here is my journey's end. . . .

he says, at a standstill, and as in a very void of time. And as the "natural" time at the play's beginning let us learn the better what he was, so relaxation to it now lets us mark the more fully the wreck that remains.

THE SCENES IN VENICE

The three opening scenes move to a scheme of their own, in narrative and in the presentation of character. The first gives us a view of Iago which, if to be proved superficial, is yet a true one (for Shakespeare will never introduce a character misleadingly) and a sample of his double-dealing. Roderigo at the same time paints us a thick-lipped, lascivious Moor, which we discover in the second scene, with a slight stimulating shock of surprise at the sight of Othello himself, to have been merely a figment of his own jealous chagrin. There also we find quite another Iago: the modest, devoted, disciplined soldier, who, though in the trade of war he has slain men, holds it "very stuff o' the conscience to do no contrived murder," and "lacks iniquity" to do himself service. The third scene takes us to the Senate House, where Brabantio and his griefs, which have shrilly dominated the action so far, find weightier competition in the question of the war, and the State's need of Othello, whose heroic aspect is heightened by this. His dignity is next matched, in another kind, with Desdemona's. And again we receive that slight shock of surprise—so stimulating to our interest in a character—when the

maiden never bold;
Of spirit so still and quiet that her motion
Blushed at herself . . .

of Brabantio's piteous pleading proves, for all that, to be as resolute and unafraid. Here is the twinned, confident nobility which is to be brought low. And Iago, conspicuously silent throughout the scene (Othello's orders to him at its beginning and end make both him and his silence conspicuous), surveys the two, and may seem to be sizing up his task—which, a moment later, with the sniveling Roderigo for listener, he begins by re-sliming them with the foulness of his mind, as a snake will with its slime the prey to be swallowed.

The scenic mobility of Shakespeare's stage permits him up to this point to translate his narrative straightforwardly into action. We pass, that is to say, from Brabantio's house, which Desdemona has just quitted, to the Sagittary, where she and Othello are to be found, and from there to the Senate House, to which he and she (later) and Brabantio are summoned. And the movement itself is given dramatic value—by its quickening or slackening or abrupt arrest. We have the feverish impetus of Brabantio's torchlight pursuit; Othello's calm talk to Iago set in sequence and contrast to it; its encounter with the other current of the servants of the Duke upon their errand; the halt, the averted conflict; then the passing-on together of the two parties, in sobered but still hostile detachment, towards the Senate House.

Note also that such narrative as is needed of what has passed before the play begins is mainly postponed to the third of these opening scenes. By then we should be interested in the characters, and the more, therefore, in the narrative itself, which is, besides, given a dramatic value of its own by being framed as a cause pleaded before the Senate. Further, even while we listen to the rebutting of Brabantio's accusation of witchcraft by Othello's "round unvarnished tale" we shall be expecting Desdemona's appearance, the one important figure in this part of the story still to be seen. And this expectancy offsets the risk of the slackening of tension which reminiscent narrative must always involve.[8]

THE ARRIVAL IN CYPRUS

Shakespeare now breaks the continuity of the action: and such a clean break as this is with him unusual. He has to transport his characters to Cyprus. The next scene takes place there. An un-

---

[8] Emilia—who is *not*, as stage usage will have it, among Desdemona's attendants; why should she be?—only acquires importance much later.

measured interval of time is suggested, and no scene on shipboard
or the like has been provided for a link, nor are any of the
events of the voyage recounted. The tempest which drowns the
Turks, and rids him of his now superfluous war, and has more
thrillingly come near besides to drowning the separated Othello
and Desdemona—something of this he does contrive to present
to us; and we are plunged into it as we were into the crisis of the
play's opening:

> What from the cape can you discern at sea?
> Nothing at all. It is a high-wrought flood;
> I cannot, 'twixt the heaven and the main,
> Descry a sail.

—a second start as strenuous as the first. The excitement offsets
the breaking of the continuity. And the compression of the
events, of the storm and the triple landing, then the resolution of
the fears for Othello's safety into the happiness of the reuniting
of the two—the bringing of all this within the space of a few
minutes' acting raises tension to a high pitch and holds it there.

Shakespeare prescriptively makes his storm out of poetry,
expands Montano's more or less matter-of-fact

> A fuller blast ne'er shook our battlements:
> If it hath ruffianed so upon the sea,
> What ribs of oak, when mountains melt on them,
> Can hold the mortise?

into the melodious hyperbole of the Second Gentleman's

> For do but stand upon the foaming shore,
> The chiding billow seems to pelt the clouds;
> The wind-shaked surge, with high and monstrous main,
> Seems to cast water on the burning bear,
> And quench the guards of the ever-fixed pole.

descending, however, for Cassio's arrival, and the news he brings,
to simpler speech; although the verse with its compelling rhythm
—touched, to keep the whole in key, with such an occasional
richness of phrase as that which ends Montano's call to the rest
to come and scan the sea for a sight of Othello's ship,

> Even till we make the main, and the aerial blue,
> An indistinct regard.

—this is retained. And it lifts again to hyperbole in Cassio's mouth, yet, be it noted, to a quite different tune, for the celebrating of Desdemona's safety:

> Tempests themselves, high seas, and howling winds,
> The guttered rocks, and congregated sands—
> Traitors ensteeped to clog the guiltless keel,
> And having sense of beauty, do omit
> Their mortal natures, letting go safely by
> The divine Desdemona.

and of his hopes for Othello's:

> Great Jove, Othello guard,
> And swell his sail with thine own powerful breath,
> That he may bless this bay with his tall ship. . . .

The scene-painting ends here; for Iago, Desdemona and Emilia appear, and Shakespeare concentrates upon character in action again. Yet these last lines have not been merely decorative. Cassio's fealty to Othello, and his reverence for Desdemona sound in them; points pertinent both to the man and the story. And if treacherous Nature may have spared her for her beauty's sake, we are warned the next instant by the sight of her

> in the conduct of the bold Iago . . .

that man's treachery will not.

The scene's vehemence abates. The storm is forgotten. The verse, deflated of metaphor, flows easily along; and its ease and simplicity benefit Desdemona's own dignity in simplicity and her courageous outward calm. As fittingly, when Iago asserts himself, the verse fractures and disintegrates, after a little, into prose.

But Othello's own safety, still in question, is too important in the story to be left for more postscriptory treatment. So Shakespeare now stimulates suspense by giving no less than a ninety-line stretch of the scene to showing us Desdemona's silent anxiety, which he frames, for emphasis, by contrast, in a bout of artificially comic distraction. The clue to his intention lies in her

> I am not merry; but I do beguile
> The thing I am, by seeming otherwise.

Our attention is centered on her. The chatter and the laughter—hers in forced accord with the rest—and Iago's scurril rhyming are but an incongruous accompaniment to her mutely eloquent fears; and they do not—this we see—by any means beguile her from them. Once the surface of the merriment is pierced by the long-repressed escaping

> There's one gone to the harbour?

the sharpness of its anxiety measurable by the comprehending Cassio's kindly reassuring

> Ay, madam.

The idle diffuseness of the dialogue, too, by contrast with its recent compression, of itself helps interpret her sense of how time lags while she waits for news.

Iago emerges from the picture (the action must be thought of in terms of Shakespeare's stage[9]) for his malignly vigilant soliloquy:

> He takes her by the palm. Ay, well said, whisper; with as little a web as this, will I ensnare so great a fly as Cassio. . . .

and her share in the scene is reduced to illustrative dumb show; but since she is the subject of the soliloquy she still will hold our attention. The scene's action is here momentarily split, so to speak, into two, its force isolated in the menacingly prominent figure of Iago. Upon his dry explicatory prose the brilliant interruption of the *Trumpet within* tells the more startlingly. Then, with his, Cassio's and Desdemona's combined swift response:

> The Moor! I know his trumpet.
> 'Tis truly so.
> Let's meet him, and receive him.
> Lo, where he comes!

—the whole coheres again, and leaps, unconstrained, to life and movement.

The suspense is over, the tension relaxes. Othello appears; and after the

> O, my fair warrior!
> My dear Othello!

---

[9] For his soliloquy he will advance to the front of the main stage; Desdemona and the rest will go towards or into the inner stage, the pictorial effect being of a fully rounded statue placed before a bas-relief.

of their reuniting, comes the nobly fulfilling music of

> It gives me wonder, great as my content,
> To see you here before me. O my soul's joy!
> If after every tempest come such calms,
> May the winds blow till they have wakened death!
> And let the labouring bark climb hills of seas,
> Olympus-high; and duck again as low
> As hell's from heaven! . . .

Here is the scene's third and superlative use of the imagery of the sea. It recalls, too, Desdemona's earlier

> downright violence and storm of fortunes . . .

They have come through both; but only, as we already know—and there is Iago surveying them to remind us of it—into a more treacherous calm. Othello's sequent

> If it were now to die,
> 'Twere now to be most happy; for, I fear,
> My soul hath her content so absolute,
> That not another comfort like to this
> Succeeds in unknown fate.

gives us the already aging, disillusioned man: Desdemona, in her youthfulness, is confident for happiness:

> The heavens forbid
> But that our loves and comforts should increase,
> Even as our days do grow!

And he, inarticulately possessed by love for her, shuts out all but that with a thankful "Amen." For a last minatory jar to the harmony we have the low snarl of Iago's

> O, y'are well tuned now!
> But I'll set down the pegs that make this music,
> As honest as I am.

—and the preparation of the tragedy is complete.[10]

~~~~~~~~~

[10] Note that if the editors in general are right—and hardly disputably they are—to follow the lineation of the Quartos, with its

> That e'er our hearts shall make.
> O you are well tuned now. . . .

then the scansion dictates this dovetailed and much elided "O, y'are . . ." and the unescapable snarl in it.

IAGO COMPASSES CASSIO'S DOWNFALL

Iago sets to work without delay; and for long to come now he will seldom be absent from the scene, since, fittingly, the action is centered on him, woven round him, even as he himself, spider-like, weaves its plot. But the attempt upon Othello will be no trifling matter, and Shakespeare lets us see him proving his quality first upon lesser and less dangerous game. His vague plan "engendered" in Venice—

> After some time, to abuse Othello's ear . . .

with scandal about Cassio and Desdemona—is consequently now shaped for a start to a prompter disgrace of Cassio, to an immediate profit by that;

> To get his place . . .

—so much to go on with!

We have sampled his protean gifts already with the transforming of the raucous cloaked figure beneath Brabantio's balcony into the frank, conscientious soldier, this again into Roderigo's coolly sceptic mentor in vice. From which nearest seeming semblance of himself it is that he now starts again, to turn, even more easily, jolly companion with Cassio, then moralist with Montano, before Othello to be once more the loyal soldier, and so on and so forth—swift to respond to the occasion's demand on him. He buys his way ahead with unstinted false coin. But the display is divided by soliloquies in which his naked mind can be seen and the course he is steering shown us, and, since he steers from point to point only, by no less than four.

Roderigo is to be his instrument; and upon the instructions which emerge from the web of words he habitually weaves about this feeblest of his victims—

> Watch you to-night; for the command, I'll lay't upon you. . . .
> do you find some occasion to anger Cassio, either by speaking too loud, or tainting his discipline; or from what other course you please. . . . Sir, he is rash and very sudden in choler; and, haply, with his truncheon may strike at you. Provoke him, that he may. . . .

—upon this precise priming of our expectation Shakespeare can afford the halt in the action of the Herald's proclamation.

Othello 19

The proclamation in itself serves several subsidiary purposes. It helps settle the characters in Cyprus. The chances and excitements of the arrival are over. Othello is in command; but the war is over too, and he only needs bid the people rejoice at peace and his happy marriage. It economically sketches us a background for Cassio's ill-fated carouse. It allows a small breathing-space before Iago definitely gets to work. It "neutralizes" the action for a moment (a Herald is an anonymous voice; he has no individuality), suspends its interest without breaking its continuity. Also it brings its present timelessness to an end; events are given a clock to move by, and with that take on a certain urgency.[11]

Now comes

Enter Othello, Desdemona, Cassio, and Attendants.

The *Attendants*, which is the Folio's addition, add a touch of ceremony to this brief passage across the stage. But while it is no more, the few lines it allows for, with their easy cadence—

> Good Michael, look you to the guard to-night:
> Let's teach ourselves that honourable stop,
> Not to outsport discretion.

—are economically made to speak of the effortless discipline which shows the good soldier in Othello, of his own temperance and self-discipline, of his affection too, as they flow on, for Cassio; "Michael" twice over. Shakespeare sounds the quiet note of the normal while he may; the strenuous action to come will tell the better against it.

Upon Othello's verse and the melodious echo of its final rhymed couplet impinges Iago's brisk prose, and his gross talk of

---

[11] But a clock whose hands move to order, so to speak. The Herald refers to "this present hour of five." A dozen lines later Iago says, " 'Tis not yet ten o' th' clock." Modern editors isolate the Herald's speech as a separate scene; and the cleared stage before and after it justifies this, and overcomes—over-overcomes, one may say—the incongruity of the leap in time. The Quartos, as usual, make no such indications. The stage is twice cleared, in fact; the effect is made. What need in print to call attention to the matter? It is only worth remarking that the editor of the Folio, inserting scene-divisions, establishes one before the speech, where no incongruity of time is in question, but not after, when, if the point could have troubled him, it is.

Desdemona strikes a yet more flagrant contrast to the uncalculated dignity of the little wedding procession we have seen pass by. Cassio in his devout admiration of her—the more incredible, by these repeated signs of it, any notion of their adultery!—is coldly unresponsive, would positively protest (we may feel, and the actor can indicate) but for his manly reluctance—upon which Iago impishly plays—to be branded Puritan. It is a like shame-facedness, a dearly-to-be-requited dash of petty moral cowardice, which betrays him a moment later in the matter of the "brace of Cyprus gallants" and "the stoup of wine."

The technical utility of Iago's sixteen-line soliloquy, which fills the gap between Cassio's departure to "call them in" and his return with them and Montano, is to allow time for the "rouse" which will bring him back a step or so advanced in tipsiness already. For, since we are to have his repentance set out at length, we do not need to see the full process of his undoing besides. Shakespeare may seem to be short of pertinent material here. We are told that the feeble Roderigo has been fortified for his provoca-tive task with a little Dutch courage too; this apart, no more than within a minute, we shall see for ourselves. But the soliloquy brings us at this ripe instant into naked touch again with Iago's quick, confident mind. And, cast for speed and impetus (by contrast with the surrounding prose) in easily flowing verse, with its final couplet—

> If consequence do but approve my dream,
> My boat sails freely, both with wind and stream.

—it whips up the scene to the spirited pitch at which Cassio's exuberantly hilarious

> Fore God, they have given me a rouse already.

is to capture it.

A tavern would, of course, be the suitable place for the carouse which follows, and the action could quite easily be transported there. But Shakespeare prefers to concentrate it all in this convenient nowhere in particular, so that it may come and go around Iago, its General in Command—who need not, therefore, now, nor for the rest of the long scene, quit the stage, nor have to relax his hold on it or us, until this battle is won and his next planned. The essentials of a tavern are as easily transported here; and a joke about the English being "most potent in potting" and a couple of ditties "learned in England" will—with an English audience—assure the illusion.

There is an edge to the foolery. As Cassio grows ridiculous in his cups Iago covertly mocks him, fanning his own jealous enmity too, with repetition of the respectful "lieutenant," "good lieutenant" (for how little longer will he need to call him so!), luring him to the jocular patronage of

> the lieutenant is to be saved before the ancient. . . . this is
> my ancient. . . .

—more food for enmity there! This flares out with Montano for one incautious moment in the contemptuous

> You see this fellow, that is gone before. . . .

flung after his "good lieutenant's" unsteady departure to set the watch, to be as quickly masked again, however, beneath kindly, comradely—but how poisonously seasoned!—reprobation:

> He is a soldier fit to stand by Cæsar
> And give direction; and do but see his vice. . . .

Another drop here into somewhat laden verse lends the passage sententious gravity; and the artless Montano is prompt to respond. For a signal of what is now imminent, Roderigo, drifting tipsily into the scene, is shot off upon his errand, is here and is gone— so swift can Iago be at a crisis—while Montano takes breath between sentences. And in another minute the mine has been sprung, and riot is afoot, with Montano also, by brilliant after-thought, involved.

Amid clamor and clangor, shouts, swords and the "dreadful bell" outtopping all, Othello appears, attended as before—by *Gentlemen with weapons*, say the Quartos; this helps depict him ruler of Cyprus. It is the second time that, by a word or so, he, the soldier, stops, not forwards, a fight. Calm restored, he begins his sternly quiet questioning: first of Iago, who looks "dead with grieving," and so is plainly a witness, not a partaker, yet answers the "Who began this?" with a frank "I do not know"—leaving the culprits scope to damnify themselves the more; next of Cassio, too shamed to speak; then of Montano, disabled by his wound. Then it is Iago's turn again, and he has only—how conveniently!—to speak the truth. He gives it convincing clarity and circumstance, falsifies it ever so slightly. It is not the whole truth, that is all. Othello's sentence follows:

> I know, Iago,
> Thy honesty and love doth mince this matter,
> Making it light to Cassio—Cassio, I love thee;
> But never more be officer of mine.

Its place in the story besides, the episode serves the unfolding of his character. Here is the heroic calm still, but with a dangerous stirring beneath:

> Now, by heaven,
> My blood begins my safer guides to rule;
> And passion, having my best judgment collied,
> Assays to lead the way. . . .

Iago and the broken Cassio are left alone. There is a moment's silence (marked after the tumult and the coming and going of guards and onlookers) while Iago quizzically surveys his handiwork. No stage direction is needed to indicate this. It is written into the text, with its breaking by the feline

> What, are you hurt, lieutenant?

—he still, most considerately, calls him "lieutenant."

There is nothing of the tragic hero in Cassio. He is as human in his repentance as in his folly, somewhat ridiculous—most enjoyably so to Iago—in the facility of his despair and the amplitude of his self-reproach, in such hyperbole as

> O thou invisible spirit of wine, if thou hast no name to be known by, let us call thee devil.

Iago, making sure by one shrewd question that his own tracks are covered, lets all this wear itself out; then, "in the sincerity of love and honest kindness," gives him the fatal advice, gratefully accepted, to importune Desdemona to plead for him with Othello, and, not omitting another cryptically ironic "lieutenant" or two, sends him away somewhat comforted. He has steered back to the main lines of his plan:

> After some time, to abuse Othello's ear . . .

with means now provided.

The soliloquy which follows:

> And what's he then that says I play the villain? . . .

is a nodal point in the play, and it adds an essential to the viability of Iago's character. Until now he has been self-seeking; and Cassio's lieutenancy is surely in sight. But how will Desdemona's ruin profit him? It is evil for its own sake that he starts pursuing now; and out of her very goodness he will

> make the net
> That shall enmesh them all.

—with which enrichment of wickedness opens a darker depth of tragedy by far.[12]

Here too would plainly be a striking finish to this long scene. But Shakespeare provides Iago instead with another exhilarating bout with Roderigo, who returns sobered—he also—by his beating, crestfallen and peevish. A few platitudes appease him. Iago has no further use for him; he has served his turn. But the despised little nincompoop will trip up his betrayer yet. That is the significance of his reappearance. He is dispatched to billet and bed. Iago, we note, needs no rest. The sun is rising. He also departs, briskly confident of adding to a good night's work a better day's.

THE ATTACK UPON OTHELLO

For relaxation before the tense main business of the tragedy begins we next have Cassio in the early morning bringing musicians to play beneath Othello's window (a pleasant custom, and here what delicate amends!), to this being added the grosser, conventional japes of the Clown. The few minutes so spent are offset by the unexpectedly close knitting of the main action when this begins again. For Iago finds no need to "set on" his wife to

> move for Cassio to her mistress . . .

Cassio having saved him thus much trouble by making bold (he is sadly humbled, so to appeal to the waiting-gentlewoman) to send in to her himself. And she comes to report that Desdemona,

---

[12] This soliloquy is more fully discussed in the section on the play's characters, p. 105.

unasked, is already speaking for him "stoutly." The economical compression strengthens the tension of the scene, and the fortuitous furthering of Iago's ends bodingly suggests to us besides that the luck is with him.

For two last strokes of preparation we have Cassio, with the weak man's impatience, bent on importuning Desdemona to do for him what he has been told she is doing already, begging Emilia to gain him the

> advantage of some brief discourse . . .

with her alone, and a passing sight of Othello, at his general's task, Iago beside him, effectively promoted lieutenant already.

Then we see Cassio with Desdemona; but not alone. Emilia is there, it is before Emilia that she promises to help him. Upon them, after a—for us—expectant minute or so comes Othello. Iago has not, needless to say, drawn him "out of the way" as he told Cassio he would, but back here to find the two; Emilia's unexpected presence, he can show, a slight vexation to him. And it is in the midst of these indeterminate comings and goings that his muttered

> Ha! I like not that.

so effectively sows the seed—this tiniest of seeds—of tragedy.

The Ambiguity in Time: A Parenthesis

IT is from this point, too, that the action passes into the ambiguity of time which has troubled so many critics. Compression of time, by one means or another, is common form in drama, and we have just seen it put to use in the speeding through a single unbroken scene of the whole night of Cassio's betrayal. But now comes—if we are examining the craft of the play—something more complex. When it is acted we notice nothing unusual, and neither story nor characters appear false in retrospect. It is as with the perspective of a picture, painted to be seen from a certain standpoint. Picture and play can be enjoyed and much of their art appreciated with no knowledge of how the effect is gained. But the student needs to know.

We have reached the morrow of the arrival in Cyprus and of

the consummation of the marriage. This is plain. It is morning. By the coming midnight or a little later Othello will have murdered Desdemona and killed himself. To that measure of time, as plainly demonstrated, the rest of the play's action will move. It comprises no more than seven scenes. From this early hour we pass without interval—the clock no more than customarily speeded—to midday dinner-time and past it.[18] Then comes a break in the action (an empty stage; one scene ended, another beginning), which, however, can only allow for a quite inconsiderable interval of time, to judge, early in the following scene, by Desdemona's "Where should I lose that handkerchief, Emilia?" —the handkerchief which we have recently seen Emilia retrieve and pass to Iago. And later in this scene Cassio gives it to Bianca, who begs that she may see him "soon at night." Then comes another break in the action. But, again, it can involve no long interval of time; since in the scene following Bianca speaks of the handkerchief given her "even now." Later in the scene Lodovico, suddenly come from Venice, is asked by Othello to supper; and between Cassio and Bianca there has been more talk of "tonight" and "supper." Another break in the action; but, again, little or no passing of time can be involved, since midway through the next scene the trumpets sound to supper, and Iago closes it with

It is now high supper-time and the night grows to waste. . . .

The following scene opens with Othello, Desdemona and Lodovico coming from supper, with Othello's command to Desdemona:

Get you to bed on the instant. . . .

and ends with her good-night to Emilia. The scene after—of the ambush for Cassio—we have been explicitly told is to be made by Iago to "fall out between twelve and one," and it is, we find, pitch dark, and the town is silent. And from here Othello and Emilia patently go straight to play their parts in the last scene of all, he first, she later, as quickly as she can speed.[14]

---

[18] Midday is not specified, but it was the usual dinner hour.

[14] The suggestion is, moreover, that in point of time, these two last scenes overlap; and, since the scene of Cassio's ambush moves so swiftly and that of Desde-

These, then, are the events of a single day; and Shakespeare is at unusual pains to make this clear, by the devices of the morning music, dinner-time, supper-time and the midnight dark, and their linking together by the action itself and reference after reference in the dialogue. Nor need we have any doubt of his reasons for this. Only by thus precipitating the action can it be made both effective in the terms of his stagecraft and convincing. If Othello were left time for reflection or the questioning of anyone but Iago, would not the whole flimsy fraud that is practiced on him collapse?

But this granted, are they convincing as the events of that particular day, the very morrow of the reunion and of the consummation of the marriage?[15] Plainly they will not be; and before long Shakespeare has begun to imply that we are weeks or months—or it might be a year or more—away from anything of the sort.

> What sense had I of her stolen hours of lust?
> I saw it not, thought it not; it harmed not me;
> I slept the next night well, was free and merry;
> I found not Cassio's kisses on her lips. . . .

mona's murder, to begin with, so slowly, this suggestion can be brought home to the audience. Quite early in the first of the two we have Othello's

> Strumpet, I come! . . .

And, during the scuffling and confusion, the stabbing of Roderigo, Bianca's bewailings, Emilia's scoldings, he is already—and the precipitancy of his departure will have implied it—with Desdemona and about his deadly work. By the scene's end, therefore, and Iago's

> Emilia, run you to the citadel. . . .

(which we shall not have forgotten when we hear her next knocking at the bedroom door) it is too late.

[15] Determination to find a possible gap in the action by which Iago's attack on Othello is entirely postponed by some weeks or months can only be rewarded by doing violence to the slight break in continuity between Emilia's offer to conduct Cassio to Desdemona with a "Pray you, come in," and Desdemona's reception of him with the

> Be then assured, good Cassio, I will do
> All my abilities in thy behalf.

And nothing can be plainer, by Elizabethan stagecraft, than a (thus much interrupted) passage here from outer stage to inner, with Othello's passage across the outer stage—

> These letters give, Iago, to the pilot. . . .
> This fortification, gentlemen, shall we see't?

—for a connecting link.

That is evidence enough, but a variety of other implications go to confirm it; Iago's

> I lay with Cassio lately. . . .

Cassio's reference to his "former suit," Bianca's reproach to him

> What, keep a week away? seven days and nights?
> Eight score eight hours? . . .

More pointedly yet, Lodovico's arrival from Venice with the mandate of recall, the war being over—by every assumption of the sort, indeed, Othello and Desdemona and the rest are living the life of Cinthio's episodic story, not at the forced pace of Shakespeare's play. But he wants to make the best of both these calendars; and, in his confident, reckless, dexterous way, he contrives to do so.

Why, however, does he neglect the obvious and simple course of allowing a likely lapse of time between the night of Cassio's disgrace and the priming of Othello to suspect Desdemona and her kindness to him—for which common sense, both our own, and, we might suppose, Iago's, cries out? The answer is that there has been one such break in the action already, forced on him by the voyage to Cyprus, and he must avoid another.

The bare Elizabethan stage bred a panoramic form of drama; the story straightforwardly unfolded, as many as possible of its incidents presented, narrative supplying the antecedents and filling the gaps. Its only resources of any value are the action itself and the speech, and the whole burden, therefore, of stimulating and sustaining illusion falls on the actor—who, once he has captured his audience, must, like the spell-binding orator he may in method much resemble, be at pains to hold them, or a part of his work will be frequently to do again. Our mere acceptance of the fiction, of the story and its peopling—we shall perhaps not withdraw; we came prepared to accept it. Something subtler is involved; the sympathy (in the word's stricter sense) which the art of the actor will have stirred in us. This current interrupted by the suspension of the action is not to be automatically restored by its resumption. Our emotions, roused and let grow cold, must be roused again—and swiftly too, if, as in this play, emotion is to be a screen for liberties taken with the logic of the story's conduct. And the effects of such forced stoking will stale with repetition, until, if the actor in difficulties be tempted to coarsen the process too much, in its crudity it may fail of effect altogether.

Hence the help to the Elizabethan actor, with so much dependent on him, of continuity of action. Having captured his audience, he can the better hope to hold it. The dramatist may profit too. He will be spared the bridging of gaps by accounts of events intervening; secondary or superfluous matter, low in tension. Shakespeare hereabouts evades this aspect of the voyage to Cyprus and its inconveniences by ignoring them, and by restarting the divided action amid the stimulating—and effacing—anxieties of the storm. But such another—and necessarily a not too similar—device would be hard to find. Were he, moreover, to allow that likely lapse of time before the attack on Othello's confidence is even begun, it would but suggest to us as we watch the equal likelihood of an aptly scheming Iago letting at least a day or two pass between each assault to give his poison time to work. And with that the whole dramatic fabric would begin to crumble. Here would be Cinthio's circumspect Ensign again, and he would leave the action stagnating, with more gaps to be bridged, more intervening events to be accounted for, if ever so cursorily, the onrush of Othello's passion checked and checked again, and he given time to reflect and anyone the opportunity to enlighten him! Give Othello such respite; and if he then does not, by the single stroke of good sense needed, free himself from the fragile web of lies which is choking him, he will seem to be simply the gull and dolt "as ignorant as dirt" of Emilia's final invective, no tragic hero, certainly.

Shakespeare has to work within the close confines of the dramatic form; and this imposes on him a strict economy in the shaping of means to end and end to means, of characters to the action and the action to the characters. If Othello's ruin is not accomplished without pause or delay, it can hardly, under the circumstances, be accomplished at all. This predicates an Iago of swift and reckless decision (qualities that, again, the compression of time both demands and heightens) that will both win him his barren triumph and ensure his downfall. Then, again, Othello's precipitate fall from height to depth is tragically appropriate to the man he is—as to the man he is made because the fall must be precipitate. And that we may rather feel with Othello in his suffering than despise him for the folly of it, *we* are speeded through time as unwittingly as he is, and left little more chance for reflection.

Not, however, that continuity of action is of use simply for the sustaining of tension, nor that, continuity being kept, tension must not on occasion be relaxed; for if it were not—and fairly often—the strain, in any play highly charged with emotion, would become intolerable. But the dramatist can better regulate this necessary ebb and flow and turn it to account in the course of the action itself than if it is obstructed by repeated stopping and starting.

In all this, truly, Shakespeare treats time itself most unconscionably. But he smooths incongruities away by letting the action follow the hourly calendar without more comment than is necessary, while he takes the longer one for granted in incidental references. And all is well while he sees that the two do not clash in any positive contradiction.

The change into ambiguity of time is effected in the course of Iago's first and decisive attack upon Othello. This is divided into two, with the summons to dinner and the finding and surrender of the handkerchief for an interlude. In the earlier part—although it is taken for granted—there is no very definite reference to the longer calendar, and Iago, until towards the end of it, deals only in generalities.[16] Not until the second part do we have the determinate "I lay with Cassio lately. . . ," the story of his dream, the matter of the handkerchief, and Othello's own

> I slept the next night well, was free and merry;
> I found not Cassio's kisses on her lips. . . .

with its implication of passing weeks or months after the morrow of the landing. But would it not also in reason be the better for the suggestion of some longer interval, during which Iago's doses of poison will have had more chance to work, than the dinner

---

[16] There is, however, one earlier incidental sign that the longer calendar is already in Shakespeare's mind, Desdemona's reference to Cassio as

A man that languishes in your displeasure . . .

—"languishes" certainly suggesting something more than a few hours of disgrace.

to "the generous islanders" can offer? But here arises again the question of continuity of action. A suggested interval would not only, from the standpoint of reason, seem to give the poison time to work but some antidote of good sense too. And from the standpoint of the play's action, such an interruption, actual or suggested, must lower its tension and dissipate interest, just when its main business, moreover, too long held back, is fairly under way. Shakespeare will certainly not feel called on to make such a sacrifice to the reasonabilities. Lowering it but a very little, he does break the tension upon Othello's and Desdemona's departure (Emilia left behind, the scene continuing, the continuity of action kept). He inserts the episode of the handkerchief. Treated by Iago, this will capture our interest. Then Othello returns, transformed from the man merely troubled in mind to a creature incapable of reason, "eaten up with passion . . ."; and a little of his emotion reflected in us will let us too lose count of time, obliterate yesterday in today, confound the weeks with the months in the one intolerable moment.

But the overriding explanation of what Shakespeare does here and at similar junctures is that he is not essentially concerned with time and the calendar at all. These, as with the actor and his behavior, and other outward circumstances, must be given plausibility. But the play's essential action lies in the processes of thought and feeling by which the characters are moved and the story is forwarded. And the deeper the springs of these the less do time, place and circumstance affect them. His imagination is now concerned with fundamental passions, and its swift working demands uncumbered expression. He may falsify the calendar for his convenience, but we shall find neither trickery nor anomaly in the fighting of the intellectual battle for Othello's soul. And in the light of the truth of this the rest will pass unnoticed.

Examination of the Play's Shaping, Resumed

AT no other moment than this, when she is pleading for Cassio with Othello, do we see Desdemona quite confidently, carelessly happy. She could beguile her fears for Othello's safe landing by

laughing with the rest at Iago's sallies; but it was empty laughter.
Into the ecstasy of their reuniting had stolen his boding

> If it were now to die,
> 'Twere now to be most happy. . . .

Their first wedded intimacy was marred by the alarms of the
broil. And when a little later she comes to call him in to dinner,
the rift between them—though she does not know it—will have
opened. Even with the tale of his headache and her

> I'm very sorry that you are not well.

her gaiety has gone.

Shakespeare gives himself this single chance, then, of showing
her, and Othello too, as they well might have hoped so happily
to be. The picture is drawn in a few strokes; in her youthfully
generous impatience of the discipline which makes Cassio "an
example"; in the hinted sense of his—for her—elderliness in the

> 'Tis as I should entreat you wear your gloves,
> Or feed on nourishing dishes, or keep you warm. . . .

in his uxorious yielding and her sensitive response to the gently
measured irony which covers it:

> I will deny thee nothing:
> Whereon, I do beseech thee, grant me this,
> To leave me but a little to myself.

with the tender

> Be as your fancies teach you;
> Whate'er you be, I am obedient.

—its pretty singsong only sharpening for us its unconsciously
tragic presage. Her artless pride, too, in her new power of place
as her "great captain's captain," shows in the bidding Cassio
stay to hear her speak, with its confidence that then and there
she can "bring him in." And her importunity seems so to publish
her innocence that, as Iago stands watching the two of them—
his first move, the muttered mock-impulsive "Ha! I like not
that," already made—we may well ask ourselves whatever matter

for a second he will manage to find.[17] Desdemona provides it
him. For it is from her mischievously merry

> What! Michael Cassio,
> That came a-wooing with you, and so many a time,
> When I have spoke of you dispraisingly . . .

that he draws his

> My noble lord . . .
> Did Michael Cassio, when you woo'd my lady,
> Know of your love?[18]

Iago, it will be remembered, is now playing for deadlier stakes
than Cassio's lieutenancy. His net is to "enmesh them all"; and
while so far he has had no more precise end in view, the evil
possessing him is no longer of the sort to be appeased by material
gain. Nor has he, in fact, the means of inflicting such disaster on
Othello. To whom could he betray him as he has betrayed Cassio?
He must bring him to be the cause of his own undoing.

Before he provokes his passions Iago means to corrupt his
mind. How to set about this? Not by direct assault; he cannot
deal with him as with a Roderigo. Here too there must be self-
destruction. The best he can do to begin with is to find some flaw
in the moral defense, some little leak in the dike, and quietly
contrive to enlarge it. Othello has unquestioning self-confidence.
Yet he is no egoist; he translates this spontaneously into confidence

---

[17] The stagecraft hereabouts is presumably as follows: Desdemona, Emilia and
Cassio are on the inner stage, where Cassio has been brought ("in") by Emilia for
the beginning of the scene, for which the curtains will probably have been drawn
back also. Othello and Iago enter on the outer stage. They re-enter rather; and the
Quartos have them still accompanied by the gentlemen who went with them, a
while since, to the fortifications, and who will now, after a moment or so, vanish
unnoticed. That the Quartos should not allow them an exeunt is nothing out of
the way, and the only slight importance in their return is that it strengthens the
continuity of the action. The outer stage now serves the purpose of a sort of anteroom (the modern editorial *Enter Othello and Iago at a distance* has no specific
warrant; we owe it to Theobald apparently), and this will account for Othello
catching only a glimpse of Cassio as he leaves. It looks as if Othello was then
meant to join Desdemona, momentarily at least, upon the inner stage while Iago
remains in the "anteroom," removed from them at any rate, and free, while he
watches them, to give expressive play to his thoughts.

[18] Additional evidence of his eavesdropping from the "anteroom." Had he been
an open listener to their talk he would be asking a question of which he obviously
already knew the answer.

in others. But the more unquestioningly it has been given the harder will any breach made in it be to restore; and to loss of confidence in the culprit will be added some latent loss of self-confidence too. He loved Cassio and his confidence in him was betrayed. He may forgive him; but not only can he never feel sure of him again, by just so much he will remain the less sure of himself. Here is a leak in the dike, which Desdemona by her pleading has already done something to enlarge; for Othello is yielding to her against his better judgment.

One way, and a swift one, to the corrupting of the mind is through a perverting of the imagination. Othello's is, even as his nature is, full-powered. But he has exercised it in spiritual solitude, and for that it is the less sophisticated and the more easily to be victimized by alien suggestion. Again, he must be induced to do himself the harm; and Iago, as the process is here illustrated and compressed, begins with words as bait; and, so to speak, he trails these words before him, sapping their integrity by questionable stress and intonation, by iteration lending them a cumulative power, setting imagination to confuse and falsify the plain thoughts which they should represent. It is a poetic practice bedeviled, and he is expert in it. And in the ensuing doubt and confusion he can the better operate.[19]

Forthwith, in answer to the sequent question he prompts Othello to ask him, he strikes the keynote of—

> But for a satisfaction of my thought . . .

augmenting it with the pejorative

> No further harm.

The combination vibrates in Othello's ear; and a rapidly reciprocated "thought . . . thought . . . think," with an echo of Desdemona's "honest" from her

> I have no judgment in an honest face. . . .

for reinforcement, issues in

> What dost thou think?
>> Think, my lord?
>>> Think, my lord!

---

[19] The student may find it convenient to have these passages of close analysis accompanied by the pertinent part of the text itself.

> By heaven, he echoes me,
> As if there were some monster in his thought
> Too hideous to be shown.

—imagination both intrigued and balked. Iago's tacit pose
provokes it further, and to the appeal:

> if thou dost love me,
> Show me thy thought.
> My lord, you know I love you.

The feint at evasion can but halt before Othello's own unequivocal

> I think thou dost. . . .

and in a moment the opportunity is offered of

> For Michael Cassio,
> I dare be sworn—I think that he is honest.

its shift from "sworn" to "think," doubling the dubiety of "think,"
making it the most provocative stroke yet.

The disintegrating play of word and thought continues. Iago,
like a tricky wrestler, slips and dodges, evades and invites attack,
nor lets himself be cornered until, upon the imperative

> I'll know thy thoughts.

he retorts with the defiant

> You cannot, if my heart were in your hand;
> Nor shall not, whilst 'tis in my custody.

and coolly casts loose, sure that he at least has stirred Othello's
imagination into a turmoil, riddled his mind with doubts.

He is skirmishing ahead behind this screen of word-play.
Emerging, who still could be more disinterested, scrupulous,
more benevolent than Iago? Trust in Cassio is inevitably flawed,
with none but himself to blame. But no slur has yet been cast on
Desdemona; unless an intonation in the sententious

> Good name in man *and woman*, dear my lord,
> Is the immediate jewel of their souls. . . .

should strike Othello's sharpening ear. And the envenoming
"jealousy" is first insinuated, incidentally, as self-reproach:

> it is my nature's plague
> To spy into abuses, and oft my jealousy
> Shapes faults that are not. . . .

Confessing to our faults wins confidence. How, after that,
should simplicity of heart suspect in a fervent warning—

> O, beware, my lord, of jealousy. . . .

—the poisonous suggestion from which jealousy may breed?
Iago quickly slips back into the impersonal upon his homilectic
"green-eyed monster. . . ." But the sting of the brutal "cuckold"—
of the word itself and the very sound of it—will rankle, and to the
invitation of the final "jealousy" Othello responds.

It is an encouragingly defenseless response; in the murmured
"O, misery!", which Iago may rather surmise than hear, yet
more so in the superficial confidence, the disdain, the apparently
robust good sense of

> Why, why is this?
> Think'st thou I'ld make a life of jealousy. . . ?

—as you, Iago, confess you do.

> 'Tis not to make me jealous,
> To say my wife is fair, feeds well, loves company,
> Is free of speech, sings, plays, and dances well. . . .
> I'll see before I doubt; when I doubt, prove;
> And, on the proof, there is no more but this,
> Away at once with love or jealousy!

But it is all too positive; the protestations are too elaborate; that
"jealousy" sticks in his mind like a burr, and will to the tip of
his tongue. And for the first time "my wife" is specifically
brought into the question. Nor does he take in the least amiss
his friend Iago's interference in the matter. He ends, indeed, with
a tacit invitation, something foolhardily like a challenge to him,
to go further if he can. It is a challenge which Iago readily
accepts.

Hereabouts, in terms of actual life, he might more wisely be
breaking off this first successful engagement, to return later to the
attack with his gains consolidated, when the intellectual poison
shall have spread, and the self-infecting fever of the imagination
risen higher yet. Shakespeare, for reasons we have argued, does
not commonly permit himself such gaps; but their admissible
places are often traceable in the close-knit fabric by little—for a

simile—knots and splicings where the threads change color or thickness.

So here. Iago, thus encouraged (as he says) by his equanimity, by (as we see) Othello's ill-concealed trepidation, shows his "love and duty" to his "dear . . . lord" with a "franker spirit" indeed. Desdemona is no longer "my lady"; we have the bluntly familiar

> Look to your wife. . . .

instead, which quickly leads, by way of the insidious

> I know our country disposition well. . . .

(hint at the alien in Othello and the seed of much misgiving) to the first thrust home:

> She did deceive her father, marrying you;
> And when she seemed to shake and fear your looks,
> She loved them most.

A twofold accusation; both aspects of it actually true; her very love for Othello turned seamy side without. A most apt thrust. And back to his mind must come—to ours also, for the moment was memorable—Brabantio's

> Look to her, Moor, have a quick eye to see;
> She has deceived her father, and may thee.

The very words; Iago had heard them.

The tormentor, from now on, has his prey intellectually broken in, and answering, compliantly or by recoil, to each touch on the rein, each flick of the whip; to such a show of unctuous devotion as the hardy mind would repel by a pitiable

> I am bound to thee for ever.

to the covertly derisive

> I see this hath a little dashed your spirits.

by the hollow

> Not a jot, not a jot.

And he winces now at the very name of Cassio.

He must be brought to admitting his distress, to fettering it on himself, so to say. Iago reiterates, therefore, the

> My lord, I see you're moved.

and is repaid by the converting of that earlier, elaborate, dignified disclaimer into the feeble protest that he is

> not much moved . . .

while a return to the perplexity of

> I do not think but Desdemona's honest.

(but it is Desdemona now, not Cassio!) shows that incipient poison to be still at work. How should Iago then resist the veiled sarcasm of

> Long live she so! And long live you to think so!

The next opening Othello volunteers:

> And yet, how nature erring from itself—

It seems to betoken a disquiet dilating more profoundly in him. Iago boldly takes advantage of it. Too boldly? he asks himself— when he has tarred Desdemona with

> a will most rank,
> Foul disproportion, thoughts unnatural . . .

—and he sidles into qualifying apologies, managing to make them, however, yet more damagingly to the point.

> though I may fear
> Her will, recoiling to her better judgment,
> May fail to match you with her country forms,
> And happily repent.[20]

But he need have felt no misgiving. Othello's

> Farewell, farewell . . .

is friendly, although he will not be deceived by its ostensible carelessness, nor by the offhand

> If more thou dost perceive, let me know more. . . .

---

20 "Will," in one of its senses, connotes carnal appetite. For us it has lost that meaning, so we lose here the effect of its use. Of what Iago means and would be understood to mean there is no doubt. But if Othello were to turn upon him he could plead the ambiguity of the word (Shakespeare continually plays upon it: for the most cited instance, see Sonnets 134-6) and take refuge in one of its politer senses. "Happily" the O.E.D. allows may stand for "haply."

Nor indeed can Othello sustain this. Despite himself there breaks
from him the shameful

> Set on thy wife to observe. . . .

—hard upon its heels the curt

> leave me, Iago.

confessing the shame. And Iago himself must find it difficult
to keep some coloring of exultation out of the obedient

> My lord, I take my leave.

Is he wise to return as he does instead of letting well alone?
It is as if he could not keep his fingers off this instrument which
now yields so fascinatingly to his touch. But he wants to make
sure that in his absence the good work will go on, Cassio be held
off, so that Desdemona in her innocence *may* "strain his entertainment," while Othello, primed just to this degree of suspicion,
will watch them but say nothing—since, of course, a few frank
words to either could still cut through the flimsy net. He meets,
for response, with a stiff

> Fear not my government.

But he is not deceived by the studied dignity of that.

Othello, the man of action, is not habitually introspective, and
Shakespeare allots him this single true soliloquy. He is used
neither to concealing nor analyzing his own thoughts and motives,
nor to conjecturing other men's. He is quite childishly impressed by Iago's cleverness at that—who

> doubtless
> Sees and knows more, much more, than he unfolds.

who

> knows all qualities, with a learned spirit,
> Of human dealings.

But he, his faith attacked, his imagination poisoned, his mind
perplexed, and now alone, is a man spiritually rudderless and
adrift. He surrenders first to panic:

> If I do prove her haggard,
> Though that her jesses were my dear heart-strings,
> I'ld whistle her off, and let her down the wind
> To prey at fortune.

next, pathetically, to the humbling thought:

> Haply, for I am black
> And have not those soft parts of conversation
> That chamberers have, or that I am declined
> Into the vale of years—yet that's not much . . .

then to precipitate despair:

> She's gone; I am abused, and my relief
> Must be to loathe her.

—relief finding its immediate expression in such commonplace sarcasms as the idealist turned misogynist will habitually have at call, talk of "this forked plague" and the like.

Then the mere sight of Desdemona—no more than that needed to dissipate these figments!—seems to be about to make all well. Yet to her simple, happily intimate

> How now, my dear Othello!
> Your dinner, and the generous islanders
> By you invited, do attend your presence.

he finds himself—despite himself—responding only with sardonically riddling evasions. The wedge of suspicion has been driven between them.

The soliloquy and this brief passage between the two form a trough in the waves of the action, allowing us a survey of Othello as Iago's first attack has left him; passions not yet fired, but mind and imagination bewildered and warped, confidence gone.

THE HANDKERCHIEF

The two depart to their "duty" dinner with "the generous islanders," and then follows the quick exchange between Iago and Emilia over the handkerchief. Thick-skinned Emilia's unscannable

> I am glad I have found this napkin. . . .

is matched, as for contrast, against the gentle melody of Desdemona's parting line. Iago comes prowling, alert for Othello's return, to vent petty spleen on his wife because he finds her here instead (that much of safety valve he may allow himself);

offering amends with a brutally indecent joke, quibbled away.
Her indifference to such usage, her concern to gratify him!
Her discrimination in dishonesty:

> What handkerchief?
> Why, that the Moor first gave to Desdemona,
> That which so often you did bid me steal.
> Hast stolen it from her?
> No, faith; she let it drop by negligence,
> And, to the advantage, I being here took't up. . . .

and her shruggingly submissive departure at his curt bidding!
Here is a pair united by very different bonds.

This makes but a forty-line interlude between Othello's departure, deeply disquieted, it is true, yet self-controlled still, and
his return, a creature possessed. Nor does Shakespeare mitigate
the inordinacy of the contrast by any pretended spinning-out
of time or incidental change of subject, or shift of place. He does
not even shift from verse to prose, and tension is fully sustained.
But there is both surprise and substance in this episode of the
handkerchief, and enough of both to secure our complete attention. So it serves equally as a solid division between the two
capital scenes and as a firm bridge uniting them.

Its pettiness, besides, will throw into relief the toweringly tragic
force of what is to come. Iago stresses this for us with his

> Trifles light as air
> Are to the jealous confirmations strong
> As proofs of holy writ: this may do something. . . .

That it can be made to do what it does, a handkerchief found
by chance and filched, that in such a trifle such deadly power
can be lodged—men's lives at its mercy!—is, of course, the
dramatic point of its use. The poignancy of the tragedy gains
by contrast with the pettiness. Further, a spice of sheer ill-luck
is involved, and this relieves the severity of what has now
become a tragedy of character, with its ordered cause and effect
steadily pointing and leading to the justified end.[21]

---

[21] It is instinctive to compare the part played in the story by this episode with
the piece of unalloyed ill-luck by which, in *Romeo and Juliet*, Friar John's journey
to Mantua is stayed. By that and that only the play's catastrophe is precipitated.
Shakespeare has much matured in art since then. In Cinthio's story the Ensign

Iago continues:

> The Moor already changes with my poison:
> Dangerous conceits are in their natures poisons,
> Which at the first are scarce found to distaste,
> But with a little act upon the blood
> Burn like the mines of sulphur.

This is the effective link between his late encounter with Othello and the one to come, and it shows signs of being arbitrarily compressed to make it so. "The Moor already changes. . . ."—a hint here that Iago has come from watching him, just possible to suggest in action, amid this telescoping of time (if he came from the direction of Othello's departure), Emilia's ten lines to herself allowing for it. "Dangerous conceits . . ."—the repeated "poisons" may even point to an elision, the gap somewhat awkwardly closed. The sentence itself sums up Iago's scheming; and promptly with that "act upon the blood. . . ." Othello reappears, by the very look of him to warrant the word.[22] Iago's elated, gratified

> I did say so:
> Look, where he comes!

both rounds off this interlude and begins the second encounter between the two.

ANOTHER OTHELLO

Othello's silence as he stands there gains import from the sultrily ominous music of Iago's commenting

himself steals the handkerchief. In the play, to involve Emilia in the matter, she is let find it and hand it to Iago. That is a halfway step to accident, but no more. Nor does the business determine the catastrophe, only helps it on. Accident may find a place, then, in tragedy, as it does in tragic life. But it had better not be pure accident, nor a decisive place.

[22] It is to be noted that the Folio puts Othello's entrance after "I did say so," thus separating this from "Look, where he comes," to avoid which (apparently) modern editors are apt to put it after *that*. But both the Quartos squeeze their stage direction into the margin at "blood." One must not attach too much importance to such things nor found serious argument upon what may be a printer's vagary. But clearly, for the effect of Iago's "I did say so," Othello should, a brief moment earlier, have appeared upon the (inner?) stage.

> Not poppy, nor mandragora,
> Nor all the drowsy syrups of the world,
> Shall ever medicine thee to that sweet sleep
> Which thou ow'dst yesterday.

Then, as he paces forward, to that bated

> Ha, ha! false to me?

the jaunty

> Why, how now, general! No more of that.

is as the setting of a match.[23]

Iago's frigid sapience, those mocking precepts for the complaisant cuckold, are now flung back at him, translated into the agony of

> I swear 'tis better to be much abused
> Than but to know't a little. . . .
> What sense had I of her stolen hours of lust? . . .
> I found not Cassio's kisses on her lips. . . .
> I had been happy, if the general camp,
> Pioneers and all, had tasted her sweet body,
> So I had nothing known.

—an agony which obliterates all else, all but itself and the moment, for us, if we feel with him, as for Othello; a factor of import, then, in the action's treatment of time.

But before he yields to his fury, Othello, in terms of what has been noblest to him in life, of

> the plumed troop and the big wars
> That make ambition virtue! . . .

takes tragic leave of what is noblest in himself. An instant later Iago's ironic concern is shocked into reality when the "waked wrath" of

> Villain, be sure thou prove my love a whore. . . .

is loosed first of all upon him.

---

[23] The Quartos have a reiterated

> false to me, to me?

The second "to me" may well be an actor's interpolation; there are, seemingly, a number of them in the play. Even so, it is some slight evidence—any being needed —that the line is meant to be throttled down in the speaking, not rung out clear.

The sudden physical retaliation upon Iago is instinctive; he is not the author only, but the very instrument of torture. The cry for proof, even if it can only be of guilt, and for "ocular proof," is for some actuality which will displace these nightmare imaginings before they riot into madness. The adjuration to Iago to

> abandon all remorse;
> On horror's head horrors accumulate;
> Do deeds to make heaven weep, all earth amazed. . . .

reflects a vision of the abyss into which, if the thing is true, he sees that he himself may fall.

He has, it is evident, his man by the throat; and it is here that, for the first time, Othello loses self-control. Nor is it only that the old quiet authority of

> Keep up your bright swords, for the dew will rust them.

has gone; the later warning to the night-brawlers:

> Now, by heaven,
> My blood begins my safer guides to rule. . . .
> if I once stir,
> Or do but lift this arm . . .

could never have issued in trumpery violence such as this. Iago is stripping him of self-respect. When he next lifts his arm it will be to strike Desdemona.

This futile violence brings no relief, a moment's exhaustion only, which lets Iago recover his jolted wits, and turn his incessantly belauded honesty to good account. An indignant protest—

> Take note, take note, O world,
> To be direct and honest is not safe.
> I thank you for this profit. . . .

—and a dignified essay at departure; and the ashamed Othello will certainly recall him. He remorsefully does; and by that will deliver himself yet more helplessly into his hands, faith in Desdemona wrecked, and none but the wrecker left for guide.

Here is, as it were, the end of one paroxysm of fever. Pending another, we see still at work the infection of mind in which the trouble was begun—

> By the world,
> I think my wife be honest, and think she is not;
> I think that thou art just, and think thou art not. . . .

—at work now upon a weakened nature. Iago can safely
administer more violent doses of poison:

> You would be satisfied?
>   Would! nay, I will.
> And may: but how? how satisfied, my lord?
> Would you, the supervisor, grossly gape on—
> Behold her tupped?

and the racked cry of

> Death and damnation!

may compensate him somewhat for the indignity of his recent
throttling. But the pure pleasure of inflicting pain so intoxicates
him that for a second or two he is at a loss:

> What then? how then?
> What shall I say? Where's satisfaction?

And had Othello still sane eyes to see and ears to hear, the
malicious savagery in the

> Damn them, then,
> If ever mortal eyes do see them bolster
> More than their own! . . .
> Were they as prime as goats, as hot as monkeys,
> As salt as wolves in pride . . .

could not but show him the man. Instead, himself bereft of
reason, he demands

> a living reason she's disloyal.

and receives instead, in even grosser picturing, only more fuel for
his frenzied imaginings; and for "proof"—Iago deftly foisting
in the word—a trivial tale of a handkerchief. And this the bank-
rupt mind welcomes with a pitiful

> Now do I see 'tis true.

The essential work is done. And now, in a kind of antiphon to
that farewell to the old Othello, is dreadfully conjured up a new:

> Look here, Iago;
> All my fond love thus do I blow to heaven:
> 'Tis gone.

Arise, black vengeance, from thy hollow cell!
Yield up, O love, thy crown and hearted throne
To tyrannous hate! Swell, bosom, with thy fraught,
For 'tis of aspics' tongues! . . .
O, blood, blood, blood!

In it he blasphemes his so prized Christian baptism, kneeling

In the due reverence of a sacred vow . . .

to call upon a "marble heaven" to consecrate his revenge. Iago
is equal to the occasion, falling upon his knees also, with
magnificently histrionic irony, to partake this sacrament of evil,
mocking its pagan piety the while. For by his practical doctrine
evil is a servant, not a god, and the "wronged Othello's service"
of his oath, his own.

Let him command,
And to obey shall be in me remorse,
What bloody business ever.

"Command," "obey"; he can afford to put it so; and note the
enticing reminder of the "bloody business." It is in cold blood
that one part of the looked-for command is given—

Within these three days let me hear thee say
That Cassio's not alive.

—and in covert delight received—

My friend is dead; 'tis done at your request. . . .

—you rid me, that is to say, of *my* rival and *your* friend. And
with this profit on his investment in villainy Iago might wisely
be content. But he has grown avid of evil for its own sake; and
shall the splendidly lethal force that Othello is, now docile to his
hand, be checked here? For a moment he fears so; until his feline

But let her live.

brings him the assurance of

Damn her, lewd minx! O, damn her!
Come, go with me apart; I will withdraw,
To furnish me with some swift means of death
For the fair devil.

—suggesting, for the scene's end and its actors' *exeunt*, intents too terrible to be published to this light of day. Finally, two pregnant strokes:

> Now are thou my lieutenant.
> I am your own for ever.

Iago has won what he set out to win and more; and the double tongue, in that "I am your own. . . ." through which so clearly rings an exultant "You are mine," proclaims the triumph of his double-dealing. But evil has him toiled as fast as he has toiled Othello, and he will trip and fall in the nets of his own weaving.

THE HANDKERCHIEF AGAIN

Enter Desdemona, Emilia and the Clown.

After the prolonged and close-knit tension some such un-qualified relief as the Clown now brings with his antic chatter will be welcome. Twenty lines of it encase besides Desdemona's unconsciously ironic message to Cassio:

> Seek him, bid him come hither; tell him I have moved my lord in his behalf and hope all will be well.

Ten more give us her vexation at the mislaying of the hand-kerchief, and Emilia's underling's face-saving fib about it.[24]

Othello reappears. His head had been aching when she came to fetch him to dinner; hence her

> How is't with you, my lord?

He surveys her in enigmatic silence for a moment. To an unexpected tang of the sardonic in his answering

> Well, my good lady. . . .
> How do you, Desdemona?

she opposes—as if they were well used so to rallying each other— the gently bantering mimicry of her

> Well, my good lord.

---

[24] The concluding

> but my noble Moor
> Is true of mind and made of no such baseness
> As jealous creatures are. . . .

may seem, in critical cold blood, to be too immediately and pointedly apposite for likelihood. But in this it is, in its own way, of a piece with the general com-pression of the action; and its likelihood passes unquestioned with the rest.

He has his fury on the curb now, but still he finds it "hardness
to dissemble," and he approaches this test of the handkerchief
fumblingly; at best his forthright nature is not apt at such wiles.

> Give me your hand. . . .

—it is actually as if the mind, clogged with inhibited rage, could
get no further than the first syllable of the wanted word and
thought. Her hand responsively in his stirs the old love and new
hate mingled in him to queer sardonic figurings. Her innocent
incomprehension leads him to the dead end of a sententious

> The hearts of old gave hands;
> But our new heraldry is hands, not hearts.

but only for the effrontery—what else!—of her

> I have sent to bid Cassio come speak with you.

to spur him promptly to a starting point:

> I have a salt and sorry rheum offends me;
> Lend me thy handkerchief

—crude, commonplace, all but comic.

> Here, my lord.
> That which I gave you.
> I have it not about me.

She is vexed that she has not; yet for her it is but a handkerchief,
to be sought for and sometime found. For him, fury seething in
him, imagination luridly aglow, its loss becomes the very emblem
of her guilt. And she can call—can she?—his anguished accusa-
tions

> a trick to put me from my suit . . .

—her brazen suit that Cassio "be received again," which she can
urge too by lovingly reproaching him with an

> In sooth, you are to blame.

Lest he lose all power of dissembling and kill her then and there,
he shakes her off and goes.

This scene is basically cast, and it must be acted, in a key of
workaday domesticity[25]; and Desdemona's share of it, more

---

[25] May not the whole play, indeed, be labeled a "domestic tragedy," Shakespeare's single essay of the kind?

particularly, should be viewed from that standpoint. It is notice-
ably detached, moreover, in tone and by an incidental touch or
so, from yesterday's arrival and the swifter march of the action.
Here they are, outwardly, as any comparable couple, married and
settled, might be. Witness the knowing Emilia's comment on his
outburst of ill-temper:

> 'Tis not a year or two shows us a man.

Desdemona's bewildered

> I ne'er saw this before.

and her later, chastened

> Nay, we must think men are not gods,
> Nor of them look for such observancy
> As fits the bridal.

She is more than vexed at the handkerchief's mislaying. But
mislaying is not loss; and he is unwell, and she will not vex him
needlessly. Besides, he is otherwise troubled already. Not until
later, regretting even her mild part in their squabble—the milder,
though, the more exasperating!—does she argue that

> Something sure of state . . .
> Hath puddled his clear spirit; and in such cases
> Men's natures wrangle with inferior things
> Though great ones are their object.

by when, truly, she is, on reflection, puzzled and troubled enough
herself to be searching for reassurance.

Was it singularly obtuse of her not at once to detect some
menace in that queer scrutiny of her hand and queerer discourse?
Here is, indeed, some light upon a factor in her character which
contributes, if but passively, to her undoing. Desdemona is utterly
unself-conscious. Othello's love for her, moreover, and hers for
him, are a part now, she feels, of the natural order of things. They
are in the air she breathes. She is uncalculating too, and it
belongs to her happiness to be so. For her, with him, to think
is to speak; and for him, with her, if the matter concerns the
two of them, surely it must be the same. Whatever, then, may
be behind his cryptic talk and conduct she will not readily imagine
herself to be concerned. Nor in wifely wisdom, if she is not, will
she aggravate an ill mood, whether by ignorantly probing or

coldly disregarding it. She responds to its equivocal play with
banter, with serious simplicity, lastly with a lightly impatient

> I cannot speak of this.

—and proceeds to speak of Cassio.

Her suicidal persistence in pleading for him can be put to the
account of her uncalculating candor too, of the frankness which
is so flawless that, by Iago's evil logic, it may equally be flawless
deceit. And here, when for once it is not quite single-minded,
bad is made worse, not better.

For Cassio and the handkerchief become gages in a domestic
tourney.

> That handkerchief
> Did an Egyptian to my mother give. . . .
>   she dying gave it me,
> And bid me, when my fate would have me wive,
> To give it her. . . .
>   there's magic in the web of it:
> A sibyl, that had numbered in the world
> The sun to course two hundred compasses,
> In her prophetic fury sewed the work. . . .

—beneath the vehemence of this, of these mordant refrains from
the tales of the days of his wooing that she had found so "passing
strange," she flinches for a moment; it troubling her too, since
the matter seems so to trouble him, that she has tripped into
telling him a little less than the truth. But she recovers as quickly.
She is no longer that wondering girl, nor a bride even, but a wife
confirmed in her status. The handkerchief is precious; but against
this extravagant intimidation Venetian dignity and civilized good
sense protest in a quietly admonishing

> Why do you speak so startingly and rash? . . .
> Heaven bless us! . . .
> It is not lost; but what an if it were?

And if unhappily it prove to be, he may the better learn that
when he is calm. But his peremptory

> Fetch't, let me see it.

mere self-respect demands she face with a firm

> Why, so I can, sir, but I will not now.

Then, suddenly, she makes the matter a trial of strength between them. Which is to prevail, reason or unreason?—with Cassio's case most unhappily chosen for an example of the reason he must show her.

> You'll never meet a more sufficient man.
> The handkerchief!
>   I pray, talk me of Cassio.
> The handkerchief!
>   A man that, all his time,
> Hath founded his good fortunes on your love;
> Shared dangers with you,—
> The handkerchief!
>   In sooth, you are to blame.

She would soften the reproof by a caress, but with an enraged "Away!" he flings her off and is gone; hers, thus, the immediate victory, yet an ill one to win.

Emilia has some warrant for her sarcastic

> Is not this man jealous?

And if her conscience as she listened has been reproaching her for her own plain lie, her guiltier silence, Desdemona's well-meant evasions may have helped to ease it. A wife may excusably do as much to please a "wayward" husband as to placate an angry one, and a maid be less scrupulous than her mistress. But Desdemona, who asks no such petty victories, stays puzzled and troubled to the point that, Cassio now appearing with Iago, she quite forgets she has sent for him.[26]

She welcomes the distraction, and her generous mind recovers poise in her real concern for "thrice-gentle Cassio's" trouble. Iago deflects her from the thought that after all Othello's anger may somehow have its aim in her.

> Can he be angry?
> Something of moment, then: I will go meet him. . . .

—for, while all is working well, explanations must be prevented.

---

[26] This will be the normal implication of

> How, now, good Cassio! what's the news with you?

But it is as possible that Shakespeare himself either momentarily forgot it, or—as is more likely—thought it more effective for Iago to bring him to her.

It is this that she modestly and magnanimously enlarges into the

> Something sure of state,
> Either from Venice or some unhatched practice
> Made demonstrable here in Cyprus to him . . .

as sufficient cause. So, without heed to Emilia's coarser wisdom
and its warning, she will go seek him too and—"If I do find him
fit . . ."—yet again plead Cassio's cause; by which time, in any
case, Iago will have him safely out of the way.

She will now be absent from the action for a while, and the fine
spirit she brings to it very markedly absent. But this short quiet
passage, which is so expressive of her—selfless, high-minded,
reasonable of heart—leaves her vivid to remembrance.

Promptly upon her going, and in sharp unlikeness to her,
appears the little trull Bianca, the very woman that Iago is
persuading Othello—his folly illuminated by the contrast—to
believe Desdemona to be.[27] Her affectations find full display in the
stale artifice of her

> Save you, friend Cassio! . . .
> What, keep a week away? seven days and nights?
> Eight score eight hours? and lovers' absent hours,
> More tedious than the dial eight score times!
> O weary reckoning![28]

And in the squabble over the handkerchief, travesty of the one
just past, we have jealousy reduced to its rightly ridiculous
stature.

---

[27] Bianca's appearance here illustrates an indefiniteness of place which fits well
with uncertainty in time. The handkerchief has been lost somewhere within the
bounds of Othello's dwelling. We are still upon that spot. What is Bianca, of all
people, doing there? Cassio's surprised and irritated

> What make you from home?

goes halfway—the negative half—to counter the unlikelihood. As to time; he has
been—this is explicit—"a week away" from her. Yesterday's landing, then, has
quite gone by the board.

[28] "Stale artifice" as she will utter it, coming when and where it does, and by
contrast with the rest of the verse. Shakespeare could make the same sort of thing
sound fresh enough in *Romeo and Juliet* and *A Midsummer Night's Dream*, when
the play itself is dominantly cast in the mold of such artifice; and he gives it
excellent comic effect in the later *As You Like It*. But here the imagery will sound,
as it is meant to, flat and false. And so will Cassio's strained apology in the same
kind.

OTHELLO AT IAGO'S FEET

For the next scene's opening Bianca's pretty clinging to
Cassio is succeeded by an Iago fastened to the heels of his
wounded victim, so to say, and aggravating the wounds:

> Will you think so?
> Think so, Iago?

—the infected mind, under ceaseless sapping, is near exhaustion.
Of argument there is no more need; the gross image will serve:

> To kiss in private? . . .
> Or to be naked with her friend a-bed
> An hour or more. . . ?

And the trumpery of the handkerchief—the word, once again,
iterated in his ear; Othello, with a feeble snatch at salvation,
exclaiming,

> By heaven, I would most gladly have forgot it.

—is now to be turned to conclusive account. Each fresh stroke
makes for the man's deeper debasing; and he welcomes them,
asks for them:

> Hath he said anything?
> He hath, my lord. . . .
> What hath he said?
> Faith, that he did—I know not what he did.
> What? what?
> Lie—
>   With her?
>   With her, on her; what you will.

—at which point he physically gives way, and collapses, babbling,
in a trance, at Iago's feet.

It is a spectacular triumph. The humiliated Ancient has
brought his General to this; the dignity, nobility, authority
dissolved in these mere debris of a man. He must enjoy it for a
moment, cannot but laud his venomous achievement with the
ironic

> Work on,
> My medicine, work!

before he turns to a businesslike recovering—for further torture—
of the stricken creature.[29]

Cassio appears (told by Desdemona to "walk hereabouts");
but after letting him show his concern Iago finds pretext to be rid
of him. The sudden "No, forbear," betokens some fresh plan;
and behind the smooth façade of

> The lethargy must have his quiet course. . . .
> Do you withdraw yourself a little while,
> He will recover straight: when he is gone
> I would on great occasion speak with you.

we may divine his brain at work on it.

Cassio gone, Othello recovering, he probably—if surprisingly!—
does not intend his opening

> How is it, general? have you not hurt your head?

to bear the scabrous meaning, which the still staggering and
obsessed brain, by the reproachful

> Dost *thou* mock me?

so pitifully lends to it. He will be the more amused to note how
compulsively his medicine does work. He will note too that, as if
from sheer exhaustion, Othello's rage seems to be flagging, since
the cynical compliments, which he next metes out to him upon
the certainty of his cuckoldom, rouse him to no more than a weary

> O, thou art wise, 'tis certain.

The fresh trick he has now prepared, with Cassio once more for
instrument and supplementary victim, will come the timelier,
therefore. It is the most puerile of tricks: to provoke Cassio to
talk scurril of Bianca and make the listening Othello believe it is
of Desdemona. But Iago, grown foolhardy with success, begins
now to jerk his puppets with contemptuous ease. He sets his
ambush. Cassio will doubtless prove ready game, and he instructs
Othello as assiduously as he might a child—who, indeed, cannot
resist a preliminary peep from his hiding-place to whisper a

---

[29] Actors of Iago are accustomed to put their foot, for a moment, upon the prostrate body, even to give it a slight, contemptuous kick. This is wholly appropriate.

> Dost thou hear, Iago?
> I will be found most cunning in my patience;
> But—dost thou hear?—most bloody.

In this passage to come Othello is brought to the very depth of indignity. Collapsed at Iago's feet, there was still at least a touch of the tragic in him, much of the pitiful. But to recover from that only to turn eavesdropper, to be craning his neck, straining his ears, dodging his black face back and forth like a figure in a farce—was ever tragic hero treated thus?[30]

Iago plays his game coolly and steadily, following his own good advice to "keep time in all," giving himself, however, the passing pleasure of pricking Cassio with a

> How do you now, lieutenant?

—the wounding word so seemingly needless a slip! He tantalizes the hidden Othello for a while with disconnected phrases and enigmatic laughter, which will make, besides, what he later does let him hear the easier to misinterpret. Bianca's unlooked-for return might well upset his calculations. But by good luck she has the handkerchief itself to fling back at Cassio with the most opportune

> A likely piece of work, that you should find it in your chamber,
> and not know who left it there! This is some minx's token, and I
> must take out the work? There—give it to your hobby-horse. . . .

and her railing departure lets him send Cassio after her and so be rid of him, his unconscious part in the game satisfactorily played out.

Othello emerges, one thought predominant:

> How shall I murder him, Iago?

He would have Cassio "nine years a-killing"; the "noble Moor"

---

[30] Most actors of Othello, I think, have shirked this scene, wholly or in part; and Salvini (by the note in the Furness Variorum) justified its omission "on the ground that it is not in accord with Othello's character," that it belittled a man of such "haughty and violent temper," was not, in other words—we may fairly gather —in accord with Salvini's own dignity either. But that is, of course, the very point of it. From the dignity of the play's beginning Othello sinks to this, to rise again to the tragic dignity of its end.

The dodging in and out of hiding and the rest of the painfully grotesque pantomime is, of course, the most striking feature of the scene.

is stripped to savagery indeed. Desdemona must be kept in the
current of his fury. Iago finds fresh obloquy for her; to be
despised by her very paramour:

> And did you see the handkerchief? . . . to see how he prizes
> the foolish woman your wife! She gave it him, and he hath
> given it his whore.

He need not fear for her fate:

> A fine woman! a fair woman! a sweet woman! . . . let her rot,
> and perish, and be damned to-night.

Nevertheless from this moment Othello's torture becomes self-
torture too. And the suffering that asks vengeance and the
suffering that breeds pity are at intricate war in him, rending
him:

> my heart is turned to stone: I strike it, and it hurts my hand.
> O, the world hath not a sweeter creature. . . . Hang her! . . . but
> yet the pity of it, Iago! O, Iago, the pity of it, Iago! . . . I will
> chop her into messes. Cuckold me!

—his nature shown naked to us; no convention of verse or set
prose intervening.

Pity, it would seem, might at least so far win as to open a way
to the truth, were not Iago there, at his coolest, to steer, by
occasional deft touches to the rudder, through this vortex. What
smarter goad to a betrayed husband than the derisive

> If you are so fond of her iniquity, give her patent to offend;
> for if it touch not you, it comes near nobody.

which does, in fact, move Othello to his ultimate

> Get me some poison, Iago; this night. I'll not expostulate with
> her, lest her body and beauty unprovide my mind again: this
> night, Iago.[31]

---

[31] Having spun out *time,* for the sake of likelihood, Shakespeare now
accelerates the *action* of the play; the distinction is to be noted. Cassio was to be
dispatched "within these three days," while for Desdemona we have had so far
nothing more precise than Othello's
> I will withdraw,
> To furnish me with some swift means of death
> For the fair devil.
which followed hard upon Cassio's sentence. Now Desdemona is to die "this
night," and Iago promptly promises news of Cassio's death "by midnight." The
effect is that of the quickening flow of a river as it enters a gorge and nears a

—for he cannot sustain these agonies longer. But Iago, though poisoning would be the safer plan, has a more pleasing picture in his eye: of Othello destroying with his own hands the beauty he has adored. How fittingly!

> Do it not with poison. Strangle her in her bed, even the bed she hath contaminated.

And Othello, not wicked at heart, yet with a wicked deed to do, snatches, as men will, at whatever vindication:

> Good, good! The justice of it pleases: very good!

the prospect of Cassio's death besides drawing from him an

> Excellent good!

And upon this a trumpet sounds, and Desdemona appears with Lodovico, on embassy from Venice, ceremoniously attended.

By just such a trumpet call was Othello's own happy advent to Cyprus heralded, and we have heard none since. The scheme for his undoing was barely shapen then. This one finds him a man betrayed and self-betrayed, in moral ruin, Iago's creature, sworn to the murder of wife and friend. Yet at the sound, and the symbolic sight in Lodovico of Venice and her sovereignty, he becomes on the instant, to all seeming, the calm and valiant Moor again—frail though the seeming is too soon to prove. It is one of the salient moments of the play, and Shakespeare thus throws it vividly and arrestingly into relief.[32]

---

cataract; our interest quickens as we watch. No inconsistency is involved. That Othello, to be quit of the intolerable strain, and Iago lest his deceit be discovered, should each grow eager to precipitate the catastrophe accords both with circumstance and character.

[32] Modern editions slightly obscure the intended effect by postponing the entrance of Lodovico and Desdemona until Iago has seen them and announced them to Othello, and so given him a second or two in which to recover his equanimity. But Q1 (commonly accepted here also for the spoken text in preference to the Folio) has

> Ia. . . . you shall heare more by midnight.
> *A Trumpet.*
> *Enter Lodovico, Desdemona, and Attendants.*
> Oth. Excellent good:
> What Trumpet is that same?

The sound of the trumpet and the simultaneous (or all but) entrance of Lodovico and Desdemona will thus surprise him in the very midst of his exulting over the murders to be done, and his effort to control himself will be given its full pictorial value.

Parenthesis: The Use of Lodovico: The Action Advancing of Its Own Momentum

WITH Lodovico's arrival the play enters a penultimate phase, worth brief consideration as a whole; of suspense, enriching of character, of full preparation for the long last scene. The horror of this has already been projected for us in the

> Get me some poison, Iago; this night. . . . Do it not with poison. Strangle her in her bed. . . . Good, good! . . .

and a lesser dramatist, bent on little else, might have cared merely to forge ahead to its consummation, tying off the main threads of the story as best he could by the way. Shakespeare, for all that he is now speeding the action to its end, is in no such haste.

Lodovico's coming weaves a fresh strand into the texture of the play. His mission, the recall to Venice, Cassio's succession—these are weighty matters; and he, bearing the mandate for them, is a figure of consequence. Despite the dire events in prospect then— Othello's murderous passion already breaking surface; Desdemona, vilely outraged, a woman in a daze—due ceremony must still be observed, the customary courtesies offered and accepted, cheerfully withal. Othello knows, the watchful Iago too, and we know, within how short a while the deeds to be done will savagely wreck this fine pattern of procedure. Meanwhile—life, as ordained, must go on.

But for the killing of Cassio—a bagatelle!—Iago's work is done. Until now we have been incessantly conscious of him urging events onward. Now, merely giving them an occasional deft touch or two, he can detachedly observe them, moving to their inevitable end. He comments regretfully—yet not hopelessly—upon their unhappy drift. It is an even more sinister aspect of him. He is pricked to activity again by the sudden reirruption of the absurd Roderigo, by the bringing home to him that he himself, even he, is lapsing into danger—and from such a quarter! He baits the fellow's death-trap with deliberate, economical care; it shall serve for Cassio's also. It is a deadlier, double-edged counterpart to the trick which undid Cassio before. It miscarries. Deprived for the first time of a cat's-paw, Iago has to handle the job himself, and he bungles it.[33] His own undoing has begun.

Thirdly, there is the so-called "brothel scene" and that of the "Willow Song." These are not necessary to the action at all; they are there to illuminate character. The first redresses a much-disturbed balance, and restores to us an Othello who is neither mere bloodthirsty monster nor degraded puppet. The second brings us unforgettably near to a Desdemona defeated in "fortune" but not in goodness, and for the last time fully herself. The play would be impoverished indeed by the loss of these closing episodes of suffering and submission.

Analysis of the Action, Resumed

OTHELLO STRIKES DESDEMONA

By Lodovico's ceremonious salutation, Othello's as ceremonious response—

> God save you, worthy general.
> > With all my heart, sir.
> The duke and senators of Venice greet you.
> I kiss the instrument of their pleasures.

(but note the oriental turn of phrase, a touch in it even of ironic humility)—the scene is set moving again upon a seemingly even keel. But beneath the compelled calm his rage will be surging only the more fiercely, we know. So does Iago, retired into watchful silence after his sardonically oracular reply to Lodovico's passing

> How does Lieutenant Cassio?

the

> Lives, sir.

—for another hour or so.

Against this morbid calm—how like, how different from, the quiet dignity of our earliest sight of him—sounds out the happy melody of Desdemona's welcome to her "good cousin Lodovico," token of Venice and home to her, who "shall make all well," who, even better, comes to recall them from the exile to which

---

[33] It turns out that he has not even, as he supposes, rid himself of Roderigo.

she had so devotedly set out. Her innocently persistent "love I
bear to Cassio" wrings from him a stifled

Fire and brimstone!

while its contradiction in her joy at their return—Cassio to be
left behind—he only ignores. For he is past reasoning; she besides
as likely now to play the whore in Venice as here. His brain,
indeed, racked by its efforts at self-control, seems near turning.
His speech, when Desdemona nears him, degenerates to a jabbered

I am glad to see you mad.

and upon her ruthful

Why, sweet Othello?

he strikes her.

She does not cry out. And this, with the amazed silence of the
rest there, sets a seal upon the atrocious thing. Her only protest:

I have not deserved this.

—then she weeps silently.

Lodovico's grave amazement shows in measured reprobation.
But Othello, the blow struck, vindicates it—

O, devil, devil!
If that the earth could teem with women's tears,
Each drop she falls would prove a crocodile.
Out of my sight!

—and augments it with the cold cruelty of

What would you with her, sir? . . .
Ay; you did wish that I would make her turn:
Sir, she can turn, and turn, and yet go on,
And turn again; and she can weep, sir, weep;
And she's obedient, as you say, obedient,
Very obedient. Proceed you in your tears.

He comes, in this zest to insult and degrade her before the world,
never nearer in spirit to the "demi-devil" who has ensnared him.

But the violent oscillation of thought begins again. As before
between pity and rage, so now between the poles of

Concerning this, sir—O, well-painted passion!
I am commanded home. Get you away;
I'll send for you anon. Sir, I obey the mandate,

> And will return to Venice—Hence, avaunt!
> Cassio shall have my place. . . .

he sways, until—Desdemona dismissed—as if clutching for very
sanity at anything of use and wont, he steadies to a

> And, sir, to-night,
> I do entreat that we may sup together;
> You are welcome, sir, to Cyprus. . . .

and, after a final outburst (lunatic to his hearers; only we and
Iago catch the connection):

> Goats and monkeys!

follows her.[34]

This long scene, with its fit of epilepsy, with Othello's degradation to eavesdropping and bloodthirsty savagery, with the outrage
upon Desdemona, has been the play's most brutal and harrowing
yet. It now ends with a quiet, gentlemanly colloquy between
Lodovico and Iago; the one so shocked, disillusioned, grieved:

> Is this the noble Moor, whom our full Senate
> Call all in all sufficient? Is this the nature
> Whom passion could not shake? . . .

—the other so regretfully making the worst of it:

> He is much changed. . . .
> What he might be—if what he might he is not—
> I would to heaven he were! . . .
> Alas, alas!
> It is not honesty in me to speak
> What I have seen and known.

Two men of the world, deploring such behavior. But what more—
in a difference too between husband and wife—what more than
deplore it can they do?

---

[34] But *do* we, across five hundred lines of speaking time, catch the connection
with Iago's

> Were they as prime as goats, as hot as monkeys . . .

Not, it is possible, very exactly. But the phrase is a memorable one, and
Othello's remembrance of it may sufficiently stir our own. To Lodovico it
suggests, with the rest of the wild talk, that he may be off his head. He very
nearly is, as the matter of the next scene, to which this phrase is a keynote,
will more amply show.

THE "BROTHEL" SCENE: DESDEMONA
AT IAGO'S FEET: EMILIA AROUSED

Othello's share in this next scene is, we noted, superfluous to the play's action; yet how impoverished would the picture of him be by the loss of it![35]

He has followed Desdemona. In contrast to the tepid end of the last scene we are admitted into the midst of a sharp cross-examining of Emilia by an Othello whom her pluck, roused for the first time, can at least set twice thinking. But here is the pathos of the matter. This questioning comes too late. He has pledged himself to a besotted belief in Desdemona's guilt. Denial of it now only tortures and enrages him; it is the offer of a comfort he can no longer take, the reminder of a happiness he has lost. Coming from Emilia it is witness to a conspiracy to deceive him; from Desdemona, it only shows her the more hardened in guilt. Committed to his error, he only asks to be sustained in it, and hardened for what he has sworn to do.

So he does his best to shake Emilia's denials, and, when he cannot, relapses upon the sneer of a

> That's strange.

—which yet (since his happiness, if lost, is not forgotten) has a tang of wistfulness in it.[36] Whereat Emilia, good fighter that she is, seizes the slight chance:

> I dare, my lord, to wager she is honest,
> Lay down my soul at stake. . . .

and hammers her daring home, leaving him without retort, but for a conclusive

> Bid her come hither. Go.

---

[35] It is comparable in this respect to the scene in *King Lear* between Lear in his madness and Gloucester in his blindness. By neither is the action advanced; the characters are enriched by both.

[36] The second sentence of his attack on her will read better if it is left a broken one:

> Yes, you have seen Cassio and she together—

some opprobrious verb implied, a present participle probably. This will also help to restore the "she" to its nominative, and remove a minor editorial difficulty.

We wait, when he is alone, for some sign that the tide of evil
in him may be turning. But all that comes is the

> She says enough; yet she's a simple bawd
> That cannot say as much. This is a subtle whore;
> A closet lock and key of villainous secrets:
> And yet she'll kneel and pray: I ha' seen her do it.

Though he can suffer still and regret, he is too weary-minded
now to rid himself of the spell.[37]

Emilia, though unbidden, returns with Desdemona, as if she
foresaw danger threatening, and takes her dismissal reluctantly.
Then twenty-five words suffice for a vivid prelude to what is to
come, and even the action they demand is made plain in them:

> My lord, what is your will?
>   Pray, chuck, come hither.
> What is your pleasure?
>   Let me see your eyes;
> Look in my face.
>   What horrible fancy's this?

—the distantly proud humility of her response to his summons;
her approach at his bidding with eyes downcast, since if he feels
no shame for the blow struck she feels it for herself and him too;
her eyes as obediently lifted, she sees in his for the first time that
which appals her.

"I'll not expostulate with her," he had told Iago, "lest her body

---

[37] It is customary, seemingly, to read this speech as if Emilia were bawd and
whore both. But it is Desdemona, surely, whom Othello assails as whore. This
is to be the starting point of his coming scene with her. It is certainly her and
not Emilia whom he has seen "kneel and pray." Hence the later, sardonic

> Have you prayed to-night, Desdemona?

To gibe at Emilia for praying is sheer dramatic waste.
  As to how to identify the

> *This* is a subtle whore. . . .

with Desdemona, that is simple enough. We are momentarily expecting her
appearance by the way Emilia has departed. Any competent actor can combine
the "this" with a gesture which will unmistakably apply to her.
  Let a difficulty be admitted in the

> closet lock and key of villainous secrets . . .

which does seem to connect in thought with the orders to Emilia to "shut the
door" and (later) to "turn the key." But Othello's mind is still flinging violently
and arbitrarily between one subject and another: and the connection is hardly
close or definite enough to invalidate the more dramatically appropriate reading.

and beauty unprovide my mind again. . . ." But he cannot, he finds, forbear. So he first, in self-defense, smirches to himself that "body and beauty" by picturing her as a whore in a bawdyhouse, traded to him for a turn. The sight of her on her knees, looking so "like one of heaven" that the devils themselves might fear to seize her, the very cadence of her protesting

> Your wife, my lord, your true and loyal wife.

exclaim against the perversity. He must then needs mesh himself yet deeper in it. Damned once for adultery, she shall "double damn" herself by swearing she is innocent. For her sin against him he will take vengeance. Her sin against herself, her goodness and beauty, and against his faith in them—that breaks his heart. He has only to believe she is innocent when she swears it; but this is the one thing he can no longer do. Nor can he reason and explain; he is as a man hypnotized, possessed. Raised here to the pitch of poetry, it is in substance the commonest of cases. Two beings who have, as have these two, reached intimate communion, cannot, once this is broken, fall back upon a simply reasonable relation.[38] His collapse in tears lets her approach him. She tries to find him excuses for his treatment of her. But what can now bridge the gulf opened between them?[39]

Only slowly has she gathered, does she force herself to understand, what is the "ignorant sin" he will have it she has committed. And not until, emergent from his self-conscious suffering, his eyes on her again, he catches that "committed" with its

---

[38] Cf. the scene between Hamlet and Ophelia, built upon much the same psychological basis.

[39] What she says of her father here—

> if you have lost him,
> Why, I have lost him too.

—is not meant to indicate that she already knows of his death. Shakespeare would not let her refer to it thus, "in passing," even at such an otherwise distressed moment as this. We learn of it later, after she is dead herself, from her uncle Gratiano, brought into the action, most inconspicuously, for, it would seem, this sole purpose. Brabantio having been too important a factor in the play to be left unaccounted for at the end. Nor, at this juncture, would Shakespeare want to add a "second string" to Desdemona's suffering. The nearer to the play's end we come, the more important it is to sustain the singleness of the tragic motive. All she means, then, by "I have lost him too" is that (as we know) her father has cast her off.

unlucky connotation of adultery, does he—iterating it, as other words have been set iterating in his hot brain; swinging it round him like a weapon—deal her blow upon blow:

> What committed!
> Impudent strumpet! . . .
> Are not you a strumpet? . . .
> What, not a whore?

—blows more grievous by far than that which must physically mark her still. But these she does not take meekly, resists them, rather, with an explicit and religious pride—

> No, as I am a Christian:
> If to preserve this vessel for my lord
> From any other, foul unlawful touch
> Be not to be a strumpet, I am none.

—which only drives him back, hardened, upon the brutal sarcasms of his brothel imagery. Resummoning the bewildered Emilia, he leaves her.

Her flash of defiance extinct, she is left spiritually stunned. Her hurt may be measured by the wan humor of her answer to Emilia's troubled question how she does:

> Faith, half asleep.

—too deep a hurt for her not to welcome a moment's stupor, not to make light of it, if she but could. She wakes, as out of sleep, to certainty of loss, sees herself in the cold light of it. What is left her but to weep?—and weep she cannot. Sensible to some fatally pending consummation of this inexplicable evil, the dire end to all their joy:

> Prithee, to-night
> Lay on my bed my wedding sheets: remember. . . .

But she sends too for the shrewd, practical Iago. While she awaits him indignation surges in her

> 'Tis meet I should be used so, very meet!

—which melts under his velvet touch to the rueful simplicity of

> Those that do teach young babes
> Do it with gentle means and easy tasks;
> He might have chid me so; for, in good faith,
> I am a child to chiding.

Nor, a moment later, kneeling there, begging him to intercede for her, is she conscious of any abasement before the two, dependents as they are.

Candor is of the very essence of Desdemona's character, a spontaneous candor, uncalculating, inconsistent; open then to all suspicion. Here what she does and says is as the reflection of passing clouds in a clear mirror. One avowal succeeds another. Each shows her differently, and all with truth.

Childishly, she cannot bring herself to repeat the "name" that Othello has called her. It is at the sound of it, rapped out by the less fastidious Emilia—

> He called her whore. . . .

—and upon Iago's so reasonably pertinent enquiry:

> Why did he so?

that she at last breaks into tears. Emilia is so filled with wrath and so lost in the satisfaction of venting it, that the solution—

> I will be hanged, if some eternal villain,
> Some busy and insinuating rogue,
> Some cogging, cozening slave, to get some office . . .

—which she hits upon within an inch, still escapes her.

For Iago this is another, and a gratuitous triumph. When Othello fell convulsed at his feet, he had taken pains for that. But to have Desdemona humiliated there too, and imploring his help, is an unlooked for pleasure. He savors it complacently.

The trumpets summon to supper. Desdemona must dry her eyes and once more play the regnant hostess at Othello's side. Iago watches her go, Emilia tending her. Surely he has achieved his end. But he turns to be confronted by an absurdly angry Roderigo.[40]

---

[40] Another instance of the usefulness of indeterminate locality. Roderigo has not much more business in a room in which Othello and Desdemona have recently been so intimately alone than had Bianca in a similar vicinity. But—unless we are reminded by scenery—we shall not consider this. And the effect to be made here depends upon Iago's sudden turn from his cold survey of the pathetically submissive figure of Desdemona to encounter Roderigo's coxcomb revolt. It would be lost by an exit, a cleared stage, or re-entrance.

RODERIGO AGAIN

Amid these crowding events we may well have—even as it seems for the moment has Iago—all but forgotten his existence; the more comically outrageous, then, the incongruity between Othello's fall, Desdemona's agony and the tale of his own wrongs, into which he so portentously launches:

> I do not find that thou dealest justly with me.

—into the horrors of this pending tragedy thrusts Roderigo, demanding justice!

But we laugh at him unfairly. He knows of no troubles but his own; and there is something pathetic in being so ridiculous in oneself. His case against Iago is strong. He has been most patient. It is time he took a high hand. He has summed up his grievances, sought choice expression for them, studiously—it is evident—rehearsed it, and for once he means to do the talking:

> Every day thou doffest me with some device, Iago; and rather, as it seems to me now, keepest me from all conveniency, than suppliest me with the least advantage of hope. I will indeed no longer endure it. . . .

He finds himself most magnificently overriding Iago's protests. The fellow is his social inferior, after all, and no better than a pimp:

> The jewels you have had from me to deliver to Desdemona would half have corrupted a votarist: you have told me she hath received them and returned me expectations and comforts of sudden respect and acquaintance. . . .

So, despite being tempted into one rather shrilly feeble parenthesis—

> Very well? go to? I cannot go to, man; nor 'tis not very well! . . .

—he reaches his peroration in fine form:

> I will make myself known to Desdemona. If she will return me my jewels I will give over my suit and repent my unlawful solicitation; if not, assure yourself I will seek satisfaction of you.

Iago gives a second or so to the assembling of the implications of this admirable combination of penitence and thrift, and then quickly comments:

> You have said now.

—as indeed Roderigo has, and pronounced his own doom.

For the time being there is only Iago's tiger smile to tell us this, although it should suffice. The revealing soliloquy is postponed to a later scene, until the plan now concocting behind the smile shall be actually in action, the ambush set. It will then be speeded through, as at that moment it must be. This both avoids delay here, and denies to the disposing of Roderigo and Cassio the fierce thought given to Othello's ruin. For Iago, flushed with success and scornful of these minor victims, is recklessly improvising now.

But he takes the floor—and the balance of the scene shifts at once—with a magnanimous

> Why, now I see there's mettle in thee; and even from this instant do build on thee a better opinion than ever before. . . .

and overrides Roderigo in turn, and ignores his ill-temper and saps his resolves, and cajoles him and maneuvers him with the old adroitness. Within a little he has the repentant libertine converted to prospective assassin. Yet Roderigo

> will hear further reason for this.

Reason and Roderigo go well together.

DESDEMONA DIVESTS HER—FOR DEATH

Between the devising of this first of the midnight murders and its execution we have a scene of ordered calm; of ceremonial courtesy, of Desdemona's divesting her for sleep.

> *Enter Othello, Lodovico, Desdemona, Emilia and Attendants.*

They come from the supper to which we heard the trumpets summon them. It will hardly have been a spontaneously gay repast, as a certain evasiveness in Lodovico's urbane

> I do beseech you, sir, trouble yourself no further.

may imply. Each line of these few is lightly pregnant; and an edge to the tone of it, the coloring of the phrase, the actor's look or gesture will tell us what is astir beneath the tension. Othello (it is Emilia's later comment)

> looks gentler than he did . . .

—she did not hear, then, his brutal command to Desdemona:

> Get you to bed on the instant; I will be returned forthwith: dismiss your attendant there: look it be done.

(the dry anonymity of the "your attendant there" emphasizing their menace) pendant to his as urbane determining of Lodovico's chivalrous courtesy by bowing him on their way together with an undeniable

> O, pardon me; 'twill do me good to walk. . . .
> Will you walk, sir?

So they depart, their escort after them.

In the passage which follows all action whatever, save for the wonted nightly "unpinning," is arrested; there is no other such in the play. Of action of every sort, and of violence and distress of speech, we have so far had plenty. This prepares, in its stillness, and in the gentle melody of the song, for the worse violence and the horror to come, and is, as we have noted, a setting against which no shade of Desdemona's quiet beauty can be lost.

The strain of self-control before Lodovico relaxed, she finds herself suddenly steeped in sheer physical fatigue. She repeats Othello's orders to her—

> He says he will return incontinent:
> He hath commanded me to go to bed,
> And bade me to dismiss you.

—without comment. And her response to Emilia's alert, alarmed

> Dismiss me!

is but the listlessly submissive

> It was his bidding. . . .

Yet the morose

> I would you had never seen him!

draws a quick

> So would not I: my love does so approve him,
> That even his stubbornness, his checks, his frowns, . . .
> have grace and favour in them.

Spiritless? It is not that. But if his love has failed her she must find refuge in her love for him.

Upon her weariness fancies and memories play freely. Reminder of the wedding sheets (imaging—so she had meant them to—the end as the beginning of their wedded joy) begets the fancy to be shrouded in them some day. From that evolves the memory of her dead mother, and of the maid Barbara and *her* "wretched fortune," and the song which "expressed her fortune"; and this recalls Venice, and for Venice stands the handsome, grave Lodovico.

The sad rhythm of the song, as she sings it, soothes her mind, if it leaves her senses still morbidly acute:

> Hark! who is't that knocks?
> It is the wind.

answers matter-of-fact Emilia. And she can note now such petty matters as that her "eyes do itch" and ask lightly if that "doth . . . bode weeping," and even half-humorously shake her head over

> these men, these men!

We are seeing the last of Desdemona, but for the midnight moment in which she will wake only to the horror of her death. So, for a finish to the scene, and a completing of her character, Shakespeare stresses the trait in it which has incongruously proved to be the fittest material for this tragedy, the goodness—the too absolute goodness—of a fiber of which Iago's enmeshing net has been made.

It is Brabantio's daughter who now speaks; the daughter of a great house, strictly, isolatingly reared, and conserving—launched into the world—a gently obstinate incredulity of its evil:

> Dost thou in conscience think—tell me, Emilia—
> That there be women do abuse their husbands
> In such gross kind?

and it will be in some incredulity of such innocence that Emilia so circumspectly answers,

> There be some such, no question.

But she is glad of the chance to cheer her mistress with a little salty humor, to agree that "by this heavenly light" she would not wrong her husband, since

> I might do't as well in the dark.

and then to treat these tenuous ideals with the hardening alloy of some good coarse common sense. But Desdemona stays unimpressed:

> Beshrew me, if I would do such a wrong for the whole world.

and, what is more,

> I do not think there is any such woman.

Emilia, her tongue once loosed, waxes eloquent upon wedded life and how to live it. Sound, practical doctrine! Expect little, overlook much; but threaten, and give, tit for tat. And as we listen, and watch Desdemona indifferently listening, and mark the contrast between the two, there may slip into the margin of our minds the thought: better indeed for her had she been made of this coarser clay. But then she would not have been Desdemona.

IAGO BEGINS TO BUNGLE

When Desdemona and Emilia have departed,

> *Enter Iago and Roderigo.*

This is the play's penultimate scene. It is thrown (as usual) into contrast with the quiet colloquy just ended; and the high organic tragedy of the scene to come will in turn stand contrasted with its turmoil. It is besides a counterpart to that other night scene which marked the arrival in Cyprus with Cassio's disgrace, and is thrown into contrast with that too. For while the chief puppets are the same, Iago no longer maneuvers them with the same enjoyable ease; and the stakes in the game are more desperate, no mere thrashing and the cashiering of Cassio, but, by one means or another, death for them both, and quickly, lest puppets turn dangerous. His capital scheme has moved faultlessly towards fruition. But even now what might not happen to stay Othello's hand, or to turn it, or Cassio's, against him? For full success, all the threads must be knotted up and cut together. Well, the "young quat" Roderigo's ire can be turned to the cutting of two at one stroke, since

> whether he kill Cassio,
> Or Cassio him, or each do kill the other,
> Every way makes my game. . . .[41]

He calculates as shrewdly as ever, but more summarily; he plays high and recklessly still. This scene is the last, moreover, of which he directs the action; and its crowding, feverish movement, after the long-sustained scheming, comes as the breaking of a dam. But, ominously, he bungles the stroke which, Roderigo having bungled his, could still rid him of Cassio. By now even *his* nerve is strained. The crisis wrings from him too that strange involuntary

> if Cassio do remain,
> He has a daily beauty in his life
> That makes me ugly. . . .

although, as if surprised by such a thought, he quickly obliterates it beneath the more matter-of-fact

> and, besides, the Moor
> May unfold me to him: there stand I in much peril. . . .

And it is a nakedly brutal scene, in which the first murderous harvest of all the complex trickery and treachery is so summarily reaped.

Ironic flattery of his "good rapier" will not make Roderigo a very competent murderer, but the "satisfying reasons" demanded have at least stiffened that once-sentimental lover to the pitch of a callous

> 'Tis but a man gone.

and a cowardly thrust in the dark. He gets in return yet better than he gives; and, after a few moments groveling agony and one last terrible flash of enlightenment, here will be the end of

---

[41] The Quartos have "game," the Folio "gaine." The Folio may in general be the better text, but the suggestion of gambling certainly fits the mood of the scene.

him.[42] He has done Iago's schooling some credit; one pities the
poor wretch, nevertheless.

Cassio, retaliating on Roderigo, is in turn served out by Iago—
who, however, having made no clean job of it, prudently
vanishes.[43] The noise brings Othello out upon the balcony above.
He has heard Cassio's voice; he knows it well. But in the silence
that has fallen and the darkness, his straining ears only catch
after a moment Roderigo's low repentant moan:

> O, villain that I am!

—a shamefully swift relapse from villainy![44] Cassio's cry, however:

> O, help, ho! light! a surgeon!

reassures him—his betrayer dying if not dead—and he exults to
the perennial infatuate refrain:

> 'Tis he. O brave Iago, honest and just,
> That has such noble sense of thy friend's wrong!
> Thou teachest me. . . .

Up to this moment it has been just possible, we may have felt,
that Othello, swinging between rage and suffering, might somehow purge himself of the evil in him. But Iago has set the
example, and the wild beast has scented blood:

> Minion, your dear lies dead,
> And your unblest fate hies: strumpet, I come! . . .

---

[42] Later it turns out otherwise. We learn in the last scene that

> even but now he spake
> After long seeming dead. . . .

and witnessed against Iago. But I suspect this to have been an afterthought on
Shakespeare's part. In this scene certainly there is no hint that he is not dead,
every evidence that he is.

Incidentally Q2 has, when Iago stabs him, *thrusts him in*. The direction
implies that there were not (when this edition was viable) two men available
to carry away the body at the scene's end, Cassio's chair having the prior claim.

[43] After "But that my coat is better than thou knowest" he does not waste
time in thrusting at Cassio's padded doublet, but slashes below it at his groin.
Iago's aim would be better and the stroke a fairly fatal one had he not to keep
his face hidden. Even so, Cassio can exclaim, "I am maimed for ever. . . . My
leg is cut in two!"

[44] Othello's "It is even so" of the Folio, could be read—the voice mistaken for
Cassio's—as a savagely sarcastic comment, and perhaps effectively. The Quartos'
"Harke, 'tis even so" simply gives continuity to his speech and serves to keep our
attention as much upon him as upon the two figures below.

And to the stuttering, choking fury of the crowded last couplet—

> Forth of my heart, those charms, thine eyes, are blotted;
> Thy bed, lust stained, shall with lust's blood be spotted.

—he goes to do the deed prepared. Desdemona is doomed.[45]

As he vanishes Cassio calls out again, and this time Lodovico and the hitherto unknown Gratiano appear.[46] We hear them mistrustfully whispering:

> Two or three groan: it is a heavy night:
> These may be counterfeits: let's think't unsafe
> To come in to the cry without more help.

—and there they stay, and nothing more happens for the moment. Cassio's cries are now reduced to an exhausted "O, help!", Roderigo is still repentantly groaning. Then Iago returns, "in his shirt," like one roused from his lawful slumbers, carrying a light, alert and helpful; just such a ready change worked in him as went with that first swift passing from beneath Brabantio's balcony to the Sagittary, from Roderigo's side to Othello's.

~~~~~~~~

[45] Another passage which producers of the play and actors of Othello conspire to omit, on the ground, presumably, that, as in the eavesdropping upon Cassio, his behavior here lacks dignity. But that, of course, as with the eavesdropping, is the very point of it. In the course of the play Othello is swung, and ever more widely, between the conviction that he is taking righteous vengeance on Desdemona and the primitive savagery which this rouses in him—and without which, it well may be, he could not so overcome his own anguish as to take it. In this stuttering, choking outburst he drops nearer to the savage than ever yet; from it he will have risen, at our next sight of him, to the tragic height of

> It is the cause, it is the cause, my soul. . . .

[46] If the stage for which *Othello* was written boasted not only the center balcony, *i.e.*, the upper stage, but one over each of the side doors as well, I think that almost certainly Lodovico and Gratiano appeared upon one of these. But the center one alone would be wide enough to allow them to enter it by one side an instant after Othello has left it by the other without seeming to be in awkward proximity to him. There is nothing against this in their own

> To come *in* to the cry . . .

or in Iago's appeal

> What are you there? Come *in* and give some help.

the "in" being merely a figure of speech; if it were not, "out" would be the appropriate word. In either case they seem to be meant to respond by descending to the lower stage: and while they pass momentarily out of sight in doing so, Iago can the better dispatch (as he thinks) the wounded Roderigo. He then confronts them below with his

> What may you be? Are you of good or evil?

He seems not to recognize Cassio; how should he look to find him here? When he does his commiseration is heartfelt:

> O me, lieutenant! what villains have done this?

—for he cannot at the moment finish his bungled job, since, he notes, there are onlookers now. But he can at least do swift justice upon the one villain who

> is hereabout
> And cannot make away.

And the prostrate Roderigo is welcome to see his face as he stabs him, for he will take care not to miss his stroke this time. He finds, indeed, some pleasure in thus winding up accounts with his dupe. And he easily drowns the aghast shriek:

> O damned Iago! O inhuman dog!

with a stentorianly indignant

> Kill men i' the dark! Where be these bloody thieves?

Roderigo, he may well suppose, will trouble him no more.[47]
For an instant, as he stands there by the body, nothing stirs.

> How silent is this town!

he says; an accusing silence which he breaks with an echoing

> Ho! murder! murder!

Those prudent onlookers approach—Lodovico he recognizes, the other is less distinguishable—and he can now, with them to witness, give undivided care to Cassio, his stricken comrade, his very "brother"; grief wrings the word from him.

He makes sure that Cassio has no clue to his assailants. Bianca's appearance, and her hysterical collapse at the sight of her lover, offer her to him for a scapegoat. The lifeless Roderigo, recognized and well wept over, may be turned to more account yet.[48] And

---

[47] See, however, p. 72, note 42, and page 94, note 61.
[48] There may be, I think, a textual error here in Iago's repetition of Bianca's

> Who is't that cried?

He can scornfully echo her; I see no other reading, nor very much dramatic point in that. It is possible, therefore, that Iago's original sentence is lost and that this replaces it.

That Shakespeare has every thread here clear in his mind is shown by Gratiano's telling Cassio that he has been to seek him. It will have been to

while he mentally assembles the factors for some fresh, plausible fiction, he is here, there and everywhere, binding Cassio's wound, summoning a chair for him, seeing him safely into it and away. He is as ready and quick as ever; but possibly too quick, somewhat emptily ready. It is easy to browbeat Bianca, and he does so with gusto, arraigning her before these Venetian dignitaries Lodovico and Gratiano:

> Stay you, good gentlemen. Look you pale, mistress?
> Do you perceive the gastness of her eye?
> Nay, if you stare, we shall hear more anon.
> Behold her well; I pray you, look upon her:
> Do you see, gentlemen? Nay, guiltiness will speak,
> Though tongues were out of use.

All very menacing! But of *what* he is to accuse her he has evidently no idea; he is searching as he speaks. Emilia's arrival and the need to repeat the tale to her give him the liar's valued chance to tell the economized truth. He pursues the Bianca trail:

> Prithee, Emilia,
> Go know of Cassio, where he supped to-night.
> What, do you shake at that?

But Bianca, by now, is in fighting trim, and can answer Emilia's

> Fie, fie upon thee, strumpet!

with a smart

> I am no strumpet, but of life as honest
> As you that thus abuse me.

Each boasts and counterboasts her respectability until Iago cuts them short with

> Emilia, run you to the citadel,
> And tell my lord and lady what hath happed.

Another blunder, thus to send her posting off! Might she not

---

inform him of his promotion to governor. Gratiano, who brings also the news of Brabantio's death, is a later arrival from Venice than Lodovico. It is the last of these compressions of the action, and very inconspicuously made. Note besides that while there are several references to the governorship, the last in Cassio's presence at the end of the play, he is never told of it directly. As with Brabantio's death, of which Desdemona is never told, Shakespeare does not want at this juncture to give a subordinate matter primary importance.

come in time to stop the murderous work afoot then? But his final

> This is the night
> That either makes me, or foredoes me quite.

(he stays behind the rest to confide it to us), with the old confident swagger marred for the first time by a strain of doubt, speaks of some sense in him that his "divinity of hell" may not have armed him quite invincibly after all.[49]

THE END

The events of the first three scenes of the play, we noted, could be presumed to pass in just about the time it took to act them, and this was time enough for an exhibition of the chief characters concerned. Then came a speeding of events and drastic com-

---

[49] At two points in this scene the question can be raised of the comparative effect to be made by implied as against actually exhibited action. When Othello departs with that savagely menacing

> Strumpet, I come! . . .

to what extent does he leave us thinking of him, as the bustling scene proceeds, on his way to kill Desdemona? The thought, I believe, will persist; because her fate is the capital issue, while the recovery of Cassio and the dispatching of Roderigo, with which the actual action is occupied, are secondary ones. But action exhibited will always command primary attention. This thought of Othello, therefore, will occupy no more than the margin of our minds; it will form a latent, though very living, link with our next expected sight of him. When Emilia is bid "run . . . to the citadel" and hastens off, the sight, coupled with this latent thought of Othello, may stimulate the question whether she can overtake him, cannot at least arrive in time, even whether (in an alertly minded audience) Iago has not therefore blundered by sending her. But the thought of her on her way will not persist with us as did the thought of Othello on his, if only because the now succeeding action involves Othello and Desdemona themselves and her murder and will obliterate thought of all else. The intended effect, indeed, is that it should. Then, when she knocks at the door we shall recall her hastening off, and the question is stimulated, with the tacit comment: Too late, after all!

But is it legitimate, and is it consistent with Shakespeare's ever most practically minded exercise of his art to provide for these secondary effects, which, it would appear, a given audience may not appreciate, fully or perhaps at all? The answer surely is: yes, as long as they *are* secondary and the primary are neither sacrificed to their success nor will be prejudiced by their abortion. They can be compared to the inner parts of a piece of orchestral music. At a first hearing only an expert may detect them and appreciate their enrichment of the whole. The rest of us may need half a dozen hearings. But the more there is to discover the greater will be the interest; and this can be as true of a play as of music.

pression of time. Now, since Lodovico's coming, the action has been only normally compressed, the scenes strung loosely along, *within* them little or no time-compression; and within this long final scene there is to be none at all. For Othello, indeed—who is never absent from it, upon whom its entire action centers—it is as if, once his sworn deed is done, time and life itself lose all momentum. We have seen him, after one storm, joyfully make port. Here, after another, is the ship slowing—his own imagery— to her "journey's end."

The scene falls into three sections: the first filled by Desdemona's murder, the second by the discovery of Iago's guilt and the killing of Emilia, the third by Othello's orientation to his own end. The murder is soon accomplished, and it is but the consummation of what has gone before. From then until he kills himself he takes little more than a passive share in the action. It eddies about him: but he has lost all purpose, and even the attack upon Iago is half-hearted. Montano (though "puny whipster" he is not) easily gets his sword from him. So the bulk of the scene is given to a survey of the spiritual devastation that has been wrought in him. Bit by bit, the "noble Moor" who was "all in all sufficient," is revealed to himself and the others as a gull, a dolt, "as ignorant as dirt," the "good" Othello as a savage monster; and the soldier, firm and renowned in action, yet guilty of *this* action, is reduced to futile gestures and inarticulate bellowings of remorse. It is a terrible, shameful spectacle, of which Shakespeare spares us nothing, which, indeed, he elaborates and prolongs until the man's death comes as a veritable relief, a happy restoring of him to dignity.

Enter Othello with a light, and Desdemona in her bed.[50]

Of all the contrasts in the play between the end of one scene and the opening of the next, or the disappearing and reappearing of a character, none is more striking than this, than the passing

---

[50] According to Q2. Q1 also has *with a light*; but the Folio omits it, and editors have, in consequence, preferred to have a light already burning in the room. This is not quite such a small error as it may seem. The intention in Q2 plainly is that Othello shall enter with the light illuminating his face; and the steadiness with which he carries the (presumably) naked candle does much to emphasize the abnormal calm which gives dramatic distinction to his appearance.

from the alarms of Roderigo's murder and Cassio's wounding, from the reciprocal scoldings of Bianca and Emilia, to the sublimity of Desdemona's sleep, and from our last sight of Othello, clothed with fury, lusting for her blood, to his entry here, as a priest might come to do sacrifice, bearing his light, uttering his oracular

> It is the cause, it is the cause, my soul:
> Let me not name it to you, you chaste stars!
> It is the cause.

He is calm as water is when near to boiling, or the sea with a surge of storm beneath. Exalted in his persuasion that it is justice he deals and not vengeance, he regains a satanic semblance of the nobility that was. He had feared "lest her body and beauty" might "unprovide" his mind. The spell of them is working in him, the first cold image of

> that whiter skin of hers than snow
> And smooth as monumental alabaster.

quickening, through vision of the living light beneath, to a full sense of them; this pursued beyond to the charnel

> Be thus when thou art dead, and I will kill thee,
> And love thee after. . . .

—the initial perverting of the mind finding such final issue; as too in the bitter

> I must weep,
> But they are cruel tears. . . .

as in the blasphemy of

> This sorrow's heavenly;
> It strikes where it doth love.

Desdemona wakes; and, as she would at any time—must have, it will seem, so many times—calls drowsily,

> Who's there? Othello?
> Will you come to bed, my lord?

A poignant incongruity: he, wrought and intent, ready to kill; she but slowly shaking free from the sleep which weariness has sent and innocence not denied her, passing, rather, indeed, from sleep to nightmare, to the incredible sight of him with eyes rolling, passion shaking his "very frame," to incredible talk of crime and killing and guilt, until, her heart palsied, she gasps,

> why I should fear I know not,
> Since guiltiness I know not; but yet I feel I fear.

Bewildered, she fences against his fierce

> Think on thy sins.

and threat of death with pretty quibbling conceits—so unreal it all still seems to her—until he beats the futile weapon down with an ultimate

> Peace and be still!

She is awake now and collected, and wifely compliance joins with womanly dignity:

> I will so. What's the matter?

The handkerchief! That this ridiculous trifle should be her death warrant, that her plain provable denial now comes too late to outweigh the "strong conception" of her guilt this madman has been brought to "groan withal"—here the play's tragic irony is sharpened to its keenest point. Add the final instance following, in which wickedness and folly together are able to "turn her virtue into pitch," her peculiar goodness, that uncalculating candor, to her harm. Cassio's death, when she hears of it, means her undoing, since his witness to her innocence will be denied her. It is in innocence that she connects the two:

> My fear interprets then. What, is he dead? . . .
> Alas, he is betrayed, and I undone!

—that blind innocence!—and her tears are a terrified child's. But Othello's distorted mind can only read in it more evidence of her guilt.[51]

---

[51] "My fear interprets then. . . ." This is the reading of the two Quartos. It contributes to a more regular, and perhaps, therefore, a more authentic line than is the Folio's "O, my fear interprets." (An initial "O," breaking the meter, itself hints at an actor's interpolation.) The meaning is, I take it—though the one reading does not make it clearer than the other, nor either very clear—that her present vivid fear interprets for her at last Othello's bewildering anger at the loss of the handkerchief, the blow, the "impudent strumpet" and the rest. Desdemona's gentle courage has been, throughout the play, a striking feature of her character. It goes with her candor and lack of suspicion, her blindness to the evil enmeshing her.

It is in cold deliberate anger that he kills her. We are spared
none of the horror, neither her panic struggles, nor the hangman
humanity of his

> Not dead? not yet quite dead?
> I that am cruel am yet merciful;
> I would not have thee linger in thy pain:
> So! So![52]

The abrupt knocking at the door and Emilia's insistent voice
can set his wits alertly on the defensive even while the fully
sentient man barely yet comprehends what he has done. His

> She's dead. . . .
> Ha! no more moving?
> Still as the grave. . . .
> I think she stirs again. No. . . .

shows a mind working detached—and the more swiftly—within
senses still benumbed. It is with the

> If she comes in, she'll sure speak to my wife. . . .

---

[52] There is a reading hereabouts in Q1, which is now generally rejected but
which nevertheless invites comment. The accepted Folio text for the moment of
the smothering runs

Des.	Kill me to-morrow, let me live to-night.
Oth.	Nay, if you strive.
Des.	But halfe an houre.
Oth.	Being done, there is no pawse.
Des.	But while I say one prayer.
Oth.	It is too late. *Smothers her.*

> *Ameilia at the doore.*
>
> *Aemil.* My Lord, my Lord? What hoa?
> My Lord, my Lord . . .

Q1, besides the omission of "Being done, there is no pawse," and such slight
changes as to *He stifles her* and *Emillia calls within*, has, after "It is too late,"

> *Des.* O Lord. Lord. Lord.

Since Dyce reproved Collier for admitting this to the edited text (Furness
Variorum: footnote, p. 302) on the grounds that the effect involved was, first,
"not a little comic" and secondly "disquietingly vulgar," no other editor appears
to have raised the question. But it is worth consideration at least. For the effect
(saving Dyce's opinion) would at least be neither comic nor vulgar, and might
prove to be very poignant indeed. Imagine it: Desdemona's agonized cry to God,
and as the sharp sound of it is slowly stifled, Emilia's voice at the door rising
through it, using the same words in another sense. A macabre duet, and un-
accountable enough to call from Othello a most distraught

> What voice is this? . . .

that he stumbles—the intimate word itself piercing him—into the light of the irrevocable fact; to cry out then in amazed agony:

> My wife! my wife! what wife? I have no wife.

The deed done, the passions so tortuously wrought up to its doing begin to unravel. From the wreck of the Othello that was emerges a man who is both the victim and the creature of the deed. His grief is as ingenuous as a child's:

> O, insupportable! O, heavy hour!

the man's awed sense of guilt is as unmeasured:

> Methinks it should be now a huge eclipse
> Of sun and moon, and that the affrighted globe
> Should yawn at alteration.

It is a furtive criminal that draws the curtains round the bed to admit Emilia with a bantering

> What's the matter with thee now?

and a callous one that answers her

> O, my good lord, yonder's foul murders done!

with the bland mockery of

> What, now?

And through the somber

> It is the very error of the moon:
> She comes more near the earth than she was wont
> And makes men mad.

speaks a spirit accursed.

The news of Cassio's escape rekindles his fury. It is quenched on the instant by the sound of that voice from the dead:

> O, falsely, falsely murdered!

—Desdemona's; she is in Emilia's arms, faintly proclaiming (as for answer to the horror-struck "O, who hath done this deed?" she gasps out her pitifully preposterous "Nobody; I myself. . . .") *his* guiltlessness too. A last corroboration of her other perjuries, if he will! Then, with the soul-searing

> Commend me to my kind lord. . . .

she is dead indeed.

The man's riven mind seems, for a moment, in the evasive

> Why, how should she be murdered? . . .
> You heard her say yourself, it was not I.

to be self-contemptuously sounding, under Emilia's accusing gaze, the depths of the ignominy of acquittal thus opened for him, to reject it by frenetically, exultantly invoking an eternal vengeance now upon the gentle dead:

> She's like a liar gone to burning hell:
> 'Twas I that killed her.

Whereupon, with volcanic Emilia, it is quick blow for blow, given and taken; from him the foul word to vindicate the brutal deed—

> She turned to folly, and she was a whore. . . .
> Cassio did top her. . . .

—from her plain "devil . . . devil." Yet out of the coarse melee rises his challenging

> O, I were damned beneath all depth in hell,
> But that I did proceed upon just grounds
> To this extremity.

soars too, in anguished remembrance, the ecstatic

> Nay, had she been true,
> If heaven would make me such another world
> Of one entire and perfect chrysolite,
> I'ld not have sold her for it.

It is not however these splendid protests that strike Emilia, but the cursory

> ask thy husband else. . . .
> Thy husband knew it all.

which slips out besides; this leaves her for an instant breathless. Then she finds herself re-echoing, her first stupidly echoed "My husband!" and again, with horror doubled and redoubled, as every echo of it draws from Othello the ever more horrible truth. And she cries to the unhearing dead:

> O, mistress, villainy hath made mocks with love!

Horror comes to a head, and clarifies:

> My husband say that she was false?
>   He, woman:
> I say thy husband: dost understand the word?
> My friend, thy husband, honest, honest Iago.

Reckless of consequence, she deals a deliberate hammer-blow:

> If he say so, may his pernicious soul
> Rot half a grain a day! He lies to the heart. . . .

Although Othello, baited and exasperated, the murderous blood still hot in him, draws sword on her now, a choking dread is rising in him. She defies him and his lowering

> Peace, you were best.

And it is she who stoutly checks and silences him and holds him there, a culprit, while she vociferates to all who may hear to come and arraign him.

A Parenthesis: The Play's Finishing

THE finishing of the play is technically not a very simple task. There are the customary conventions to fulfill. Iago's treacheries must be disclosed, and not only to Othello; they must be published to the rest of this mimic world also. Such a methodical completing of the story seems on a stage such as Shakespeare's, where illusion is uncertain, to confirm its credibility; it resembles the old-fashioned "proving" of a sum. This outcry from Emilia will assemble everyone concerned. If story were all, the threads could now be combed out and tied up expeditiously enough. But the play is a tragedy of character; and Othello's—even though no spiritual salvation will dawn for him—is not to be left in mere chaos. The dramatist's task, then, is to restore him as much to himself, and to such a consciousness of himself, as will give significance to his end, and to do this convincingly without pursuing the action beyond appropriate bounds.

Consider, for comparison of treatment, other such Shakespearean partnerships in death. Romeo and Juliet die from simple mishap, divided by a few minutes of time; and the completing of the story follows as a long—and rather tiresome—anticlimax. This is early work. *Othello, Antony and Cleopatra, Macbeth*;

these are all three mature, and in each case the method of the ending fits story and characters appropriately together. Between Antony's death and Cleopatra's, action is interposed that lends hers an importance matching his, even as in life the two are matched; and this can be very suitably done since the scope of the story is so wide. Lady Macbeth, on the other hand, has been reduced, well before the play's end, to the wraith of the "sleep-walking" scene; and she dies actually "offstage." But from the moment of Duncan's murder she has been a slowly dying woman, the battlefield is no place for her; and her death, made much of, might, the action close-packed as it is, inconveniently outshine Macbeth's.

As to Othello and Desdemona; if he is to be restored to dignity his death must not come as an anticlimax to hers. Yet, as in cause, so in effect, it must closely depend on hers. Shakespeare makes, then, no break in the action; and he keeps Desdemona's murdered body the motionless, magnetic center of it, silently eloquent until the end. Again, Othello cannot be let actively dominate the scene until his end is imminent. It would never do, for instance, to have him personally dragging the truth from Iago, Emilia or Cassio, tritely reversing in epitome the process of his deception. To avoid such recapitulation, Iago, before he appears for the second time as a prisoner, has already "part confessed his villainy," and will obstinately refuse to say more, while Cassio will not appear till then, when there is nothing much left for him to say. For a channel of disclosure we have the impetuous Emilia, who herself has it all to learn, for an instrument the handkerchief, which she set on its fatal course. Nor can Othello himself do justice on Iago. As requital for Emilia's death it would be inappropriate; he does not care whether she lives or dies. And to kill him a moment before he kills himself would be a discounting of the effect of his own end. What initiative is left him, then, until the time comes for him to do justice on himself? It follows that the tension of the scene must be sustained for the most part without him. Yet he must never be deprived of his pre-eminent place in it. The dramatic task involved is by no means an easy one.

Analysis of the Action, Concluded

To the Folio's

Enter Montano, Gratiano and Iago.

the Quartos add, *and others*; and there is gain in the sudden irruption of half a dozen or more figures, from among which Emilia picks out, even before we may, the one that counts, with her keen

O, are *you* come, Iago? . . .[53]

Yet he is her husband; and he must clear himself. Desperately she bids him

Speak, for my heart is full.

But her fiery challenging brings instead only sourly evasive admissions, and to the damning

My mistress here lies murdered in her bed. . . .
And your reports have set the murder on.

no answer at all, except (amid the appalled murmurs) for Othello's suddenly weary, strangely empty

Nay, stare not, masters: it is true indeed.

And for a helpless moment it even seems as if, the deed irrevocable, Othello, the man he is, with vengeance on a guilty wife— one woman's voice alone swearing her guiltless—not unpardonable, here might be coming an end to the whole matter.[54]

It is the one woman who will not have it so. While Montano and old Gratiano deplore the thing done, Emilia, with her

Villainy, villainy, villainy! . . .

is flinging herself on the track of the true doer, frantically, incoherently flogging her every faculty into use:

I think upon't: I think: I smell't: O villainy!
I thought so then: I'll kill myself for grief:
O villainy, villainy!

---

[53] The Folio's later speech-heading "*All*" gives countenance to the Quartos' "*and others*," since it can hardly be meant to indicate Montano and Gratiano alone.

[54] It should be noted, however, that Lodovico, the man of authority, is not present.

As cool as she is frantic, Iago marks a danger signal in that "I thought so then . . . ," and he orders her home, out of the way. He will mark another in her stricken

> Perchance, Iago, I will ne'er go home.

—since she is ready now for the worst. But Othello's sudden collapse in inarticulate agony takes all eyes and ears, and for the moment she is stayed. His savage rage dissolved in savage grief, she finds relief from her own anguish in the sight of his, a satisfaction even:

> Nay, lay thee down and roar;
> For thou hast killed the sweetest innocent
> That e'er did lift up eye.

And they unite in grief for the dead Desdemona. Even Othello's exculpatory

> O, she was foul! . . .

laments her; and in the echoing

> 'Tis pitiful. . . .

compunction wells again. And Gratiano's gentle

> Poor Desdemona! I'm glad thy father's dead. . . .

takes no account of guilt or innocence. He and the rest there stand and gaze.

Only Iago holds frigidly, vigilantly apart, the sight of him so reminding us that where he is evil is brewing still. Then Othello's

> but yet Iago knows . . .

turns every eye on him again.

> That she with Cassio hath the act of shame
> A thousand times committed . . .

—this, with its frenzied "thousand times" raising the scene to fever pitch again—

> Cassio confessed it:
> And she did gratify his amorous works
> With that recognizance and pledge of love
> Which I first gave her. . . .

Iago can tell what is coming, and there is no stopping it. He has a wary eye on Emilia—

> I saw it in his hand:
> It was a handkerchief. . . .

—and, when he sees the light of this break on her, a dangerous one. But there is a deadlier power left in that "trifle light as air"— and a livelier danger to *him*—than he would suppose; witness for response, upon a note she has never sounded till now, Emilia's deep searching

> O God! O heavenly God![55]

This handkerchief, then, has been the instrument of Desdemona's death; she the cat's-paw to handle it; her pleasuring of Iago, her petty lie, her silence, all means to the appalling end. And God above has permitted this. What shall she do?

Iago, alert to a fresh force in her, gives her full warning; first with a sharp

> Zouns, hold your peace.[56]

(But " 'Twill out, 'twill out. . . ." she cries; her strong spirit crying through her); then, after a moment, with a cold and clear

> Be wise, and get you home.

And would she be so wrong to be wise? She can no longer mend the matter. What profit therefore now in pinning guilt upon Iago—and he her husband after all? She can read besides in his look what will befall her if she does. She might well choose to be wise. But if she cannot restore Desdemona to life, to honor and

---

[55] The Q1 reading; the Folio (also, substantially Q2) having

> Oh Heaven! oh heavenly Powres!

The difference, at this point, is not a slight one; Q1 striking the far stronger note. It is generally admitted that the text of *Othello* bears many marks of the 1605 "Act against Swearing" (and one has but to glance at the Concordance, with its two entries under "God" and its long list under "heaven"). The line in the Quarto has, therefore, that much inferential claim to be what Shakespeare first wrote. But a more important argument in its favor is its challenging intent, so closely akin to Laertes' "Do you see this, O God?"; to Macduff's "Did heaven look on and would not take their part?" (which should surely read "God," the whole scene hereabouts being enfeebled by repeated "heavens"); and, of course, to more than one passage in *King Lear*—where, however, Shakespeare escapes difficulties with the Censor by expressly "paganizing" the play. But this challenging attitude towards divinely permitted evil is characteristic of the mature tragedies.

[56] Q1 also.

her innocent name she can. Therefore, without need to question what she shall do, she answers that cold, clear "Be wise. . . ." as clearly with a resolute, deliberate

> I will not.

—and, for the dead Desdemona's sake, faces her fate.

Then and there Iago draws his sword. It is not the most plausible of ways, this, one would suppose, to confute Emilia. But guile, failing, turns into foul abuse, and "honest Iago" into the trapped beast, fangs bared. To which monster it is that Gratiano makes gentlemanly protest:

> Fie!
> Your sword upon a woman!

Emilia speaks on. If the words are to be her last she will leave nothing in doubt:

> O thou dull Moor! that handkerchief thou speaks't of
> I found by fortune and did give my husband. . . .
> She give it Cassio! No, alas, I found it,
> And I did give't my husband.

—nor minimize (witness the stressed and repeated "my husband") her own blind partnership in the villainy. With all eyes on the two of them, Iago is kept at bay. But when—coming, indeed, like a very clap of it!—the tremendous

> Are there no stones in heaven
> But what serve for the thunder?

turns attention to Othello, he slips through the defense, wreaks vengeance on her and is gone.

But for kindly old Gratiano, Emilia would fall and die there unheeded; and, after a moment's care of her, even he leaves her for dead. The rest have still only eyes for Othello, whom Iago's escape leaves balked, silenced, motionless, yet with such giant menace in the very look of him that Montano must wrest his sword away, and, General though he be, set drastic guard over him till the fugitive can be caught and justice done. So sentries are set without the door; and they leave him there, disarmed and imprisoned, alone with the dead Desdemona and the dying Emilia.

He sinks into impotence:

> I am not valiant neither,
> But every puny whipster gets my sword.
> But why should honour outlive honesty?
> Let it go all.

—into an oblivion which even Emilia's dying words do not pierce. She, dragging herself to Desdemona's side, her mind wandering—back to the refrain, the "Willow, willow, willow," which was her mistress' last sad gift of herself to her—can yet rally strength to take the death-witnessed, never-doubted oath:

> Moor, she was chaste; she loved thee, cruel Moor;
> So come my soul to bliss, as I speak true;
> So speaking as I think, I die, I die.

But it is all unregarded that she dies.
His mind is elsewhere. He says to himself,

> I have another weapon in this chamber;
> It is a sword of Spain, the ice-brook's temper;
> O, here it is. Uncle, I must come forth.

Whereupon he proceeds to play a grimly comic little practical joke upon Gratiano, who is on guard without, armed with the sword Montano had secured. The old man's voice protests confidently:

> If thou attempt it, it will cost thee dear;
> Thou hast no weapon. . . .

Othello is actually wielding his new-found one as he answers with boyish cunning:

> Look in upon me then, and speak with me,
> Or, naked as I am, I will assault thee.

And when Gratiano innocently does so, there stands the prisoner, formidably rearmed.[57]

If he meant, as it will seem, to pursue Iago, the impulse is dead in him already. But his soldierly dignity must be retrieved from

---

[57] A typically Shakespearean device: to follow the tragic moment of Emilia's death by this semi-comic trick, so both separating it from the tragedy still to come, and heightening this by contrast.

that momentarily humiliated depth of "I am not valiant
neither . . . ," even if to the

> I have seen the day
> That with this little arm and this good sword
> I have made my way through more impediments
> Than twenty times your stop. . . .

he must now add a bitter

> O, vain boast!

He stands there an awe-inspiring figure still, in outward seeming
still the Othello who had but to lift his arm for the best of them
to sink in his rebuke. But the fire within is cold, the purpose gone:

> Be not afraid, though you do see me weaponed;
> Here is my journey's end, here is my butt
> And very sea-mark of my utmost sail. . . .

wan echo, this, of the ardent

> O, my soul's joy!
> If after every tempest come such calms . . .

of the whelming

> Like to the Pontic sea,
> Whose icy current and compulsive course . . .

—the mighty and untamable sea that has been throughout the
image most consonant to his nature.

Then he turns to the dead Desdemona:

> Now, how dost thou look now?[58]

and takes, with Gratiano for witness (whose grave compassion
will exemplify our own as we listen), another and very different
farewell of her. The up-wrought

> whiter skin of hers than snow
> And smooth as monumental alabaster.

becomes a simple

> O, ill-starred wench!
> Pale as thy smock!

---

[58] And he must, I think, pull back the curtains of the bed, and, if need be,
raise the body, so that the dead face can be plainly seen.

For his murderer's look which so terrified her we have now

> When we shall meet at compt
> This look of thine will hurl my soul from heaven,
> And fiends will snatch at it.

and, for his mortal assault on her with its "Strumpet . . . strumpet!", the timid touch of his finger on her breast or cheek, and the dull

> Cold, cold, my girl!
> Even like thy chastity.

It is their last communion: her visionless gaze, his unavailing words.

With a quick twist his thoughts pursue Iago:

> O, cursed, cursed slave!

to be flung back upon his own maddening guilt:

> Whip me, ye devils,
> From the possession of this heavenly sight! . . .

(his macabre

> Be thus when thou art dead, and I will kill thee,
> And love thee after. . . .

has ripened into this). It is his last and stormiest fit of such passion

> Blow me about in winds! roast me in sulphur!
> Wash me in steep-down gulfs of liquid fire! . . .

It subsides into the deep, measured diapason of

> O, Desdemona! dead Desdemona: dead!

—the irrevocable indeed in that last word, and in a softly added

> Oh, oh!

dumb suffering and remorse.[59]

~~~~~~~~~

[59] The Folio reading. Most editors here follow the Quartos'
   O *Desdemona, Desdemona* dead. O, O, O.
(Q2 replacing Q1's comma after the second "Desdemona" by a semi-colon).
   Too much importance must not be attached to minor phrasing or to punctuation, which may in fact be either the prompter's or the printer's. But the Folio reading here happens to be substantially preferable, both in its repetition of "dead" (the added emphasis being of much dramatic value) and for the weightier rhythm and melody, which help to make the line the solemn

In the ensuing silence Lodovico appears, escorted, and embodying once more the majesty of Venice itself. Montano is with him, and behind them is the captured Iago, disarmed and guarded. The wounded Cassio comes too, carried in a chair. And the scene which follows has the semblance of a tribunal, over which Lodovico authoritatively presides.[60]

He addresses the one culprit indirectly, considerately, commiseratingly:

> Where is this rash and most unfortunate man?

and Othello accepts disgrace:

> That's he that was Othello: here I am.

He treats the other as fittingly:

> Where is that viper? bring the villain forth.

and the two are confronted.

Iago is silent, and his face a mask. Hence (at one remove of thought) Othello's baffled

> I look down towards his feet: but that's a fable. . . .

A swift stroke at the pinioned creature—

> If that thou be'st a devil, I cannot kill thee.

---

apostrophe I think it is meant to be instead of giving countenance to yet another mere outcry.

It is interesting to compare this whole passage with that in which Lear apostrophizes the dead Cordelia. We have the same intimate simplicity of phrase. Death, and the death of one so dear, is no matter for rhetoric. And even for Cleopatra, attired in all her splendor, Charmian finds the simplest of terms: "a lass unparalleled." And Macbeth, when the news of his wife's death is brought him, can find no words whatever. How far we are in all these from Romeo's grief, and almost as far from Horatio's "flights of angels."

[60] From now until the beginning of Othello's last speech Lodovico should dominate the scene. Actors of Othello are too apt to believe that, even from "It is the cause, it is the cause, my soul. . . ," to the end, the responsibility rests upon them. But Shakespeare has been careful to relieve them from such a strain, and the scene itself from the monotony involved. Emilia's masterful intervention, Iago's attack on her, his flight and her death provide such relief. And now, for a while, Othello remains an all but passive figure, and, for a little, before his

> Soft you; a word or two before you go. . . .

is an all but silent one. By which passivity the dramatic value of his last speech, when he does make it, is notably increased.

—should answer the question one way or the other. But at Lodovico's peremptory

> Wrench his sword from him.

he is for the second time disarmed; and Iago, though he wince, can vaunt diabolically enough:

> I bleed, sir, but not killed.

The tension is relaxed by Othello's rueful, sardonic:

> I am not sorry neither: I'ld have thee live;
> For, in my sense, 'tis happiness to die.

This kindles the compassionate reproach of Lodovico's

> O, thou, Othello, that wert once so good,
> Fallen in the practice of a damned slave,
> What shall be said to thee?

which finds answer in the terse

> Why, any thing;
> An honourable murderer, if you will;
> For nought I did in hate but all in honour.

An honorable murderer! Is there more to be said?

Lodovico continues his inquest. Each there has his part in it, and by an individual touch or two helps to sustain and diversify the fabric of the scene. The wounded Cassio's response to Othello's single-syllabled, abased avowal of intent to murder him, is but a grieved

> Dear general, I never gave you cause.

As unaffected a

> I do believe it, and I ask your pardon.

recalls—if nothing could restore—the old frank comradeship between the two.

And what more cause had this other?

> Will you, I pray, demand that demi-devil
> Why he hath thus ensnared my soul and body?

Does Iago even know the answer? "I hate the Moor," rabidly, senselessly, profitlessly; a search through the ruin of his tricks and lies would add nothing real to that. And in the light of the consequences—for him also—such an answer must seem almost less tragic than absurd. Incorrigibly he wraps himself in the shreds of his satanic conceit, as self-deceived in this, it may be, as were his victims in their "honest" Iago:

> Demand me nothing; what you know, you know.
> From this time forth I never will speak word.

And if the ordeal will be sharp, the hardihood of vanity is great. Lodovico's shocked

> What, not to pray?

Gratiano's exasperated

> Torments will ope your lips.

are, at each extreme, the habitual human response to such contumacy. Othello's indifferent

> Well, thou dost best.

speaks of weary readiness to have done with it all.

But he must be held to life's business still; so the magistral Lodovico, showing him some respect, insists:

> Sir, you shall understand what hath befallen,
> Which, as I think, you know not. . . .

The last is heard of the paltry handkerchief. He confirms Emilia's judgment:

> O, fool! fool! fool!

Then the rest turn, as men will with grave matters concluded, to talk more volubly of the lesser. Here it is of the

> letter
> Found in the pocket of the slain Roderigo . . .

and of "another discontented paper," and of the trick played on Cassio which led to his disgrace, and of Roderigo's wonderful recovery. And how much more of the sort would there not be to say, but that Lodovico once more gives orders.[61]

------

[61] This diverting of our attention at such a moment from Othello to the papers found in Roderigo's pocket has been a matter of distress to certain commentators. Koester, in particular, to quote from the Furness Variorum, finding here "in the needlessness of these letters, and in the fact that they rehearse only what is

Othello must to prison. As they prepare to conduct him there he speaks:

> Soft you; a word or two before you go. . . .

The old quiet authority is his again in fullest measure; a touch of irony added here. Before *they* go. Give orders now who may, he will not. Then:

> I have done the state some service and they know it. . . .

—his one dispassionate comment upon his downfall from what he was. For the rest, let them speak the truth of him, and of those "unlucky deeds"; and the mild detachment of the phrase tells them that he himself knows it, as a man may when nothing is left him of either hope or fear. They are to speak

> Of one that loved not wisely but too well;
> Of one not easily jealous, but, being wrought,
> Perplexed in the extreme . . .

It is the truth.

> of one whose hand,
> Like the base Indian, threw a pearl away
> Richer than all his tribe; of one whose subdued eyes,
> Albeit unused to the melting mood,
> Drop tears as fast as the Arabian trees
> Their medicinal gum. . . .

already known to the audience, a proof that the scenes, in which the events related in these letters occur, were omitted in the representation."

But it is, of course, only another example—of which the play holds several—of preparing for a passage of supreme tension, such as Othello's last speech will be, by one in which the tension is slack. That Shakespeare did not think of the letters and of Roderigo's recovery until he suddenly found he had need of something of the sort—of this there are signs. Was the letter that "imports the death of Cassio" written by Iago? When?—not to mention why? And was he, the tried soldier, such a bungler with sword and dagger that he could not competently dispatch the already wounded Roderigo?

But these are idle arguments. The dramatic purpose of the passage is plain enough: to take our attention temporarily from Othello, so that when he recaptures it he will do so the more impressively. Material for such a passage must not be of first importance, or the tension will not be slackened; nor, at such a critical moment, can it be of merely extraneous interest, or our attention will be dissipated. The Roderigo-Iago-Cassio complication, with a final reference to the handkerchief, seems, then, to fill the need and suit the occasion fairly well. And far from the inconsistencies involved and the pedestrian style being evidence that Shakespeare did not write the passage, admit its dramatic utility, and they could perhaps better be pleaded as evidence that he did.

No longer cruel tears; and the crude horror of the deed done already tempered a little—Nature's healing sadness would be at work. But not in him. He knows better than they can tell him or Venice decide what is due to an Othello, traitor to his Christian self, from him who is now that self again; and this they shall see. Therefore,

> say besides, that in Aleppo once,
> Where a malignant and a turbaned Turk
> Beat a Venetian, and traduced the state,
> I took by the throat the circumcised dog,
> And smote him, thus.

—twice they have disarmed him, but he had kept a dagger hidden.

Gratiano and Lodovico cry out at the sight. Cassio does not; his comment comes later:

> This did I fear, but thought he had no weapon;
> For he was great of heart.

—homage to his lost hero overriding prescribed disapproval. Othello, the while, lies dead, with the dead Desdemona in his arms:

> I kissed thee ere I killed thee; no way but this,
> Killing myself, to die upon a kiss.

The simple rhyme and the simple sentiment harbor peace in oblivion.

But Lodovico turns our eyes once more upon Iago:

> O, Spartan dog,
> More fell than anguish, hunger, or the sea.
> Look on the tragic loading of this bed;
> This is thy work. . . .

In Iago's stressed silence, as he looks, is the last stroke of the action. His face is an inscrutable mask. What lies behind that but the stupidity of evil?

Act and Scene Division

Q1 and F1, near of a date in their printing, which was some eighteen to twenty years subsequent to the play's writing and staging, agree—but for a slip or so, fairly patent as such—upon its act and scene division.

The scene-division is in any case indicated in the action itself by the "cleared stage."[62] Localization, except for the first three scenes and the last, is less than precise. But the action demands this.[63]

As to the act-division; this has (exceptionally) sufficient purely dramatic validity, is sufficiently a part of the play's articulation, for it to be at least claimable—despite the twenty-year lag—as Shakespeare's own. Act I is indubitably a unit of action. Act II may be accounted one also, if not so completely, since Iago's "By the mass, 'tis morning. . . ." and Cassio's later "The day had broke before we parted. . . ." link II and III closely together. Act V has unity of subject. It compasses all the murderous consequences of Iago's scheming, and in it the whole action is wound up. There seems only to be no good reason why Acts III and IV should be divided as they are—or indeed at all—unless it be to make up the classic count of five. If this should be the purpose, the division is doubtless as good a one as may be. It shares the total matter of the two acts approximately in halves, and the flow of the action can be said to move more swiftly and fatally towards catastrophe—and markedly so—in Act IV than in Act III.

But act-division may be made to mean, in the actual staging of a play, more than one thing; a short formal pause of relaxation, or a prolonged interval in which the audience can move about and the sympathetic contact established with the actors will be broken, or anything between the two; and the effect upon the performance will be very different. What the practice of the theater was, either at the time of the play's writing or of its printing twenty years later, we do not know. Five acts smacks somewhat of the respectability of editing and printing, and F1 has certainly imposed the formula upon some plays that Shakespeare himself never so shaped. But it does not follow that he never so shaped any. *Henry V* at least, in fact, he did. Nor does it follow that three acts or four may not have suited him as well if that suited his subject. He and his theater were not bound to the classic rule for its own sake, and it can have meant little to his audience. Why indeed—so free was he—should he plan his

---

[62] The trivial complication concerning the Herald is noted in its place.
[63] Cf. p. 51, note 27; p. 65, note 40.

plays to any so unyielding a measure as "acts" at all? To some significant pattern, inevitably, his play must be shaped. If this allowed for a relaxing pause or so convenient to actors and audience and of benefit to its performance, so much the better. And if in time the five acts became an established formula for the theater as for the printed page, and four interrupting intervals in a performance promised to be too many, the superfluous ones had only to be formalized, even to vanishing point—Shakespeare and his immediate inheritors were masters enough in a theater of their own making for that; and that, I suggest, is how they would view the matter.

The producer of Shakespeare's plays today, in this as in more important questions, must distinguish the essential from the incidental. Where direct evidence is lacking as authority for what he aims to do he must fall back on circumstantial, judging the worth of it. He must, on occasions, boldly deduce the particular from the general; this being his own general knowledge of the essentials of Shakespeare's art, his title to produce the plays at all. He need not claim to be impeccably correct in what he does. He cannot wait for positive proof over this or that disputed point; he must do something. In the small matter of this play's act-division his course is, however, both easy and pretty plain. He should not, very certainly, introduce act-divisions of his own devising; nor does he need to, with four already provided, which are on the whole more likely to be Shakespeare's than not. He need not, on the other hand, give the value of a prolonged interval to what may have in Shakespeare's own theater counted merely as a formal pause. Nor if—the evidence being what it is— he overrides an act-division altogether (say, that in particular between Acts III and IV) will he commit any deadly sin; for he can plead that he is but emphasizing the general continuity of action, which is one of the "essentials in ordinary" of Shakespeare's art.

The Characters

IAGO

IF Iago presents something of a problem to the critic, so did he to Shakespeare. It was not a question first of imagining the man and then of finding the appropriate thing for him to do. What was to happen had already in the main been settled—by Cinthio; Shakespeare's task was to devise a character who could take his allotted share in this, convincingly and effectively.

Cinthio is in no difficulty. He warrants his "wicked Ensign" capable of every necessary crime simply by describing him as "a man of the most depraved nature in the world," and thereafter telling us that this or the other happened in the tone of one who—the events being over and done with—fears no contradiction. But the dramatist is by no means so taken at his word. His characters, under our scrutiny, must convince us of the likelihood of what they do even as they do it, while every word they speak is compulsory evidence of what they are. Carried through on such terms, the Ensign's task in the story—Iago's in the play, and Shakespeare's—can be no easy one.

Out of Cinthio's Moor Shakespeare molds to his own liking the heroic Othello, confident, dignified, candid, calm. He sets up an Iago in total contrast to him; a common fellow, foul-minded and coarse-tongued, a braggart decrying in others the qualities he himself lacks, bitterly envious, pettily spiteful, morbidly vain. He has abounding vitality, a glib tongue and a remarkable faculty of adapting himself to his company, as we see when the cynical swagger which so impresses Roderigo—that portentous "I am not what I am" and the like—turns to sober soldierly modesty with Othello. Since Iago in the course of the play will attitudinize much and variously, and not only before his victims but to himself, will exhibit such skill and a seemingly all but supernatural cunning, Shakespeare, for a start, gives us this unvarnished view of him, of the self, at any rate, that he shows to Roderigo, whom he despises too much to care to cheat of anything but money.

We could take it, too, that this opening view of Iago, the first impression he is to make, was meant to be the true one, if only because Shakespeare, in first presenting a character, never deliberately misleads us, is accustomed, rather, to sketch in its chief features, then and there, as unmistakably as possible, so as to leave us in no doubt from the start as to the sort of man or

woman he is.[64] He likes, moreover, to state his case—so to say—
as soon and as clearly as possible. And here, in the first two
scenes, in the contrast between the men, and in the boasted hate
and its masking, are the main factors of the play already defined
and set in motion. We shall, besides, soon become aware that
a play is in the making differing in important aspects from its
neighbor tragedies. With Macbeth, with Antony, amid the
clashes of *King Lear*, the destructive force is one of the nobler
human ardors turned to evil, and the battleground—as so notably
with Hamlet—is the hero's soul. Here the evil impulse is
externalized in Iago; and if Othello's soul be a battleground, he
himself puts up no fight on it. Nor can the jealousy which un-
does him be properly called a degrading of the love it supplants;
it is an aberration rather, and an ignoble one. Iago inoculates him
with it, as with a disease, and after the feeblest of struggles
against it—he is lost.[65] Othello is not, therefore, a spiritual
tragedy in the sense that the others may be called so. It is only the
more painful; an all but intolerable exhibition, indeed, of
human wickedness and folly, which does not so much purge us
with pity and terror as fill us with horror and with anger that such
a shoddy creature as Iago, possessed by his mountebank egoism,
his envy and spite, should be able unresisted to destroy an Othello
and bring Desdemona to her death. This incongruity is the keynote of the tragedy, and Shakespeare, therefore, strikes it clearly
to begin with. And the actor who tries, here or later, to present
Iago as a sort of half-brother to Milton's Satan only falsifies both
character and play.

To begin with he is not planning Othello's ruin at all. While
he protests that

> I do hate him as I do hell pains. . . .

yet for an aim:

> I follow him to serve my turn upon him. . . .

[64] I can think of no instance to the contrary. It will be partly, of course, a
question of economy. He has much to do with his characters—their talk and
action make up his sole medium—and not overmuch time in which to do it. He
cannot afford to turn them first in one direction, then in another, and so
complicate his task.

[65] Cf. Leontes, whom Shakespeare, writing later, treats as a purely pathological
case.

and he admits that Brabantio's anger can at most only

> gall him to some check . . .

Roderigo do no more than

> poison his delight , . .
> And though he in a fertile climate dwell,
> Plague him with flies. . . .

Spite; nothing deadlier! And when later, left alone, he asks himself how he may best serve his turn upon him, it will be by filching Cassio's place; and simply to this end it is that he intends

> After some time, to abuse Othello's ear
> That he is too familiar with his wife.

It will no doubt gratify his malice merely to see Othello vexed by jealousy (that being, it seems, the one sort of barb by which his own hide might be pierced); and a finer-drawn second thought ensues, another vista is opened in the·

> and to plume up my will
> In double knavery . . .

—to flatter and foster, besides, that is to say, his egregious conceit of his own wickedness.[66] But he is still aiming in the main at his own material advantage. Well for him, it will seem in retrospect, had he looked no further and known when to "cash in" on a success. For within a while, by his plausible tongue and his gangster's skill, he will most brilliantly have maneuvered Cassio

---

[66] Bradley, after much debate, finds in the "plume up my will . . ." the master-key to Iago's mind, his inmost motive. To agree one must add, I think, that Iago is hardly aware of it—nor Shakespeare. This is not necessarily the paradox it may sound. An imaginative author, steeped in his subject, will sometimes write more wisely than he knows. One need only insist, then, that Shakespeare is not here intentionally presenting us with any such master-key; for if he were he would give the phrase an appropriate saliency, whereas it is so placed in the speech that it cannot well be made either arresting or memorable. In the "double knavery" does come the first hint of the will to do evil for its own sake (as well as for the profit of it) that carries Iago both to triumph and disaster, but one cannot recognize the tune from this single note heard in passing.

Bradley was a most enlightened critic and one hesitates to differ from him. But his habit of treating the characters in a play as if they had once lived actual lives of their own (he says elsewhere, for instance, that Iago's intellect cannot be compared to Napoleon's; but one must not, surely, even begin to compare an imaginary Iago to a real Napoleon), while it lends his pages great vitality, is apt to blind him to mere dramatic technicalities such as this.

into disgrace, and still be "honest Iago" to all the world, his victim included. And there is the lieutenantry ripe and ready to fall to him. But by then he must be appeasing the hunger of his quite profitless hate for Othello. Here are deeper waters. Success exhilarating him, he plunges in, to find that seemingly he can navigate them as brilliantly. He wins his will, and no hate could be more fully satisfied. But it is at the price of his own torture and death; no part of the program, this! There is this tragedy of Iago to be considered too, though it will hardly appeal to our pity.

What is the secret of his success—and failure? If it rests, as is likely, in his being what he is, he cannot tell us, and we listen to those many soliloquies in vain. Of his opinions and desires and of what he means to do they will tell us truly; but as to what he *is*, less than another can the man who lives by deceiving others know the truth about himself. We observe and must judge for ourselves. He vaunts his doctrine of "reason," and seemingly wiser ears than Roderigo's have approved that

> 'tis in ourselves that we are thus or thus. . . . If the balance of our lives had not the one scale of reason to poise another of sensuality, the blood and baseness of our natures would conduct us to most preposterous conclusions. . . .

—as, in fact, the blood and baseness of Iago's nature ultimately do. He owes it, then, to his intellectual vanity to make a show of finding good reason for wreaking his hate on Othello. But it is a very poor show. He cannot trouble even to decide whether he thinks that Othello has cuckolded him or no.

> I know not if't be true,
> But I, for mere suspicion in that kind,
> Will do as if for surety.

Suspicion of "the lusty Moor" (about the last epithet, incidentally, to apply to Othello) is, however, of itself so encouraging, that he returns to it, yet to admit besides in the very next breath that

> The Moor, howbeit that I endure him not,
> Is of a constant, loving, noble nature;
> And I dare think he'll prove to Desdemona
> A most dear husband. . . .

—to which incongruous testimony he tags a fantastic notion of
fastening upon Desdemona himself; since

> I do love her too,
> Not out of absolute lust . . .
> But partly led to diet my revenge. . . .

next contributing to this mental chaos a sudden parenthetic

> For I fear Cassio with my night-cap too . . .

(the recent, frank, merrily gallant kiss of greeting offered
Emilia twisted to that account!). Needless to say we hear no more
of his "love" for Desdemona or fear of Cassio. And his suspicion
of Othello's lechery, stoked up to

> the thought whereof
> Doth like a poisonous mineral gnaw my inwards;
> And nothing can or shall content my soul
> Till I am evened with him, wife for wife. . . .

collapses, inconsequently and ridiculously, then and there, into

> Or failing so, yet that I put the Moor
> At least into a jealousy so strong
> That judgment cannot cure. . . .

By the light of his reasoning, then—this being a specimen of it
—Iago would not seem likely to get very far. Nor is his judgment
of Othello's character oversound. Nor, when he turns to Desdemona—with

> That Cassio loves her, I do well believe it;
> That she loves him, 'tis apt and of great credit. . . .

—does he come nearer the mark; and even as to Cassio he is
astray. And the soliloquy's ending, its

> 'Tis here, but yet confused. . . .

suggests that he is not wholly unaware of all this himself. It is not
"reason" that serves him, though he would like to think it did.
We note, too, that his projects are continually changing. It is on
the spur of the moment that he is at his best, when he trusts to
its inspiration.

Swinburne, refining upon Hazlitt, calls Iago "a contriving
artist in real life," and the phrase is illuminating. Here indeed is
the key—and was there need of any other?—to the problem

Shakespeare set himself when he decided that his heroic Othello was not to be destroyed by an opponent of the same caliber, but dragged down by an Iago. He will not, that is to say, exalt such wickedness. That Iago himself should do so—the clever, but essentially stupid fellow, the common man of common mind—is quite another matter. But how equip such a one for his task, with genuine capacities denied him? By endowing him with the intuition of the artist, and the power of counterfeiting them. And Shakespeare will have a further need, which an artist Iago can satisfy, of a villain pursuing wickedness for its own sake.

The artist in leading-strings, writing or painting or making music to order, may be a happily harmless creature enough. Love of his art for its own sake turns him egoist. This is inevitable. In normal human love for a person, a country or a cause, we find egoism and devotion combined, the egoism storing up no more force than will be spent in devotion. But the artist's devotion to his evolving work is to something that is still a part of him, and his egoism will thus be fed and fed until the completing of the work discharges him of its burden. Being ill-fed or over-fed, it may grow diseased and monstrous. The force of a passion so self-fulfilling as to be self-forgetful is likeliest, perhaps, to carry him cleanly through the adventure; and this, at its most powerful, can so mobilize his faculties that their functions will seem to fuse—imagination and thought and skill working together as one—to an incommunicable magnifying of their power. The artist-egoist, minding nothing but his art, can, of course, be as harmless a creature—unless to himself and his friends and relations—as the artist in leading-strings, and his work may have its peculiar value. But set such an occult and lawless force operating in real life, and it can prove dangerous indeed; this force in Iago, for instance, of a love of evil for its own sake, vivified by the artist's powers, pursued with the artist's unscrupulous passion.

The medium in which Iago works is the actor's; and in the crude sense of pretending to be what he is not, and in his chameleonlike ability to adapt himself to change of company and circumstance, we find him an accomplished actor from the beginning. These rudiments of the art of acting most people learn to practice a little—and harmlessly—in real life; but Iago is an expert to the point that pretense is second nature to him. In his earlier maneuverings, moreover, he is on familiar ground. "Honest Iago," with his sympathetically parasitic faculty of being all things to all men, knows, without thinking, how his fellow soldiers Cassio and Montano (Roderigo is a nonentity), the Cyprus gallants and Othello will think and act when events pass—with a very little help from him—as they do. So all goes well. Then, under their stimulus of success, and triflingly perhaps of wine,[67] his inherent hatred of Othello begins to pulse more urgently, and then it is that the artist in Iago takes effective command. For his profit in Cassio's ruin, already achieved, is forgotten, and it is the thought of Othello's that obsesses him, profitless though this may be. Here is the artist who will do the thing for its own sake, and out of sheer delight in the doing let himself be carried beyond all bounds of "reason" and prudence. Desdemona shall be ruined too, though he has no hatred for her. And, beaconlike, there at once flashes on him—as inspiration visits the artist—a solution to the problem that his reason left so confused. An error to speculate, as his own nature bade him, upon Cassio's treachery to his friend, Desdemona's to Othello. It is the very virtues of the virtuous that can best be turned against them. While Cassio, therefore,

> this honest fool
> Plies Desdemona to repair his fortunes,
> And she for him pleads strongly to the Moor,
> I'll pour this pestilence into his ear,
> That she repeals him for her body's lust;
> And by how much she strives to do him good,
> She shall undo her credit with the Moor.
> So will I turn her virtue into pitch;
> And out of her own goodnesss make the net
> That shall enmesh them all.

Iago feels—as at such a moment the fervent artist will—that a very revelation has been vouchsafed him, sent direct from the Devil himself, so exhilarating is it. And Shakespeare has found, in part at least, the Iago he needs. And the way is now open to the play's tragic end.

---

[67] That which hath made Cassio drunk hath made him bold. Lady Macbeth had the same head for liquor.

But given the unqualified purpose, what of the task itself and the means? To undermine Othello's faith in Desdemona! What part can Iago play which will best let him attempt that? Of the hectoring admonition which serves with Roderigo there can naturally be none, nor much, to begin with at any rate, of the frank comradely helpfulness which is bait for Cassio. Can any sort of frontal attack, indeed, be made on that superb authority? Somehow, then, he must find his way behind the defenses, and from there, in the friendliest fashion, help Othello to achieve his own ruin. Hate, moreover, dictates this, since there is no ill worse than self-inflicted ill. But how insinuate his way into that very sanctuary of Othello's being where love for Desdemona is lodged? How discover in his own base nature enough understanding of Othello's to admit him there? How qualify for the playing of this part?

Play-acting is pretense, and as an art it is more than that. The actor is the dramatist's mouthpiece, and as an artist he is something besides. His share in their mutual work is to give bodily life to what has until then existed only as thought recorded in words. The career of a character in a play from its imagining to its presenting on a stage has something in common with the begetting and birth of a child, and the particular shares of the parents in their offspring may both seem as obvious and prove as hard to analyze. But an actor will acquire certain specialized and somewhat anomalous faculties. Being neither mere mouthpiece nor mere puppet, he interprets a character—the material the dramatist gives him—in the terms, more or less disguised, of his own personality. Yet it will not be his true personality. He cannot, strictly speaking, know more of the character than the dramatist has told him, and this, though it be the essential part, can never be much. But he must seem to know much more, and in many ways, if we are to think of the two as one. Yet this need be but seeming. He need acquire no knowledge but apparent knowledge, cultivate in this respect no ability but to seem able, nor build up, of this composite personality demanded, anything but a painted façade. Note that it is not a question of trivial knowledge or poor ability, still less of evil or good, but of knowledge and ability merely reflected as in a mirror—which reflects the best and the worthless alike. The actor's is, above all, the faculty of sympathy; found physically in the sensitive ear, the receptive eye, the dancer's body that of itself responds, emotionally in the tears or laughter ready at call, and intellectually in a capacity not only seemingly to absorb some product of another's thought, but to reproduce the effects of understanding it without necessarily having understood it in the least. The mirror upheld to nature is a long-accepted image for the art of the theater. As the art matures the mirror is brought to reflecting from beneath the surface; and in the character and skill of an Iago is pictured to us—a reflection from art back to life again—how bedded in human nature and active in real life the actor's faculty can be. In real life also it *may* be innocuously exercised; the worst to be urged as a rule against the parasite intelligence—to which dishonorable status the loss of artistic sanction reduces the actor's—a certain complacency in futility. But with hate to give it purpose, it can be made, as Iago makes it, an instrument of deadly corruption.

He has most sensitive material to work upon. Othello—it is the countervailing trait to his soldierly calm—is as quick in response to a touch or a hint as the high-mettled barb he would ride. And if Iago wisely cannot, neither has he need to accuse Desdemona directly and brutally. A little eavesdropping gives him for a starting point matter which is in Othello's mind already, a known answer to his artless question whether Cassio knew of the wooing. From there he feels his way—as delicately at first as an insect by its tentacles—into that field of the man's affections in which he means to make havoc; and he surreptitiously takes and ever so slightly twists the form of the matter he finds there and reflects it back to Othello, who sees his own thought again as in a distorting mirror, receives back thoughts and words obscured and perverted. He cannot dominate Othello yet, but he can misinterpret him to himself.

The finer the nature the more fragile its defense; when thicker skins would be but chafed, the poison permeates Othello. For a measure of his susceptibility: it needs but the provocative intonation of that single word "Indeed" to set him questioning, and again questioning; insistent to be answered, and to leave him to self-questioning. Here is the intuitively feared requital for the "content so absolute" of his reunion with Desdemona; no halfway for him between that and a very helplessness of doubt. And Iago, admitted to intimacy, can not only proffer, for bad example, his own failings in jealousy and suspicion, but—his parasite mind feeding on Othello's, his coarse spirit gaining perception from contact with Othello's fine spirit—can soon learn to detect rifts in the texture of its confidence made ready for his widening that Othello will then himself the more effectively widen again. "By heaven," he exclaims, "he echoes me"; and words and thoughts are indeed flung back and forth between them until it would be hard to say whose they first were. And note how Iago seizes on the vague misgiving in the unfinished thought of Desdemona's nature "erring from itself—" to shape and color it into a vivid image of her, rank of "will" and foul of mind; it is such a verdict on her very love for him that he renders back to Othello, to be digested and turned about, and to re-emerge, its stigma on them both, in the bitter "Haply, for I am black. . . ."

In this passage of less than two hundred lines we are shown Othello's moral disintegration. But it owes its compressed form and continuity to dramatic convenience only. Actually to be imagined is a protracted, many-sided, disjunctive process of chicanery, in which Iago gathers, mainly from Othello himself, how best to cheat him, a complexity which Shakespeare clarifies and orders into the form of a few minutes' talk, into no greater a space than the action allowable can animate.

Iago is enjoying himself. He has the artist's faculty for doing well whatever he takes pleasure in doing, and for no solider reason than that. He is even amusing himself. The trick with the handkerchief—"This may do something"—should prove a pretty one. He has yet to see the effect of his poison on Othello. It will doubtless soon begin to "Burn like the mines of sulphur," but he can hardly look suddenly to find his obliging self in the clutch of that "waked wrath," and being shaken as a rat by a dog.

He is a passionless creature. Cinthio gives his wicked Ensign some motive for evil-doing in jealousy, and a love for Desdemona ignored and so "changed into the bitterest hate." But Shakespeare admits neither love nor lust into Iago's composition, nothing so human; shows him to us, on the contrary, frigidly speculating upon the use such indulgence might be to him, and as frigidly deciding: none. Even his hate is cold, and will be the more tenacious for that, its strength not being spent in emotional ebb and flow. His endeavors then to respond suitably to Othello's outbursts—the flamboyant "Take note, take note, O world . . ." and the kneeling to echo and to mock the oath by "yond marble heaven"—are simply histrionic, and overdone at that. And this, made plain to us, might be plain to Othello, were he not "eaten up with passion." For of intellectual excitement Iago *is* capable, and, elated by swift success, he begins to run risks. That stirs his cold blood; it is all that does. And the pleasures of the game, as it develops, are multiplying. He has the noble Moor stripped now, but for a rag or so, of his nobility; no stimulus to savagery seems to be too strong for him. Iago can, consequently, admit more of himself into the part he is playing, can, in the actor's phrase, "let himself go," while the actor faculty enables him still to keep a cool enough eye upon whither he is going. He can thus vent the full foulness of his mind, in itself a relief and a pleasure: and there is the sheer pleasure of seeing Othello suffer and madden beneath the spate of it. And his daring pays. The success of the enterprise betters all expectation. Not merely is Cassio's death to be granted him—and he had schemed for no more than his disgrace—but at that zestful crisis, with the artist in evil in him strung to perfect pitch, one timely phrase assures him of Desdemona's thrown in too.

But in the very ease and abundance of his success, in his complacent enjoyment and exploitation of it, looking neither ahead nor around, lie the means to his ultimate ruin. To harry the distraught Othello until he actually collapses at his feet in a fit, then to rally the unlucky cuckold and condescendingly urge him to "be a man"; to be able to jerk him, like a black puppet, back and forth from his eavesdropping—what could be more amusing? And having once had to defer for his ends to each changing shade of Othello's mood, now to find the victim swaying to every sinister touch, even to be able—artist in evil as he is—to devise that felicitous strangling of Desdemona "in her bed, even the bed she hath contaminated"—this is gratifying too. There are secret satisfactions besides. To see Desdemona struck and be the hidden force behind the blow, to deplore Othello's conduct and be the unsuspected prompter of it; this is meat and drink to thwarted, perverted vanity. And that the blind fools who have ever

galled him by their patronizing praise should be deaf to the irony
in his

> Alas, alas!
> It is not *honesty* in me to speak
> What I have seen and known.

—he finds egregious pleasure here.

Then comes, as an unlooked-for gift, the most delectable
episode in his clandestine triumph. He has seen Othello collapsed
at his feet; now it is Desdemona kneeling there, innocently
begging the humble Ensign to rescue her from the very misery
—did she but know it, worse!—into which he, even he, has
plunged her. He savors her anguish, gently encourages the pitiful
delusion. Could his tortuous "Divinity of hell" be more gracious
to him—yet, fittingly, and as invariably under surfeit of good
luck, more beguiling? For in the cold, complacent arrogance of
his success he disregards and dismisses with a dozen contemptuous
words, with a final "You are a fool: go to," the threat that, at this
very moment, emerges so plainly and sounds so insistently in
Emilia's questing anger. Here again shows the radical stupidity
of the man, that other aspect of the adroit, intuitively extem-
porizing artist-actor-charlatan, who until now has played his
deadly part so well. He misjudges Emilia, even as by the light of
his vaunted "reason" he misjudged Desdemona and Cassio as
likely lovers and traitors to Othello. He may know the Emilia of
a marriage to him. How should such as he divine what fellowship
with Desdemona has made her?

This complacency adds even to the careless contempt with
which he customarily treats Roderigo, now unexpectedly rebellious. When he sees that the trouble is serious he schemes its
liquidation—and Roderigo's—smartly enough; and Cassio's death
in addition will round off events very comfortably. But his luck
proves to be a little out, that "devil's own luck" which has carried
him round so many awkward corners—which is perhaps but
another term for the quick sense of the effective moment that
has marked him at his best. Roderigo blunders. He blunders. It
is not irretrievable blundering, but it rattles him. And he, whose
cue it is to be always so cool and detached, finds himself
bustling, too, amid the bustle and confusion, and bluffing and

giving orders at random. And for the very first time—although
not until he has said it does he really recognize it:

> This is the night
> That either makes me, or fordoes me quite.

—he is touched by fear.

When Emilia turns on him and speaks out and stands her
ground he is utterly at a loss, can find nothing to do but stupidly,
since uselessly, to kill her.

In the Folio's list of characters Iago is ticketed "a Villaine," as
he might be in the program of the crudest of melodramas today;
and he himself rejoices in his claims to the title. Even so, and yet
more explicitly, does Richard III announce in his first soliloquy
that he is "determined to prove a villain," proceed accordingly,
and, in his last, argue at some length the metaphysical issues of
his conduct. But between the writing of the two plays Shakespeare
has developed other methods. He has learned to take these
theatrical types and to give them, not merely more individuality,
but an inward verity as well. Out of the conventional Jew comes
Shylock; Falstaff out of Prince Hal's butt and buffoon; out of
the "melancholy man" Hamlet. And out of Cinthio's "wicked
Ensign," and his theatrical match, the melodramatic "villaine,"
evolves Iago.

Points of view will remain, from which a line drawn between
Iago and the villain of melodrama is so fine as to be invisible.
But melodrama is not necessarily false to life; it may only unduly
simplify it. And Shakespeare's problem was to retain the melodramatic simplicity with the strength which belongs to it, and to
give this an inward verity too. He solves it, as we have seen, by
making his Iago something of a melodramatic actor in real life.
The result is a highly complex, and at moments a very puzzling,
character; but in it the reconciliation between verity and melodrama is achieved. There are plenty such people in the world,
who borrow, as actors do, their working material, may add bits
of themselves to it, will make a superficially brilliant use of the
amalgam, yet remain worthless within. But, as a rule, they lack
force of character (again, as do actors, they "live to please"), and
the Iago of the story must be exceptionally endowed with some

sort of force. Shakespeare sees this begotten by hate, and by a hate which will have only the more force for being unreasoning and motiveless.[68] In its stupidity—there is to be no glorification of such wickedness—it can well bring him at last to his doom, but by a blinkered persistence which belongs to unreason it may first attain its ends. Iago—it belongs to the part he is playing— sees himself above all as a man of reason. He reminds us rather, behind his intellectual antics, of a hound on the trail, sensitive and alert, nose to the mud, searching and sampling, appetite and instinct combining to guide him past error after error to his quarry. His hate possesses him. It rewards him. But when it has had its will of him he is left—a swaggering mountebank still. The broken, bewildered Othello asks:

> Will you, I pray, demand that demi-devil
> Why he hath thus ensnared my soul and body?

Why, indeed! The true answer, spuriously qualified, he has long ago given us—and Roderigo. Repeated amid this holocaust, would it not sound even to him so incongruous as to be all but comic? "I hate the Moor"—there has been no more to the whole elaborately wicked business than that.

But with passion and persistence and some plausibility and the narrowness of purpose that belongs to evil, what cannot stupidity achieve?

OTHELLO

We have seen how, to make the story dramatically viable, the mainspring of the play's action has to be drastically compressed. It follows that the fatal flaw in the hero's character must be one which will develop swiftly and catastrophically too. The story has provided in sexual jealousy about the only one which will.

Of vanity, envy, self-seeking and distrust, which are the seeds of jealousy in general, Othello, it is insisted from the beginning, is notably free, so free that he will not readily remark them in others—in Iago, for instance, in whom they so richly abound.

---

[68] Cinthio gives his "wicked Ensign" a motive in a one-time love for Desdemona, which, ignored, has "changed into the bitterest hate." But Shakespeare— instead of seizing on it as a human contribution to his villainy—rejects this.

And he has never yet cared enough for a woman to be jealous of her; that also is made clear. It is a nature, then, taught by no earlier minor failings of this kind to resist a gross attack on it, should that come.

But sexual jealousy, once given rein, is a passion like no other. It is pathological, a moral lesion, a monomania. Facts and reason become its playthings. Othello does at first put up a feeble intellectual resistance, in a single soliloquy he struggles a little with himself; but, after this, every defense is swept away, and the poison rages in him unchecked. Here, then, is the sudden and swift descent to catastrophe, which the story, as Shakespeare dramatizes it, demands. A bad business, certainly, yet, to this extent, shocking rather than tragic. Indeed, did not Othello suffer so and dispense suffering, the spectacle of his wholly baseless duping and befooling would be more comic than otherwise, a mere upsetting of his confidence and dignity, as enjoyable to us as to Iago; and, in a ghastly fashion, it for a few moments becomes so when he is set eavesdropping upon Cassio and Bianca. Shocking, that it is, and pitiful, for all perplexed suffering is pitiful. But there is more to true tragedy than this.

The writing and rewriting of *Hamlet* must surely have shown Shakespeare the limits to the dramatic use that can be made of the purely pathological. For while little was to be done in exhibiting the character of a man consistently aping madness who would not reveal himself, even less was practicable if he were really mad and could not. With Hamlet it is the land near the borderline which proves peculiarly fruitful, since there we have him so acutely conscious of himself as to be at his readiest for that work of self-purgation by which the tragic hero finds significance in his fate.

With Othello neither the planning of the play, nor his character, nor the jealous mania which is foreign to every other trait in it, will allow for this. He cannot reason with himself about something which is in its very nature unreasonable, nor can Shakespeare set him searching for the significance of events which exist only in Iago's lies—we, the audience, should resent such futility. He is betrayed and goes ignorantly to his doom.

And when, at last, Desdemona dead, he learns the truth, what can he have to say—or we!—but

O, fool, fool, fool!

The mere sight of such beauty and nobility and happiness, all wickedly destroyed, must be a harrowing one. Yet the pity and terror of it come short of serving for the purgation of our souls, since Othello's own soul stays unpurged. Hamlet dies spiritually at peace; Lear's madness has been the means to his salvation; by interpreting his life's hell to us even Macbeth stirs us to some compassion. But what alchemy can now bring the noble Moor and the savage murderer into unity again? The "cruel tears" and the kiss and the talk of justice are more intolerable than the savagery itself. Nor can remorse bridge—though too late—the gulf between the two; they were and remain beings apart. Othello wakes as from a nightmare only to kill himself, his prospect hell. And the play's last word is, significantly, not of him, but of tortures for Iago; punishment as barren as the crime. It is a tragedy without meaning, and that is the ultimate horror of it.

But Othello, when it is too late, does at least become conscious of this cleavage made in his nature. Hence his submission to Lodovico as

he that *was* Othello . . .

The Othello that was could never have done such a deed; an ignorant brute in him has done it. Yet it is still he, the Christian Othello, accepted, trusted, loved, who has proved viler even than "the circumcised dog" that he smote "in Aleppo once." It is the fellow to this dog in him that he now smites "thus" to end all.

If he cannot be let elucidate his calamities, Shakespeare can at least make him the very kind of man who could not. To begin with, he is "the Moor," and in this alone, a strange, removed, enigmatic figure. Before we see him we hear him only vilified as "thick-lips" and "lascivious Moor"; it is a way of adding by slight surprise to the effect he will make upon us when he does appear, so plainly nothing of the sort, but—even before we learn he is of royal blood—an aristocrat, a chief of men and the ripe soldier, sparing of words, their tone level and clear, not to be flustered or overawed. He will have no street-brawling; that is not how he fights when he must fight. Nor will he wrangle here in public;

he does not even notice Brabantio's abuse of him. To the Duke himself and the Senators he yields no more than the respect due to his

> very noble and approved good masters . . .

They shall hear his "round unvarnished tale"; he will call one witness, Desdemona; and upon her word—nor when she comes does he even first speak to her lest he seem to bias it—will he be judged.

By touch after touch Shakespeare builds up the figure, and upon its present calm and poise the lightest is effective. Since he was a very child—since his arms had "seven years' pith"—he has known only war and adventure. And, but for love of Desdemona, he would not now put his "unhoused free condition" into "circumscription and confine." War calling, they must both obey; he leaving her then and there, she following him into danger if she may. His austerity protests that it will not be

> To please the palate of my appetite . . .

her courage that it is even

> to his honours and his valiant parts . . .

that she has consecrated "soul and fortunes." It is no ordinary marriage. There is nothing commonplace in either of them.

There is little tenderness in their parting:

> Come, Desdemona; I have but an hour
> Of love, of worldly matters and direction,
> To spend with thee. . . .

—that is all. But she accepts it so, the soldier's wife already. It is only after their separation, when he finds her safe in Cyprus, preserved from the dangers of war and shipwreck, that he realizes how much she and this new and strange thing happiness mean to him.[69] He is awed—

> If it were now to die,
> 'Twere now to be most happy; for, I fear,
> My soul hath her content so absolute,
> That not another comfort like to this
> Succeeds in unknown fate.

---

[69] Dangers more present to the Elizabethan mind—the minds of the play's first audience—than to our own. Yet in January 1940, as I write, this is hardly so.

—and amused—

> O, my sweet,
> I prattle out of fashion, and I dote
> In mine own comforts.

by its hold on him. But he is as strict in discipline with himself as with others. It is his wedding night, but his parting orders to Cassio are:

> to-morrow with your earliest
> Let me have speech with you.

Unhappily for Cassio, he finds cause to speak with him still earlier. When the noise of the unpardonable broil has been quelled; quietly, sternly, curtly it is:

> Cassio, I love thee;
> But never more be officer of mine.

For in judgment he is swift and uncompromising. This is the last capital touch given to the picture of a still unscathed Othello. In retrospect we may recognize the danger that lay in a too inflexible perfection of poise; once upset, hard to regain.

It is the picture of a quite exceptional man; in high repute and conscious of his worth, yet not self-conscious; of a dignity which simplicity does not jeopardize; generous in praise of those who serve him; commanding respect without fear; frank and unsuspicious and ready to reciprocate affection. Yet he has been a man apart, alone. He is not young, has fought and adventured the world over, striking root nowhere. And he is black. The Venetians, truly, not only value his soldiership, but Brabantio, he says:

> loved me, oft invited me . . .

They seemed to be treating him in everything as one of themselves. But to have him marry Desdemona! That would be quite another question. Neither he nor she was of the eloping kind; evidently no other way looked open to them. Lay a part of Brabantio's anger to the elopement itself, of the Duke's appeasing attitude to his wish, with the Turks attacking Cyprus, not to offend his only competent general. Yet that the daughter of a Venetian Senator should

> to incur a general mock,
> Run from her guardage to the sooty bosom . . .

—even of the renowned Othello—is conduct unnatural enough for her bewitching

> By spells and medicines bought of mountebanks . . .

to be a very likely way of accounting for it. Shakespeare does not need to spend much explanatory speech on all this. Othello's exotic figure and the contrast between the two will in themselves be eloquent of it. And should we, under the spell of his nobility, be inclined to forget it—since Desdemona could!—reminder will not be lacking. For Iago's defiling eye sees only this, reads only foulness and perversity into such enfranchisement.

But Desdemona

> saw Othello's visage in his mind . . .

That we may see him as she did the story of his life is repeated before the Senate and to us even as she heard it. And, says the Duke,

> I think this tale would win my daughter too.

It is in her fine faith in this vision of him that she goes forward, first to a happiness justifying and fulfilling it, then to its inexplicable shattering. He finds in happiness with her a self unrealized before. It is a self created by her love for him, and will be the more dependent, therefore, upon his faith in that. It will be, besides, a dangerously defenseless self, since he is no longer a young man when it comes to life in him, and between it and the rest of his character, fully formed and set in far other molds, there can be no easy interplay. This division between old and new in him—between seasoned soldier and enraptured bridegroom!—presages the terrible cleavage to come. He does not bring to his love for Desdemona, nor wish to, the measured wisdom which experience has taught him. It is against his judgment that he yields to her pleading for Cassio with a

> let him come when he will;
> I will deny thee nothing.

The romantic Cassio himself had acclaimed her as "our great captain's captain," of which Iago's acid version is that "our general's wife is now the general." He is, in fact—the elder husband, the young wife!—uxorious; yet less from weakness than in tribute to this miracle she has wrought in him. Could it prove illusion—he is at the height of happiness, challenging fate, Iago at his side—"chaos is come again." But even now, and for all their love, they see life differently. Adventure behind them, she has settled down to the workaday joys of a home, in which she can be confidently, merrily, carelessly herself, so confidently, we note, that his exasperation over the handkerchief gives her only passing concern. But he is still an uncharted stranger in this world, inapt, despite his quality, at its defense—which yet needs only the simple, natural instinct in a man, loving and so beloved, that all is well.[70]

Othello has a quick and powerful imagination. It is a gift which in a man of action may make either for greatness or disaster. It can be disciplined and refined into a perceptiveness, which will pierce to the heart of a problem while duller men are scratching its surface; it can divorce his mind from reality altogether. How is it that, even under stress, Othello does not unarguably perceive Desdemona's innocence and Iago's falsity? Instead his imagination only serves to inflame his passion. He is conscious of its unruliness.

> I swear 'tis better to be much abused
> Than but to know't a little.

—since imagination will multiply "little" beyond measure; that, when passion has dislodged reason in him, is his first cry. Imagination begets monstrous notions:

> I had been happy, if the general camp,
> Pioneers and all, had tasted her sweet body,
> So I had nothing known. . . .

And Iago keeps it fed with such kindred matter as the tale of Cassio's dream, with picturings increasingly physical, of her "naked with her friend a-bed," of Cassio's confessedly lying "with her, on her; what you will!"—until the explicit obscenity leaves imagination at a loss, and nature suspends the torment in

---

[70] Shakespeare shows us the two, upon the very edge of calamity, living together—as Cinthio tells us that his Moor and Desdemona were living—in "harmony and peace"; he contrives to insinuate thus much of this telling introduction to the story into the play.

the oblivion of a swoon. Later, self-torment takes the obscurer, perverser form of the "horrible fancy" which sees Desdemona as a whore in a brothel, himself among her purchasers; imagination run rabid.

But, in his right mind, he can be master of his imagination too. Call Iago an "artist in real life," if a spurious one; Othello is the poet born. While the soldier he is must hold to realities, the poet in him is free in a metaphysical world in which these find a rarer meaning. The tales that won Desdemona will have been of a poet's telling—anthropophagi and "men whose heads do grow beneath their shoulders" being mere curiosities in themselves—and the more roundly told and unvarnished the more befitting the matter and the man. We are still far from the Othello who hysterically charges a lost handkerchief with the very "mighty magic" he mocks at here.

From the beginning, when the occasion stirs him, the poet's mind shows. It shows in the delicate balance of idea and phrase, in the irony blended with beauty of

> Keep up your bright swords, for the dew will rust them.

It is a poet that seeks refuge from dishonor among imaged memories of a glory indefeasibly his, of

> the plumed troop and the big wars
> That make ambition virtue! . . .
>   the neighing steed and the shrill trump,
> The spirit-stirring drum, the ear-piercing fife,
> The royal banner and all quality,
> Pride, pomp and circumstance of glorious war!

then to renounce them as a man renouncing life itself. This is not an exercise in rhetoric. The trumpet and drum, the fife and the banners, were themselves tokens of the metaphysical world, in which Othello found his life's meaning. The words are tokens too, which, in the melody and rhythm of the mounting phrases, he is setting to do all that words made musical may do to unveil that world for him again.

It is a world in which one lives alone. Iago—being what he is—has listened in amazed incomprehension. He will be ready, however, at its next unveiling, upon the black vision of

> the Pontic sea,
> Whose icy current and compulsive course
> Ne'er feels retiring ebb, but keeps due on
> To the Propontic and the Hellespont . . .

with a fine histrionic pretense to fellowship in it. Desdemona is given a horrifying glimpse of it as an anarchy of grotesque and infected images; flies quickening in the shambles, a winking moon, the bawdy wind—a world to which he brings the miseries bred in him. He reaches towards his metaphysical world once more in the rapt calm of

> It is the cause, it is the cause, my soul:
> Let me not name it to you, you chaste stars!
> It is the cause. . . .

to enter it, his murderous passion sated, and find it void:

> Methinks it should be now a huge eclipse
> Of sun and moon, and that the affrighted globe
> Should yawn at alteration.

—no lesser figure will serve.

Othello's, we said, is a story of blindness and folly, of a man run mad. As the play is planned, evil works all but unquestioned in him until it is too late. Of battle between good and evil, his soul the battleground, even of a clarifying consciousness of the evil at work in him, there is nothing. Not until the madman's deed is done, does "he that was Othello" wake to sanity again; his tragedy, then, to have proved that from the seemingly securest heights of his "soul's content" there is no depth of savagery to which man cannot fall. Yet, in face of the irrevocable deed savage and man are one.

Shakespeare paints us a merciless picture of the awakened, the broken Othello; of the frenetically repentant creature of Emilia's scornful

> Nay, lay thee down and roar. . . .

of the man with all strength for evil or for good gone out of him, remorse mere mockery as he looks upon the dead Desdemona; of an Othello crying

> Whip me, ye devils,
> From the possession of this heavenly sight!

> Blow me about in winds! roast me in sulphur!
> Wash me in steep-down gulfs of liquid fire! . . .

—sheer horror this; the howling of the damned! He speaks his
own epitaph before he dies; a last echo of the noble Moor that was.

DESDEMONA, EMILIA, BIANCA

Desdemona's part in the play is a passive one. The single
fateful step she takes has already been taken at the start. We have
only to be told—and this we are told most explicitly—that she
took it wholly of her own free will. Emilia, but for the sneaking
of the handkerchief and one aimless explosion of wrath, remains
passive until at last she unmasks Iago. Bianca is a cat's-paw. The
economy of the action allows for no extraneous adventuring into
the character of any of the three. They respond illuminatingly
to its events; and by setting them in strong contrast each to the
other Shakespeare makes them, all three, the more vivid. Desdemona and Bianca never even meet. But Cassio, turning so
differently from the one to greet the other so cavalierly, links the
two; and what Bianca is and what Desdemona—what in the face
of Iago's slanders she so transparently is *not*—springs thus into
higher relief. The three provide the play with something like a
pattern of womankind—motherhood and old age omitted: Desdemona's fine nature set beside Emilia's coarseness, with the little
trull Bianca, who

> by selling her desires
> Buys herself bread and clothes . . .

for their ape and counterfeit.

DESDEMONA

Desdemona appears in one scene only of the three which pass
in Venice and speaks just twenty-seven lines. But the action and
debate center on her, and when she has at last had her own say
a very clear picture of her emerges.

What has happened is extraordinary enough in itself to rivet
our attention. The tale of it is flung at us for a start in the crudest
and most rancorous terms. Their rancor discounts them somewhat; still more does the sight of Othello himself, so evidently
neither "gross" nor "lascivious," nor is he even found, as he

might more suggestively be, in Desdemona's company. Brabantio's angry chatter about drugs, charms and witchcraft sounds overdone. But his talk of her as

> a maid so tender, fair and happy,
> So opposite to marriage that she shunned
> The wealthy curled darlings of our nation . . .

as

> A maiden never bold;
> Of spirit so still and quiet that her motion
> Blushed at herself . . .

has a likelier ring, and we expect explanation. Othello's may suffice the Duke, concerned for those Cyprus wars; but it takes Desdemona's own appearance fully to enlighten us. And the effect of it is unexpected. This "maiden never bold" is intimidated neither by her father nor "all this noble company." She does not turn to Othello for support, nor plead irresistible love for him, nor, indeed, offer any excuse whatever for her conduct. She speaks of duty, but as divided between past and future; once owed gratefully to her father, now, she challenges—there is defiance in the word!—due to her husband. Whatever else, here is no helpless maiden enticed away, whether by foul means or fair. Small wonder that, before such impassivity, Brabantio's distress freezes to a

> God be with you! I have done.

—after which, while he and the Duke exchange their neat, not too engrossing, "sentences," we can observe her mutely standing there. The war's threat to part her from Othello gives her speech again; as impassive in its admission of her father's final loss of her, but lucid and fervent—her heart bared without false shame—in the plea for her rights in the love for which she has dared so greatly. Again, here is a Desdemona unknown to her father, unknown, we may suppose, to Othello too, now stirring him for the first time from his soldier's restraint to an echo of her plea. But between the explicit calm with which she can speak her determined mind and this rare favor lies in her nature a reticent and inarticulate zone, unguarded, and to prove of mortal peril to her.

Brabantio's
> She has deceived her father, and may thee.

—which Othello so trenchantly flings back at him, which Iago
stores in his memory—is more false than true. He was deceived
in her, as, with less excuse, Othello will be. She was to blame for
letting him stay too long self-deceived. But there was he who
should have known her best, knowing her so little as never even to
suspect what ardor and resolve might lie beneath her accustomed
quiet. Hard to confide in him in any case, all but impossibly hard
to tell him that she loved the alien "black" Othello. How convince
him but by doing as she did? It has taken the unexpected threat
of separation to make her speak her heart out even now; but,
speaking out, it is with no apology. Under vile accusation later on
she will swear to her innocence. But if this and no more sounds
better evidence of baser guilt—why, of explanations, arguments,
self-justifyings, of any of the means of defense commonly used
by those who might be guilty though they are not, she, who
could not be guilty, is incapable. Even as Othello went unpro-
tected against the poison of mistrust of her, so she gives never a
thought to protection against—how should she expect it?—his
mistrust. It is she, in truth, who does not wear her heart upon
her sleeve; confessing that

> I am not merry; but I do beguile
> The thing I am, by seeming otherwise.

and thereupon, to deaden her fears for Othello's safety, even
letting Cassio flirt with her a little. She is no precisian in candor.
To smooth down that unwarranted commotion over the mislaid
handkerchief she does slightly economize the facts. Moments of
great joy may leave her at a loss. Upon their reuniting all her
response to Othello's eloquent ecstasy is a sober

> The heavens forbid
> But that our loves and comforts should increase,
> Even as our days do grow!

She does not try to find words to express her deepest feelings;
they are lodged too deep in her, they are too real. That she can
plead as fluently as frankly for Cassio should be one sign at least—
were any needed—that no more than her kindness is engaged.

Moments of misery leave her dumbfounded too. Out of her clear sky of happiness it comes, with no more warning than the pother about the handkerchief; before all the world Othello strikes her. And she has nothing to say but

I have not deserved this.

Then, first dismissed as a servant might be, when later she is summoned to him again, she does not reproach him, nor even refer to the incredibly terrible thing. She cannot. She is as helpless, too, to draw reasons for his anguished passion from him as he to give them. And when at last, lashing her with "strumpet" and "whore," he leaves her and the alarmed Emilia asks her how she does, her answer is

Faith, half asleep.

She will not talk of what has passed even to Emilia. When she sends Iago to Othello to plead for her, she cannot bring herself to speak the word that has so shamed her.[71] Childish of her; but, as she says, she is "a child to chiding." Has she no pride, that she, Brabantio's daughter, who could face Duke and Senate with composure, is on her knees before Iago? But innocence has a dignity of its own, a courage too. When, at this instant, the trumpets sound to supper, she does not need his admonition to "go in and weep not" to embolden her to do her ceremonial duty with perfect calm. Supper done, and Lodovico having taken formal leave of her, she falls back again into an obedient humility.

But, alone with Emilia, the blow, and the worse blow of

that cunning whore of Venice
That married with Othello.

seem to have numbed her mind. One might suppose that she no longer cared even to learn of what she is accused. But it is largely sheer fatigue; and beneath the surface, where reality lies, she is as sensitively alive as ever, and to what is, for her, the

---

[71] It may well seem that Shakespeare has here stretched a psychological point in his wish to complete the pattern of Iago's triumph; first, Othello senseless at his feet and now Desdemona kneeling there. Would she have sent him to Othello? Such unlikelihood as there may be is lessened a little by the stress laid on the fact that he is Emilia's husband, she by this her mistress' friend. But one suspects that, as with the plainly imported meeting between blind Gloucester and mad Lear, it was the effectiveness of the pattern which counted.

essential thing. She is a great lady, and has been publicly insulted
—and worse. She is innocent, and has been foully slandered. She
is a Venetian, and has surely but to appeal to Lodovico and
Venice to protect her from this alien, this Moor—against whom,
how rashly, she would not be warned. But she makes no such
move, advances no such claims. She holds still by the faith in his
"very quality," for which she clairvoyantly came to love him. For
better or worse he is now her lord; and to her

> even his stubbornness, his checks, his frowns . . .
> have grace and favour in them.

Nor will proper pride, nor just resentment with all the arguments
in the world for aid, change that. Better pleading will be those
emblems of her chastity, her wedding sheets—to the obtuse Emilia
they are just "those sheets!"—laid tonight on their bed. And when
the time comes, what fitter shroud! She is not conscious, as we are,
that her death is near; only that, if sorrow cannot change her, nor
will time. Emilia tries to rally her with a robust

> Come, come, you talk!

She finds expression for her "wretched fortune," not in its
own bewailing, but in the melody which expressed poor Barbara's,
and in that an anodyne. And so little does she anticipate calamity
that, quitting her cryptic spiritual solitude, she can idly turn her
thoughts to Lodovico, play the tolerant married lady with
shrugging "O, these men, these men," and, in the sequent

> Dost thou in conscience think—tell me, Emilia—
> That there be women do abuse their husbands
> In such gross kind?

be suspected by Emilia of playing—and overplaying—the innocent
too.

But Emilia hardly understands her here, nor she fully perhaps
herself. If she is now to live a life deformed by jealousy and
suspicions, it will not suffice her simply to be sure that she does
not deserve them, would not

> do such a deed for all the world.

Self-complacency is cold comfort. But some habitation of faith
she must have; so she will exchange the glory of her lost ideal

for the companionable shelter of that gently obstinate delusion:

> I do not think there is any such woman.

But Desdemona's truth outshines such ingenuous streaks of self-deceptions, or the scared fib about the handkerchief, even as it transfigures the incredible lie of her dying answer to Emilia's

> O, who hath done this deed?

—the heart-rending

> Nobody; I myself. Farewell.
> Commend me to my kind lord. . . .

—into a shaming of the mere truth. Emilia finds the word:

> ' O, she was heavenly true!

—not simply true to Othello, but to herself and her faith in him. This is betrayed, and she is wantonly and savagely killed. No ray of light pierces there. But they could not kill her faith—in the Othello that remained to her, for her still the true Othello, and the beauty of this.

EMILIA

Emilia is coarse clay. She is of Shakespeare's own invention, no kin to the Ensign's wife in the story. He develops her—with the economy of his maturer stagecraft—by the measure of his need for her. An attractive young woman, from whom Cassio finds it good fun to claim a kiss, Iago's pretended fears for his "night-cap" being given that much color; such is our first impression of her. She stays mumchance enough for the moment to bear out Desdemona's bantering defense of her:

> Alas, she has no speech.

But—while what Iago may say is no evidence—she will later amply corroborate his

> In faith, too much!
> I find it still when I have list to sleep. . . .

by showing that she can chide very much more trenchantly than "with thinking" if she is stirred to it.

Shakespeare already has clearly in mind what he wants of her; and upon the

> I am glad I have found this napkin. . . .

and in the short exchange with Iago (their single scene alone
together) he more definitely shapes her to it, and briskly, with the

> This was her first remembrance from the Moor:
> My wayward husband hath a hundred times
> Wooed me to steal it; but she so loves the token—
> For he conjured her she should ever keep it—
> That she reserves it evermore about her
> To kiss, and talk to. I'll have the work ta'en out,
> And give't Iago. What he will do with it
> Heaven knows, not I;
> I nothing but to please his fantasy.

Beside the neighboring subtleties of Iago's dealing with Othello
the packed utility of this may seem technically a little crude. But
Shakespeare will not interrupt that chief issue for long; and since
there is little subtlety about Emilia, the artlessness of the soliloquy
pictures her the better:

> My wayward husband . . .

—her incurious, tolerant, pedestrian mind finds this the aptest
term for Iago's restless exigence and uncertain temper—

> hath a hundred times
> Wooed me to steal it . . .

—to which point she would not go, and will not, as she answers
him, admit to be going now:

> No, faith; she let it drop by negligence,
> And, to the advantage, I being here took't up.

It is a nice distinction. But she that can make it will have the less
difficulty in setting down her honest Iago's share in the business
to "fantasy." Better to please him too, and to find herself his
"good wench" for a change from his perpetual chiding (he greets
her testily; her first words to him are "Do not you chide": these
jolly fellows, such good company abroad, are often less so at
home); and better, by far, she must have found, not to cross him
or question him if his "wit" begins to turn "the seamy side without," as it does when, misgiving seizing her, she begs the handkerchief again. "'Tis proper I obey him" is her wifely code, and
the mere tone of his present

> Be not acknown on't; I have use for it.
> Go, leave me.

must warn her that she will be wise to obey him pretty promptly in this. Yet she must be conscious too that there is mischief in the matter. What licit use could he have for the handkerchief? But she chooses to shut her mind and hold her tongue.

Having thus committed her to a peccadillo which she will be loath to avow he runs the less risk of her betraying him; and, in fact, the occasion soon arising, she lies smoothly and efficiently. It is before Othello's clamor over the loss that she does so. After this it is even less easy to recant and confess; nor could she without involving Iago and incurring his anger, since she no longer has the handkerchief to restore. But Desdemona's own fib about it seems, by comparison, to lighten hers; nor, apparently, is the handkerchief the real cause of the clamor, a pretext only for such a fit of truculent ill-temper as any wife must learn to expect from any husband. Once again, then, she shuts her mind.

Not that the diabolical truth could come at present within the range of her most vigilant suspicions. She does not think very highly of the masculine nature, nor express herself very delicately about it:

> 'Tis not a year or two shows us a man:
> They are all but stomachs and we all but food;
> They eat us hungerly, and when they are full
> They belch us.

But if lack of imagination leaves her blind to the heights it lets her ignore the blacker depths around her too. The Iago of the play's opening, envious and false beneath his honest surface, she will long enough have known for her husband; but of the demi-devil committed to Cassio's death and Desdemona's, and to Othello's ruin, how should she have an inkling?

While she herself, however, is hardened to jealousies and "chidings"—and of these can give as good as she gets—her lady, she soon sees, is not so thick-skinned; nor, she suspects, would Othello's jealousy, once roused, be likely to end in mere bluster. Hence her "Pray heaven" that "no conception nor no jealous toy" "possess him" and her "Lady, amen!"—graver by far than Desdemona's own conscience-free

> Heaven keep that monster from Othello's mind!

And her fears are soon justified. Then it is another facet of

Emilia that we see, standing stubbornly up to Othello in defense
of a mistress she has learned to love, ready to stake her soul that

> if she be not honest, chaste and true,
> There's no man happy; the purest of their wives
> Is foul as slander.

He dismisses her. But she has not, we find later, been above
listening at the door to the terrible invective thrown on Desdemona; and her loyal indignation rises the higher at it and its
meek receiving, and the higher yet upon encountering Iago's
disconcertingly tepid sympathy—and some instinct seems suddenly to set her on a trail:

> I will be hanged, if some eternal villain,
> Some busy and insinuating rogue,
> Some cogging, cozening slave, to get some office,
> Have not devised this slander. . . .

We are at one of the play's crucial moments, and it is upon
Emilia—upon what she will now do, what fail to do—that the
event turns. Iago's dry

> Fie, there's no such man; it is impossible.

is a plain caution to her to follow that trail no further. Later,
rent by remorse, she will avow that "I thought so then," and the
"then" is now. She has, of course, no reason to suppose Desdemona in mortal danger, she merely sees her suffering more keenly
what other wives suffer; and if Iago is drawing some still hidden
crooked profit from it, his tart

> Speak within door. . . .
> You are a fool; go to.

is yet plainer warning that the less she says or knows the better
for her. So she satisfies her outraged feelings with a few high-
sounding words, and for the third time, and this time fatally, she
obediently shuts her mind. If her conscience is uneasy it will be
lightened when she remarks, upon her next sight of Othello, that
"he looks gentler than he did." And then she relaxes, despite
misgivings, into her habitual matter-of-fact mood, administering
to her wounded, delicate Desdemona a good-night dose, not of the
compassion she feels, but of a cheerful toughening conjugal
doctrine of give and take, prophylactic for the future.

To the shock of the murder upon this night of murders is added the poignancy of Desdemona's death in her own arms—by so little is she too late to save her! To this succeeds stupefaction:

> O, who hath done this deed?
> Nobody; I myself. . . .

and to that, under ban of the devoted, incredible lie, the moment's helplessness of

> She said so: I must needs report the truth.

Then Othello's

> She's like a liar gone to burning hell:
> 'Twas I that killed her.

sets her anguished wrath free to rage—until it is checked as by a blow at his

> Thy husband knew it all.

For a stunned while she can only repeat and repeat

> My husband ! . . My husband ! . .
> My husband say that she was false?

—each answer the tearing of a screen from before that closed mind. Yet when Iago appears he must—he, her husband!—clear himself if he can, as surely he can. He does so, sufficiently:

> I told him what I thought, and told no more
> Than what he found himself was apt and true.

—and a woman of common sense might well leave it at that. Desdemona is dead. What is her good name worth? Emilia will not.

> But did you ever tell him she was false?

He can hedge no further. Othello is listening. He faces her, this unsuspected Emilia, with a blunt "I did," and she brands him before them all as a liar.

But Desdemona's innocence so proclaimed and believed, might she not now at least "charm her tongue" and excusably let things go their way? Again she will not. There is worse hidden, and out it shall come, and she will purge herself too of her own share of the guilt—

> I thought so then: I'll kill myself for grief. . . .

—of the guilt of the blind eye and closed mind. What this may cost her she has time to reckon while Othello lies there prostrate with remorse and Gratiano recites his mild elegy, clear warning of it in Iago's tensely vigilant silence; he has already bidden her be gone. She has only to hold her tongue as before about that tragically ridiculous handkerchief. Yet again she will not. The threatening sword is half-drawn; she might still save herself; she will not. She brings his crime home to him, confesses her ignorant share in it, and he kills her.

The coarse-grained, conscienceless, light-minded Emilia proves capable of this. She could love an Iago; she gives her life in testimony of the dead Desdemona's innocence. She passes from her merrily cynical

> Why, who would not make her husband a cuckold to make
> him a monarch? I should venture purgatory for't.

to a

> Moor, she was chaste; she loved thee, cruel Moor;
> So come my soul to bliss, as I speak true. . . .

Othello does not heed. She prays to be lifted to her mistress' side, but they let her lie where she has fallen. Her senses failing, she can only cry pitifully

> What did thy song bode, lady?
> Hark, canst thou hear me?

Desdemona can no longer hear. The memory of a melody, of that "Willow, willow, willow . . ." must serve for communion between them. But Emilia has won herself a place in the play's tragic heaven.

BIANCA

The little hussy Bianca is Desdemona's very opposite, and our first sight of her is meant to make this plain. For Cassio, taking respectful leave of the one in her gentleness and dignity, turns to find himself at once accosted by the pretty, flaunting impudence of the other—who actually is to him, moreover, what Iago, abusing Othello's ear, would have Desdemona to be. And the mocking, scurrilous talk of her which Othello, eavesdropping, overhears is made to seem talk of Desdemona.

Iago, as his nature is, speaks brutally of her and to her; of her

"selling her desires," addresses her, when he wants to implicate
her in the midnight ambush laid for Cassio, as a "notable
strumpet," and wags a moral head over such "fruits of whoring."
But it is the respectable Emilia's gratuitously added

> Fie, fie upon thee, strumpet!

which touches the young woman on the raw, and evokes the
shrilly protesting

> I am no strumpet; but of life as honest
> As you that thus abuse me.

She is, of course, a trull, no better, and ill-behaved at that.
She pursues her lover in the streets, makes scenes there, flies into
tantrums, turns as jealous as her betters. The gallant Cassio, more
than a little vain of her infatuation for him, treats her as such
creatures must expect to be treated. But she is shrewd and witty.
To the gallant cant of Cassio's

> Not that I love you not.

she retorts with a neat

> But that you do not love me.

She is plucky; she stands up to Iago's bullying. She may even love
her lover in her disreputable way. For Shakespeare she is at
least a human being.

BRABANTIO, CASSIO, RODERIGO

BRABANTIO

Brabantio is redeemed from the convention of the hoodwinked
father by a few specific strokes. He swings between extremes,
from his high regard for Othello to insensate abuse of him,
through a chill pardon for Desdemona, in which past tenderness
still echoes, to the cutting farewell:

> She has deceived her father, and may thee.

He seems exceptionally credulous about

> spells and medicines bought of mountebanks . . .

but he takes a detached view of his own nature, "glad at soul"
that he has no other child, since Desdemona's escape would teach

him "tyranny, to hang clogs on them." He passes from a frantic bustle of pursuit:

> Raise all my kindred. . . .
> Call up my brother. . . .
> Some one way, some another. . . .
>   At every house I'll call. . . .

to quiet, solitary dignity before the Senate, as from clamor for vengeance on Othello to the magnanimous

> If she confess that she was half the wooer,
> Destruction on my head, if my bad blame
> Light on the man!

And then and there, despite grief and defeat, he is capable of capping the Duke's encouraging platitudes with some very smooth irony. But it looks as if the shock and the strain may have broken him, and when he speaks of his "bruised heart" he means it. And later we hear that Desdemona's loss

> was mortal to him, and pure grief
> Shore his old thread in twain.

CASSIO

The Folio's list of characters calls Cassio *an Honourable Lieutenant.* He is seemingly a man of gentle birth, and of education; Iago mocking at his "bookish theoric." He is the unwitting implement of evil, its stalking-horse, and his place in the play's scheme is that of an average, unheroic, well-meaning man caught between tragic extremes—of wickedness and of the nobility it betrays. His faults are failings, redeemable by his own recognition of them. But here he sways, haplessly, somewhat ridiculously, between extremes within himself. He knows that he has "very poor and unhappy brains for drinking," yet he yields from good nature to the claims of good fellowship, though he says, even as he does so, "it dislikes me." He is sensitive even to self-consciousness, and, beyond that, to the point of self-display. Having listened in disciplined silence to Othello's sentence on him, in his heartfelt outburst to Iago, the

> Reputation, reputation, reputation. O, I have lost my reputation!
> I have lost the immortal part of myself, and what remains is
> bestial. My reputation, Iago, my reputation!

we remark that he is listening, not unappreciatively, to the sounds of his own despair. Such misery does not strike deep, nor last long; its enjoyment is soon exhausted. Iago tactfully gives it scope, and Cassio, disburdened, not only accepts his optimistic advice without question, but will "betimes in the morning . . . beseech the virtuous Desdemona" to plead his cause.[72] For may not Othello's anger dissolve as easily—so this mood bids him hope—as has the bitterness of his own remorse? The man is mercurial. He is a lightweight. But there is with that something boyish about him, and appealing. Despite his despair, he thinks to bring musicians to play the customary nuptial *aubade* beneath Othello's windows; an ingenuous piece of propitiation.

He is a romantic soul. We have him, during those first moments in Cyprus, rhapsodizing over "the divine Desdemona." He is gaily gallant, finds it good fun to claim a kiss of welcome from Emilia. And Iago's "profane and liberal wit" having served its purpose while they all wait anxiously for news of Othello, he takes his turn at distracting Desdemona, more delicately and intimately, yet openly and respectfully, galling Iago with envy of his address in "such tricks," in kissing his "three fingers" and playing "the sir," having already—how thoughtlessly—patronizingly disparaged his Ancient's good breeding to her, with that

> He speaks home, madam: you may relish him more in the soldier than in the scholar.

But he has a finer sense than all this shows of Desdemona's quality. She is for him—the epithet springs spontaneously—"the virtuous Desdemona." Nor will he join in the accepted marriage pleasantries, meets Iago's ribald

> Our general . . . hath not yet made wanton the night with her, and she is sport for Jove.

with a cold snub. And her "bounteous" compassion on him when he is in trouble raises respect to very reverence.

His attitude towards Bianca is of a piece with the rest of him. She is his mistress, she is "a customer," and he scoffs merrily at "the monkey's" pretense that he means to marry her. But he

---

[72] Note how Cassio's impulsiveness helps give the needed speed to the action.

treats her, even as Shakespeare does, decently and humanely. He does not care to have her pursue him in the street—who would? —and, being what she is, she must put up with a blunt

> leave me for this time. . . .
> I do attend here on the general;
> And think it no addition, nor my wish
> To have him see me womaned.

nor does he scruple to round on her pretty sharply when she vexes him. But, this apart, she is his "most fair Bianca," his "sweet love." He excuses himself with courteous insincerity for a week's neglect of her, protesting that he loves her, paying her in that coin too. He is a gentleman, and she, as the phrase goes, is no better than she should be. But he would never be guilty, to her face or behind her back, of the grossness of Iago's "This is the fruits of whoring."

The weakness which lets him drink when he knows he cannot carry his liquor is matched by his broken resolve to break with Bianca. He has kept it for a week; and, confiding to Iago what an infatuated nuisance she is, he protests:

> Well, I must leave her company.

Yet a moment later, after she has told him in a fit of tantrums to come and sup with her that same night or see her no more, Iago dryly demanding if he means to, he answers shruggingly:

> Faith, I intend so.

the full truth being, it would seem, that he is both secretly flattered by her scandalous infatuation for him—he makes the most of it:

> She falls me thus about my neck. . . . So hangs and lolls and weeps upon me; so hales and pulls me. . . .

—and not a little afraid of her. It is at this point in the play that he, with Othello, is brought to the lowest pitch of indignity; puppets the two of them in Iago's hands, the one turned eavesdropper, the other fatuously vaunting his conquest of a light-o'-love.

But a worthier finish is reserved him. For his would-be murder he utters no harsher reproach than

> Dear general, I never gave you cause.

and his epitaph upon Othello is fitly felt:

> For he was great of heart.

And—though here, if the story were to have a sequel, we might question Senatorial judgment—he is left to rule in Cyprus.

RODERIGO

The Folio is as exact with its "Roderigo, *a gull'd Gentleman*"; but to this stock figure also Shakespeare gives human substance. It tells another tale of moral degradation; Iago the unresisted instrument. For Roderigo begins as an honorable suitor for Desdemona's hand; and, for his service in sounding the alarm, he converts Brabantio straightway from the

> In honest plainness thou hast heard me say
> My daughter is not for thee. . . .

to a

> good Roderigo, I'll deserve your pains.

And what could be more correct than the long, elaborate, pedantically parenthetical address to the newly wakened and distracted father at the window, with which he justifies his interference?

> I beseech you,
> If't be your pleasure and most wise consent,
> As partly I find it is . . .

—a mild effort at sarcasm—

> that your fair daughter,
> At this odd-even and dull watch of the night,
> Transported with no worse nor better guard
> But with a knave of common hire, a gondolier . . .

—as who might say today: carried off in a taxi-cab, not even a private car!—

> To the gross clasps of a lascivious Moor—
> If this be known to you, and your allowance . . .

—sarcasm again!—

> We then have done you bold and saucy wrongs;
> But if you know not this, my manners tell me
> We have your wrong rebuke. . . .

—a neat antithesis!—

> Do not believe,
> That, from the sense of all civility,
> I thus would play the trifle with your reverence:
> Your daughter, if you have not given her leave . . .

—he fancies his sarcasm—

> I say again, hath made a gross revolt,
> Tying her duty, beauty, wit and fortunes,
> In an extravagant and wheeling stranger . . .

—his vocabulary too!—

> Of here and everywhere. . . .

—and could listen to his own eloquence all night. We see Iago in the background, a-grin at the foolish exhibition.

Roderigo's renewed hopes soar high, then, as he sticks by the grateful Brabantio and follows him to the Senate, but only to collapse again utterly upon the surrendering of Desdemona to Othello. He stands there mute, would be left alone and ignored even by Iago, did he not at last utter a plaintive

> What will I do, thinkest thou? . . .
> I will incontinently drown myself.

—the "silly gentleman" at his silliest, most pitiable, least unlikable.

He goes to the devil with his eyes open, yet blindly. His poor mind is no better than a sounding board for Iago's sophistries. Yet he takes each step downward most advisedly, and even in admitting his folly he persists in it. He is an incorrigible fool. To put money—for Iago—in his purse, to follow the wars—and Desdemona—he will sell all his land, uproot and leave himself to the mercy of events.[73] And his moral sense is as feeble and obscure as his mind is muddled. Since he cannot win Desdemona for his wife, he may get her—Iago persuades him—as a mistress, may cuckold Othello. There will be manly satisfaction in that. But when he hears that she is in love with Cassio:

> Why, 'tis not possible. . . . I cannot believe that in her; she's full of most blessed condition.

[73] This final flourish to his scene with Iago:
I am changed: I'll go sell all my land.
had a significance for Shakespeare's audience that it cannot have for us.

And it is not, seemingly, that he thinks his own charms, given their chance, would make way with her, for he listens, unprotesting, to their most unflattering comparison with Cassio's. A less convinced, a more unconvincing, libertine there could hardly be. Finally, however, patience and cash exhausted, he protests, and, in a prepared oration, following the one he launched at Brabantio's window, he calls Iago to account. He has been let in—such is the tone of it—for a pretty poor investment, financially and morally too, and must now save what he can from the wreck:

> The jewels you have had from me to deliver to Desdemona would half have corrupted a votarist: you have told me she hath received them and returned me expectations and comforts of sudden respect and acquaintance; but I find none. . . . I will make myself known to Desdemona. If she will return me my jewels, I will give over my suit and repent my unlawful solicitation; if not, assure yourself I will seek satisfaction of you.

Is there, after all, any real vice in the creature? He sees himself handed back his jewels while he makes Desdemona yet another carefully prepared little speech of polite regret for ever having dreamed of committing adultery with her. And his amorous advances, we may suspect, would have been hardly more formidable.

But if there is no passion in him, evil or good, to stimulate, such little mind as he possesses Iago does most successfully corrupt. The denigration of Desdemona is left to sink in; the less he believes in her virtue, the readier he will be to continue his pursuit of her; his final complaint is that the jewels have had no effect. The "satisfying reasons" he has received for Cassio's death we do not hear; but an echo of them can be caught in the callous

> 'Tis but a man gone.

with which, craven in his ambush, he draws a clumsy sword. With Iago for guide, he has traveled from the lovelorn folly of

> I will incontinently drown myself.

to this. Even so, he is no more of a success as a murderer than he has been as an adulterer; and his bravo's

> Villain, thou diest!

is promptly changed, with Cassio's sword between his own ribs instead, into an abjectly repentant

> O, villain that I am!

A last disillusion is due; his mentor's face mockingly grinning, his friend's dagger stuck in him—

> O damned Iago; O inhuman dog!

Disillusion indeed! But he is so futile a fool that we spare him some pity.

The Verse

OUT of an inheritance, in the main of blank verse and the ten-syllable couplet, but with the octo-syllabic and even the "old fourteener" never quite forgotten, and with a generous place left for prose, Shakespeare develops the dramatic speech of his art's maturity. He makes it an instrument which is both supple and powerful and of a wide range of effect, sensitive to the interpreting of thought charged with emotion, and allowing a sufficiently seeming spontaneity of expression without loss of coherent form. *Julius Cæsar*, with its virile chorus of conspirators, Cassius' passion, Brutus' calm and Antony's adroit modulations from mood to mood, may be said to see him master of the means to it. Then comes *Hamlet*, with Hamlet himself to give it greater freedom and a new intensity.

For with *Hamlet* Shakespeare breaks bounds, to enter and make his own—and no one has followed him there—a land of rarer and harder drama altogether. The dominant figures of the great post-*Hamlet* plays live and move in a larger imaginative area. Lear scales heights as Macbeth descends to deeps without precedent. The Antony brought to bay at Actium stands a giant, a "triple pillar of the world" indeed, beside the clever fellow who outplayed Brutus and Cassius. And Shakespeare has need of more powerful and resourceful means of expression still.

Of any revolution in his stagecraft there could be little question. Though the theater for which he has learned to work is grown richer, its mechanical and pictorial aspects remain fundamentally and unaccommodatingly the same. Nor has he ever made much

of its shows and tricks, such as they are. His plays depend upon
more essential things.

He might have followed Jonson's precepts and practice—who
would, incidentally (some later critics to prove heartily in accord),
have counseled him to leave such a subject as that of *King Lear*
alone—and have entrenched himself in a strict formula, within
which expression gains even an intenser power because it cannot
expand. But one does not see him bartering freedom for security.
It had not become him, as an aspiring "shake-scene," and a mere
theater hack, to dwell upon theory and rule. It was for him to
turn to account any convention whatever that might suit a
particular occasion. And having learned all "the tricks of the
trade," he will not, in these days of his mastership, discard from
his store a single one of them. The Chorus, the Presenters, the
Dumb Show, a Prologue or an Epilogue—devices not to be de-
pended on, but there may be fitness and utility in them still. A
Chorus proves but an encumbrance to the swift movement of
Romeo and Juliet, and is rejected, seemingly in midcourse; but
he can turn one to good use as a courier for the heavily equipped
Henry V, and as the best and simplest means by which to "slide
o'er sixteen years" in *The Winter's Tale*. The first part of *Henry
IV* asks, to his thinking, no prologue; but "Rumour, painted full
of tongues" makes a useful mnemonic link with the second.
Rosalind's epilogue pays overt homage to convention; its dramatic
use is to reconcile the comedy itself with the concluding masque.
A dumb show would go ill indeed with the intense actualities of
Hamlet; it is quite in place in *The Murder of Gonzago*, and
markedly distinguishes the play within the play from the play.
And even presenters, let vanish from the early *Taming of the
Shrew*, make a short and qualified reappearance—as if to acknowl-
edge the play's sophistication—in *Cymbeline*.[74] So too with his
verse. He soon shook free of cramping or unmanageable meters
and overelaborate artifice, strung-out alliteration, classical tags,
multiple puns and the like. But with his art at its ripest, his verse
at its freest, he still does not forbid himself a neat little passage

---

[74] The episode of the apparitions and Jupiter's descent has, I know, been labeled
spurious. But, in its main lines at least, it may, I think, be called Shakespeare's,
and with the more likelihood, perhaps, if this aspect of it is considered.

of stychomythia in *Antony and Cleopatra*, a few octosyllabics in
Measure for Measure; and in *King Lear*, as a fitting auxiliary
to Lear's madness, we have a very medley of vernacular song,
mime and antic.

From *Othello* we can pick in this category, the Clown, the
Duke's "sentences" and Iago's extempore rhyming.[75] Shakespeare
has fitting use for each. As to the first; the strain of the play's
action is continuous and at times intense, and the identifiable
characters are all caught into its rapidly flowing main stream.
The strain upon an audience will, moreover, be greater if, in
performance, there are no marked intervals between acts and
scenes. The anonymous Clown with his conventional jokes
(coarse for the minstrels, innocuous for Desdemona) is the only
completely contrasted "relief" afforded us. And it is to be noted
that, of his two appearances, one occurs when our attention has
been closely held by Iago throughout the long scene of the night
of Cassio's downfall and just before the yet longer passage, in
which Othello travels the entire distance from cloudless happiness
to the savage dooming of Desdemona to death (a passage in which
concentration and strain will be at their closest and tensest) and
the other just after this.

The Duke's sententious "sentences" make on us and in the
scene the effect they fail to make more directly on Brabantio, of
"a grise or step" between the concluded turmoil of the elopement
and the ardor for the coming departure to Cyprus and the wars.
The Duke pronounces them from his chair of state as an informal
and kindly judgment upon the case brought before him; the
artifice of their form befits this, their smooth cadence the emollient
content, while the couplets sound a full close. And Brabantio's
ironically echoing reply—respectful, acquiescent; but he is as good
at "sentences" as the Duke!—provides him with a dignified and
effective retreat from the action. Shakespeare wants, without any
too sudden change in the steering, without upsetting its balance,
to set his scene upon another course; and this is as legitimate a
way as any other.

Iago's six couplets of impromptu rhyming are semi-comic relief

---

[75] It would be pedantry to add the Herald; the convention of his speech will
pass unobserved upon any nonrealistic stage.

to the strain—not on the audience, but on Desdemona while she waits for news of Othello's safety. Therefore they can be fully "dramatized"; the accomplishment, such as it is, being accounted an item in Iago's equipment, and well it becomes his intellectual swagger.

Utility is Shakespeare's sole test. He will employ any sort of device, however old and worn, if he can make it dramatically useful. The cumulative effect of the iteration of some single significant word; he has inherited this as a formula habitually carried to mechanical extremes. He never abandons it, only reduces it to the point at which it colorably reunites with our natural habit, upon which supposedly it was built, of recurring again and again under the stress of suffering, to the one thought that dominates our trouble. In *Othello* under various forms he makes frequent use of the device; directly, but within the limits of the spontaneous; oftener by inserting the iteration into the main body of speech; sometimes by using the significant word as "honest" and "honesty" are used—by the play's end what changes in tone and color, application and implication, have not been rung upon Iago's selected epithet![76]

The first noticeable bout of iteration is Cassio's in his lament for his lost reputation; and the sextuple repetition—though it is partly blended into his speech—gives the needed, in this case slightly comic, turn to his exaggerated grief. It can be matched and contrasted with Othello's tragic outcry when he suddenly wakes to the meaning of his terrible deed:

> If she come in, she'll sure speak to my wife;
> My wife! my wife! what wife? I have no wife.

and with Emilia's whelming

> Villainy, villainy, villainy!
> I think upon't: I think: I smell't: O villainy! . . .
> O villainy, villainy!

---

[76] It is Iago, speaking to Roderigo, who first employs the word for the "honest knaves" who are loyal to their masters. It is Othello who first attaches it to him with the

> So please your Grace, my Ancient;
> A man he is of honesty and trust. . . .

The epithet then sticks, with Iago himself acutely and angrily conscious of it.

Then there is the more complex, and so it will seem intentional

> Ay; you did wish that I would make her turn:
> Sir, she can turn, and turn, and yet go on,
> And turn again; and she can weep, sir, weep;
> And she's obedient, as you say, obedient,
> Very obedient. . . .

And since it habitually serves for the underscoring of some excess of emotion we shall in consequence find the device put oftenest to Othello's own use. It shapes his very first passionate outpouring; the

>   O, now for ever
> Farewell the tranquil mind! farewell content!
> Farewell the plumed troop and the big wars
> That make ambition virtue! O, farewell!
> Farewell the neighing steed and the shrill trump . . .
> Farewell! Othello's occupation gone!

And, after this, instance upon instance of its employment can be found; the iterated word being either woven into a speech, when it not only heightens but controls the emotion, as with the

> It is the cause, it is the cause, my soul: . . .
> It is the cause. . . .

and with

> Put out the light, and then put out the light. . . .

—the word and idea, to be thrice more repeated, binding this section of the speech together as does a recurring note a passage in music—or it may be given the simple cumulative emphasis of

> O, blood, blood, blood! . . .
> O, fool, fool, fool! . . .

Finally, we have iteration turned to a far-related use; a word and the idea distributed over the greater part of a scene, and recurring later, played upon with varying intonations and implications, as Iago plays upon "think" and "thoughts," "jealousy" and "honesty," until he has Othello repeating them too and letting them have their way—Iago's way—with him.

But Shakespeare's verse is the master-medium of his stagecraft; and to make it the comprehensive means of expression which it now is, and which he operates with such freedom and ease, he has absorbed into it—and will often transform until they are hardly to be recognized—not a few conventions and forms. Take the verse of any scene in the play, and try to determine its normal measure. The ten-syllable, five-beat line is still there, if not manifestly, then—and more often—embedded in the dominant rhythm. But the speaker—and it is a question of speech—who sets to work upon a finger-tapping basis of rule and exception, with account to be taken of the use of extra syllables, of the curtailed or overrun line, of weak endings and the like, will soon find himself at a feeble and tangled halt. Let him rather acquire an articulate tongue, an unfailing ear for the pervasive melody and cadence of the verse, let him yield to its impetus, and—provided, of course, that he knows more or less what it is all about, and this sympathetic self-surrender will aid him there—Shakespeare can be counted on to carry him through.

Not that the verse, freely and variously though it may flow, escapes into any excessive metrical latitude, such as, in later post-Shakespearian days, will bring the weapon that it is, meant to command attention, to breaking from simple weakness in the actors' hands. There is never the lack of a stiff short line for the forcible punctuating of any overambulatory passage, nor of a few successive lines of strict scansion to restore, for just so long, an exemplary discipline; or the border can be crossed into a stretch of the contrasted discipline of prose. For if Shakespeare will not barter freedom for sheer strength, neither will he sacrifice strength to freedom; and a play demands some overriding unity of treatment, some force which will bind it together, if it be only to counterbalance the naturally disintegrating tendency of the individualities and diverse methods of its actors. Variety must not be let deteriorate into patchwork.

The enriched vocabulary, the bolder syntax, the unconfined rhythm, those are the more patent attributes of the maturer verse; its intrinsic virtue lies in the ready power, now developed in it, to paint and reveal character—he turns his freedom to that use. The verse of a play may be shaped and colored as a whole by the nature of its subject and setting, as, very notably, is the verse of *Coriolanus*; or—another means to a like end—it may be in large part keyed to the interpreting of the play's central figure;

and the rest within range, demands of character and the action allowed for, will be responsive. The dominant influence upon the verse of *Othello* is Othello himself. At his appearance he sets it a tone very much—and appropriately—as an officer commanding can give a tone to his regiment. The "round unvarnished tale" is exemplary: speech that moves forward to a steady rhythm; the epithetic picked and significant, yet never in sound or sense over-weighting the verse and retarding it; the imagery sparse, nor ever merely decorative, but bred always of the matter in hand and the moment's imagination. And if Cassio and Iago (on duty) and, later, Montano seem spontaneously to pattern their speech upon his, there is truth to character in that; and Desdemona, before the Senate, Othello beside her, will be, after her own fashion, as naturally responsive.

It is, so to say, upon another plane that the Duke and Senators respond in their kind. As characters they are not sharply individ-ualized; there is nothing in them to combat such domination. This is so too with Lodovico, appearing towards the play's end as a figure of importance to the action, but of no more specific character than is indicated by the dignity of his mission, Desde-mona's

> This Lodovico is a proper man.

and Emilia's gayer hint. Gratiano is in the same category. But by now a mold for the run of the verse has been formed, and the speech—no demands of character or action to the contrary—tends to flow into it. The Othello influence is neither exact or constraining. It initiates a tone and rhythm, and some measure in the use of imagery, and, on those within his immediate reach, will inevitably be strong. But it allows ample scope for individual expression; Desdemona's, in character attuned to his; Emilia's, late awakened to the matching of his anger with her own.

The opposing factor is Iago—the Iago of the soliloquies and of the unguarded scenes with Roderigo. His speech at the play's opening—its impetus and forceful rhythm and lack of all melody, regular and irregular lines chasing and ousting one another—is eloquent of this first aspect of him, of his greedy malice, the itch of his envy. In the very vowels and the dry distastefully reiterated

consonants of "be-lee'd . . . calmed . . . debitor .. . . creditor . . .
counter-caster" sounds his contempt for Cassio:

> But he, sir, had the election;
> And I . . .
> must be be-lee'd and calmed
> By debitor and creditor: thus counter-caster,
> He, in good time, must his lieutenant be. . . .

His pretentious cleverness is painted thick for the start of his
first lesson to Roderigo:

> Our bodies are our gardens; to the which our wills are
> gardeners: so that if we will plant nettles or sow lettuce, set
> hyssop and weed up thyme, supply it with one gender of herbs,
> or distract it with many, either to have it sterile with idleness or
> manured with industry, why, the power and corrigible authority
> of this lies in our wills. . . .

—and so on. It impresses Roderigo. And from out the verbiage,
the talk of "carnal stings" and "unbitted lusts," of which love, he
takes it, is "a sect or scion," its satisfaction now "as luscious as
locusts" to be "shortly as bitter as coloquintida," there does at last
emerge an admirably plain "Put money in thy purse."

Roderigo's lessons in worldly wisdom are mostly framed to
this pattern, and in prose, the best medium in which to call a
spade a spade. Only once, when he is bewailing Cassio's cudgeling,
does Iago hearten him with the swing and color of verse:

> Does't not go well? Cassio hath beaten thee,
> And thou by that small hurt hast cashiered Cassio:
> Though other things grow fair against the sun,
> Yet fruits that blossom first will first be ripe. . . .

—the melody as efficacious as the argument!

Iago's soliloquies are in verse. That befits their impulsive
confidence. But there is little or none of the imaginative stuff of
poetry in them; and this noticeable incongruity is as befitting.

He can always, when he chooses, suit both the matter and
manner of his speech to the occasion and his company; "honest
Iago" is to be seen, actorlike, under any aspect demanded. And,
at grips with Othello, so supply and swiftly does he shift his
address, giving and taking, advancing and yielding, now deform-
ing Othello's thoughts, now shaping his own to their shape, that

Iago the actor would seem to be, as the phrase goes, "lost in his part." But in that capacity lies his talent; and behind it there *is*, indeed, no Iago, only a poisoned and poisonous ganglion of cravings after evil.

The expressive range of the play's verse with its auxiliary prose is in its entirety a wide one. There are the utilitarian units of the messengers and the Herald who speak after their kind; there is the conventional Clown who speaks and acts after his; and the First, Second, Third and Fourth Gentlemen paint us the storm and the landfall as, it is recognized, such things may effectively be painted, this being the aim and end of their existence. Then, beneath its exotic setting and warlike trimmings, the play is, at its core, a "domestic tragedy"—and Shakespeare's only essay in this kind. So in the more familiar scenes the verse falls readily into a semblance of the to-and-fro of habitual talk. But, dominating all, is the heroic figure of Othello himself, built to an heroic scale of expression and able to animate the noblest poetic form.

The gamut must run, with no incongruous gap appearing, between the squabble over the handkerchief—

> Is't lost? is't gone? speak, is it out o' the way?
> Heaven bless us!
>   Say you?
> It is not lost; but what an if it were?
> How!
> I say it is not lost.
>   Fetch't, let me see it.
> Why, so I can, sir, but I will not now. . . .

—up to the highest pitch of imaginative emotion. The unity of the action makes of itself for unity of treatment, and its sustained tension will not let even the most loosely woven verse be altogether slackened. In the stress of his suffering the firm athletic temper of Othello's speech breaks; but through this it is to a natural and characteristic superlative that he lifts it in such a passage as

> Like to the Pontic sea,
> Whose icy current and compulsive course
> Ne'er feels retiring ebb, but keeps due on
> To the Propontic and the Hellespont . . .

Nor, in its setting and at its moment, will the sacrificial

> It is the cause, it is the cause. . . .

seem hollow magniloquence beside the simple factual horror of Desdemona's murder; nor, after this, the tremendous

> Methinks it should be now a huge eclipse
> Of sun and moon. . . .

nor the dazzling

> Nay, had she been true,
> If heaven would make me such another world
> Of one entire and perfect chrysolite,
> I'ld not have sold her for it.

reduce Emilia by comparison to commonplace. The scene's charge of tragic emotion is enough for the fusing of whatever the range of its means of expression.

As he returns to sanity so Othello returns also to the old sober, lofty equilibrium of thought and speech. We have it in that

> Here is my journey's end, here is my butt
> And very sea-mark of my utmost sail. . . .

with its memory of "the sea's worth" which could be no more to him than the worth of Desdemona's love, of the storm which spared them for the calm joy of their reuniting, of the icy current of the Pontic sea which imaged to him his implacable revenge. And in his valediction, with the remoter memories of Aleppo and the Arabian trees, the

> then must you speak
> Of one that loved not wisely but too well;
> Of one not easily jealous, but, being wrought,
> Perplexed in the extreme . . .

we have it brought to simplicity itself, and the beauty of that.

NOTE A

OTHELLO'S COLOR

"Haply for I am black . . ."; it is Othello himself who says so. Certainly the word then and later was given wide range in such connection; it could be used to denote dark hair and complexion merely. But in this case the meaning is surely plain: he is a black

man, not a white one. Roderigo's "thick-lips" on the other hand
is simply abusive; and no actor of Othello is called upon to make
himself repulsive to his audience—although, as to this, taste will
vary both with time and clime. The dramatic point of the matter
lies in Desdemona's

> I saw Othello's visage in his mind. . . .

and all that it conveys of the quality of her love for him, its
courage and clairvoyance. His looks at least must stress this, not
minimize it.

NOTE B

OTHELLO'S CHRISTIANITY

Shakespeare could not, of course, make much of this if he
would, since religion was a subject forbidden to the theater; but
the references to it are more than casual. It is implied in
Brabantio's "Are they married, think you?" and in Iago's
quickly sequent question to Othello: "Are you fast married?"
Othello's appeal to the rioters is:

> For Christian shame, put by this barbarous brawl. . . .

And in Iago's next soliloquy he speculates upon the ease with
which Desdemona could

> win the Moor, were't to renounce his baptism,
> All seals and symbols of redeemed sin . . .

The "sacred vow" by "yond marble heaven" may or may not
be intended to indicate a backsliding towards his "paynim" past
—I doubt if an average audience would seize the point. But the
tragic irony of his command to her to say her prayers and be
reconciled to Heaven before, in her innocence, he murders her, is
patent, and could have been made more so by the stronger
stressing of his conversion to Christianity. And his final likening
of himself to the "circumcised dog" whom he smote in Aleppo
once for beating a Venetian and traducing the state, just such
a one as in his own person he smites now—here the reference
to his Christianity and his betrayal of it is unmistakable, even
though Shakespeare would not risk making it more definite.

Coriolanus

CORIOLANUS cannot be ranked with the greatest of the tragedies. It lacks their transcendent vitality and metaphysical power. But while neither story nor characters evoke such qualities, those they do evoke are here in full measure. The play is notable for its craftsmanship. It is the work of a man who knows what the effect of each stroke will be, and wastes not one of them. And while ease and simplicity may sometimes be lacking, an uncertain or superfluous speech it would be hard to find. Was Shakespeare perhaps aware of some ebbing of his imaginative vitality—well there may have been after the creation in about as many years of *Othello, King Lear, Antony and Cleopatra* and *Macbeth*! and did he purposefully choose a subject and characters which he could make the most of by judgment and skill?

The play follows close, it would seem, upon *Antony and Cleopatra.* Between the two there is the general likeness of a setting in Roman history. For the rest, the contrasts are so many and so marked as hardly to be fortuitous. To that large picture of an imperial Rome and a decadent Egypt and of

> The triple pillar of the world transformed
> Into a strumpet's fool.

succeeds this story of earlier and austerer days, of a Rome still challengeable by her neighbors, and of a very different hero. Antony and Caius Marcius are men of action both. But Antony is the astute politician too, and by that talent could save himself from disaster if he would—does save himself and has the game in his hands, only to throw it away because

The beds i' the East are soft.

Antony—and Othello and Macbeth too—are soldiers, famous generals; but that is not the side of them we come to know. Coriolanus is the man of action seen in action, and among the heroes of the maturer canon unique in this.[1] He is the younger man, a fighter and a brilliant one, but effectively no more. He is at heart—and despite his trials remains to the end—the incorrigible boy, with "Boy!" for the final insult flung at him by Aufidius that he will at no price swallow. And save in physical valor (of which in the elder, by the plan of the action, we hear but see nothing) in every trait he and Antony radically differ. To the one his men are "my good fellows." He jokes with them, praises them impulsively and generously for their pluck. The other is curt, even to friends and equals, self-conscious, and incapable of the least appeal to the populace he despises. In his contempt for spoils and rewards, in his stubbornness, his aristocratic pride, in his chastity—Virgilia greeting him on his minatory return, it is

> Now, by the jealous queen of heaven, that kiss
> I carried from thee, dear; and my true lip
> Hath virgined it ever since.

—in every significant feature the two stand contrasted.

Then in Cleopatra's place we have Volumnia; for the exotic mistress the Roman mother. Yet each in her fashion brings ruin, to lover or son. And for the Egyptian Court, in which, says Enobarbus,

> Mine and most of our fortunes to-night shall be—drunk to bed.

we exchange that picture of the simple Roman home, its great ladies content to

> set themselves down on two low stools and sew.

The contrasts are pervasive too. In the one play the action is spacious and varied beyond comparison; Shakespeare's every resource is drawn upon, his invention finds full scope. In *Coriolanus* it is disciplined, kept to its single channel, and the story moves lucidly and directly to its retributive end. And in one

---

[1] And even Henry V, at war, is not seen fighting. He is the didactic hero, and this is far less mature dramatic work.

major difference most of the rest are rooted: in the part played in
each by the idea of Rome. In each, of course, it is a vital part.
Antony early forecasts his own ruin in that reckless

> Let Rome in Tiber melt, and the wide arch
> Of the ranged empire fall!

Cleopatra's first note of alarm lest she lose him sounds in the

> He was disposed to mirth; but on the sudden
> A Roman thought hath struck him.

and throughout she is a prey to her jealousy, hatred and dread
of Rome. Still, this is little more than a background for the
personal passion. But in *Coriolanus* everything centers upon
Rome. It is the play's one sounding board. The springs of the
action are there. Coriolanus himself sinks at last by comparison to
something like second place. He returns for his revenge, and all
thoughts and eyes are on him. He departs, self-defeated; and it is
Volumnia who re-enters the city in triumph, hailed by a

> Behold our patroness, the life of Rome!

And his death thereafter in Corioles even approaches anticlimax.

But this fidelity to the larger, less personal theme lends the play
a very Roman strength and solidity, which compensates to some
degree, and in its kind, for the lack of such plenary inspiration as
has given us Lear or Macbeth, colossal and then stripped to the
soul. The play gains strength too from the keying of its action
throughout to strife of one sort or another. Of no other of the plays
can it be said that, but for an incidental scene or so, and for the
stilled suspense in which we listen to Volumnia's ultimate
pleadings, the quarreling and fighting scarcely cease from beginning to end. It is dramatically the more important, then,
that the opposing stresses should be kept fairly balanced, in
sympathy as well as in force. Amid mere ebb and flow of
violence the interest of the action could not be sustained. But the
balance is adjusted and continually readjusted, the tension never
quite relaxed. And the skill of the play's workmanship shows
largely in this.

The story allows for scene after scene of actual fighting, and
Shakespeare contrives for these every sort of variety: ranging in
the war with the Volscians from the amazing sight of Marcius

pitted against a whole city-full to the duel with Aufidius; in the struggle with the citizens from the victory where, sword in hand, he leads a handful of his friends against the rabble, a victory he is persuaded not to pursue, to the defeat in which this same rabble, better disciplined by the Tribunes, combine to banish him. And in the play's closing passages, the happy shouts of the Romans, freed from their fears, are contrasted with the spurious triumph of the Volscians.

The balance of sympathy also is fairly adjusted, neither side capturing—and keeping—overmuch. Shakespeare has been freely charged, in an age apt to be prejudiced in its favor, with bias against the populace. Allow for a little harmless ridicule and it is really not so. They are no match for Menenius in a contest of wit—although one of them, to his surprise, gamely stands up to him—but they see through Marcius' mockery, for all that they are too polite to tell him so. In that scene of the "garment of humility," indeed, his manners contrast most unfavorably with theirs. Individually, they seem simple, kindly creatures; collectively, they are doubtless unwise and unstable. They are human. Marcius has been their enemy, and they do not forget it. He declares that he remains so, and when he attacks them, they retaliate. They follow their leaders blindly, are misled and turn on them savagely at last. It is not a very sentimental survey, certainly. But why should it be?

The Tribunes are left the unqualified "villains of the piece"; a surface of comic coloring—which by making them amusingly contemptible may make them a little less detestable—is the only mitigation allowed them. But not one of the characters with a capital share in the melee of the action is very sympathetically drawn. Not, certainly,

> Worthy Menenius Agrippa; one that hath always loved the people.

—so acclaimed by them at our first sight of him, but in fact, as we soon find, cajoling them and sneering at them by turns. Not Aufidius, unstable in good and ill. The untender Volumnia remains so to the last, heedless in her triumph of the price her son must pay for it; a point made implicitly only, but clearly enough to leave us feeling cold towards her. And Shakespeare treats Caius Marcius himself detachedly, as a judge might, without creative warmth. Both sides of his case are to be heard; and we see him first at his worst (an unusual introduction for a titular hero), bullying the hungry citizens. The balance is soon adjusted by evidence—the fighter seen actually fighting—that his valor exceeds all tales of it; in battle and after it he stands out as hero supreme. And his trial of character, when this begins, is lifted, at its crisis, to high ground. It is not his ill-conditioned egoism but his fervent championship of an unpopular faith that gets him driven from Rome. The balance shifts violently when he seeks recreant revenge for this, to be shifted again when at the last moment he abandons it and pays the penalty. Finally, something like justice is done.

The play's range of characters is not a wide one, for it is kept closely relevant to the demands of the action, and these do not by much overspread the direct channel of the story. But within this range Shakespeare works with complete surety. We have that most leisurely of openings, the tale of the Belly and the Members, and Marcius' first attack on the citizens—much of a distractingly different sort having to happen before that full quarrel is joined— is given good scope. The geography of the battle-scenes by Corioles is schemed for us as concisely as clearly. But we have their action at length; for this serves to fill out the characters of Marcius, of Cominius and Titus Lartius too, each the more himself by contrast with the others; the prudent Consul and the old warrior, so young at heart, who will

> lean upon one crutch and fight with t'other,
> Ere stay behind this business.

generously happy, both of them, in their arrogant young hero's glory. The dispute that leads to the banishment is thrashed out at fullest length, argued back and forth, and yet again, nothing significant left uncanvassed. Later, in the scene at Antium, which brings us the renegade Coriolanus, we note that Shakespeare gives as much space to the sly, flunkey commentings of Aufidius' servants upon the amazing business and their master's romantic aberration as he has to the encounter itself. This, besides lowering the tension, helps resolve the new combination into the unheroic key in which it will be worked out.

Shakespeare has now come to ask for more sheer acting from his actors than he did, for more meaning and feeling to be compressed occasionally into half a dozen words than would once have flowed from a rhetorical hundred, for expressive listening as well as expressive speech, for silence itself sometimes to be made eloquent.

Holds her by the hand, silent.

—the play's most tragic moment, in which Marcius accepts defeat and in the sequel death at his mother's hand, confided to a simple stage direction.[2] Throughout the play action and words are expressively keyed together, the action of as great an import as the words. Marcius' share in the scene of the wearing of the gown of humility is as much picturing as speaking; and the mere sight of him later in his Roman dress, surrounded by the Volsces in theirs, sitting in council with them, marching into Corioles at their head—the graphic discord vivifies the play's ending.[3] The sight of the silently approaching figures of Volumnia, Virgilia and Valeria makes double effect; directly upon us, and upon us again through the effect made upon Marcius. And little though Virgilia says (and Valeria not a word), Volumnia so insistently joins them to her plea that their simple presence has an all but articulate value; while the actual spectacle of Marcius fighting singlehanded "within Corioles gates" is better witness to his prowess than any of the "acclamations hyperbolical" which he somewhat self-consciously decries. The memory of it, moreover, will not fade, only lie dormant until at the last it is rekindled by the magnificently trenchant

---

[2] And it is pretty certainly Shakespeare's own. Such moments of eloquent silence are to be found indicated, more or less explicitly, in all the later plays. A very notable one comes with Macbeth's hearing of his wife's death. Another follows upon the blow that Othello publicly deals Desdemona.

[3] In *Cymbeline*, certainly, costume marks the difference between Roman and British, and in *Macbeth* between Scots and English; in *Antony and Cleopatra*, probably, between Roman and Egyptian. We may take for granted, I think, that Volscians and Romans were dressed distinctively. A "realistic" reading may suggest that Marcius would cast off his Roman garb with his allegiance. But I believe that, quitting the "mean apparel" in which he went to encounter Aufidius, he would reappear as a Roman general, the dramatic effect being worth more than any logic.

"Boy"! false hound!
If you have writ your annals true, 'tis there,
That, like an eagle in a dove-cote, I
Fluttered your Volscians in Corioles:
Alone I did it.

Here, then, we have a play of action dealing with men of action; and in none that Shakespeare wrote do action and character better supplement and balance each other.

The Characters

CAIUS MARCIUS

MARCIUS is by no means a sympathetic character, and Shakespeare's attitude towards him seems, as we say, to be less that of a creator than a judge. There is a sense in which—brought to it by the art of dramatist and actor—we can come to "sympathize" even with the murderer Macbeth, as we can pity the murderer Othello, having learned to put ourselves imaginatively in their place. But we are left detached observers of Coriolanus; now admiring his valor, now exasperated by his harsh folly, touched occasionally by the flashes of nobility, the moments of gentleness. Yet we are never wholly at one with him, never made free of the inward man. And the juncture which could best bring this into play, the spiritual crisis in which he decides for his renegade revenge on Rome, is boldly and neatly side-stepped. It is strange, says Marcius in that one short soliloquy, how quickly enemies may become friends and friends turn enemies.

So with me:
My birth-place hate I, and my love's upon
This enemy town.

We are (this is to tell us) past the play's turning point already. The crucial change in the man has already taken place; and of the process of it we learn nothing. But this is not necessarily a shortcoming on Shakespeare's part—as were Marcius a Hamlet it would be. *Was* there any such explicable process? He is not a man of reason, but of convictions and passionate impulses, which can land him in a sudden decision—and he will not know how he came by it. That may help make him a good fighter, less good,

probably, as a general, certainly a poor politician. And it justifies
Shakespeare's treatment of him here. By his mere looks, in the
bitter humility—the old pride so quickly breaking through, as the
unlucky Third Servingman discovers—with which he encourages
Aufidius' servants to mock him, we are to discern the sufferings
of his lonely exile, and surmise the pent-up wrath, vented at last
in that blind resolve to be revenged on his own ungrateful
people or let the Volsces take revenge on him. Shall we now, on
such evidence, sufficiently surmise all this? That the thing, when
it did happen, will have happened in a flash; we have seen amply
enough of him by now to believe so. Critics have combed the text
for some sign of the actual moment of its happening; since
surely, they argue, Shakespeare could not have let such a
significant one slip by unmarked; and one has been found hidden
in an exclamatory "O, the gods!" wrung from him at the very
time of his banishing when he is taking leave of his mother and
his wife. But this will not do. Tell the actor concerned that he
is expected to convey to his audience in those three detached and
unacknowledged words a sudden resolve to be revenged on the
ungrateful city, and he will reasonably reply that it cannot be
done. And while the maturer Shakespeare may certainly present
his actors now and then with all but insuperable difficulties—
creative imagination beckoning the interpreter towards very steep
places indeed—never does he ask of them the impossible. What
he does in this instance by a mere stroke of omission may seem to
the *reader* of the play only to leave a rent in the texture of story
and character. But in effect, and to the *spectator*, it is not so.
Marcius could not appropriately be made to argue himself into
such treason, as a Hamlet might, or discover the seeds of it in
his nature, as might Macbeth. But picture and action significantly
"placed" are as legitimate and often as important a dramatic
resource as the spoken word can be. And what, at this juncture,
could be more fittingly eloquent than the simple sight—and the
shock it must give us—of this haggard, hardly recognizable
figure? It will flash into our imaginations, as words might not,
a sense of the suffering that has brought him to such a pass.

Shakespeare does not shirk the less tolerable aspects of the
character. Indeed he stresses them, since he first shows us the man
at his worst—strange treatment for a hero!—and in the theater

first impressions cut deep. After the long and exceptionally leisurely opening of the tale of the Belly and the Members comes Marcius, like a tornado, bullying and abusing the hungry citizens; and while what he says of them may be true, it is no satisfying answer to their empty stomachs. But if this is the worst side of him the best side of that is turned to us a minute later, and within a few more the various contending forces of this most contentious of plays have been deployed, their differences established, Marcius in the center of them.

Word comes that the Volsces are in arms, threatening Rome. He turns happily to welcome the news, and the war itself, which he has shrewdly foreseen. It will help "vent our musty superfluity"; here is something quite other than the complaint that has driven the despised citizens (who listen in glum silence) to mutiny. To "our best elders," the Consul Cominius and the Senators, who now appear, he is all disciplined deference, accepting, though, besides, their tributes paid to him as if these were his right, nor forgetting as he goes to fling a parting sneer at the "worshipful mutiners."

The new-made Tribunes, Brutus and Sicinius, have been listening in silence too; and now we have their comments on him, as unfriendly, truly, as his own conduct to the people they are to stand for has been unfair—unfair to the best in his nature, but an undeniable part of that truth about him which the play is so judicially to unfold. Proud, disdainful, insolent; the three notes are hit hard. The Tribunes attach to him by implication besides— as such men are apt to—some of their own politician's cunning. But in this, it will soon be made plain, they mistake him. Better for him had he had that sort of weapon with which to fight them.

The battle-scenes bring his most trenchant qualities into play. The amazing spectacle of his singlehanded fight "within Corioles gates" is to be matched by his duel with Aufidius in which he takes on "certain Volsces" too who come to their leader's aid, *till they be driven in breathless*, later by his stand against his fellow Romans, drawing his sword with a "No; I'll die here," and contrasted with the yet later sight of him, truly alone, *in mean apparel, disguised and muffled*. Throughout the battle he is in his glory, and at his happiest, outshining and outtopping all the rest; hero indeed. But the more portraying strokes are not

neglected. When his troops fall back he abuses them as roundly
as he did the citizens; still this is in the stress of the fighting.
When he calls inspiringly for volunteers to follow him in a
desperate venture—

> If any such be here,
> As it were sin to doubt, that love this painting
> Wherein you see me smeared; if any fear
> Lesser his person than an ill report;
> If any think brave death outweighs bad life,
> And that his country's dearer than himself . . .

—these surly cowards of such a short while since, now *all shout
and wave their swords; take him up in their arms, and cast up
their caps.*[4] Marcius could win men if he would, it is plain, had
he but a tithe of the confidence in them that he has in himself.
Nor is it that he is mere cold-hearted egoist. At the very instant
of victory he can remember the "poor man," a prisoner, who once
used him kindly, even as later, in the midst of his triumph he
can think of the widows left in Corioles and the "mothers that
lack sons." He shows contempt for the spoils of war, honest
distaste for the praises his prowess wins him, and under their
lavishing an all but boyish self-consciousness.

This last trait (of Shakespeare's own importing: it has no
place in Plutarch) is turned to varying account throughout the
play. In the boyishness, the reckless high spirits with which he
flings himself into battle, there is saving grace; even the thrasoni-
cal bragging to Aufidius before they fight is purged of offense if
it comes as their mere overflow.[5] The question is not one of
years. Marcius' actual age is not determined, and in North is
only implied by the fact that he first went to the wars "being but
a strippling," and that when he stands for Consul he has seen
seventeen years' service. He might then, by this, be about thirty-
two, and as mature a man as the maturer Hamlet. But more than
one thing in the story gives color to youthfulness of temper. His

---

[4] It was not, truly, this division of the army which fled and left him to his
fate "within Corioles gates." But while we shall remark the contrast in spirit
and conduct, we shall not, I think—and are not meant to—make the nicer
distinction.

[5] Note, too, that there is something of the duelists' conventional salute in this,
as it might be a clashing of sword against shield.

boyish prowess, repeatedly stressed, suggests it; so do his rash decisions; so does his continued deference to his mother. And Shakespeare takes and enlarges on this means of mitigating the harshness which makes him—as North has it—so "churlish, uncivill and altogether unfit for any man's conversation," to touch him with an unruly charm instead.

It is in the self-consciousness that the flaw lies. His repeated protests against the praises lavished on him become somewhat less then genuine. During the traffic of the battle, to generous old Titus Lartius:

> Sir, praise me not;
> My work hath yet not warmed me. . . .

And again:

> Pray now, no more: my mother,
> Who has a charter to extol her blood,
> When she does praise me, grieves me. . . .

And yet again, in protest to his general, not very graciously:

> You shout me forth
> In acclamations hyperbolical;
> As if I loved my little should be dieted
> In praises sauced with lies.

—this is not modesty (as Cominius kindly calls it), rather an inverted pride. Neglect to praise him; he will be the first to resent that!

We are shown one aspect after another of this obsessing self-consciousness. He will not even make himself sit still and listen respectfully to the Senate's official tribute to him, but must be up and away in the middle of it with a

> I had rather have one scratch my head i' the sun
> When the alarum were struck than idly sit
> To hear my nothings monstered.

His desperate discomfort standing in the market place in the gown of humility is positively comic.

> May I change these garments?

—his first request when the ordeal is over. He pictures himself with dramatic clarity returning there shamefaced to ask pardon of the despised citizens; he cannot resist, even at this critical moment, the false modesty of

> Scratches with briers;
> Scars to move laughter only.

when his friends once more be-laud his "war-like service" and cite his many wounds. Later, he is most conscious of the effect he is making in his picturesque disgrace upon Aufidius and the lackeys. Lastly, he provokes his own death by losing all control under the petty insult of Aufidius' "Boy!"

Yet such self-consciousness is not self-knowledge. Possessing but a spice of *this*, would he ever have taken his rash, revengeful vow to destroy Rome?—which, put to the ultimate test, proves no more stable than does Aufidius' febrile conversion to his cause. At the critical moment he stands firm against Cominius, certainly. But with Menenius—though he dismissed him harshly— he has afterwards to own that, under guise of firmness, he *has* yielded, even if it be only "a very little." And the mere news of the coming of his wife and mother seems to paralyze him:

> Shall I be tempted to infringe my vow
> In the same time 'tis made? I will not.

—the desperate "I will not" telling us plainly that in his heart he knows already that he will. He is no true renegade. Striving to be false to Rome, he is false to himself. And this his instinct—his unclouded, unself-conscious self-knowledge—has warned him more than once that he cannot afford to be. He was so—if harmlessly; for it was a trivial matter, and Shakespeare stresses the comic aspect of it—when after swearing he never would he *did* put on the gown of humility. He is about to be again, and in a matter of more consequence, when, under protest—

> Would you have me
> False to my nature? Rather say I play
> The man I am.

—he is letting Volumnia persuade him to recant before the people the faith he has just so ardently professed to them. But he finds when he tries to that he cannot. And it is in the violent recoil from this attempt to be other than he is that he strikes his most genuinely heroic note, with the ineffably proud retort to his sentence of banishment, the "I banish you."

Wrong-headed, intolerant and intolerable in his dealings with the citizens he may be, but upon the actual issues between them is he so wrong? He foresaw the first Volscian attack when the Senators—"our best elders"—did not, and the hungry populace could think of nothing but their hunger. Victory won and a "good" peace granted the enemy (a little to his impatience), himself made Consul, he foresees another attack—

> So then the Volsces stand but as at first,
> Ready, when time shall prompt them, to make road
> Upon's again.

—not imagining, however, who, in the amazing irony of events, will lead it! He has foreseen, besides, from the beginning, that the new-made Tribunate

> will in time
> Win upon power, and throw forth greater themes
> For insurrections arguing.

And who is to say that he is wrong in his protest against the "popular shall . . . the greater poll . . . the yea and no of general ignorance" being let outweigh experienced wisdom. What answer is there to his passionate

> my soul aches
> To know, when two authorities are up,
> Neither supreme, how soon confusion
> May enter, 'twixt the gap of both and take
> The one by the other.

Wrong or right, however, he must abide by his own convictions: honestly he can no other. He foresaw that too from the beginning, when Volumnia first held him out hopes of the consulate and he told her:

> Know, good mother,
> I had rather be their servant in my way
> Than sway with them in theirs.

For a man can do no better than be himself at his best. Sometimes it may even strangely seem that his quality lies rather in the worse than the better part of him; then we must take the rough with the smooth.

Play and character become truly tragic only when Marcius,
to be traitor to Rome, must turn traitor to himself. The actual
turning, as we said, we do not see, we are shown the thing already
inwardly done. And the tragedy is uncovered in something like
a reversal of the process, in the tragic failure to undo the thing
once done, once begun even. It is ironic tragedy, too. Marcius has
been used to meet fortune, good or bad, in the open. But from that
dark moment in Antium, of the bitter

> My birth-place hate I, and my love's upon
> This enemy town.

everything with him and within him turns to mockery. Aufidius'
extravagant homage to him will soon show itself a cheat. It is a
false façade of him seeming to sit there

>   in gold, his eye
> Red as 'twould burn Rome . . .

And when he has finally yielded to his mother's prayers he looks
up to find that

>   the heavens do ope,
> The gods look down, and this unnatural scene
> They laugh at.

He could go back to Rome—the "clusters who did hoot him out
o' the city" now as ready to "roar him in again"—thanked for
his weakness and kindness, and forgiven—he Coriolanus forgiven! But nor is that his nature. He is at least no weathercock.
He has turned aginst the Romans, he will stay loyal now to the
Volsces.[6]

Mockery piles on mockery in Corioles. The people there are
something the same problem that they were in Rome. Aufidius,
with his great repute, has still to observe their temper. And of
Coriolanus, even of him, it can be said that he

> Intends to appear before the people, hoping
> To purge himself with words . . .

And—though first, truly, to the lords of the city—so, *the Com-*

---

[6] Tennyson finds a similar thought for

> His honour rooted in dishonour stood
> And faith, unfaithful, kept him falsely true.

moners being with him, he does, boasting of the spoils and the
full third part
The charges of the action . . .

he has brought back. When till now did he value such pinchbeck
glory? In Rome he was plunged from triumph into obloquy.
Now it is the fickle commoners of Corioles that turn on him,
cheering him back at one moment, tearing him to pieces the next.
When last these same Volsces swarmed round him he was one
against all of them, and victor. They make better business of it
now.

Coriolanus, then, is a character not inwardly evolved, as the
greater tragic characters are, but seen from without. Seen and
molded, however, in the round; and as consistent and solid a
figure as Shakespeare ever put in motion.

VOLUMNIA

The relations between mother and son and the likeness and
difference between them are at the core of the play. The likeness
is patent. It is she, he is wont to say, whose praise first made him
a soldier. She rejoices in his prowess, gleefully in his very wounds,
has the tale of them by heart, could dance for joy at his return for
the third time with the oaken garland, wounded yet again. If
martial spirit were all she would seem to be almost more soldier
than he. And when the fateful struggle between them comes it is
the grimmer for this.

As a woman she has no overt part in the political quarrel with
the Tribunes; and, in that phase of the action, it is not until, amid
the violence of its crisis, Marcius seeks a breathing-space in his
house and hers, that we see or hear from her at all. But then she
astonishes us—and him. For until now she has seemed as stiff, and
stiffer than he, in pride. As to the Tribunes and their kind, she
has ignored them, but had been wont, he says,

> To call them woollen vessels, things created
> To buy and sell with groats, to show bare heads
> In congregations, to yawn, be still and wonder
> When one but of my ordinance stood up
> To speak of peace or war . . .

Yet now, when trouble comes, from unashamed policy she

would have him humble himself to them, recant his word and
cheat them even in recanting, "mountebank their loves." He is to
be, he protests, false to his nature; and she is setting him an
example by being false to hers. She persuades him to it: yet
fruitlessly since, tested, his nature rebels. It will take more than
this: defeat and banishment and, later, suffering and blind anger,
to trap him into swearing that oath of unnatural vengeance
which it will prove beyond his power to keep. She will set out
again to persuade him to break it, and, spending her last ounce
of strength and influence, she will succeed. And then it will bear
fruit; salvation for Rome, but, for him, bitter fruit indeed.

In a central scene, then, and at one of the play's chief turning
points, we have this truly unexpected exhibition of difference
between the two. Willful and stubborn he may be, but, to his
credit, he is not the mere overgrown spoiled child which the
extravagance of her praise might so easily have made him. He
turns from praise with the touch of affectation we have noted;
from hers the more genuinely, remembering how much he once
owed to it. But in his quarrel with the Tribunes he stands fear-
lessly for a cause. This is enshrined in egoism doubtless, but is
not, he proudly feels, the poorer for that; since he stands, in
what he has done and is, for what is best in Rome and he will
never shrink from proclaiming it and his faith in it, no matter the
moment's consequence. Volumnia, astonishingly the opposite,
shows herself at once shrewdly critical, worldly-wise—

> O, sir, sir, sir,
> I would have had you put your power well on
> Before you had worn it out.

—and shrewder yet:

> You might have been enough the man you are
> With striving less to be so. . . .

with irony to follow for the deflating of his anger, and the cold
realism of

> I have a heart as little apt as yours,
> But yet a brain that leads my use of anger
> To better vantage.

—a calculated use of it. And it will no more dishonor him (she easily argues) to maneuver a crooked way back into his fellow countrymen's favor than it would in wartime to

> take in a town with gentle words.

She herself, here and now, lavishes the gentlest on him; these failing, tries her "use of anger," pretended or real, with a

> At thy choice, then:
> To beg of thee it is my more dishonour
> Than thou of them. Come all to ruin. . . .
> Do your will.

He is the cause she stands for—that is the truth; and that he will not help her, and himself, by unscrupulously putting it before all other, exasperates her. He pays in banishment the penalty of his scruples. She is passionately for him in defeat as in victory, and but the more enraged with his enemies for their profiting by his high-minded unwisdom. After this, again, she is absent from the action for many scenes; and again, re-entering it, she sounds an unexpected note.

Mark now the dramatic strategy, as Shakespeare plans it, of her share in the women's appeal to Marcius for mercy upon Rome. Simply the sight of her and of his wife and son stirs him. She does not speak at first; only

> My mother bows,
> As if Olympus to a molehill should
> In supplication nod. . . .

The constricted figure has an eloquence of its own. His wife, softly reproachful, wins the first response from him. Not until he kneels does Volumnia speak, outdoing him then by herself kneeling, a shade of irony—no more!—in the ostentation of her gesture. After which, as with a certain confidence in this their meeting again, the plea is launched. She can be eloquent now, as never before. It is an eloquence inspired by that clarity of vision which imminent tragedy brings:

> for how can we,
> Alas! how can we for our country pray,
> Whereto we are bound, together with thy victory,
> Whereto we are bound? Alack! or we must lose
> The country, our dear nurse, or else thy person,
> Our comfort in the country. We must find

An evident calamity, though we had
Our wish, which side should win; for either thou
Must, as a foreign recreant, be led
With manacles through our streets, or else
Triumphantly tread on thy country's ruin,
And bear the palm for having bravely shed
Thy wife and children's blood.

The new note follows; a new note indeed:

If it were so that our request did tend
To save the Romans, thereby to destroy
The Volsces whom you serve, you might condemn us
As poisonous of your honour: no; our suit
Is that you reconcile them: while the Volsces
May say "This mercy we have showed"; the Romans,
"This we received"; and each in either side
Give the all-hail to thee, and cry "Be blest
For making up this peace!"

If he "mused" before at her indifference to his heroic stand
against the mob for his proud conscience' sake, what will his
retort be now to this talk of peace—of peace for its own sake; to
such a warning from her as

Thou knowest, great son,
The end of war's uncertain. . . .

to her disparaging

Thou hast affected the fine strains of honour. . . .

her

Think'st thou it honourable for a noble man
Still to remember wrongs?

It has taken truly a terrible revolution to bring her to this: no
less than the sight of her son, his country's hero, turned his
country's enemy, her own son, her enemy. And she begins to feel
nevertheless that she is beaten, that her high arguments are
breaking against his stubborn silence. Yet she is as tenacious a
fighter in her way as ever we have found him to be, and she flings
herself and the forces with her—mother, wife, child, the whole
womanhood of Rome—desperately into the struggle:

Daughter, speak you:
He cares not for your weeping. Speak thou, boy:

> Perhaps thy childishness will move him more
> Than can our reasons.

Their silence had begun it, as they stood ranged accusingly before him; by some means they must break his silence now. Volumnia chides and clamors:

> There's no man in the world
> More bound to's mother; yet here he lets me prate
> Like one i' the stocks. Thou has never in thy life
> Shewed thy dear mother any courtesy. . . .

By whatever means let her win! But she can fight a losing battle as fiercely as he could a winning one:

> Down, ladies; let us shame him with our knees.

Then with a Parthian scorn:

> Come, let us go:
> This fellow had a Volscian to his mother:
> His wife is in Corioles, and his child
> Like him by chance.

Yet she has won. Throwing her strength in to the very last, even at the admitted moment of defeat—

> Yet give us our despatch:
> I am husht until our city be a-fire,
> And then I'll speak a little.

—she had already won.

The very moment during his tenacious silence when his will yielded has been covered by silence too. And now she does not answer his low, searching

> O, mother, mother!
> What have you done?

when it emerges from the silence, nor respond at all to the unequivocal

> O, my mother, mother! O!
> You have won a happy victory to Rome;
> But for your son, believe it, O, believe it,
> Most dangerously you have with him prevailed,
> If not most mortal to him.

So possessed by her victory, is she, as to be incapable of a second thought? Is she so spent with the strain of her pleading that she faces Rome again a little later, and its frenzied welcome, in a very daze? Marcius, in any case, as with a new-learned magnanimity, shepherds away more talk of his defeat, thoughts of his fate. And her part in the play is done.[7]

It ends, as does her son's—as may be said of the whole play—amid the ironic laughter of the gods; she is unaware, that is all, of the successive mockeries in the event, made at last so bitterly plain to him. She has bred him to be at once Rome's hero and Rome's enemy. She has begged Rome's life of him, and, in

[7] What exactly is the effect that Shakespeare means to have made here? The mere suggestion of his danger in Marcius'

> O, mother, mother!
> What have you done? . . .

Volumnia, not yet certain of her victory, might easily overlook. But the repeated

> O, my mother, mother! O!
> You have won a happy victory to Rome;
> But for your son, believe it, O, believe it,
> Most dangerously you have with him prevailed,
> If not most mortal to him.

—to ignore this practically plain statement that he is most likely to be going to his death she must be prostrated indeed. And that I think on the whole is the intention. He then turns and goes to Aufidius, and Volumnia, left among the women, quickly recovers. She has not fainted, there must be no such weakness; it is simply a moment's reaction from the extreme strain of the victory. He turns back, and apostrophizes them from where he stands:

> O, mother! wife!

and stands still gazing while Aufidius speaks his aside. This is the heartfelt farewell he takes.

Editors hereabouts insert

The Ladies make signs to Coriolanus.

presumably to account for the "Ay, by and by . . ." with which he breaks the silence of his gaze. They stand expectantly where he has left them; there is no need of more. Then he joins them, as if bidding them dismiss all forebodings, gallantly congratulating them on their victory; and our query, if there was risk of one: why does not Volumnia see that in saving Rome she has sent her son to his death? has been fended off. It may return on reflection when the play is over. It probably will not. And if it takes the shape of the memory of a Volumnia as peremptory and passionate as her son, as stubborn in her own cause and as oblivious to all besides, that is a not unjust one.

Shakespeare the practical playwright, having had his full use of a character, and the whole action being near its end, will add nothing needlessly. Volumnia has saved Rome, and the action asks no more of her. Care for her son's fate would prolong or complicate it, and, in doing so, upset the balance of interest. It must suffice, then, that we do not remark any such omission; and circumstance and character are shaped so that we shall not. It is in these instances of dramatic tact that Shakespeare the playwright shows at his most skillful.

winning it, is obviously sending him to his death. And we last
see her welcomed triumphantly back to Rome even as he once
was, flowers strewed before her, amid cries of

> Unshout the noise that banished Marcius;
> Repeal him with the welcome of his mother. . . .

But it is too late for that. And tragedy of character does not
work out in such happy confusions of popular acclaim.

It is a chill parting, this with Volumnia; our last sight of her—
nothing nearer—parading through Rome, her back turned upon
Marcius himself and the essential tragedy's imminent consummation.

AUFIDIUS

It takes all Shakespeare's skill to make Aufidius fully effective
within the space which the planning of the action allows him—
and perhaps he does not wholly succeed. For a while it is not so
difficult. He is admitted on all hands to be Marcius' rival and
to come short of him by little. Marcius' first word of him is that

> I sin in envying his nobility,
> And were I anything but what I am,
> I would wish me only he.

He is secondary hero. And when within a moment or so we see the
man himself he is telling the Senators of Corioles:

> If we and Caius Marcius chance to meet,
> 'Tis sworn between us we shall ever strike
> Till one can do no more.

Volumnia, imagining glorious things, can see her Marcius

> pluck Aufidius down by the hair . . .

In the battle the Corioles taunt the Romans with

> There is Aufidius: list, what work he makes
> Amongst your cloven army.

while to Marcius, whether far off—

> There is the man of my soul's hate, Aufidius. . . .

—or within reach—

> Set me against Aufidius and his Antiats. . . .

—he is an obsession. And when they do meet and fight, Aufidius, if bettered, is not beaten. To this point, then, however little we may see of him, he is brought to our minds in each succeeding scene, and is emphatically lodged there when he is so unconsentingly rescued in the duel with his famous enemy by "certain Volsces" (anonymous: common soldiers presumably, therefore):

> Officious, and not valiant, you have shamed me
> In your condemned seconds.

And, since we shall not see him thereafter for some time, this note of shame, and of the crooked passion it can rouse in the man, is enlarged and given what will be memorable place in a scene coming but a little later.

> Five times, Marcius,
> I have fought with thee; so often hast thou beat me,
> And wouldst do so, I think, should we encounter
> As often as we eat.[8]

Frank confession! But now

> mine emulation
> Hath not that honour in't it had; for where
> I thought to crush him in an equal force,
> True sword to sword, I'll potch at him some way
> Or wrath or craft may get him. . . .
> Where I find him, were it
> At home, upon my brother's guard, even there,
> Against the hospitable canon, would I
> Wash my fierce hands in's heart.

We shall certainly recall that—and be given good cause to—when, all amazingly, the event so falls out. The scheme of the action allows Aufidius very limited space; but we have thus far been kept conscious of him throughout. From now, even until he emerges into it again, he does not go quite without mention, and we shall have lodged in mind what he may mean to it when he does. It is able stagecraft.

In a cruder play Aufidius and the Volsces might be made to serve as "villains of the piece." But Shakespeare is not painting in such ultra-patriotic black and white. We are on the Roman

---

[8] Later on, in Antium, Aufidius makes it "Twelve several times" that he has been beaten. But nothing hangs on the precise number, and he is not on his oath.

side, and they are "foreigners"; so their worse, not their better, aspect is naturally turned towards us. The victorious Romans give them a "good" peace, Titus Lartius being commanded to send back from their captured city

>   to Rome
> The best, with whom we may articulate,
> For their own good and ours.

They, when their victorious turn comes, so we hear,

>   looked
> For no less spoil than glory . . .

Shakespeare shades them somewhat. But the balance is not unfairly held.

Aufidius, then, re-enters the action at its most critical juncture, and to play for the moment a surprising part in it. Here, in this wine-flushed host to the nobles of Antium, is quite another man; and not only in the look of him but, yet more surprisingly—suspense resolved—in the deep-sworn enemy turned ecstatic comrade. From that

>   Nor sleep, nor sanctuary,
> Being naked, sick, nor fane nor Capitol,
> The prayers of priests, nor times of sacrifice,
> Embarquements all of fury, shall lift up
> Their rotten privilege and custom 'gainst
> My hate to Marcius.

we are at a glowing

>   Let me twine
> Mine arms about that body, where against
> My grained ash an hundred times hath broke
> And scarred the moon with splinters: here I clip
> The anvil of my sword, and do contest
> As hotly and as nobly with thy love
> As ever in ambitious strength I did
> Contend against thy valour.

It is a turning point indeed, and doubly so; the revolution in Marcius is barely set forth before it is matched with this. The two revolutions differ as the two men do; the one a plunging through defeat and misery from confident pride to obdurate bitterness; that in Aufidius a sudden emotional overthrow, sprung by this startling proffer, this attack upon a weakness in him which he would never think to defend. Yet there is a likeness between them too. And they are in keeping, both, with the rest of the play, its extremes of passion and their instabilities; the weathercock-swaying of the citizens, Volumnia's violence and arbitrary shifts. Marcius himself we shall see will be unable to abide by his treason to the end; and Aufidius, we shall very quickly guess, will not long sustain this unnatural change. Recurring ironies fitting into the scheme of tragic irony which informs the whole action.

This "strange alteration"—reflected too in the freakish comment of the servants—gives us a fresh, and, for the moment, an alert interest in Aufidius. From now to the end the stagecraft actuating him remains as able; and if here and there the figure seems to lack vitality, to be a little word-locked, why, livelier development of this new aspect of the man might well make more demands on the play's space than could be spared, or such a turn of inspiration as Shakespeare (even he!) has not unquestionably at command. But he does not dodge nor skip a step in the completing of the character. And, within a scene or so, to begin this, we see Aufidius again—quite disillusioned.

Thinking better of things is a dry business; and this ancillary scene, shared with an anonymous Lieutenant, will appropriately be none of the liveliest. But the matter of it is a strengthening rivet in the character scheme of the play. Aufidius' sobered reaction from his rhapsodies to the coldest common sense—hints dropped moreover of revengeful traps already laid for Marcius; Aufidius to be revenged on him for his own access of too generous folly, the hardest thing forgivable—this will redress any balance of sympathy lost between the two for the action's last phase. We have no violent swing back to the fanatically sportsmanlike hatred with which they started. On the contrary, to Aufidius is given in the scene's last speech the most measured and balanced of summarizings of his rival's qualities and failings. And for Marcius it is in this quiet reasonable accounting that his worst danger can be foreseen. Mastery in soldiership—who has ever denied him that? He has not even to exercise it now:

> All places yield to him ere he sits down;
> And . . .

—despite his treason; because of it indeed—

> the nobility of Rome are his:
> The Senators and Patricians love him too. . . .
> I think he'll be to Rome
> As is the asprey to the fish, who takes it
> By sovereignty of nature. . . .

Aufidius, lacking just that sovereignty, could not look his own problem more fairly in the face. For, indeed, he had better know just where he has the worse of it, that being the second-rate man's due approach to getting the better of it after all. He may next encourage himself by listing—though with every scruple and reserve—Marcius' failings too: pride, temper, intolerance and the rest, and by recognizing that in this discordant world men have the defects of their qualities and the qualities of their defects; and that at best, what is more,

> our virtues
> Lie in the interpretation of the time. . . .

—which may prove for us or against us; and whichever way

> One fire drives out one fire; one nail, one nail;
> Rights by rights founder, strengths by strengths do fail.

Fortune, with a little patient aid, is ever ready to turn her wheel:

> When, Caius, Rome is thine
> Thou art poor'st of all; then shortly art thou mine.

Both speech and scene demand of their audience close attention, closer, perhaps, than such detached argument will currently command at this juncture in a play unless it be embodied in some central, radiating figure. It is the more notable that Shakespeare should here, so to speak, be forcing his meaning through the recalcitrant lines.[9] But his aim, it would seem, is to give a rational substance to the figure, of such a sort as will keep us an Aufidius expressively if cryptically observant through succeeding scenes while we await the due restoring of the natural open enmity between the two.

It comes with relief.

> How is it with our general?

---

[9] One or two lines in this last speech are doubtless corrupt. But rectify them as we may, we shall hardly make them lucid.

his fellow conspirators ask.

> Even so
> As with a man by his own alms empoisoned,
> And with his charity slain.

But he is free now of his false position and on his own ground
again, and the ills done him are glib upon his tongue. He must
be cautiously in the right at all points:

> And my pretext to strike at him admits
> A good construction. I raised him, and I pawned
> Mine honour for his truth. . . .

More than so, he

> took some pride
> To do myself this wrong . . .

—he is fueling up with virtuous indignation, until, at the touch
of a match, Coriolanus himself can be trusted to fire out in fury,
no moral excuses needed. "Traitor . . . unholy braggart . . . boy
of tears . . . boy!"—it is the last spark that sets all ablaze.

Aufidius' philosophic mind has not endured; nor does the
one-time gallantry. "My valour's poisoned . . ." —we are back at
that. He is no coward, we know; has ever been ready to fight.
It is only that, now or never, he must have the best of it, and he
has made all sure. So, duly provoked

> *The Conspirators draw, and kill Coriolanus, who falls.* . . .

Upon which, though, he cannot resist it:

> *Aufidius stands on him.*[10]

Shakespeare, in the maturity of his skill, knows how to give
as much meaning to a significantly placed gesture as to a speech
or more. There are two gestures here, the insolent treading of
the slain man under foot, with the quick attempt in face of the
shocked outcry to excuse it:

> My noble masters, hear me speak.

then the response to the reproach:

> O, Tullus!
> Thou hast done a deed whereat valour will weep.
> Tread not upon him. Masters . . .

---

[10] Shakespeare's own stage direction, we may once more be pretty sure.

which can but be its shamed and embarrassed lifting, the more
eloquent of Aufidius, this. The more fittingly unheroic, besides,
the ending. The lords of the city have been honourable enemies.

> Peace, ho! no outrage: peace!
> The man is noble and his fame folds in
> This orb o' the earth. His last offences to us
> Shall have judicious hearing.

The sight of the outrage done him horrifies them. But as Aufidius
promptly argues,

> My lords, when you shall know, as in this rage
> Provoked by him, you cannot, the great danger
> Which this man's life did owe you, you'll rejoice
> That he is thus cut off.

and, truly, as they'll in fairness soon admit:

> His own impatience
> Takes from Aufidius a great part of blame....

Common sense supervenes:

> Let's make the best of it.

And Aufidius can say with truth, the man being safely dead:

> My rage is gone,
> And I am struck with sorrow.

MENENIUS

Menenius makes one in the ironically figured pattern of
character. He is set outwardly—and at the play's very start—in
sharp contrast to Coriolanus himself:

> Worthy Menenius Agrippa; one that hath always loved the
> people.

—so even the disgruntled citizens admit. Jovial, humorous,
reasonable; what could be less like the intolerant, rough-tongued
young soldier, whose pride it is that

> He would not flatter Neptune for his trident,
> Or Jove for's power to thunder.

But soon enough we notice that behind the cajoling

> Why, masters, my good friends, mine honest neighbours ...

and the merry tale that sets them laughing—at each other it is, too!—his complete indifference to their troubles. Marcius, storming, would have had

> the nobility lay aside their ruth,
> And let me use my sword.

Menenius has taken the cannier way; and here already, at no cost but fair words,

> these are almost thoroughly persuaded;
> For though abundantly they lack discretion,
> Yet are they passing cowardly.

Nor does he scruple, it would seem, to say so in their hearing.

Menenius is to pervade the play, yet as an auxiliary character only. This full and vivid shaping of the figure so early has one incidental advantage then; the lightest future touch—and however slight be its connection with the main action—will be effective. And in all the plays there are few livelier or more individual characters.

An old gentleman of "character," an "original," to his friends the best of friends; his fighting spirit has not flagged either with the years, and he fights the more cleverly with his tongue for his sole weapon, if the more spitefully now and then. Would Marcius but profit by it his counsel might steer him to safety. He loves him as a man his own son, delights in his prowess and fame. He knows him too, better than does Volumnia, and is quick to persuade him that, willy-nilly, he must don that vext "gown of humility," sticks to him too till he has it on, shepherds him to the very verge of the actual ordeal, only quits him then with almost comic misgiving, to return at the first moment as proud as a nurse of a well-behaved child at a party.

The rioting in the market place tells on his age. While he stands loyally by Marcius he pleads breathlessly with each disputant in turn, flatters even the loathed Tribunes. But he never loses his head, nor his sense of humor either, gives a savingly comic twist to Marcius' militant

> On fair ground
> I could beat forty of them.

(as indeed we know and see) by his own merry

> I could myself

Take up a brace of the best of them; yea, the two Tribunes.

Nor does he ignore his own side's failings. Of Marcius, momentarily relieved of his incendiary presence:

> His nature is too noble for the world. . . .
>   What the vengeance!
> Could he not speak 'em fair?

—into which combination of tempers do these heroes drive us. But here he is at his best, with that frank

> As I do know the Consul's worthiness,
> So can I name his faults.

and in his plea for Rome's honor, threats of death and banishment overhanging the man who has so fought for her:

>   Now the good gods forbid
> That our renowned Rome, whose gratitude
> Towards her deserved children is enrolled
> In Jove's own book, like an unnatural dam
> Should now eat up her own! . . .
> What has he done to Rome that's worthy death?
> Killing our enemies, the blood he hath lost—
> Which, I dare vouch, is more than that he hath,
> By many an ounce—he dropped it for his country;
> And what is left, to lose it by his country,
> Were to us all, that do't and suffer it,
> A brand to the end o' the world.

—the artful old man with his crotchets turned to the grave patrician; the verse as fittingly strong and clear.

But to the last moment he is pliably for give-and-take, real or pretended, wailing to his self-wrecked hero a despairing

> Is this the promise that you made your mother?

and past the last moment staying faithfully by him, till he finds place in that sad journey to the gates.

>   Thou old and true Menenius,
> Thy tears are salter than a younger man's,
> And venemous to thine eyes.

—yet more quickly dried to calm, it seems. (Here comes one of Shakespeare's incidental touches of veracity.) The fight finished

and lost, the women—Volumnia, even Virgilia—pass from tears
to anger, Menenius to all that is most pacific. There is no more
to be done, and he is very, very weary; though if he

> could shake off but one seven years
> From these old arms and legs . . .

he'd tramp it too by Marcius' side with the best. But Marcius
gone, not even the sight of the swaggering Tribunes rouses him.
Finally, for the distraught and shaken mother and wife he has
nothing but a kindly

> Peace, peace! be not so loud.

unless it be, as Brutus and Sicinius sheer off, the consolation of

> You have told them home,
> And, by my troth, you have cause. . . .

with the yet solider comfort of

> You'll sup with me?

It is unheroic, doubtless, thus to finish such a day. But he is
not heroic!

Tit for tat is hard to resist; nor, certainly, is Menenius a man
to miss a chance of it when it comes. While Marcius is banished
and the Tribunes are in power he keeps a stiff lip in opposition,
foxing enough to warrant their sarcastic

> O! he is grown most kind
> Of late. Hail, sir!

But when the sudden, startling turn of fortune comes, tidings of
Marcius' and Aufidius' dread approach, the old Menenius
reappears, lively and ready as ever:

> What news? what news? . . .
> What's the news? what's the news? . . .
> Pray, now your news? . . .
> Pray, your news?

News suiting his ironic temper in defeat, of the prospect of his
hero's sacking of his city; a pretty contradiction, however deserved.
But here even Menenius' sense of irony will be stretched a little.
He can turn, however, sarcastically on the Tribunes:

> You have made good work,
> You and your apron men. . . .
> You and your crafts! You have crafted fair!

If they shirk the blame, what can the answer to that be but

> How! was't we? . . .

But it was.

> We loved him; but, like beasts
> And cowardly nobles, gave way unto your clusters,
> Who did hoot him out o' the city.

And will mere words now win pardon for either lot of them? Menenius takes delight in assuring the wretched citizens—a troop of them arriving at this juncture—in assuring them under the crestfallen Tribunes' very noses that

> not a hair upon a soldier's head
> Which will not prove a whip: as many coxcombs
> As you threw caps up will he tumble down,
> And pay you for your voices.

He once more finds himself, indeed, the old racily tongued Menenius of our first acquaintance, haranguing the biddable crowd. Brutus and Sicinius make a last effort to regain their followers' confidence, but with little enough left in themselves, it seems. The one-time winners throw in their hands, and the losers are left to make the best of a bad job between them.

Menenius does not fancy suffering himself the great man's treatment of Cominius. It was Cominius' business (who preceded him as Consul) to be the first to go begging forgiveness. Once

> He called me father:
> But what o' that? . . .
> Nay, if he coyed
> To hear Cominius speak, I'll keep at home.

But what he wants is to be pressed into going; and for that he flagrantly plays, until flattery in full measure sends the old man off, breezily confident that with him to do it the task is as good as done.

Menenius makes, dramatically speaking, a good end. He plays the statesman with the soldiers guarding Coriolanus, they, enjoyably, the soldier with him. He is "an officer of state," and he and Rome, things at the worst, retain, one hopes, their dignity. But he's not the first to come (here the close-packing of the action, the tale of Cominius' attempt, adds to the effect of this); and

> our general
> Will no more hear from thence.

Then begins the tussle, familiar to any wartime, between soldier and civilian, the Somebody in peace and Nobody in war, whose condescending

> Good my friends,
> If you have heard your general talk of Rome,
> And of his friends there, it is lots to blanks,
> My name hath touched your ears: it's Menenius.

earns from a sentry under orders no more than a cool

> Be it so; go back: the virtue of your name
> Is not here passable.

Menenius adds to his credit one civilian virtue after another:

> I tell thee, fellow,
> Thy general is my lover: I have been
> The book of his good acts, whence men have read
> His fame unparalleled, haply amplified:
> For I have ever verified my friends,
> Of whom he's chief. . . .

—and it is true!—

> with all the size that verity
> Would without lapsing suffer . . .

each as unavailingly as the last. Indignation does not serve.

> Sirrah, if thy captain knew I were here, he would use me with estimation.
> Come, my captain knows you not.
> I mean thy general.
> My general cares not for you. Back, I say, go; lest I let forth your half-pint of blood. . . .

—the soldier's conclusive argument. Marcius' own appearance, with Aufidius in quiet partnership, puts the matter to the proof.

Nowhere in the play do we find the pattern of its character-planning more effectively turned and colored. The comic charged with emotion; what more human? Old Menenius fatuously insisting upon the sentries discomfiting him, yet heartbroken in his pleading; and it is—we see it—with a cracked heart that Marcius repulses him, that harsh "Away!" little better than a blow in the face. And he must accept Aufidius' praise for it, the dry

> You keep a constant temper.

The sentries allowed their mockery, if they fancy they can out-mock this gallant old patrician in defeat they are vastly mistaken. He can still give back better than he gets:

> I neither care for the world, nor your general: for such things as you, I can scarce think there's any, y'are so slight. . . .

Civilian though he be, he has a weapon of which they cannot rob him:

> He that hath a will to die by himself, fears it not from another. Let your general do his worst. For you, be that you are, long; and your misery increase with your age! [His does!] I say to you, as I was said to, Away!

—and he is gone; bearing off the honors with him, thinks one of these Volscians, duly impressed:

> A noble fellow, I warrant him.

the other of tougher mind:

> The worthy fellow is our general: he's the rock, the oak not to be wind-shaken.

The closely contrived action allows for yet one small turn more in the pattern of character, and typical—fully so—it shall be. The trembling Sicinius awaits tidings; not to be mitigated. But if Menenius has been beaten, let there be no belittling the battle lost; and, if *he* cannot come home winner, who may? Did not Cominius tell them how

> The tartness of his face sours ripe grapes; when he walks he moves like an engine, and the ground shrinks before his treading. . . . He sits in his state, as a thing made for Alexander. . . .

Sicinius may bleat that

> He loved his mother dearly.

Forlornest of hopes, retorted on by

> So did he me; and he no more remembers his mother now than an eight-year-old horse. . . . Mark what mercy his mother shall bring from him: there is no more mercy in him than there is milk in a male tiger. . . .

Menenius, be it remembered, does not know what has passed since his plea was repulsed. For all that he does know it is the right sort of medicine he is administering—having first swallowed it himself with that cheerful courage, which it is lets him in turn so enjoy forcing it down the unhappy Tribune's own throat. Once more comes the solacing refrain:

> and all this is 'long of you.

with, for a closing chord, each striking his own note, Sicinius' pitiful

> The gods be good unto us!

the old politician, gamer:

> No, in such a case the gods will not be good unto us. When we banished him we respected not them, and, he returning to break our necks, they respect not us.

Take the rough with the smooth and look facts in the face; as wholesome a lesson in politics as lay in the tale of the Belly and the Members. Whereupon, the concluding good news brought and confirmed, Menenius can take this also as coolly—for all that he'll let the two scurvy cowards of Tribunes discover! And with this he is caught back into the ending central stream of the play's action, lively to his last word.

THE TRIBUNES

Brutus and Sicinius make a listening and a not promptly identifiable first appearance. The aristocrats, assembled by the rumors of war, depart elated, the humiliated citizens steal away, leaving these two—the new Tribunes, will they be?—to savor their comments:

> Was ever man so proud as is this Marcius?
> He has no equal.

They are not of the simple caliber of their followers, that is at once made plain; the craftiest of politicians, rather, with Brutus to belittle—and slander—Marcius, true politician-wise:

> Fame, at the which he aims,
> In whom already he's well-graced, can not
> Better be held nor more attained than by

> A place below the first; for what miscarries
> Shall be the general's fault, though he perform
> To the utmost of a man; and giddy censure
> Will then cry out of Marcius, "O, if he
> Had borne the business!"

Sicinius joining in. The twenty-five-line interchange of cynical judgment stamps them vividly enough on our memory: a binding-up of the story; for between now and our next encounter with them the whole Volscian war is to pass.

We find them again still in Rome (where they are is always Rome); of consequence now, evidently, among the people, but uneasily awaiting the hero's return, decrying him, fearing for their chances beside him. It is now that they take color as comic villains; this thanks to Menenius, who finds ridicule, in which he is bluffly expert, the best weapon with which to torment them. One effect of this will be that while we, with the more sympathetic Menenius, may detest and make fun of them, in other bearings they are still the two sharp politicians. Shakespeare disposes his sides for the coming combat with great address. Here are these two, playing the game by its rules, yielding smoothly to their mastery, condoning no smallest breach of them, pursuing that, indeed, as far and as bitterly as vengeance may. It will be at no point a pretty picture. Set against it we have the cool comment of the neutral Senate House officials upon Marcius as he opens his political career:

> That's a brave fellow; but he's vengeance proud, and loves not the common people.
>
> Faith, there have been many great men that have flattered the people, who ne'er loved them; and there be many that they have loved, they know not wherefore: so that, if they love they know not why, they hate upon no better a ground. Therefore, for Coriolanus neither to care whether they love or hate him manifests the true knowledge he has in their disposition; and out of his noble carelessness lets them plainly see't.

"Noble carelessness"—that phrase alone, with what we have seen of him besides, would weight the sympathy well upon Marcius' side. But the yet cooler, the ironic

> but he seeks their hate with greater devotion than they can render it him . . .

caps it. A political play; the hero, under this aspect of it, with no more skill at the game than makes him his own worst enemy—a fruitful theme. Nor will he take counsel; Menenius could save him more than once. It is between him and the Tribunes that the earlier maneuvering mostly proceeds; Marcius—if he would but let himself be so!—a glorious figurehead, the citizens poor puppets. And it is not so easy to pick holes in the Tribunes' conduct at first. They demand their people's rights: that is only their duty. Is it their fault if Marcius so grudgingly grants these? They slyly incite them to test him at his weakest point. Are they to blame if he not merely yields under the test, but unrepentingly proclaims that here he is, to their despite, at his strongest instead? It is something of a trap, but need he so recklessly walk into it?

But from now on they grow ever more contemptible. They promptly abuse the success they so easily win. Says Marcius scornfully,

> I do despise them;
> For they do prank them in authority
> Against all noble sufferance. . . .
> It is a purposed thing, and grows by plot. . . .

and—though they may safely deny it—we know this is true.

They overplay their hands when they demand Coriolanus' death, show their last sign of political good sense when they'd accept Menenius as mediator in the quarrel. Otherwise they had better have pressed for death, since exile is but to bring back revenge. And something of this they do actually, in the midst of the turmoil, perceive—

> To eject him hence
> Were but one danger, and to keep him here
> Our certain death. . . .

—it being only that their insensate vanity, bred in the flush of success, so blinds them. Marcius gains tragic dignity in defeat and departure; they, tarring the rabble on to hoot him "out at gates," swaggering ludicrously through the streets themselves—"our noble Tribunes"!—touch depth.

When the tide of fortune has turned, although we know what is coming, we see them still sunning themselves fatuously for a while

> i' the present peace
> And quietness o' the people . . .

Then, foolishly, futilely, denying the plain unpleasant fact, feebly protesting, when they cannot, against Menenius' mockery. Nor that the worst. While one still tries, and yet again, to argue facts away:

> *Enter a Messenger.*
> Sir, if you'd save your life, fly to your house:
> The plebeians have got your fellow-Tribune,
> And hale him up and down: all swearing, if
> The Roman ladies bring not comfort home,
> They'll give him death by inches.

Such politics have their revenges.

The Action of the Play

> *Enter a company of mutinous Citizens, with stones,*
> *clubs and other weapons.*

But let not the unwary producer be led by that *mutinous*, and by the *stones, clubs and other weapons*, into projecting a scene of mere quick confusion, violence and high-pitched noise. Shakespeare has further reaching intentions. These citizens form a collective character, so to call it, of capital importance to the first half of the play; at its very start, therefore, we are to be given a fully informing picture of them. A homespun lot, but with a man or so among them that can both think and talk. They are certainly in an ugly temper at the moment and ripe for mischief, since plaints and a fortnight's threats have, it seems, proved futile; and they are not of the breed (Roman or British) that sits down to starve in patience. So if nothing is left them to do but to rid themselves and the world of this man they take to be their "chief enemy," Caius Marcius—why, no more speech-making, nor parliamentary acclamations of "Resolved, resolved!": let the thing be done! But they can be halted and made to listen yet once more. First it is to the chief rebel amongst them ruthfully justifying their intent, protesting that

> the gods know I speak this in hunger for bread, not in thirst
> for revenge. . . .

then to a last-minute defender Marcius finds among them, bidding
them remember the "services he has done for his country." For
even though he be "a very dog to the commonalty," all that can be
said for him must be heard.

The distant shouts of some kindred company of mutineers
rouse them again; such temper is infectious. And they would be
off to make common cause with these others; but Menenius
Agrippa's arrival once again quiets them. They like old Menenius.
He is "one that hath always loved the people." Even the First
Citizen will grudgingly admit that

> He's one honest enough: would all the rest were so!

"Honest," perhaps; but little proof of his love for the people is
in fact ever forthcoming, and the chief token of his honesty
would seem to be that he speaks his mind bluntly to them. But
he does so in a sort of rough good fellowship, giving himself no
high and mighty airs. How far with them even a show of
kindliness will go! He knows how to tackle them. They are his
"countrymen," his "good friends," his "honest neighbours"; and
within a few minutes he has this mutinous mob quietly gathered
round him while he tells them a fairy tale. It is the parable of the
Belly and the Members. Only that ruthful rebel the First Citizen
is mildly recalcitrant:

> you must not think to fob off our disgrace with a tale. . . .

—which, of course, is just what Menenius means to do. And
most readily he does it, going his own leisurely pace, giving the
homely humor its full value; and while he holds them there
absorbed the mutinous mood ebbs out of them. With the
recalcitrant First Citizen he spars offhandedly. A dash of ironic
flattery (but indeed the creature is intelligent!), a tolerant snub,
flooring him finally amid the merriment of his fellows with a
stroke of something less than good-humored ridicule:

> What do you think,
> You, the great toe of this assembly? . . .
> being one o' th' lowest, basest, poorest
> Of this most wise rebellion . . .

After which Caius Marcius himself—Coriolanus to be—strides in.
It is for Shakespeare an unusual opening—the plays offer indeed

none comparable to it—with its hundred and sixty lines of abortive revolt and elaborate parable; he will habitually have swung his main theme into action within half the time or less. But it accomplishes a variety of purposes. The mutinous entry having furnished initial impetus enough, its slackening, the debate, and their equivocally mild response to Menenius' bluff bullying, give us a fair view of the citizens not yet in leash to their Tribunes, a sample of their native quality, upon which the lash of Marcius' contempt is next so precipitately to fall. The telling of the parable holds back the action, even as Menenius means it to hold up the revolt, yet bears directly on it, is no mere digression (that, at the play's outset, would be a weakness), but enlarges it at, so to say, one remove. This factor of the citizens and their condition is thus given ample preparatory display. Marcius' castigation will cow them now to silence. While the war with the Volsces is waging they will be absent from the scene. When they return to it Brutus and Sicinius will be their spokesmen, maneuvering and coloring their cause for them.

Marcius, abruptly appearing, at once spurs the action to the swift pace his dominance of it befits. To Menenius' affectionately admiring tribute of a

> Hail, noble Marcius!

he—though young man to old—returns no more than a curt "Thanks," so impatient is he to round on the mutineers. Plainly, Menenius' milder methods have already prevailed; but he must still vent his spleen. They are rogues and curs, hares in cowardice, geese in folly, ingrates, their own worst enemies, inconstant and perverse. They say, do they, that there is grain enough in the city, yet they are hungry, that though they be dogs, yet dogs must eat? But

> Would the nobility lay aside their ruth,
> And let me use my sword, I'd make a quarry
> With thousands of these quarter'd slaves, as high
> As I could pick my lance.

Doubtless! And all he says of them and more may be true; but such scorn for starving fellow-countrymen has no very chivalrous ring. Nor is Menenius' placatory

> Nay, these are almost thoroughly persuaded;
> For though abundantly they lack discretion,
> Yet are they passing cowardly.

the most generous comment possible upon their surrender to his wiles. Marcius, it may be, is the angrier with them since the other "troops," whose shouts we heard, whom he has just quitted, have by their plaints prevailed with this same nobility to grant them

> a petition . . . a strange one . . .
> Five tribunes to defend their vulgar wisdoms . . .
> S'death!
> The rabble should have first unroofed the city
> Ere so prevailed with me. . . .

He foresees, shrewdly enough, that

> it will in time
> Win upon power and throw forth greater themes
> For insurrection's arguing.

There lies, indeed, the obstacle against which he is to bruise and break himself, and it is embryonic already in this group of sullen, silenced, confuted men over which he now rides so contemptuously roughshod. Marcius is about the least sympathetic of Shakespeare's heroes, and he is first shown to us in his unloveliest light.

He is happy to be freed from these cankerous domestic politics by the sudden news of war:

> we shall ha' means to vent
> Our musty superfluity. . . .

And "our best elders," whose coming follows the news—Cominius the Consul, old Titus Lartius and other Senators—will have worthier duties to perform than playing blackmail to the populace. He himself is consequently in great credit:

> Marcius, 'tis true that you have lately told us;
> The Volsces are in arms.

He can smell the chance of a fight, from wherever the wind of it blows. And at once, in sharp contrast, he is at his best: his sword his country's, no questions asked; chivalrous tribute paid to its chief enemy:

Tullus Aufidius . . .

he is a lion
That I am proud to hunt.

It may all go to a somewhat too self-sufficient tune, yet pardonably stimulated, this—were stimulus needed—by the deference Rome's great men offer him. He cannot resist, moreover, a parting gibe at the "worshipful mutiners," become sullenly silent onlookers, bidding them follow him to play rats among the abundant Volscian corn, which such a little valor will win. But, says the stage direction,

Citizens steale away.[11]

(the empty stomach not being one for fighting), while Marcius, and old Titus, who'd

lean upon one crutch and fight with t'other,
Ere stay behind this business.

and Cominius the Consul and the Senators, depart high-heartedly to the Capitol, their place of honor and authority; from it to proclaim the war.

There have been two other onlookers, silent so far, who now remain behind: Brutus and Sicinius, the newly appointed Tribunes. And in the twenty-five lines or so with which they finish the scene Shakespeare etches them in memorably for the caustic element in the play they are to prove; politicians sizing up their destined adversary and, dispassionately, cynically, the weakness and the strength of his position. Nothing to be done now. They must "wait and see."

THE VOLSCIANS

The succeeding scene shows us the Senators of Corioles in council of war, Aufidius bringing news to them of the Roman preparations, and receiving his commission as general in the field. The scene is but forty lines long; yet we learn besides that much "intelligence" passes between Rome and the Volsces—a point to be made more than once; Rome, civilly distracted, has her fifth column—and from Aufidius, clinchingly, that

---

[11] For the argument that those and other stage directions are Shakespeare's own, see p. 295ff.

If we and Caius Marcius chance to meet,
'Tis sworn between us we shall ever strike
Till one can do no more.

The Senators are airily confident:

Let us alone to guard Corioles. . . .

The clash is nearing.

With the scene which follows all the main factors of the play
will have been assembled, and its opening stage direction is
illuminating:

VOLUMNIA AND VIRGILIA

Enter Volumnia and Virgilia, mother and wife to Marcius.
They set them down on two low stools and sew.

This note of puritan simplicity is struck at once by nothing
more elaborate than the two low stools and the sewing. For these
are great ladies, and live in state, as the attendant Gentlewoman
announcing the Lady Valeria, and the Usher and the Gentlewoman to show her in, will help show us within another minute
or so.[12] We remark too the formality of their manners to each other
in the "sweet madam," "good madam," "my ladies both," "your
ladyship." Volumnia dominates the household. It is to her that
Valeria's visit is announced, and Virgilia asks her for permission
to retire. Valeria, by contrast, will seem a very frivol; yet it is for a
no wilder gaiety she would have Virgilia lay aside her "stitchery"
than to "go visit the good lady that lies in."

The scene gives us Volumnia's Spartan temper, harsh at its
kindliest, her son's tones—his very words—echoing through hers;
Virgilia's gentler spirit, her tremulous courage, her soft stubbornness; Valeria, witty and merry, primed with her news of the war.
The opening prose is austere; it paints Volumnia. For the
picturing of Marcius in the field comes colored and moving verse.
Valeria's chatter about the child brings prose again, easy and
decorative, in which medium the scene ends. By reference, Valeria's
news:

---

12 For the implicit contrast with the scene between Charmian, Iras, Alexas and
the Soothsayer in *Antony and Cleopatra*, see p. 151.

> the Volsces have an army forth; against whom Cominius the
> general is gone, with one part of our Roman power: your lord
> and Titus Lartius are set down before their city Corioles. . . .

advances us several steps in the war; and the next scene's opening:

> *Enter Marcius, Titus Lartius, with drum and colours, with*
> *Captains and Soldiers, as before the city Corioles.*

with the later

> *Enter two Senators with others on the walls of Corioles.*

THE WAR WITH THE VOLSCIANS:
BEFORE CORIOLES

—the walls being simply the upper stage—asks no further
explanation.

The earlier scene has ended with a gentle little tussle between
Valeria and Virgilia, and the gentler of the two has won. Now
begins, under every form of contrast, the man's war. Marcius and
Titus Lartius are in the highest spirits, the old soldier as youthful
as the young, and laying bets—an English trait if not a Roman!—
upon the news the Messenger, just sighted, will be bringing:

> A wager they have met.
> My horse to yours, no?
> 'Tis done.
> Agreed.
> Say, has our general met the enemy?

and, the horse so sportingly lost and won, the bet is then, as
between comrades, generously discounted.

This scene, and the three which follow, are to be predominantly
scenes of action. Marcius is above all a fighting hero, and, most
effectively to warrant him his title, Shakespeare lets us see him
fight. Henry V, Antony, Othello, Macbeth, they also are soldiers;
but—even with Henry V—that is not the aspect of them most
vividly lighted. With Coriolanus, it is his personal prowess in war
and its unlucky linking to as trenchant a pugnacity in peace that
make and mar him. We have heard him for a start at his worst.
We are now to see him at his best, winning valiantly to the
summit of his fortunes. He will thus hold our regard the better
along the descent to his tragic end.

For the battle without its walls, a Roman reverse and recovery, and the taking of Corioles; for a second wavering battle, Marcius to the rescue, and final victory, Shakespeare's material resources are little other than those of the old inn-yard, although doubtless the Globe Theatre at the height of its fame can enrich their quality and be more lavish with them. But *drum and colours* still sufficiently betoken an army on the march, and a recognized code of alarums, trumpet flourishes and the sounding of parleys and retreats illustrate the course of a battle or a siege. It is indeed only by the use of such tokens that the extension and swaying confusions of a battle can be made clear. For with hand-to-hand combat realism's limits are reached.

Shakespeare, using both speech and action, sets his board and makes his moves on it, with exactitude and economy. Marcius and Titus Lartius before Corioles learn that Cominius with his army facing the army of the Volsces are

> Within this mile and half.

Marcius' comment is that

> Then shall we hear their 'larum, and they ours.

When, therefore, a little later we hear the *Alarum afar off*, its meaning is at once plain to us, and distracting explanations are saved. For by then the Senators of Corioles are upon the walls, defying the Romans, and—as drums from within the city help inform us—about to anticipate their assault by a sortie. That Aufidius is not in the city we have at once been told. To the noise of the distant fight is added word that he is a captain in it. Marcius here, then, he there; they are not to meet yet.

> *Enter the army of the Volsces. . . . Alarum. The Romans*
> *are beat back to their trenches.*

The hiatus is filled by a seven-line speech from Marcius, both indicating and interpreting the accompanying action:

> They fear us not, but issue forth their city.
> Now put your shields before your hearts, and fight
> With hearts more proof than shields. . . .

That allows, if barely, the symbolic army time to enter and form line, the Romans to start to face them:

Advance, brave Titus:
They do disdain us much beyond our thoughts,
Which makes me sweat with wrath. . . .

—impetuous, impatient!—

Come on, my fellows:
He that retires, I'll take him for a Volsce,
And he shall feel mine edge.

rating them for cowards too, even by anticipation. Fighter but no
leader! Then battle is joined and the Romans are beaten back.[13]
After which

Enter Marcius, cursing.

---

[13] The ordering of the action upon Shakespeare's stage must be gathered by
piecing together text, stage directions and our yet imperfect and disputed
knowledge of the mechanics of the Globe.

The stage directions are for the most part figurative and recommendatory, not
set down by the book-holder or in his fashion (see p. 295ff.). The curtains to
the inner stage could no doubt be made to serve, but it looks as if this
Corioles had solid gates.

Enter the army of the Volsces.

might, by convention, mean that these opened to discover the dozen men or less
who made the army standing there; and this, for the short time the text allows,
would be convenient. It fits, too, the First Senator's

our gates,
Which yet seem shut, we have but pinn'd with rushes;
They'll open of themselves.

They could—wide enough to let the men through, and close behind them. This
looks likely, and that they reopen later to accommodate the retreat—

The Volsces retire into Corioles and Marcius follows them to the gates.

—and then stay open, to suit Marcius'

So, *now* the gates are ope: now prove good seconds:
'Tis for the followers fortune widens them,
Not for the fliers. . . .

until they shut on him.

The Romans are beat back to their trenches apparently through one of the
side doors, the Volsces following them. It would need to be of some width to
allow for the melee of men, swords and shields, and they might more conveniently
be fought to a standstill on the stage. But *Enter Marcius, cursing*, contradicts this
possibility. He has been beaten off too, the last of the Romans to go. Further,
Titus Lartius is absent when he is shut in the city.

A textual note. In the line

we'll beat them to their wives,
As they us to our trenches follows.

(some editors preferring "follow," others "followed"). The "follows" has
probably slipped in by some accident from the neighboring stage direction,
Marcius follows them to the gates. Neither sense nor verse accommodates its
speaking.

and the Romans rally; whether thanks to his magnificent vituperation we are free to judge. What is made plain, however, is that when he calls on them to follow him into the city in pursuit of the flying enemy—

> mark me, and do the like.

—none of them do. His is no way to win just such devotion from his soldiers.

> Fool-hardiness; not I!
> Nor I!

And when the gates close on him, for all comment comes a

> See, they have shut him in.

with the grim humor of

> To the pot, I warrant him.

added. Then, Titus Lartius reappearing, Shakespeare stages his great "effect." The gates open, and there stands Marcius

> *bleeding, assaulted by the enemy.*

alone, at cut and thrust with the whole Volscian "army"; and the amazing sight, and Titus Lartius' call to them, shame the recalcitrant Romans—honest fighters enough—into rescuing him, and so to taking the city.

The stage stays empty for a breathing-space. Then

> *Enter certain Romans, with spoils.*

and we have a three-line tokening of the customary sack of a town:

> This will I carry to Rome.
> And I this.
> A murrain on 't! I took this for silver.

while the

> *Alarum continues still afar off.*

to remind us that Cominius and Aufidius, a "mile and half" away, are battling still. Marcius and Titus Lartius return, Marcius fuller than ever of angry scorn for the common soldier, "these movers . . . these base slaves" that

> Ere yet the fight be done, pack up. Down with them!

he cries, down with these paltry prizes they are pilfering.[14] The distant alarums continue.

> And hark, what noise the general makes! To him!
> There is the man of my soul's hate, Aufidius,
> Piercing our Romans: then, valiant Titus, take
> Convenient numbers to make good the city;
> Whilst I, with those that have the spirit, will haste
> To help Cominius.

His wounds still bleed. The veteran Titus counsels prudence, some respite. He will have none of that. He is off. Titus returns to the city.

The stage is again empty. Then

COMINIUS' PART OF THE BATTLE

Enter Cominius, as it were in retire, with soldiers.[15]

to a very different tempo.

> Breathe you, my friends; well fought! We are come off
> Like Romans, neither foolish in our stands,
> Nor cowardly in retire. . . .

Cominius is Consul and General in Chief, a steady, responsible soldier; and this has indeed quite the tone of an official bulletin, issued in mid-battle. For

> believe me, sirs,
> We shall be charged again. . . .

And news of Titus Lartius and Marcius is lacking, and when, long delayed, it comes, is bad. With clarity and economy Shakespeare connects the one fight and the other. Cominius has heard the alarums of the besiegers even as they have heard his. It is "above an hour" since the Messenger left the Romans "to

---

[14] The *exeunt* occasionally marked for the spoilers after "I took this for silver" is an editorial interpolation and not in the Folio.

[15] How, in the terms of Shakespeare's theater, is this vacating of the stage, which marks the end of a scene and change of place, differentiated from that of a few lines earlier, before the entry of the soldiers with their spoils, which indicated neither? In the first instance, probably, the open gates still confront us; in the second, after Titus Lartius and his attendants have passed through them, not only will they be closed, but the curtain masking the inner stage will be drawn too.

their trenches driven"; and *we* know what has happened since then, and that Marcius himself is now upon his way here.[16] And when he arrives, so masked in blood that Cominius does not recognize him, we appreciate the effect to the full, since we have already seen him so, and it is as if we had a share ourselves in astonishing Cominius.

No more waiting now, with Marcius here, to be "charged again," if he has aught to say in the matter.

> Where is the enemy? are you lords o' the field?
> If not, why cease you till you are so?

He has left Titus Lartius to do the "mopping-up" in Corioles, is too impatient to be at it again to tell the story of the fight that is over, can scarce spare breath for further railing at "the common file" he so detests. He begs to be set against Aufidius without more delay, and appeals for volunteers to follow him into what must prove a desperate struggle in nobler tones than have sounded from him yet:

> If any such be here,
> As it were sin to doubt, that love this painting
> Wherein you see me smeared; if any fear
> Lesser his person than an ill report;
> If any think brave death outweighs bad life
> And that his country's dearer than himself . . .

and—though momentarily touched by doubt of it when it comes—wins as generous a response.[17] Cominius, we note, without

---

[16] Time, as usual with Shakespeare in such cases, is elastic. We are to picture the Messenger and Marcius dashing across country; so they are allowed likely time for this. As to Titus Lartius' work of making good the city, issuing decrees and the rest of it, that, like the unquestioned minutes of a meeting, we "take as read."

[17] There is corruption of the text hereabouts. When the soldiers take him up in their arms:

> Oh, me alone, make you a sword of me?

has found (to my mind) no very satisfactory interpretation or amendment.

> If these shows be not outward . . .

marks the touch of doubt; and there may be some connection of thought between this and the corrupt line.

Another corruption must be in the line

> Please you to march;
> And four shall quickly draw out my command. . . .

Why "four"? The "Please you to march" is worth noting too, with its unusual suavity.

throwing more doubt upon its zeal, adds solid inducement:

> Make good this ostentation, and you shall
> Divide in all with us.

And so they march—thanks to Marcius, with fresh spirit—to renew the fight.

BACK TO CORIOLES

Titus Lartius, having set a guard upon Corioles, going with Drum and Trumpet toward Cominius and Caius Martius, enters with a Lieutenant, other Soldiers and a Scout.

The scene's action and its seven spoken lines help—and most economically—both to space out and knit together the movements of the siege and the battle as a whole, do so in time and place too. Titus Lartius gives final orders to the Lieutenant for the holding of the town and the sending of reinforcements for the battle still in progress if they are needed. The Lieutenant retires within the gates, which are finally closed; and Titus Lartius with his symbolic Drummer and Trumpeter, the Scout for "guider," and a selection of soldiers takes the road that Marcius more hastily took a while before. The stage is empty again. The curtains before the inner stage (and the gates of Corioles) can now close.

BACK AGAIN TO COMINIUS' SIDE OF THE BATTLE: CAIUS MARCIUS AND AUFIDIUS MEET

Alarum as in battle.

—much such a sound as that which went with the fighting under the walls, the Alarum afar off brought close, and to its most startling and insistent. After which preparation·

Enter Marcius and Aufidius at several doors.

It is for each the peculiarly critical moment of the day. But before they come to blows they go to it with words, the one out-scorning and outbragging the other. There is something of convention in this, doubtless; but it follows not so much Shakespeare's accustomed "high Roman fashion" as that of Trojan

Coriolanus 199

and Greek in the scurril *Troilus and Cressida*. And it again gives us Marcius at his crudest, excusable by a certain boyishness in him, of character if not of years, of the unlicked cub in the man. Yet it is a flaw of character, which future subtler fighting than this will fatally widen. Nor is the outcome of this duel to prove lucky. Clean conquest of his enemy might serve him well. But

> *certain Volsces come in the aid of Aufidius.*

Marcius has little choice but to turn on them, and he

> *fights till they be driven in breathless.*

But for Aufidius to be left (since he can hardly make yet another in such a melee) to stand there a looker-on, or to follow after while Marcius so magnificently drives the fellows before him—

> Officious, and not valiant, you have shamed me
> In your condemned seconds.

—will he ever forgive that?[18]

THE VICTORIOUS ROMAN FORCES REASSEMBLE

Flourish. Alarum. A Retreat is sounded. Enter at one door Cominius with the Romans: at another door Marcius with his arm in a scarf.[19]

The battle is over. The strenuous beat of the action relaxes to

---

[18] Once more Shakespeare, by an incidental stroke, regulates the clock of the action.

> Within these three hours, Tullus,
> Alone I fought in your Corioles walls. . . .

The echo from *Troilus and Cressida* is in

> Wert thou the Hector
> That was the whip of your bragged progeny. . . .

It may even perhaps echo Hector's own

> You wisest Grecians, pardon me this brag. . . .

[19] So, but for amended spelling, the Folio. Capell, it seems, added . . . *and other Romans*, and some editors have copied him. But Shakespeare evidently wishes—be it by an arbitrary effect only—to contrast Cominius and his officers and men, with the solitary figure of Marcius, once more wounded.

The stage directions hereabouts tend to be emblematic. How precise a meaning Shakespeare's audience would read into *Flourishes* and *Alarums*. *A Retreat is sounded*, and the like, it is hard for us to estimate. A few lines later, moreover, we have *Enter Titus with his Power from the Pursuit*. Could there have been any means of illustrating . . . *from the Pursuit*? I fancy this is simple narrative.

the soberer measure of Cominius' stately praise. The threads of the play's other themes begin at once to be woven back into the fabric. Cominius, addressing Marcius, speaks of

> the dull Tribunes
> That, with the fusty plebians, hate thine honours . . .

Marcius, in deprecating response, of

> my mother,
> Who has a charter to extol her blood . . .

And here we have him at his best; not too mock-modestly belittling his own feats, genuinely generous to his comrades:

> I have done
> As you have done; that's what I can; induced
> As you have been; that's for my country:
> He that has but effected his good will
> Hath overta'en mine act.

rejecting reward without a second thought; acknowledging the supreme honor of

> For what he did before Corioles, call him,
> With all the applause and clamour of the host,
> Caius Marcius Coriolanus! Bear
> The addition nobly ever!

with humorous, becoming simplicity:

> I will go wash;
> And when my face is fair, you shall perceive
> Whether I blush or no: howbeit, I thank you.

Still more attractive is his plea amidst this triumph for the poor Volscian, some time his host, whose name he only finds himself too weary now to remember. He wants a drink of wine. And so we part from him, happy and magnanimous in victory; free too for the moment—or all but—from that self-conscious egotism which so besets him.

But the war is not to finish upon this note.

THE STANDPOINT OF THE VANQUISHED

A flourish. Cornets. Enter Tullus Aufidius, bloody, with two
or three soldiers.[20]

Here are the defeated Volscians, and the shamed Aufidius.
Cominius the Consul in the scene just past had ordered Titus
Lartius back to Corioles, and from there to

> send us to Rome
> The best, with whom we may articulate,
> For their own good and ours.

But Aufidius scoffs at confidence in such a peace, in Rome's
surrender of the conquered city:

> Condition!
> What good condition can a treaty find
> I' the part that is at mercy? Five times, Marcius . . .

—There it is!—

> I have fought with thee; so often hast thou beat me,
> And wouldst do so, I think, should we encounter
> As often as we eat.

From this sense that he will never now by fair means prove
himself the better man springs the mistrust, and hatred, and will
the treachery at last to come.

> My valour's poisoned
> With only suffering stain by him. . . .

—the keynote to Aufidius' spiritual tragedy, which time and the
event are to work out.

ROME REJOICES

The entry of Menenius and the Tribunes, Sicinius and Brutus,
shows that we are back in Rome. Their acrimonious banter—
Menenius an expert at it, the other two doing their humorless
best—opens a prospect of the civic war, which is to be rekindled
now that the Volscian war is won. But the factors will differ, and

---

[20] It is likelier that *A flourish. Cornets.* rightly belongs to the end of the scene
before rather than to the beginning of this, which certainly seems not to call
for any sort of "flourish."

the people, with the Tribunes to lead them, prove tougher combatants than before. We have a revaluing of the forces to be engaged, a fresh adjustment of sympathy. Menenius lures the two on. Marcius is blamed for his pride. But

> do you two know how you are censured here in the city, I mean of us o' the right hand file? do you? . . . You talk of pride: O! that you could turn your eyes toward the napes of your necks, and make but an interior survey of your good selves. O! that you could. . . . Why, then you should discover a brace of unmeriting, proud, violent, testy magistrates, alias fools, as any in Rome.

and then, before they can retort on him, he paints his own faults to his liking; an old trick in debate:

> I am known to be a humorous patrician, and one that loves a cup of hot wine with not a drop of allaying Tiber in 't. . . . What I think I utter, and spend my malice in my breath. . . .

with which excuse he goes on to tell them in comically colored terms just what he thinks of them, of their exploiting of the people, and their pretentious folly in general:

> When you speak best unto the purpose, it is not worth the wagging of your beards; and your beards deserve not so honourable a grave as to stuff a botcher's cushion, or to be entombed in an ass's pack-saddle. Yet you must be saying Marcius is proud. . . . God-den to your worships: more of your conversation would infect my brain. . . .

And he turns from them, leaving them glowering, to accost Volumnia, Virgilia, Valeria—a high contrast, in dignity and beauty both—who are hastening across the stage. The news due tonight has come already (Shakespeare's habitual device for sharpening our expectation): the victorious army is approaching, with Marcius, who

> comes the third time home with the oaken garland . . .

Acrid old Menenius transformed to a cheering schoolboy, his cap flung in the air; he and Volumnia, the two elders, competing in extravagant glee; Virgilia and Valeria the staider in joy, Virgilia shrinking from the thought of the wounds

> I' the shoulder and i' the left arm: there will be large cicatrices to show the people when he shall stand for his place. . . .

—this hint of what is to come another habitual device for the sharpening of our expectation. The Tribunes stay glowering in the background; Menenius cannot forbear a passing gibe at them. But suddenly from the distance comes a shout and the sound of trumpets, cutting sharply into the ferment of their jubilation. Volumnia, in a flash, responds; the Roman matron, and inspired:

> Hark the trumpets!
> These are the ushers of Marcius: before him he carries noise,
> and behind him he leaves tears:
> Death, that dark spirit, in's nervy arm doth lie;
> Which, being advanced, declines, and then men die.

A bold and masterly transition; from the familiar and excited prose of the exchanges with Menenius to the portentous trumpet-echoing

> These are the ushers of Marcius. . . .

and the measured music of the conventional "sentence."[21]

> *A sennet. Trumpets sound. Enter Cominius the general, and Titus Lartius; between them Coriolanus, crowned with an oaken garland, with Captains and Soldiers, and a Herald.*[22]

—with all possible pomp and circumstance, that is to say; and dialogue and stage direction now combine to make a notable and most eloquent effect. Nor is it eloquence of words alone;

---

[21] Shakespeare has been by no means sparing of space in this scene so far. In particular he could have lessened the passage between Menenius and the Tribunes by half and kept all its substance. Is there any reason for this? He may, one suspects, have been sure of an exceptionally good actor for Menenius. Throughout the play he indulges the character and spaciously—in incidental opportunities. Unfounded surmise, no more; but it is somewhat as if he felt he safely could. Another and more technical reason here, if any at all be needed, is at least worth canvassing. We have left Marcius bloody and unkempt after his fighting. The actor must have time to put himself in proper array for his triumphal entry. Will the speaking of 190 lines allow him more than enough? And here the question of act-division—between I and II—is also involved. Is this Shakespeare's, or an editor's? And if Shakespeare's, and to be marked in performance, was an appreciable interval allowed or no? Speculative questions, and of no capital importance; pertaining to the play's study, nevertheless. For the main question of act-division, see p. 294ff.

[22] *Titus Lartius?* A slip, apparently, on Shakespeare's part. Menenius tells us later that he has been sent for, and, a scene later still, he arrives, to be questioned by Coriolanus about Tullus Aufidius and the Volscian preparation for revenge.

Shakespeare's stagecraft has outpassed that. Ringing speech pertains to the Herald:

> Know, Rome, that all alone Marcius did fight
> Within Corioles gates. . . .
> Welcome to Rome, renowned Coriolanus!

and to the response, in unison, of the nameless onlookers:

> Welcome to Rome, renowned Coriolanus!

The flow of sound—trumpets, the Herald's trenchant tones, the volume of voices—suddenly ceasing, creates, so to speak, a silence in which Coriolanus' or Volumnia's simplest phrase, spoken in all simplicity, will tell to the height of its value.

> No more of this; it does offend my heart:
> Pray now, no more.

he begs them. The distaste is again genuine, barely tainted by mock-modesty. But the self-consciousness which sets him so continually insisting on it shows a crack in character, if a slight one.

The three women, becomingly, do not press forward; this, to the end, is soldiers' business. Cominius himself must intervene with a

> Look, sir, your mother!

And Marcius steps from his place of honor to kneel to her. For once her sterner self dissolves in emotion. There is tenderness in the pride of the

> Nay, my good soldier, up . . .

and thereupon he is her "gentle" Marcius, her "worthy" Caius, the pride returning almost shyly in the

> What is't? Coriolanus must I call thee?

as if she scarce dare trust the gloriously earned title on her tongue. Then she yields her mother's claim to the wife's.

Virgilia stands quietly, happily, crying. Marcius, to mask his own emotion at their reuniting, rallies her with a loving, but half-humorous

> My gracious silence, hail!

with the gentle irony of

> Wouldst thou have laughed had I come coffin'd home,
> That weep'st to see me triumph? . . .

The thought follows:

> Ah, my dear,
> Such eyes the widows in Corioles wear,
> And mothers that lack sons.

none better befitting the poignant gravity of such a triumph. It is Marcius' noblest moment.

Menenius recalls them to their rejoicings. These center on this group of the people of consequence in Rome, exchanging greetings, so content with themselves and their world. Says Marcius:

> Ere in our own house I do shade my head
> The good patricians must be visited. . . .

He ignores, that is to say, the Tribunes, although Menenius, with another merry gibe, points them out to him. Volumnia voices more positively now her high hopes of the consulship for him. His response is cold. Then *Flourish. Cornets. . .* , and the procession, Volumnia and Virgilia joined to it, passes on its way, leaving the neglected Brutus and Sicinius to discuss the situation.[23]

First, Brutus must vent his spleen. And if the coloring of his picture of Rome's greeting to her hero is dyed deep in jealousy of Marcius, it reflects contempt too for the people whose champion he is, as little kindness for "the kitchen malkin" who

---

[23] There is an inconsistency in the stage directions here to be noted. The Folio marks an *Enter Brutus and Sicinius,* having accorded them no certain *exeunt.* Nothing very out of the way in this; both Folio and Quartos abound in such apparent slips. But it opens up a question of the movements and the placing of the two during the interchange between Menenius and Volumnia, and next while Marcius dominates the scene. They are still there, of course, when Menenius addresses them with his

> God save your good worships! Marcius is coming home.

But are they when he cites them to Marcius for the

> old crab-trees here at home that will not
> Be grafted to your relish. . . .

If not, but for a responsive shrug or the like, Marcius' neglect of them will be purely negative. It looks, however, as if they were intended still, at this moment, to be thereabouts, glowering in the background. And probably they go off with the procession, hang back from it, and immediately return. This will at least justify the Folio's stage direction and give point to Brutus' sequent speech, his description of the hero's greeting by the crowd.

> pins
> Her richest lockram 'bout her reechy neck,
> Clambering the walls to eye him . . .

as for the "seld-shown flamens" who "press among the popular
throngs" and "our veiled dames" with "their nicely-gawded
cheeks." A man of no rose-tinted illusions, Brutus, except, possibly,
about himself!

Sicinius has his mind on realities. In a dry seven words he states
them:

> On the sudden
> I warrant him Consul.

and Brutus, rancor indulged, is as shrewd:

> Then our office may,
> During his power, go sleep.

Very coolly the two then canvass the prospect: Marcius' failings,

> He cannot temperately transport his honours. . . .

—the unstable temper of the commoners, which, in his pride, he
is sure soon to provoke again. So

> At some time when his soaring insolence
> Shall touch the people—which time shall not want,
> If he be put upon't; and that's as easy
> As to set dogs on sheep—will be his fire
> To kindle their dry stubble; and their blaze
> Shall darken him for ever.

They themselves have but meanwhile to "suggest" to the people—
the word is twice used—

> in what hatred
> He still hath held them . . .

and wait, not for long.

The scene ends upon a Messenger's summoning them to the
Capitol, for

> 'Tis thought
> That Marcius shall be Consul. . . .

and he breaks, his commission done, into a rapturous

> I have seen the dumb men throng to see him, and
> The blind to hear him speak: matrons flung gloves,

Ladies and maids their scarfs and handkerchers,
Upon him as he passed; the nobles bended,
As to Jove's statue, and the commons made
A shower and thunder with their caps and shouts:
I never saw the like.

It is Brutus' tale again, but by this young hero-worshiper how differently told; its enthusiasm gall to the hearers, who, bracing themselves for the coming struggle, depart.

MARCIUS' FIRST STEP IN POLITICS

So much for the hero's greeting by his patrician equals and by the populace. Shakespeare now provides a passing comment on him from a third standpoint.

Enter two Officers, to lay cushions, as it were, in the Capitol.[24]

Here is—to modernize it somewhat—the permanent official's detached view of the politician, with its somewhat cynically critical discrimination. Coriolanus is

> a brave fellow; but he's vengeance proud, and loves not the common people.

Who, then, in Rome will not say that of him? Detached analysis follows:

> there hath been many great men that have flattered the people, who ne'er loved them; and there be many that they have loved, they know not wherefore: so that if they love they know not why, they hate upon no better a ground. Therefore, for Coriolanus neither to care whether they love or hate him manifests the true knowledge he has in their disposition; and out of his noble carelessness lets them plainly see it.

True enough, and "noble carelessness" no doubt becomes a hero. But, comes the answer, is it only that?

---

[24] *To lay cushions, as it were* . . . is one among the play's "suggestive" stage directions. A cushion can mean "the seat of a judge or ruler" (though the reference for this definition in the O.E.D. is dated 1659). Presumably the officers have a couple of actual cushions, or more, to lay. But the phrase has, I fancy, a further implication; it tells us—even as the subsequent dialogue shows—the sort of persons they are, not menials, but men of a definite dignity, the equivalent, possibly, in Shakespeare's mind, to officers of Parliament, who may bring to their covenanted respect for its members, Lords or Commons, a very critical private view of their individual worth.

he seeks their hate with greater devotion than they can render in him, and leaves nothing undone that may fully discover him their opposite. Now, to seem to affect the malice and displeasure of the people is as bad as that which he dislikes, to flatter them for their love.

"He seeks their hate. . . ." Shrewd comment! And it is the seamy side of this aspect of the man, the impulse which sets him upon his road to disaster. For his defense:

> He hath deserved worthily of his country. . . .

and not to let such deeds excuse his faults were gross ingratitude. Finally, "He's a worthy man"; on that they agree. Again—and here upon the verge of the action's chief struggle—Shakespeare has trimmed the balance of its sympathies.

> *Sennet. Enter, with Lictors before them, Cominius the consul, Menenius, Coriolanus, Senators, Sicinius and Brutus. The Senators take their places; the Tribunes take theirs by themselves. Coriolanus stands.*

The Lictors before the Consul, the Senators and Tribunes in their respective places, Coriolanus standing facing them, as one about to be harangued—this paints the occasion accurately enough; and Menenius' opening

> Having determined of the Volsces, and
> To send for Titus Lartius, it remains,
> As the main point of this our after-meeting . . .

enlarges the circumstances, and, by suggestion, lengthens the apparent time events have been taking, lending them more reality.[25]

Marcius is to be publicly thanked for his "noble service" to the State. The question of the consulship, which is in everyone's

---

[25] At Cominius' command the procession moved "on to the Capitol." Brutus and Sicinius, after a fifty-five-line talk, are summoned there also, because

> 'Tis thought
> That Marcius shall be Consul.

and the thirty-five-line talk between the Officers lets them arrive in time for the business. Menenius' "This our after-meeting . . ." implies that more has been happening, and associates the public thanks to Coriolanus and his proposal as Consul with the general business of the State, and lends them verisimilitude and importance thereby.

mind, will be canvassed later, and with no voice to the contrary, supposedly, and so hard upon the praise with which Cominius will crown his triumph. Wherefore the Senators' confident request to the Tribunes, as "Masters o' the people," for their "kindest care," and their

> loving motion toward the common body,
> To yield what passes here.

But parliamentary courtesy between the parties is even now at a strain. Note Sicinius' canting

> We are convented
> Upon a pleasing treaty, and have hearts
> Inclinable to honour and advance
> The theme of our assembly.

continued smoothly into Brutus' sarcastic

> Which the rather
> We shall be blest to do, if he remember
> A kinder value of the people than
> He hath hereto prized them at.

and Menenius' temper tetchily shortening with these "Masters o' the people" ("*your* people"—he cannot disguise his contempt). And while Cominius, ready with his Consular speech, is thus kept waiting, Coriolanus himself, hero of the occasion, declaring that

> I had rather have one scratch my head i' the sun
> When the alarum were struck than idly sit
> To hear my nothings monstered.

hardly improves it by abruptly departing. Altogether, an unpromising beginning to a political career!

But Cominius' speech, its recalling of what this man has done for Rome, must surely obliterate all petty differences about him. Says the chief Senator:

> He cannot but with measure fit the honours
> Which we devise him.

And when, brought back, Menenius announces to him without more ado:

> The Senate, Coriolanus, are well pleased
> To make thee Consul.

there is at least no dissentient voice. The business being on the crest of the wave, then, he adds at once—a monitory hint to Marcius, one fancies, in his tone:

> It then remains
> That you do speak to the people.

But—as is to be expected—without a moment's heed comes back the

> I do beseech you
> Let me o'erleap that custom. . . .[26]

and Sicinius is as quick with his

> Sir, the people
> Must have their voices; neither will they bate
> One jot of ceremony.

Menenius, however, all conciliation in success, would be closing the gap:

> Put them not to 't;
> Pray you, go fit you to the custom. . . .

And the self-conscious Marcius'

> It is a part
> That I shall blush in acting. . . .

is a yielding plea—were that all. But he must needs add:

> and might well
> Be taken from the people.

and play into the Tribunes' hands. Brutus'

> Mark you that!

is exultant. To cover the blunder and halt the dangerous argument, Menenius and the Senators, without more delay, in due form recommend him Consul to the Tribunes, through them to the people, themselves, moreover, positively acclaiming him:

---

[26] "Without a moment's heed . . .": this is sufficiently indicated in the continuity of the verse. Marcius' "I do beseech you . . ." completing Menenius' line. Besides which (the actor will remember) Brutus has

> heard him swear,
> Were he to stand for Consul, never would he
> Appear i' the market-place, nor on him put
> The napless vesture of humility . . .

> to our noble Consul
> Wish we all joy and honour.

—and every voice in the Senate answers

> To Coriolanus come all joy and honour!

It is one of the play's salient and most significant moments.
Marcius has sworn (Brutus says he heard him, reiterates, "It was
his word") that never, to be chosen Consul, will he stand in the
market place, show his wounds and beg the people's voices. Yet
plainly he now means, after a little persuasion, to do so. Shakespeare will not, in other words, bring him to grief upon a point of
mere stubbornness and vanity. And the Tribunes would so far
be facing defeat did he not in the very same breath—and how
gratuitously!—open up the larger quarrel. Such a privilege

> might well
> Be taken from the people.

Thus jauntily he throws the gauntlet down. It is upon what
grows from this, issues of statecraft, nothing petty and egotistic—
however egotistically and arrogantly he may urge them—that he
will take his stand, and will fail. Here is indeed the play's turning
point, from which it develops into true tragedy, with Marcius'
character, given that scope, itself rising to heroic stature.

The political war ahead, in which Coriolanus is to be worsted,
asks for other qualities than those which so well served in him to
beat the Volsces. Brutus and Sicinius will prove to be the successful generals now, and their tactics are to await for the while the
adversary's errors. The Senators and their hero departed; says
Brutus,

> You see how he intends to use the people.

And they set off themselves to anticipate Coriolanus in the
market place and do what may seem wise to bias the proceedings
there.[27]

---

[27] But here Shakespeare performs one of his occasionally convenient feats of
sleight of hand. The Tribunes quit the stage with this intention; but immediately
after the citizens enter, as in the market place, expecting Marcius, who shortly
arrives. There has been no opportunity, then, for interference by the Tribunes—
unless some break in the continuity of the action, some imaginary passage of
time between the two scenes is to be conceded, and that can be counted out of

THE TROUBLES IN THE MARKET PLACE
BEGIN

Enter seven or eight Citizens.

In the few lines spoken before Marcius appears we renew
acquaintance with them, and sample their present mood.

Once, if he do require our voices, we ought not to deny him.

—the First Citizen is quite positive about it.[28] The Second
Citizen insists on their rights:

We may, sir, if we will.

The Third Citizen enjoys arguing things out, and the sound
of words, and, possibly, of his own voice:

We have power in ourselves to do it, but it is a power that we
have no power to do. . . . Ingratitude is monstrous, and for the

the question. Moreover, there is no sign in the talk of the citizens among themselves, or to Marcius, that Brutus and Sicinius have recently been at them. Yet,
arriving later, when the ordeal is over and the "voices" have been accorded, the
two pointedly refer to the good advice they gave, and scold their already disillusioned followers for neglecting it.

Could you not have told him
As you were lessoned . . . ?
Thus to have said,
As you were fore-advised . . .

We probably do not detect the trick. But what brings Shakespeare to playing
it? Is it that, having dispatched the Tribunes (so to say) to the market place, he
sees how much better it may be to let the citizens encounter Marcius in his
"gown of humility" without their interference? Yet there is value in the present
subsequent passage in which they expound and deplore the errors that, all
against their advice, have been made, and undertake to relieve them. For it is
in this that they give evidence of being "masters o' the people" indeed. It will
then become important not to prejudice its effect by staging shortly beforehand a
similar passage of the actual giving of the good advice. Very well; that can be
omitted, advantageously from other points of view also. And if it is also
important to have the Tribunes reproach the citizens for ignoring their advice,
let them do so. We are unlikely to remark later that the advice was never given,
nor, as the action ran, could have been.

[28] I doubt if any consistency of character can be established between the First
or Second Citizens of the play's opening and of this scene, or between them in
this and any of the later ones. Within the boundary of a single scene there will
be consistency; they will be ineffectual figures otherwise. But to push the matter
further would be to make each a character in his own right, so to speak, and to
rob the populace of its collective strength. No matter how diverse the opinions
and feelings to be vented, a crowd must remain dramatically a single if a
multiple unit.

multitude to be ingrateful were to make a monster of the
multitude. . . .

They are not forgetful:

> for once we stood up about the corn, he himself stuck not to
> call us the many-headed multitude.

Yet they bear no malice; let bygones be bygones.

> if he would incline to the people, there was never a worthier
> man.

—upon which Marcius appears, as demanded, in the gown of
humility, shepherded by a Menenius who is plainly most ap-
prehensive of what may happen when in a moment his fatherly
and restraining influence is withdrawn.

As with the scenes of battle, the passages which now follow
between Coriolanus and the citizens are as eloquent, or all but,
in their action as in their speech; and disposition and movement
ask careful perceiving. Both parties at first shirk the encounter.
The citizens, at the sight of the man who has heretofore never
met with them but to abuse them, herd together for mutual
support, until the sapient Third Citizen protests that

> We are not to stay all together, but to come to him where he
> stands, by ones, by twos and by threes. . . .

and stiffens their backs a bit. And Coriolanus, that bold fighter,
at his most miserably self-conscious as he shows himself in the
detested gown, would bolt, it seems, from these despised boors if
he might, like a shy schoolboy. There is a generous measure of
the comic in the scene, contributed by no means by its simpletons
only. Shakespeare does not scruple now, should it suit him, to add
to a tragic hero's diet a taste or two of the bitter sauce of ridicule.

Coriolanus takes his stand, to await assault. It is a queer caricature of the picture we so recently had of him, fighting "all
alone . . . within Corioles gates." He now has instead of Volsces
these kindly fumbling fellow Romans, offering him a victory
which the arrogant demon in him does everything to spurn.
Fatherly Menenius is in despair:

> You'll mar all:
> I'll leave you: pray you, speak to 'em, I pray you,
> In wholesome manner.

and Marcius' response is certainly not reassuring:

> Bid them wash their faces,
> And keep their teeth clean.

—let them hear it if they like; what does he care![29]

It looks, indeed, an embarrassing business enough: the hero, stripped of his martial trappings, his oaken garland, and appearing, it must be owned, a little ridiculous in this gown of humility. Not so ridiculous as he himself fears, and in the eyes of these simple, serious-minded citizens, not at all. But Marcius, his martial glory disregarded, has not—it is the fatal flaw—the humane and inward dignity which can outshine appearances.

It is distressing, also, to see him so smartly sparring at these simple folk, unable to resist the puzzling repartee, the adroit seizing of a vantage-point, the covert insolence. One gentle stroke pierces his harness. The Third Citizen has ventured the artlessly cunning, joke-in-earnest of

> You must think, if we give you anything, we hope to gain by you.

upon which Marcius pounces with

> Well then, I pray, your price o' th' consulship?

Says the First Citizen very quietly:

> The price is to ask it kindly.

That goes home. It does not soften him. He is no sentimentalist. But at least he next responds as one man allowably may to another—

> Kindly! Sir, I pray, let me ha't: I have wounds to show you, which shall be yours in private. Your good voice, sir; what say you?

—if, even so, he cannot keep derision from his tones, inverted arrogance from the concluding

> I have your alms. Adieu!

___

[29] A point obscured in most modern editions by their setting the entrance of the citizens after the line has been spoken, whereas the Folio has them enter just before. It does not follow that he definitely intends them to hear it; he does not see them until immediately after. But they were there a moment before; he knows they are about. The point is that he does not care.

They have not the wit nor the wish to retort on him in kind. But they are none the less conscious of his mockery, and resentment will secrete in them only the more abundantly.

These three are replaced by a Fourth Citizen and a Fifth, the Fourth plain-spoken:

> You have deserved nobly of your country, and you have not deserved nobly. . . . You have been a scourge to her enemies, you have been a rod to her friends; you have not indeed loved the common people.

The candidate counters with irony:

> You should account me the more virtuous that I have not been common in my love. . . .

But by all means, if they prefer it, he will flatter his

> sworn brother the people, to earn a dearer estimation of them . . . practise the insinuating nod . . . counterfeit the bewitchment of some popular man, and give it bountiful to the desirers. . . .

Could he—were they not such impervious clods!—do more positively to induce them to reject him? Nor will he frankly show these two his wounds; only, since he must, beg them for their "voices"—which they promise him "heartily." He is then left a breathing-space.

Marcius is no more given to reasoning coolly with himself than with others. Inward conviction is his only strength; and, erring against it, as he is erring now, he becomes like an animal caught in a net, frantic, struggling, self-strangled.

> Better it is to die, better to starve . . .

—by test of reason, certainly, a somewhat overcharged outburst. The protest against custom's tyranny,

> What custom wills, in all things should we do't,
> The dust on antique time would lie unswept,
> And mountainous error be too highly heaped
> For truth to o'erpeer. . . .

comes with unconscious irony from the conservative mind in rebellion. But, having brought himself thus far to "fool it so"—

> I am half through;
> The one part suffered, the other will I do.

—resentment would seemingly fade into shrugging self-contempt, did there not at this point

Enter three Citizens more.

The sight of them stirs him to a very self-scourging of mockery:

> Your voices! For your voices I have fought;
> Watched for your voices; for your voices bear
> Of wounds two dozen odd; battles thrice six
> I have seen and heard of. . . .

But, their own stolid simplicity unaffected, the scourge flags, the mockery peters out—

> for your voices have
> Done many things, some less, some more: your voices. . . .

—into the final surrender of

> Indeed, I would be Consul.

That he should come to this! They give him his reward:

> He has done nobly. . . . Therefore let him be Consul. . . . God save thee, noble Consul!

and as Menenius returns, the Tribunes with him, these simple folk inconspicuously depart; Marcius, released, venting an incorrigible

> Worthy voices![30]

Menenius is triumphant. His man wins; and the rest of the business can be pushed through without more delay. Sicinius stiffly assents. Marcius only demands: will it be decently done in the Senate House, not here in the vulgar market place; and

> May I change these garments?

—this ridiculous "gown of humility"? He may. Then all's well; and he and Menenius both are off in high feather. Diplomatic Menenius does not forget to ask their good colleagues the Tribunes to go along with them. No; they prefer to "stay here for the people"; their people. Sicinius' smooth "Fare you well" has an inauspicious ring.

Brutus thinks all is lost for the time being, and would dismiss

---

[30] For the technical treatment of this soliloquy, see the section upon the play's verse, p. 276ff.

the people. Sicinius will wait and see. And, sure enough, when
the plebeians reassemble, the tide of their favor towards Marcius
is already on the turn. Did he suppose, because they did not
retort then and there, that they were insensible to his sarcasm?

> To my poor unworthy notice,
> He mocked us when he begged our voices.

says the Second Citizen; and the Third, thus encouraged:

> Certainly.
> He flouted us downright.

But attack again brings defense. The First Citizen, in a minority
of one though he may be, stands out:

> No, 'tis his kind of speech; he did not mock us.

As in that old quarrel over the corn, Marcius must have fair play.

Brutus and Sicinius know better than to join in the attack while
it is strong enough without them. There are better ways of
fomenting it. Surely he can never have refused—Sicinius won't
believe it—his fellow citizens their right to see

> His marks of merit, wounds received for 's country.

The Third Citizen is effectively roused:

> He said he had wounds, which he could show in private;
> And with his hat, thus waving it in scorn,
> "I would be consul," says he: "aged custom,
> But by your voices, will not so permit me;
> Your voices therefore."

Not a derisive phrase nor a scornful twist of the tongue did he
miss, it seems:

> When we granted that,
> Here was, "I thank you for your voices: thank you:
> Your most sweet voices: now you've left your voices
> I have no further with you." Was not this mockery?

The rest mutely agree. They have behaved like fools. The
Tribunes now read them—and not for the first time, upon this
very subject!—a sound political lesson.[31]

Admitting that his recent "worthy deeds" gave him a claim

***

[31] "Not for the first time": see p. 211, note 27.

upon them, they should have reminded him of his ancient enmity towards them. Clearly, they should have said, they could not risk his remaining a "fast foe to the Plebeii." They should indeed have demanded from him a pledge for his future good behavior—which, if he had given it, they could have held him to; and if, as was more likely, the mere demand had "galled his surly nature," then, "putting him to rage," they could have

> ta'en the advantage of his choler,
> And passed him unelected.

For do they suppose that a man who can treat them as he has now done when he needs their votes will prove very considerate when he no longer needs them? And are they, who have " 'ere now denied the asker"—the candid, honest asker—to bestow their "sued-for tongues" in thanks for such treatment as this? The appeal is to sound sense and self-respect. And it needs but a single evasive

> He's not confirmed; we may deny him yet.

to stampede the rest:

> And will deny him:
> I'll have five hundred voices of that sound.

And the rot will spread:

> I twice five hundred and their friends to piece 'em.

Brutus has the demagogue's sense of a crowd's mood and the critical moment:

> Get you hence instantly, and tell those friends,
> That they have chosen a Consul that will from them take
> Their liberties. . . .

—rate them for fools as we are rating you. But Sicinius is for putting a more temperate face on the affair:

> Let them assemble,
> And, on a safer judgment, all revoke
> Your ignorant election. . . .

—let them confess it to be so. Then he builds them up their case; against Marcius' pride, and his old hatred of them, which in the light of his great deeds they had been so ready to forget

as not to note the mocking scorn, sure sign that he hated them
still. Upon which draft Brutus is quick to improve:

> Lay
> A fault on us, your Tribunes, that we laboured—
> No impediment between—but that you must
> Cast your election on him.

A brilliant maneuver from the Tribunes' standpoint! The people
will save their faces, and they win credit for a patriotic effort to
heal this old unhappy quarrel. So excellent seems the notion that
they enlarge on it until they find themselves lauding, not Marcius
alone, but his ancestors also for their services to Rome and its
people; very practical, popular services; for

> Of the same house Publius and Quintus were,
> That our best water brought by conduits hither. . . .

So Sicinius must steer back to the point, that

> you have found . . .
> That he's your chief enemy, and revoke
> Your sudden approbation.

while Brutus encourages them again with another

> Say you ne'er had done it—
> Harp on that still—but by our putting on. . . .

for already the tide of their resentment has ebbed to the
uncertainty of an

> *almost* all
> Repent in their election.

But they depart to do the bidding of these political masters, who
linger a moment, themselves, before taking their shorter way to
the Capitol, to reflect that, mildly as it yet promises,

> This mutiny were better put in hazard
> Than stay, past doubt, for greater. . . .

and that, arriving "before the stream of the people," the threat of it
can be made to

> seem, as partly 'tis, their own,
> Which we have goaded onward.

THE BATTLEGROUND IS BEFORE THE CAPITOL NOW

Cornets. Enter Coriolanus, Menenius, all the Gentry, Cominius, Titus Lartius, and other Senators.

All the Gentry is to be noted, with the completeness of the contrast it indicates between this gathering and that of the home-spun group of citizens. The cornets, elaborately sounding, tell us that the ceremonies of the election are not yet over. Coriolanus is once more fitly attired for them. And he is already deferred to as Consul—Titus Lartius, back from Corioles, but still in fighting trim, calls him "my lord"; Cominius addresses him as "Lord Consul"—and spontaneously, confidently, so asserts himself. He nurses no illusions, as the more pacific Cominius does, that Rome has finished with the Volscians, points a prompt finger towards the source of trouble to come with his

> Saw you Aufidius?

is as boyishly himself as ever in the eager

> Spoke he of me? . . .
> How? What?

Aufidius has retired to Antium, has he, there to bide his time? This by triple repetition is impressed on us. Then, says Marcius:

> I wish I had a cause to seek him there. . . .

—and the words will lodge in our memory.

So here is Coriolanus on the very crest of the wave, Rome's leader elect, and just such a leader as she may most need, with war, as is hinted, likely to threaten her again. Supported by the Senate and the gentry, he is now on his way back from the Capitol to the market place for the final act of the election, the people's confirmation of their acceptance of him. The Tribunes enter as from the market place. They do not speak at once; and Marcius apparently is not unwilling that, as they stand there, they should overhear his comments on them:

> Behold, these are the tribunes of the people,
> The tongues o' the common mouth: I do despise them;

For they do prank themselves in authority,
Against all noble sufferance.[32]

The Tribunes do not mean to be provoked into losing their tempers. They are come, on the contrary, to prevent disorder. Coriolanus must not proceed to the market place:

The people are incensed against him.

Brutus confirming Sicinius with a solemn

Stop,
Or all will fall in broil.

Coriolanus, needless to say—and the Tribunes have counted on it—flares into anger at once, and first against the Tribunes themselves for failing to control their "herd":

What are your offices?
You being their mouths, why rule you not their teeth?

"Rule"—the first thought to his mind; and a minute later he is inveighing against

such as cannot rule
Nor ever will be ruled.

(Brutus and Sicinius could tell him if they would that while they get their own way with their "herd"—and better than he knows how to—it is not by rule.)

His tactic, in this sort of fight as in another, is at once to force the acutest issue:

Have you not set them on?

—let them deny it if they can. Theirs is to lure him aside. The vexed, one-time question about the corn, Brutus neatly casts that into the arena. Marcius scoffs:

Why, this was known before.

and—the quarrel then widening to admit Cominius and Menenius to a share in it—one hopes he may have the sense to drop the subject. But no!

Tell me of corn!
This was my speech, and I will speak 't again—

---

[32] If he is not at least willing for them to overhear, there is little or no point in the lines. But here is the schoolboy side of him, very similarly shown in the scene of the gown of humility.

and not Menenius nor the Senators can stay him.

Nor is this the worst. Though his friends beseech him not to, he must needs go on to raise the whole question of these privileges that have been granted to "the mutable, rank-scented meynie"— political disapproval and personal fastidiousness combined!—for

> I say again,
> In soothing them we nourish 'gainst our Senate
> The cockle of rebellion, insolence, sedition,
> Which we ourselves have ploughed for, sowed and scattered,
> By mingling them with us, the honoured number. . . .

Brutus' acid comment,

> You speak o' the people
> As if you were a god to punish, not
> A man of their infirmity.

is a not altogether surprising one.

Marcius had been ready with this protest, and was fended by but a little from making it, upon the verge of the prescribed appeal in the gown of humility on the market place. In hot blood he has, to their faces, denounced the people yet more fiercely; and Menenius urges the Tribunes not, in fairness, to take advantage of his choler now. Marcius consents to no such excuse:

> Choler!
> Were I as patient as the midnight sleep,
> By Jove, 't would be my mind.

And it is at this juncture that, a graver note sounding, we become aware of him grown to more heroic stature, to take his stand for a cause of greater import than his own:

> O good, but most unwise patricians! why,
> You grave but reckless Senators, have you thus
> Given Hydra here to choose an officer. . . ?

For of two things one: the hydra-headed people will rule, or he— this Sicinius or the like—in their name; and

> If he have power,
> Then veil your ignorance; if none, awake
> Your dangerous lenity. If you are learned,
> Be not as common fools; if you are not,
> Let them have cushions by you. You are plebeians,
> If they be Senators: and they are no less. . . .

> By Jove himself,
> It makes the Consuls base: and my soul aches
> To know, when two authorities are up,
> Neither supreme, how soon confusion
> May enter 'twixt the gap of both and take
> The one by the other.

—it is a note never sounded by Marcius before; the rare note of selfless intellectual passion.

This is the juncture too at which he begins to alienate his friends. Little do the Senators want less—they are as apt politicians as the Tribunes—than to have such an issue raised. Cominius would evade it with a

> Well, on to the market place.

But that only sets this incorrigible Consul-elect to prove his case by revising the well-worn quarrel about the corn—and, since he will, why, adroitly he argues it as could the most proficient politician of them all. And that brings him to lashing at the people yet once more for their wartime cowardice, and Menenius cannot stop him.

He finds himself at last upon the higher ground again, for him the highest. What can go well in a state

> where gentry, title, wisdom,
> Cannot conclude but by the yea and no
> Of general ignorance . . .

Even for the people's own sake

> at once pluck out
> The multitudinous tongue; let them not lick
> The sweet which is their poison. . . .

Dangerous ground! Brutus and Sicinius have no more need of their façade of indignation. It sputters from them:

> Has said enough.
> Has spoken like a traitor, and shall answer
> As traitors do.

But it is not in Marcius to retreat. Here, indeed, he is, in the sort of situation that most delights him, singlehanded against odds, reckless of consequence. And with the happy, schoolboy ribaldry of the question:

What should the people do with these bald Tribunes. . . ?

he is ready to

throw their power i' the dust.

Not for this was he to be elected Consul. It is, as Brutus says, "Manifest treason." But revolutions do not always come from below.

Such a quarrel started, each must line up on his own side. And the summoning of the Aediles to apprehend Rome's hero

as a traitorous innovator,
A foe to the public weal . . .

—the Tribunes will carefully keep their law-abiding and conservative footing—rallies the troubled Senate round him.[33] Sicinius, violently excited, is for arresting Marcius with his own hands; Cominius, scandalized, protesting; Marcius, at his senile touch, with a

Hence, rotten thing, or I shall shake thy bones
Out of thy garments.

sending him yelping off in terror. Hullaballoo ensues; Coriolanus alone standing silent and unmoved.

The first thing is to quiet it; and this only the Tribunes, who have roused it, can well do. Menenius, outshouted, helpless, is reduced to begging "good Sicinius" to speak to the people. If he thinks he has a peacemaker in him he is much mistaken. Sicinius but repeats quietly and more clearly what he has already called aloud:

---

[33] There is significance in the two stage directions: first

Enter a rabble of Plebeians, with the Aediles.

The people were assembled in the market place ready to disavow their choice of Coriolanus, but prepared—neither they nor the Tribunes—for no such business as this. So, called upon for help, they appear as a "rabble." It will be a very different matter when, for the later encounter, they have been "collected . . . by tribes" and drilled in the required behavior.

Secondly, while the plebeians are mustering to the support of their Tribunes, the direction to the Senators is

They all bustle about Coriolanus.

It is one of the play's characteristically descriptive stage directions; and it suggests a certain embarrassment and fuss, the Senators little less perturbed than the Tribunes are.

> You are at point to lose your liberties:
> Marcius would have all from you; Marcius,
> Whom late you have named for Consul.

And to the shocked reproach from the Senate side that

> This is the way to kindle, not to quench.
> To unbuild the city and to lay all flat.

he launches at Marcius, who would throw the popular power "in the dust," the tit-for-tat

> What is the city but the people?

with its powerful chorus of popular response:

> True,
> The people are the city.

And thus can the political pendulum swing once it is started swinging.

For the Tribunes, cooler now and confident with their followers ranged behind them, this is a chance not to be missed, of pushing their power to its utmost. It marks them and their kind that they cannot resist the temptation. Their enemy, attacking them, has rashly talked treason too; and, says Sicinius:

> This deserves death.

Brutus adds categorically,

> Or let us stand to our authority
> Or let us lose it. We do here pronounce
> Upon the part o' the people, in whose power
> We were elected theirs, Marcius is worthy
> Of present death.

And, without more ado, the sentence ends, he is to be flung from the Tarpeian rock. Menenius—violence imminent, his side outnumbered—beseeches lenity. Marcius, silent till now, simply draws his sword, and says,

> No, I'll die here.

He adds, more sportingly,

> There's some among you have beheld me fighting:
> Come, try upon yourselves what you have seen me.

Urged by the Tribunes, they tumultuously do; and

> *In this mutiny, the Tribunes, the Aediles, and the People,*
> *are beat in.*

—as, with Marcius at the head of even a handful of men of good fighting quality (Cominius is there, and Titus Lartius), such a rabble might look to be.

But it is to be noted how the impromptu victory is taken: Menenius' first thought is for Marcius to profit from it by retreating to his house and leaving the reasonable rest of them to patch up the best peace they can. One or two are left fighting keen.[34] But

> Shall it be put to that?

—Romans at war with Romans—

> The gods forbid!

In affection for his hero the old man mitigates the effect of Marcius' grimly vaunting

> On fair ground
> I could beat forty of them.

with the humor of his own

> I could myself
> Take up a brace o' the best of them; yea, the two Tribunes.

But it is a relief to have him gone. Comment is practical:

> This man has marred his fortune.

—this is *not* the way to campaign for the consulship in Rome.[35]

~~~~~~~~

[34] Cominius, apparently, one. But I fancy that the

> Stand fast:
> We have as many friends as enemies.

is misascribed to him. For if not, he changes his mind barely a moment later; and, a little later still, a six-line speech conclusively puts him among the prudent ones. Further, he and Coriolanus depart together.

[35] The Folio has marked an *exeunt* for Coriolanus and Cominius only; and the minor speeches immediately following are given to *Patri*, translated by later editors into First and Second Patrician, instead of to the Senators who have fulfilled this need till now. One queries at first an (unrecorded) departure of the Senators too; but at the end of the scene there still remains one Senator at least. A possible explanation is that the Senators in their robes—whatever on Shakespeare's stage these were—are meant to be withdrawn to the background, the gathering to lose the last of its ceremonial aspect. This will add, by contrast,

And through Menenius' loyally laudatory

> His nature is too noble for the world:
> He would not flatter Neptune for his trident,
> Or Jove for 's power to thunder. . . .

can be heard, perhaps, the man of the world's sigh of exasperation at being left to clear up if he can the mess this noble nature has made of things. It issues in a final

> What the vengeance!
> Could he not speak 'em fair?

But a breathing-space at least has been gained, in which Menenius himself can "speak 'em fair," can try, as he said,

> whether my old wit be in request
> with those that have but little . . .

and here we may recall our first sight of him at the play's opening, and the skill with which he quieted the mutiny over the corn. This is a harder task. Brutus and Sicinius are not to be so cajoled. They possess authority, moreover, to which he takes care to show deference, while Marcius has put himself indefensibly in the wrong. And the people are for the moment—wherefore the Tribunes are astutely demanding death without delay—authentically incensed against him, witness the full chorus of reiterated "No, no . . ." which greets his mere tentative naming as "the Consul Coriolanus." He must make for him, then, must Menenius, such a place with the people as the Tribunes dare not, for shame— will not, for policy—obstruct.

First, it is to a regard for Rome's good name:

> whose gratitude
> Towards her deserved children is enrolled
> In Jove's own book . . .

Then:

> What has he done to Rome that's worthy death?
> Killing our enemies, the blood he hath lost—
> Which, I dare vouch, is more than that he hath,
> By many an ounce—he dropped it for his country;

---

to the semblance of authority worn by Brutus and Sicinius, reappearing at the head of their rabble.

> And what is left, to lose it by his country
> Were to us all, that do 't and suffer it,
> A brand to the end o' the world.

"Were to us all"—they are one in citizenship with him, and all are Rome.

The Tribunes see that they must put a stop to this, must let loose the pent wrath of the people, before, under such soothing, it abates altogether. But—each minute a gain—Menenius begs for

> One word more, one word.

And of full effect he makes it; with its warning whither "tiger-footed rage" may lead, his repicturing to the people of their soldier

> bred i' the wars
> Since he could draw a sword . . .

and his final promise to bring him back to them compliant in spirit. And the Senatorial

> Noble Tribunes,
> It is the humane way. . . .

solidly supports him.

They are practiced politicians, are the Tribunes, and can quickly tack and veer, and turn moderation to account as well as rage. If they do not now give Marcius another chance, they may well, under the effect of such appeals for him, split their own party. If they do, and he does not take it, he will probably split his own, and they will have him the more at their mercy. Besides, Menenius will almost certainly fail to bring him tamely to heel. So Sicinius generously consents; a touch of sardonic humor in his

> Noble Menenius,
> Be you, then, as the people's officer . . .

And the

> Masters, lay down your weapons.
> Go not home.
> Meet on the market place. . . .

is but a menace postponed. To Menenius and the Senators, indeed, Sicinius is coldly explicit:

> Where, if you bring not Marcius, we'll proceed
> In our first way.

Menenius' "old wit" has won him somewhat; but despite the jovially confident

> I'll bring him to you.

he knows how precariously little yet. And the scene ends upon the ominous muted note of his

> He must come,
> Or what is worst will follow.

as he and the Senators depart to fulfill the no easier second half of their task—if they can!

Coriolanus absent, and his violent stimulus to the action lacking, its pulse has kept a steadier beat. There is no slackening, the tension is sustained; and we are stirred to question: will he once more yield to persuasion, or no?

VOLUMNIA'S SHARE IN THE QUARREL

Finding him at his house, the young nobility around him, high-mettled and willful as he, truly it does not seem likely.[36] He is at the highest pitch of indignant wrath:

> Let them pull all about mine ears; present me
> Death on the wheel, or at wild horses' heels;
> Or pile ten hills on the Tarpeian rock
> That the precipitation might down stretch
> Below the beam of sight; yet will I still
> Be thus to them.

flattered in it by these young supporters of his own breed and mind whom conflict begins to gather to him—one of them exclaiming,

> You do the nobler.

---

36 The Folio's stage direction speaks here only of his entering *with Nobles*; actually it is later, on his way to banishment, that he is said to be accompanied to the city gate by *the young Nobility of Rome.* But the distinction implied at both points between them (whether called *Nobles* or *young Nobility*) and the rest of his party is the same, and its meaning is, I think, clear. At first he has, of course, the Senate on his side; and among the variously termed Patricians, Gentry, Nobles, some will be Senators, some not. Step by step, in his intransigence, he alienates the Senators, and—if it can be shown, if the theater company can muster sufficient numbers—possibly some of the elders among the mere gentry too. But the young nobility—men more or less of his own age—side with him to the last. And it is at this point in the action that—though not much is made of it—they begin to be distinguished from the rest.

—pricked the more to it by a most unexpected crossing just encountered:

> I muse my mother
> Does not approve me further. . . .

We may note how Shakespeare here concentrates his action, dovetails it, coils it like a spring to give it strength. Marcius left the Capitol with Cominius, who has now, apparently, gone elsewhere; we shall learn where and why later. He himself has been at home long enough for a first encounter with Volumnia, the result of it shown in the outburst with which the scene opens, the violent recoil from her sober counsel; and that this *is* the result of it to be surmised from the sight of her as she slowly follows him and stands, disapproval in her attitude, until he turns to discover and ask,

> Why did you wish me milder?[37]

Here too the depicting of Marcius takes a more intimate turn. Man of action, of impulse, and of quick response to his fellows whether in anger or affection, we do not find him reflecting in solitude. Shakespeare allots him but one short soliloquy, and that to mark his loneliness and defeat.[38] He is brought nearest to consciousness of himself—the boyish self-consciousness that plagues him a very different thing!—when he looks, as now, in the glass of his mother's opinion of him. This has been satisfyingly flattering so far; he "muses" the more that she should now wish him to be false to himself. And the tragedy of character gains shape.

He yielded to persuasion and was false to himself when he put on the gown of humility and stood begging for votes in the market place. But at least he did it ill; and he atoned to himself, moreover, when the chance came, by giving Tribunes and people a fuller taste of his true mind than otherwise he would have done —gave it to his own prejudice too. This new temptation to go back upon himself finds him at first more violent in resistance, yet the less able to resist.

---

[37] A simple effect, lost in the modern editorial delaying of her entrance by nine lines.

[38] The exclamatory "Better it is to die, better to starve . . ." in the scene in the market place is hardly a soliloquy.

Having vented in defiance his astonishment that Volumnia
should so rebuke him, he listens to her respectfully, lovingly; to
Menenius and the Senators, coming in hope and doubt from their
parley with the Tribunes; to Cominius, who later reports from
the market place that the issue must be faced—to all their politic
advice. But it is a chilling change from his mother's accustomed
fervors to the biting

> You might have been enough the man you are
> With striving less to be so. . . .

apt and deserved though this may be. That he is right in what
he has said, but that he should wait, should he, to say it until
those that hold him wrong are in his power?—it is foxy doctrine.
He has been, protests genial old Menenius, "too rough, something
too rough. . . ." From Volumnia, again, who claims for herself

> a brain that leads my use of anger
> To better vantage.

(not that, tested so little later, this appears) he faces a

> You are too absolute.

He, then, their hero, if he is to be their Consul, has some most
unheroic lessons to learn. To return to the Tribunes and publicly
repent what he has spoken—which he would not do to the gods!
But he listens still. He has no taste for argument. Strange that it
should be his mother cleverly proving to him, his friends ap-
plauding, that a lie told to his fellow Romans here to gain his
ends no more dishonors him than it would in war thus

> to take in a town with gentle words,
> Which else would put you to your fortune and
> The hazard of much blood . . .

But a good argument doubtless. Not a very admirable picture,
though, that she sketches of him for his copying:

> with this bonnet in thy hand . . .
> Thy knee bussing the stones—for in such business
> Action is eloquence, and the eyes of the ignorant
> More learned than the ears—waving thy head,
> (Which often) thus correcting thy stout heart,
> Now humble as the ripest mulberry
> That will not hold the handling. . . .

And, even more than in his donning of the gown of humility, does it put him to a part which, he protests, he never can "discharge to the life." But, waging this sort of war, his friends have him at their mercy as never had his enemies when he faced *them* sword in hand. For his wife's sake, his son's, in the Senators' cause and the nobles', it is his duty, so it seems, to forswear himself. And Volumnia, argument unavailing, coaxes and chides him like a child, and, as a last resource, treats him to a hot fit of the very temper she has so disastrously bred in him.

He is swung from a baited

> Well, I must do 't.

and from his own yet sorrier filling-in of her sorry picture of him—

> Away, my disposition, and possess me
> Some harlot's spirit! my throat of war be turned,
> Which quired with my drum, into a pipe
> Small as an eunuch . . .
> > a beggar's tongue
> Make motion through my lips, and my armed knees,
> Who bowed but in my stirrup, bend like his
> That hath received an alms! . . .

—to the violent revolt of

> > I will *not* do 't
> Lest I surcease to honour mine own truth,
> And by my body's action teach my mind
> A most inherent baseness.

but, finally, as she rounds on him, to a boylike

> > Pray, be content,
> Mother, I am going to the market place;
> Chide me no more. . . .

It is the endearing side of him.

> > I'll mountebank their loves,
> Cog their hearts from them, and come home beloved
> Of all the trades in Rome. Look, I am going:
> Commend me to my wife. . . .

The invincible soldier! Vulnerable in the simplicity of his affections, as son, husband, father, friend! Pure patriot, by his unquestioning lights; his life his country's! As a politician, a fool! He is foredoomed to fail in this coming test, with which the long strain of his campaign for the consulship is to end. It does not lie in him to be cynically false to his nature. He knows only how to be true even to its faults. Still, he will please them if he can; to have his mother turn her back on him in anger distresses him. So, with "Mildly" for his watchword—a wry irony evolving from the sound of it as he and Menenius pass it between them— he sets out again at the head of his party.

BANISHMENT

Sicinius and Brutus (the appointment was for the market place; when we see them enter, then, we shall presume them there) have not wasted time. While Senators and nobles have been at odds with their candidate and leader, they, by contrast, have been drilling their followers and developing their tactics. Coriolanus can still be best accused of aiming at tyrannical power; and, says Brutus,

> In this point charge him home. . . .

But "if he evade us there. . . ," if, that is to say, Menenius has succeeded in making him see reason, why, to tax him with having, in his hatred for the people, deprived them of their share of the spoil "got on the Antiates," will certainly rouse his wrath again. He is coming, they hear; accompanied, of course, by old Menenius

> and those Senators
> That always favoured him.

There are others, then; and his party can be divided. Then come their last-minute instructions to the Aedile. The people have been organized in their legal groups? Good. Let them listen for their leaders' voices; and, says Sicinius,

> when they hear me say "It shall be so
> I' the right and strength o' the Commons," be it either
> For death, for fine, or banishment, then let them
> If I say fine, cry "fine," if death, cry "death". . . .

—for only with such docile followers can a democratic leader do himself full credit, reap the moment's maximum harvest. But there are, besides, the opposite uses to which a crowd can be put:

> And when such time they have begun to cry,
> Let them not cease, but with a din confused
> Enforce the present execution. . . .

Then Brutus, kindling to the opportunity:

> Put him to choler straight.

and the rest will follow. The unhappy Coriolanus is no better
than a child in their hands. Sicinius, beneath the surface, is as
excited:

> Well, here he comes.

It is a tense and a pregnant moment.

Menenius, on the way here, has been harping, seemingly, on the
single string, its note varied only from the parting "Mildly" to
this

> Calmly, I do beseech you.

—Marcius' muttered answer not reassuring! The opponents face
each other like duelists with a ceremonious salute; and what
could be more exemplary than Marcius'

> The honoured gods
> Keep Rome in safety, and the chairs of justice
> Supplied with worthy men! plant love among's!
> Throng our large temples with the shows of peace,
> And not our streets with war!

Menenius applauds, as might a proud tutor his pupil:

> A noble wish!

The Tribunes duly proceed:

> Draw near, ye people.

And the Aedile sustains their dignity:

> List to your Tribunes! Audience! Peace, I say!

Now comes maneuvering for position. Is this to be the end of the
dispute? Marcius demands; Sicinius in turn:

> If you submit you to the people's voices,
> Allow their officers, and are content
> To suffer lawful censure for such faults
> As shall be proved upon you?

"Submit ... censure ... faults ..."; it is a bitter pill. The Tribunes hope, the Senators fear, that he will never swallow it. With a Spartan

> I am content.

he does. Upon which, his friends cannot in prudence but see, the business had best be brought to a quick finish. Yet Menenius, though he himself sees it—

> Lo! citizens, he says he is content. . . .

—cannot resist pleading once more the cause that is already won, so well has he pleaded it; the advocate's common fault! "War-like service" and "wounds" must again be commended; and Marcius himself, as before, must mock-modestly protest,

> Scratches with briers;
> Scars to move laughter only.

And the fresh tribute to his soldiership stirs him, despite Cominius' caution, to reopen the quarrel:

> What is the matter
> That being passed for Consul with full voice,
> I am so dishonoured that the very hour
> You take it off again?

—then he sees his error, and checks himself. But, if the Tribunes have failed so far to "put him to choler," they will not now:

> We charge you, that you have contrived to take
> From Rome all seasoned office, and to wind
> Yourself into a power tyrannical;
> For which you are a traitor to the people.

A two-edged thrust!

> The fires i' the lowest hell fold in the people!
> Call me *their* traitor! . . .

—no holding him after that!

The people are ahead of their leaders here. Spontaneously the cry rises:

> To the rock, to the rock with him!

So now the supple demagogue can play the moderate man, gain credit with the moderate men of the other side, and insure himself

against reaction, should that come. The people are right. Marcius'
treachery to them

> Deserves the extremest death. . . .
>   But since he hath
> Served well for Rome—

(Brutus is more than a little patronizing) sentence on him
shall mercifully be commuted to banishment for life. Neither
Menenius' comically frantic

> Is this the promise that you made your mother?

nor Cominius' noble plea, can turn Coriolanus from his defiant
wrath, the Tribunes from their triumph. And in their lessoned
unison the people echo once and again:

> It shall be so! It shall be so!
> Let him away!
> He's banished, and it shall be so.

Against such a chorus the single voice sounds nobly:

> You common cry of curs! whose breath I hate
> As reek o' the rotten fens, whose love I prize
> As the dead carcasses of unburied men
> That do corrupt my air . . .

and the superlative pride is warranted of the

> I banish you.

To his grim presage of what must be in store for such a mob
and for their Rome the Tribunes listen in complacent silence, the
people heedlessly, awaiting but the sight of his departure—

> Despising,
> For you, the city, thus I turn my back:
> There is a world elsewhere.[39]

---

[39] It is just possible, I think, that F's quaintly corrupted stage direction:
Exeunt Coriolanus, Cominius, with Cumaligs (due to a muddled deletion in the
MS evidently) has to do with the several other stage directions and hints in
the text meant to indicate the growing division among Coriolanus' supporters (see
p. 229, note 36, and page 239, note 40). Was the *with* to have been followed
by particulars of those that accompanied him and those that did not, and did
Shakespeare, for lack of room or any other likely reason, content himself rather
with the *cum aliis*, leaving the fact that some went one way, some another to be
deduced (and implemented by the actors) from the opening stage direction of
the next scene: *Enter Coriolanus . . . with the young Nobility of Rome*; the

—to take their time once more from the fugleman-Aedile with a
jubilant

> Our enemy is banished! He is gone! Hoo! hoo!

though its ending is mere wolfish clamor.

"Despising, for you, the city . . ."; there is the first faint sound—
if the actor can accent it, and we are quick to hear—of the
deeper and more tragic discord to come.

Brutus and Sicinius meanwhile will lose nothing of a popular
triumph, nor of their revenge. The hero, cheered but a few hours
since, shall now be hooted through those same streets:

> Go, see him out at gates, and follow him,
> As he hath followed you, with all despite;
> Give him deserved vexation. . . .

—it is the mob's part. For the assertion of their own inflated
dignity:

> Let a guard
> Attend us through the city.

THE DEPARTURE

Marcius is at once more likable in adversity than in triumph.
Of the cheering crowds that greeted, so short a while back, his
conqueror's entry, of the gathered Senate praising and honoring
him, out of all Rome nothing friendly seems left him as he takes
his way to exile, but his mother, his wife, two tried friends, and
this silent, useless handful of the young nobility, reluctant though
they are to see their hero depart; and these he will leave behind.
But he makes no complaint, has no word against the Tribunes—
in that omission the perfectest contempt!—and, for the people,
only the humorously bitter

> the beast
> With many heads butts me away.

He can rally his mother's spirits by retorting on her a choice few
of the precepts with which she was wont to load him, and with
a bantering

elders, but for Cominius and Menenius, having definitely deserted him? Mere
conjecture, and the point a small one; but the very smallest may have its worth
in a reconstructing of the play's intended staging.

> What, what, what!

when anger breaks from her—

> Now the red pestilence strike all trades in Rome
> And occupations perish!

even as his own, to her reproving, was so apt to do. His harsher

> Nay, I prithee, woman!

vented upon his wife, is rather curb to himself lest he give way
to grief as she is doing. Menenius—

> Thou old and true Menenius . . .

—already in tears, he comforts with kindly affection. Cominius,
of sterner mettle, he calls on to

> tell these sad women
> 'Tis fond to wail inevitable strokes
> As 'tis to laugh at them.

To the wreck of his own fortunes there is no more reference than
the boyishly simple

> I'll do well yet.

But this is the Marcius passingly glimpsed, who remembered,
amid the acclaiming shouts, the poor man in Corioles who had
once used him kindly, and, after victory, the widows there, and
the "mothers that lack sons."
But beneath the cheerful courage, the buoyancy of

> I shall be loved when I am lacked.

we become conscious of a dark, of a sinister sorrow, its shadow
apparent in the

> I go alone,
> Like to a lonely dragon, that his fen
> Makes feared and talked of more than seen. . . .

of a suffering repressed, but up-welling in that single

> O, the gods!

He will go to his exile alone, as befits his pride; and whatever
they hear of him it shall be

> never of me aught
> But what is like me formerly.

No regrets, therefore, no compunction! He is the same Marcius still; and what cannot soften will but harden him the more.[40]

THOSE LEFT BEHIND

Brutus and Sicinius follow at his heels, the Aedile attending them. Their amiable plan to have a mob hoot him "out at gates" is thwarted. He has gone. The sooner, therefore, their violence having served its turn, the people are quieted and sent home the better. This is the Aedile's task. Besides, a change of policy is called for now.

> The nobility are vexed. . . .

—and doubtless will repent their weakness in letting Coriolanus go.[41] Therefore, says the sagacious Brutus,

> Now we have shown our power
> Let us seem humbler after it is done
> Than when it was a-doing.

Neither do they fancy an encounter with Volumnia as she now returns—a lowering thundercloud!—with Virgilia and Menenius from the farewell at the gate. But they dodge unavailingly. For the cruel strain of that parting asks fuller relief than in tears—and here they are, very much to the purpose.

Marcius has gone, ominously self-controlled, to nurse his

---

[40] The young nobility, "my friends of noble touch," here also left behind, are evidently closely related to the "three or foure of his friends only" who, in North's Plutarch, did accompany him. The main point of the change is, of course, to bring Marcius, without more complication, to Antium all alone. A lesser dramatist might, then, have rid himself of the young nobility altogether. But to Shakespeare the enrichment of Marcius' character, slight as it is, by his dismissal of them is worth while. And it costs him but half a line of text.

[41] It is likely, I should say, that the sight of the young nobility returning from their farewell to Coriolanus at the city gate (to be followed in a minute by Volumnia, Virgilia and Menenius) and their demeanor when they see the Tribunes suggests this

> The nobility are vexed. . . .

to Sicinius. They would merely cross the stage. Cominius would presumably be with them. There is nothing, of course, either in text or stage direction to indicate this; but it fits with the rest of the scene's business. Clearly they should have appeared to follow Marcius to the gate, for he has said to them

> *when I am forth,*
> Bid me farewell, and smile.

wrongs and breed them into—we shall see what monstrous shape. With Menenius what's done is done. Why waste more words on the fellows? So he finds himself pleading to Volumnia—and as fruitlessly as to her son. For the touch of the unexpected with which Shakespeare is wont to reinforce such eddies in the action as this: Virgilia too, foregoing her "gracious silence," sets about Sicinius, seconds Volumnia valiantly. The wretched Tribunes take refuge from the volleying words, at first in scandalized astonishment:

> Are you mankind? . . . O blessed heavens!

then in cant; their answer to Volumnia's

> I would my son
> Were in Arabia, and thy tribe before him,
> His good sword in his hand.

to Virgilia's

> He 'ld make an end of thy posterity.

to Volumnia's

> Bastards and all!
> Good man, the wounds that he does bear for Rome!

a smooth, white-of-the-eye,

> I would he had continued to his country
> As he began, and not unknit himself
> The noble knot he made.
>   I would he had.

To which her retort comes plumply:

> "I would he had!" 'Twas you incensed the rabble:
> Cats . . .

Only a dignified departure is left them:

> Pray, let us go.

appropriately tinged with malice:

> Why stay we to be baited
> With one that wants her wits?

They gone, and the storm past, he trusts, Menenius essays for solace:

> You have told them home;
> And, by my troth, you have cause. You'll sup with me?

—old age's comfort in the commonplace! Virgilia, spent by unwonted wrath, is in tears again. But Volumnia:

> Anger's my meat; I sup upon myself,
> And so shall starve with feeding. Come, let's go:
> Leave this faint puling and lament as I do,
> In anger, Juno-like. . . .

These are the natures—like mother, like son—to be broken, never bent; born to catastrophe.

TRADERS IN THE IGNOBLE

Enter a Roman and a Volsce.

Before we see the noble and heroic fallen, infatuate, into infamy, Marcius, amazingly, a traitor to his country, we are given—for edification!—this marginal passage of cheerful trading in the ignoble. The Roman is a Fifth Column fighter, a Volscian spy, on his way to his masters to tell them that, Coriolanus banished, now is the time for them to take their revenge on Rome. His name, it appears, is Nicanor. He luckily encounters a Volscian comrade, one Adrian, who, being in something the same line of business, has been sent to discover him in Rome. He knows Adrian at once, who does not recognize him in his present guise— or disguise:

> You had more beard when I last saw you. . . .

his quizzical apology. The Roman bringing good news, the couple warm to each other:

> the nobles receive so to heart the banishment of that worthy Coriolanus, that they are in a ripe aptness to take all power from the people, and to pluck from them their Tribunes for ever. . . .

—which is not true, we shall learn later; but no matter, since it is good news, not necessarily the truth, that curries favor for your Nicanors.

> I shall, between this and supper, tell you most strange things from Rome, all tending to the good of their adversaries. . . .

continues this pleasant specimen of them, preening himself on the sensation he will make. Coriolanus banished, Aufidius and his Volscians ready to strike:

242 Prefaces to Shakespeare

> I am joyful to hear of their readiness, and am the man, I think,
> that shall set them in present action. So, sir, heartily well met,
> and most glad of your company.

And renegade Roman and Volscian go their way together, arm
in arm, and as merry as grigs.

The scene forms a bridge between Coriolanus' departure from
Rome and his appearance in Antium, suggests some likely period
of time passing between the two. Also it shows us a seamier side
to the magnificent and tragic treason he is about to commit. He
will at least not draw sordid profit from it, and be merry over it.

ANTIUM

Enter Coriolanus, in mean apparel, disguised and muffled.

From now to its end the tone of the play is changed. Marcius
is changed, or rather—since men do not change—he seems no
longer himself. The vengeance incarnate he becomes is but an
empty simulacrum of himself; "a kind of nothing," Cominius
calls him later. His troubles until now have come upon him because he could not learn to be false to his proudly faulty nature.
But he has at least been honestly himself in struggling with them
—and with the tricky Tribunes—however faultily. Now, under
defeat, his untried soul will abjure the spontaneous loyalty, the
faith, that had chiefly made him what he was; and he will be the
mere tool of his vengeance, until, abjuring this, he is himself
again. Meanwhile the passionate and unstable, temptation-tossed
Aufidius will be covertly compassing his destruction. By such
twisted and blind paths is it that the action now proceeds.

Marcius appears alone. It is the first such solitary appearance
in the play, and will be the more striking because of that.[42] Till

---

[42] The first and the last for that matter, even as the scene thus begun
contains the play's sole soliloquy. A play of action, not reflection; by its nature
it does not run to soliloquies.

One may note, in passing, the baldness of the introductory

> A goodly city is this Antium.

Shakespeare, in his maturity, is master of a dozen or more different ways of
indirectly locating his scenes, as vaguely or as exactly as he may choose. But he
will still use means as plain and direct as Sir Philip Sidney's notorious (and
possibly apocryphal) placard, if they happen to be dramatically effective also.

now, too, we have seen him only either in fighting trim or in the
panoply of his triumph and his consulship, except for the
grotesque interlude of the *gown of humility*; his present *mean
apparel* is a grimmer variation of it. Outcast, destitute, unarmed,
in this city where—pride bitterly reminds him—discovery could
mean death, he is seeking his chief enemy Aufidius.[43] And from
a soliloquy—short, and the only one allotted to him—we learn
why.

He is here to enlist with the Volscians against Rome. It has
come to that with him. Neither now nor later are we told of any
process of debate within him, any struggle or yielding to temptation. He simply comments now—coldly, cynically—upon the fact
that such spiritual revolutions do occur, from hate to love, and
love to hate; and

> So with me:
> My birth-place hate I, and my love's upon
> This enemy town.[44]

[43]   At Antium lives he? . . .
> I would I had a cause to seek him there. . . .

—the unconsciously ironic words, spoken at the very height of his good fortune,
may well have lodged in our minds.

Destitute, unarmed: Shakespeare does not stress the point of poverty, "my
misery" covering much more than that, if that; but the "meanness" of his
apparel, superfluous to mere disguise, seems meant loosely to suggest it. And it is
evident that, in the encounter with Aufidius' servants, he at least wears no sword.

[44] The phrase

> Some trick not worth an egg . . .

recalls Hamlet's

> delicate and tender prince,
> Whose spirit with divine ambition puffed
> Makes mouths at the invisible event,
> Exposing what is mortal and unsure
> To all that fortune, death and danger dare,
> Even for an egg-shell . . .

It is not to say that there was, as he wrote, any constructive connection between
the two in Shakespeare's mind, but the parallel is there; between Fortinbras the
happy and Coriolanus the unhappy man of action, the one that (says Hamlet
enviously) is ready

> greatly to find quarrel in a straw,
> When honour's at the stake . . .

his sense of honor exalting him, the other coming to see men and friends

> On a dissension of a doit, break out
> To bitterest enmity . . .

while his extravagant sense of his honorable duty to himself only betrays him to
deep dishonor.

But it is of a piece with the rest of him that there should have been no such debate or struggle. Of the faculty of introspection he most certainly has none. Not once do we hear him question himself. He acts upon conviction, and is never less than fully convinced. That has helped to make him a fine fighter. Moreover, he must act; inaction is against nature with him, and exile has condemned him to it. And in what he does there will be no compromise, no middle course taken. His soldier's genius and his love of country have inspired him to the doing of great deeds, and the thwarting of these forces in him deprives him of all purpose in life. It is no argument that has turned him traitor. But the present sight of him—so altered and worn that Aufidius, who has five times fought him foot to foot, does not know him— speaks eloquently enough of the lonely misery endured, until, in some dark moment, natural love dead in him, he sought salvation in hate.

Of this sight of him so altered Shakespeare makes much. Deferential enquiry for "great Aufidius'" house takes him to its hall-fire, to stand there, a gaunt, muffled, forbidding figure, while, contrastingly, cheerful music plays within and the liveried servants pass to and fro on the business of the feast. Ironically submissive to his first rebuff,

> I have deserved no better entertainment,
> In being Coriolanus.

it is the old Marcius that answers with an ominous

> Away!

to the temerity of the Second Servant coming to oust him. What to make of him and that humbly dignified

> Let me but stand; I will not hurt your hearth.

A third servant, with the first two to back him, will deal with the fellow:

> What are you?
> A gentleman.
> A marvellous poor one!
> True, so I am.

But another rash move to oust him brings the Third Servant within reach of that formidable arm, to be sent spinning by a

touch from it. These are matters for their master. But awaiting
Aufidius, the Third Servant holds his jack-in-office course:

> Where dwell'st thou?
> Under the canopy.
> Under the canopy?
> Ay.
> Where's that?
> I' the city of kites and crows.

while Marcius, the fateful moment nearing, finds a sardonically
trivial satisfaction in mystifying these blockheads, a solider one
when, turning on the unlucky Third Servant with a

> Thou prat'st; serve with thy trencher: hence!

he whacks him over the head with it.

Aufidius appears; he also, in his feasting finery, little like the
man we saw last, bloody with his wounds, savagely sullen in
defeat. Genial, flushed with wine, he surveys the uncouth
stranger. He has drunk enough to allow for an obstinate repeating
of

> What's thy name?

a petulantly willful

> I know thee not.

while the haggard gaze is leveled at him. And when at last the
steeled voice says,

> My name is Caius Marcius. . . .

he sobers to very dumbness, listens at first stupent. Nor is
Marcius, nor are we, to know until the whole tale has been
rigorously told, how he will take it, what he will do.

Marcius is as absolute as ever, and as proud, still prouder in
ill fortune than in good. He does not excuse, nor condescend to
justify, nor find fine phrases for what he is ready to do; "in
mere spite" to fight against his "thankless country," his

> cankered country, with the spleen
> Of all the under fiends . . .

and with as fierce a hate for the "dastard nobles," his own party,
who have suffered him

> by the voice of slaves to be
> Hooped out of Rome.

as for the slaves themselves.

He stoops to no flattery of Aufidius, pretends to no more thought for him and his Volscians than as mere instruments of revenge. A callous bargain; scornfully provokes Aufidius if he will not strike it:

> if so be
> Thou dar'st not this, and that to prove more fortunes
> Thou'rt tired, then, in a word, I also am
> Longer to live most weary, and present
> My throat to thee and to thy ancient malice,
> Which not to cut would show thee but a fool. . . .

Not in mercy then, but as callously, and to his own profit and content, let Aufidius end an enemy's misery here and now. This, in Marcius, is no bravado, but a sober measuring of the worth of revenge to him. He clinches his argument—

> Since I have ever followed thee with hate,
> Drawn tons of blood out of thy country's breast,
> And cannot live but to thy shame, unless
> It be to do thee service.

—and awaits, as uncertain as are we, the issue.

Aufidius, come to credit eyes and ears, has heard dumbfounded these amazing things unfolding, while within him one responsive impulse ousts another; until at last:

> O, Marcius, Marcius!
> Each word thou hast spoke hath weeded from my heart
> A root of ancient envy. . . .

—the generous emotion gushes forth, playing like a warm stream upon the ice, this ice that is Marcius. But he, for his part, yields, nevertheless, with little grace to the rhapsodies and embraces of his so suddenly converted foe, nor responds at all to such flowery rhetoric as the

> Know thou first,
> I loved the maid I married; never man
> Sighed truer breath; but that I see thee here,
> Thou noble thing, more dances my rapt heart
> Than when I first my wedded mistress saw
> Bestride my threshold. Why, thou Mars! . . .

Only when he hears of the "power on foot," of the Volscian plan already made for

> pouring war
> Into the bowels of ungrateful Rome . . .

does he tardily, sternly, utter that

> You bless me, gods!

—and the thankfulness must sound strange in his own ears. For the rest: the leadership proffered, the welcome from the "friendly Senators" awaiting him, Aufidius' superlative

> A thousand welcomes!
> And more a friend than e'er an enemy . . .

—he accepts it all in silence, passing in to the feast, little like a man so lavishly granted his desire. He goes—already—as to his doom.[45]

Withdrawn to a respectful distance, First and Second Servant have been listening prick-eared:

> Here's a strange alteration!

---

[45] "Such flowery rhetoric": to Marcius, at any rate, in such a mood as he is, it will seem so. The contrast between the dry, angular phrasing of his speech to Aufidius and the rich, decorative and flowing melody of Aufidius' response is marked. A distinguished critic has connected—and somewhat carpingly—the dry angularity with the fact that Shakespeare took entire phrases for the speech from North's Plutarch, and used them unaltered. But this effect of a man speaking not spontaneously, as Aufidius does, but after long and bitter brooding with painful thought given to what he should say, speaking moreover not out of the fullness but the very emptiness of his heart, is, I suggest, precisely the effect meant to be made. And if Shakespeare found he could best make it by tacking together phrases from Plutarch he would certainly do so.

Marcius, at the thrilling moment of joining forces with Cominius on the battlefield before Corioles, had launched into something the same imagery that Aufidius uses now. But he was happily himself then as he will never be again. And, even so, that

> O, let me clip you
> In arms as sound as when I wooed, in heart
> As merry as when our nuptial day was done,
> And tapers turned to bedward.

denoted a harder temper than sounds from Aufidius'

> never man
> Sighed truer breath; but that I see thee here,
> Thou noble thing, more dances my rapt heart . . .

Shakespeare, in writing them, may or may not have had the likeness between the two passages in mind. It is unlikely that an audience will remark it.

—and readily do they adapt their artlessly servile minds to it. A great man; they might have known that, of course, despite his rags, from his high-minded way with them. And if great, if, in the next breath "the rarest man i' the world," why, another must be the lesser. Promptly begins the comically pitiful little shuffle of loyalties, their servile version of the tragic treason upon which they have been eavesdropping.

> a greater soldier than he, you wot on.
> Who? my master?
> Nay, it's no matter for that.
> Worth six on him? Nay, not so neither: but I take him to be the better soldier.
> Faith, look you, one cannot tell how to say that. . . .

—for in prudence we must both commit ourselves, or neither. And to Third Servant strutting excitedly in—happy to have been knocked over the pate with his own trencher by so great a man— and to his reckless

> here's he that was wont to thwack our general. . . .

First Servant makes shocked protest:

> Why do you say "thwack our general"?

reducing him to double-quick recanting:

> I do not say "thwack our general. . . ."

But, with a wink and a wag of the head from Second Servant,

> Come, we are fellows and friends. . . .

the three are in a tale together.

The consummation of Coriolanus' welcome, the sight of him

> set at upper end o' the table; no question asked him by any of the Senators, but they stand bald before him. . . .

while

> Our general himself makes a mistress of him; sanctifies himself with's hand, and turns up the white o' the eye to his discourse. . . .

—this we see through the simpleton eyes of Third Servant, puffed with the pride of coming fresh from the very sight of it. The comic coloring of the picture heightens, by irony of contrast, its

tragic import. The blundering parroting of the talk at table over
the noble renegade's prospects—

> for, look you, sir, he has as many friends as enemies; which
> friends, sir, as it were, durst not, look you, sir, show themselves,
> as we term it, his friends, whilst he's in directitude. . . . But
> when they shall see, sir, his crest up again, and the man in blood,
> they will out of their burrows like conies after rain, and revel
> all with him.

—embellishes its cynical shrewdness. And already, while Aufidius
is still erecting his fragile fane of devotion to his late enemy, this
belittling of him by these faithful followers is providing for its
wreck.

The scene ends with a noncombatants' chorus in praise of war,
coming from Volscians too, who have just been soundly beaten
and accorded by their conquerors a merciful peace.

ROME ONCE MORE

The Tribunes Sicinius and Brutus reappear; we are in Rome
again. They are pluming themselves upon

> the present peace
> And quietness o' the people . . .

upon—at this most appropriate moment!—having heard no more
of Coriolanus, while

> Here do we make his friends
> Blush that the world goes well, who rather had,
> Though they themselves did suffer by 't, behold
> Dissentious numbers pestering streets than see
> Our tradesmen singing in their shops and going
> About their functions friendly.

It may be so. But there are men—politicians and others—who
learn, whether by experience or from the book of their own natures, to think the worst of everyone. Menenius, passing by, out-
faces their complacency—

> Your Coriolanus is not much missed
> But with his friends: the Commonwealth doth stand.
> And so would do, were he more angry at it.

—with a glum, blunt

> All's well, and might have been much better if
> He could have temporised.

After which they take the opportunity that offers of edifyingly patronizing a group of humbly grateful citizens—who beseech the gods preserve them, who for

> Ourselves, our wives and children, on our knees,
> Are bound to pray for you both.

to be unctuously repaid by a showering of

> Good den our neighbours.
> Good den to you all, good den to you all. . . .
> Live and thrive!
> Farewell, kind neighbours. . . .

with—a sting for Menenius!—a

> we wished Coriolanus
> Had loved you as we did.

It is for a beginning to the play's ending that we are given this passage of sharp contrast with its beginning; the genial bullying of the citizens by Menenius, their brutal rating by Marcius, here replaced by the soft smiles of their Tribunes—from which official fool's paradise they are very quickly to be expelled.

From its beginning to the moment of Marcius' banishment the play has abounded in physical action, in battles and rioting. From now to the verge of its concluding catastrophe we shall have only the increasing tension of the threat of his reprisals; then, suddenly, their frustration. The battle to be fought now is one of moral forces, culminating in the struggle between Marcius and Volumnia, in which, silently at the last, he accepts defeat. The two sections of the play stand in nearly every respect contrasted. The scene with Aufidius in Antium may be called a bridge between the two; that of Marcius' death is in the nature of an epilogue.

The drama of Coriolanus' approach to his revenge begins at a very zero point, that of Brutus' fatuous

> Rome
> Sits safe and still without him.

Promptly an Aedile appears, to convey, with due official dignity,

the news, brought by "a slave, whom we have put in prison . . ."
that

> the Volsces with two several powers
> Are entered in the Roman territories. . . .

For Menenius, it is Marcius' banishing that has brought them,
Aufidius, doubtless, at their head. For Brutus, such an unpleasant
thing simply "cannot be" and the slave must be whipped for
saying so. "Cannot?"; but it has been, thrice within Menenius'
memory. Sicinius is as blandly confident:

> Tell not me;
> I know this cannot be.

Whereupon

Enter a Messenger.

Shakespeare gives a hundred lines more to the completing of
this scene of the Tribunes' discomfiture, and the whole is a
minor masterpiece of treatment. He employs the economical
convention of the Messenger, which gives drama the continuity
of narrative. But, to vary and enrich it, the story to be told is put
into four mouths instead of one, differing in temper and quality,
each supplementing or revising the other. The Aedile is un-
hurried and correct. He has taken order with the slave; he reports
the matter; his duty is done. The first Messenger is precipitate
and perturbed; wide-eyed. Is it to be believed, this rumor

> that Marcius,
> Joined with Aufidius, leads a power 'gainst Rome,
> And vows revenge . . .

Menenius, for a moment, is at one with the Tribunes in disbelief.
But the pendulum is swung violently back by the coming of a
second Messenger in all haste to summon the pair without
ceremony to the Senate, the ill news cumulated into worse:

> A fearful army, led by Caius Marcius,
> Associated with Aufidius, rages
> Upon our territories; and have already
> O'erborne their way, consumed with fire, and took
> What lay before them.

And, before they can take breath to protest, comes finally Co-

minius, not only to confirm it but, with grimly humorous satisfaction, to point them out as the culprits:

> O, you have made good work.

Trouble not to be mended by the whipping of a slave! The
Tribunes are struck dumb.

Cominius does not spare them, keeps Menenius impatiently
demanding his news while he loads them with terrors:

> You have holp to ravish your own daughters, and
> To melt the city leads upon your pates,
> To see your wives dishonoured to your noses—

and—this is the fruit of their rule in Rome—

> *Your* temples burned in their cement, and
> *Your* franchises, whereon you stood . . .

Menenius—his still incredulous

> If Marcius should be joined with Volscians—

extinguished by the sardonic acclaim of

> If!
> He is their god; he leads them like a thing
> Made by some other deity than Nature,
> That shapes man better; and they follow him
> Against us brats. . . .

—takes up the refrain too:

> You have made good work,
> You, and your apron men . . .
> You have made fair work!

until Brutus at last finds a meek and fearful tongue:

> But is this true, sir?

Satisfaction with the vengeance to fall on the Tribunes—capable
themselves now of little but agonized grimaces—mingles in
Cominius and Menenius with genuine alarm for Rome.[46] This is
shot through with renewed pride in Marcius—one of themselves—

---

[46] Brutus and Sicinius are semi-comic characters, and the actors of them were,
I think, expected to make their conspicuous silence here even more conspicuous
by facial play.

and the power of his name, this again with the shameful memory
that they, his friends, abandoned him.

> We loved him; but, like beasts
> And cowardly nobles, gave way unto your clusters,
> Who did hoot him out o' the city.

The theme of betrayal and self-betrayal permeates the play.
Some "clusters" gathering round—

> *Enter a troop of Citizens.*

—Menenius can relieve his mind with a little of his old frank
abuse of them. Echoing from past clashes,

> Now he's coming. . . .
> as many coxcombs
> As you threw caps up will he tumble down,
> And pay you for your voices. . . .

Cominius echoing him with a

> Ye're goodly things, you voices!

they leave the poor citizens to their pitiful excuses—

> That we did we did for the best; and though we willingly
> consented to his banishment, yet it was against our will.

—and the Tribunes, freed from their daunting presence, to the
flattering futility of

> Go, masters, get you home, be not dismayed:
> These are a side that would be glad to have
> This true which they so seem to fear. . . .

Spiritless all, they go their several ways. Menenius and Cominius:

> Shall's to the Capitol?
> O, ay; what else!

The Second Citizen to the rest:

> But come, let's home.

Sicinius to his fellow:

> Pray, let's go.

While as to Brutus, his rueful

> Would half my wealth
> Would buy this for a lie!

reminds us, incidentally, that politics and the leadership of the poor can be made to pay.

AUFIDIUS DISILLUSIONED;
MARCIUS SCANNED

The scene between Aufidius and his Lieutenant prepares the play's final stroke without discounting this by telling us too clearly what it is to be. The impulsive generosity to a fallen enemy has soon burned out in him, and Aufidius, recovered from the experience and ready to treat Marcius as an enemy again, can estimate his virtues and failings the more fairly, even though he is now but the more set to "potch" at his prodigious rival by

> some way
> Or wrath or craft may get him.

For generosity repented has hardened him,

> I do not know what witchcraft's in him. . . .

says the Lieutenant. Well, Aufidius himself has been its victim, and, beside him, will doubtless be

> darkened in this action . . .

—which, however, since there's to be Volscian profit in it, must be carried through. It is only too true that

> All places yield to him ere he sits down;
> And the nobility of Rome are his;
> The Senators and Patricians love him too:
> The Tribunes are no soldiers, and their people
> Will be as rash in the repeal as hasty
> To expel him thence. I think he'll be to Rome
> As is the osprey to the fish, who takes it
> By sovereignty of nature. . . .

But—! Now follows the coldly, carefully, qualified verdict of second-rate success upon first-rate failure:

> First he was
> A noble servant to them, but he could not
> Carry his honours even. Whether 'twas pride . . .
> whether defect of judgment . . .
> or whether nature,

Not to be other than one thing . . .
> but one of these,
As he has spices of them all—not all,
For I dare so far free him—made him feared,
So hated, and so banished. . . .

Let the greatly gifted man remember, then, that

> So our virtues
> Lie in the interpretation of the time. . . .

and, their turn served, are apt to be canceled out. It will be so
with Coriolanus:

> One fire drives out one fire; one nail, one nail;
> Rights by rights founder, strengths by strengths do fail.

Aufidius, nursing his plans, his last lethal stroke conceived, is
oracular:

> When, Caius, Rome is thine,
> Thou are poor'st of all; then shortly are thou mine.[47]

The scene allows incidentally for the time taken by Cominius'
intercessory visit to Coriolanus, now encamped before Rome. This
is over when the next opens, with the tension notably increased by
its failure.

NEMESIS NEARS

*Enter Menenius, Cominius, Sicinius, Brutus, the two
Tribunes, with others.*

—*with others,* listeners and onlookers; a token of the general
anxiety.

Grave as they saw it to be, their enjoyment in saddling the

---

[47] Such now unusual phrases as "not moving from the casque to the cushion"
and "even with the same austerity and garb as he controlled the war" increase
for us the difficulty of following Aufidius' analysis of Coriolanus' virtues and
defects, its repeated "whether . . . s" making it already difficult enough. (The
trick of the speech, one notes, is much that of Hamlet's "So oft it chances in
particular men. . . .") And in quoting it here I have had, so as to isolate the
continuity of thought, to reduce it to an ugly skeleton. Then, when it comes to
the more general comments on success and failure, we meet with a corruption of
the text—"hath not a tomb so evident as a chair . . ."—which no one yet, as far
as I know, has been able satisfactorily to clarify. Altogether, it is a troublesome
speech to the modern actor; and Aufidius, as a whole, may be called a troublesome character in the acting. Shakespeare, it seems, found him interesting, but
would not afford space for his expansion. (Cf. p. 173.)

Tribunes with the blame for it was some sign that Cominius and
Menenius had not, despite all, thought the situation quite hope-
less, had underlyingly felt, rather, that even though they had
deserved Marcius' hate, "and therein showed like enemies," yet
they were the men to redeem it. But Cominius has been on his
mission since: and

> He would not seem to know me.

Once, indeed, he did call him by his name. But thereafter,

> Coriolanus
> He would not answer to, forbad all names;
> He was a kind of nothing, titleless,
> Till he had forged himself a name o' the fire
> Of burning Rome.

Plea following plea, none moved him, nor will; Cominius is
hopelessly sure of it.

Menenius, on the other hand, protesting that he never can
succeed if Cominius has failed—

> He called me father,
> But what o' that? . . .
> Nay, if he coyed
> To hear Cominius speak, I'll keep at home.

—is plainly "coying" himself, and only waiting to be pressed
harder to consent, in his turn, to go. He is cheerful enough still
to be mockingly reminding the now quite crestfallen Brutus and
Sicinius that they

> have made good work!
> A pair of Tribunes that have racked for Rome,
> To make coals cheap . . .

There is no spirit left in them. Sicinius, begging him to go, is
reduced to the pitiful

> if you refuse your aid
> In this so never-needed help, yet do not
> Upbraid's with our distress. . . .

An "instant army" will be all they can muster for Rome's
protection.[48] They fall to wheedling and flattering him. Even if

---

[48] It is implied in more than one passage that the Tribunes now rule Rome,
and Aufidius has just remarked of them that they "are no soldiers." Theirs is, in

he fails, Sicinius says:

> Yet your good will
> Must have that thanks from Rome, after the measure
> As you intended well.

—which puts him on his mettle. A final show of diffidence, for tribute to "good Cominius" and his failure, and he is the buoyant old Menenius still:

> He was not taken well; he had not dined.
> The veins unfilled, our blood is cold, and then
> We pout upon the morning, are unapt
> To give or to forgive; but when we have stuffed
> These pipes and these conveyances of our blood
> With wine and feeding, we have suppler souls
> Than in our priest-like fasts. . . .

—the imagery characteristically recalls our first hearing from him with the fable of the Belly and the Members—

> therefore I'll watch him
> Till he be dieted to my request,
> And then I'll set upon him.

And, cheerily confident, off he goes.

Cominius has listened in silence. He shakes his head, strikes the stern note again:

> He'll never hear him. . . .
> I tell you, he does sit in gold, his eye
> Red as 't would burn Rome, and his injury
> The gaoler to his pity. . . .

pictures and prepares us for the pitiless figure we are soon to see.

Then, to end the scene, the step beyond the next is forecast:

> So that all hope is vain,
> Unless his noble mother and his wife,
> Who, as I hear, mean to solicit him
> For mercy to his country. . . .

As the crisis nears the action is knit the closer, that our attention may be the more closely held.

---

fact, what would be called today a "pacifist" government, quite unprepared for war.

MENENIUS TRIES, AND FAILS

Enter Menenius to the Watch or Guard.

Yet another encounter between patrician and commoners, and a scene of ebb and flow of emotion and humor before—it will be a contrast—the powerfully sustained tension of the trial to come. Menenius deploys his tact. He answers the sentry's sharp challenge with affable praise:

> You guard like men, 'tis well. . . .

asserts his own quality with accustomed ease:

> but, by your leave,
> I am an officer of state, and come
> To speak with Coriolanus.

—in vain. The sentries disappointingly deserve his praise.

> You may not pass, you must return. . . .
> You'll see your Rome embraced with fire before
> You'll speak with Coriolanus.

He tries the flattery of familiarity:

> Good my friends,
> If you have heard your general talk of Rome,
> And of his friends there, it is lots to blanks,
> My name hath touched your ears: it is Menenius.

is brought to vaunting his own with the great man—

> I tell thee, fellow,
> Thy general is my lover. . . .

—and, in euphemistic phrase, the unconscionable services he has done him:

> Therefore, fellow,
> I must have leave to pass.

Hectorings and wittiness alike get plain answer:

> Faith, sir, if you had told as many lies in his behalf as you
> have uttered words in your own, you should not pass here. . . .

But the old gentleman persists, to be given finally a sound and most disrespectful talking to:

> You are a Roman, are you?
> I am, as thy general is.

Then you should hate Rome, as he does. Can you, when you have pushed out your gates the very defender of them . . . ?

Truly these Volscian sentries know their own minds and can speak them; the dose no pleasanter to Menenius for its likeness to his own recent medicining of the Tribunes. And if it is to come to an issue between fretful dignity on one side and discipline with cold steel to warrant it on the other—

Sirrah, if thy captain knew I were here, he would use me with estimation.
Come, my captain knows you not.
I mean thy general.
My general cares not for you. Back, I say, go: lest I let forth your half-pint of blood. Back; that's the utmost of your having: back.
Nay, but fellow, fellow—!

At which moment Coriolanus and Aufidius pass.
After a sharp, soldierly
What's the matter?

Coriolanus waits in silence, fulfillment of Cominius' picture of him. Menenius, tossed between emotions, lets the lightest first possess him; tit-for-tat with impudent sentries will restore him his confident good humor.

Now, you companion . . . you shall perceive that a Jack guardant cannot office me from my son Coriolanus. . . .

He is himself again in the jaunty extravagance of

guess but by my entertainment with him, if thou standest not i' the state of hanging, or of some death more long in spectatorship, and crueller in suffering; behold now presently and swoon for what's to come upon thee.

It gives him time, too, in which to face this changed Marcius, distant, mute, hostile, companioned there with Aufidius. But he neither hesitates nor calculates. Eloquence overflows in affection and tears:

The glorious gods sit in hourly synod about thy particular prosperity, and love thee no worse than thy old father Menenius does! O my son! my son! thou art preparing fire for us: look thee, here's water to quench it. . . .

and, for a final fillip, into the familiar humor:

> The good gods assuage thy wrath, and turn the dregs of it
> upon this varlet here; this, who, like a block, hath denied my
> access to thee.

The one word of the answer, spanning the space between them—

> Away!

—falls like a blow. The old man staggers under it. Had he ears for
aught else he might note in the sequent

> Wife, mother, child, I know not. . . .

the flaw in the armor of which that too rigid figure is himself
aware, might even read in the strain of the

> Yet—for I loved thee—
> Take this along, I writ it for thy sake
> And would have sent it. . . .

in this letter with which he is dismissed, defense ready to crumble.
But pride, if not affection, is now too wounded for him to think
of aught else.

Coriolanus and Aufidius pass on their way:

> This man, Aufidius,
> Was my beloved in Rome; yet thou beholdst!

to which utterance of twisted, tortured pride Aufidius pays
sardonic tribute:

> You keep a constant temper.

But Menenius can take a blow gallantly still, and pay back
mockery with mockery. To the sentries' jubilant

> Now, sir, is your name Menenius?
> 'Tis a spell, you see, of much power. You know the way home
> again.
> Do you hear how we are shent for keeping your greatness
> back?
> What cause, do you think, I have to swoon?

he returns as good as he gets, and better:

> I neither care for the world, nor your general: for such things
> as you, I can scarce think there's any, y'are so slight. . . .

—but it is graver defiance than that—

Coriolanus 261

He that hath a will to die by himself, fears it not from
another. Let your general do his worst. . . .

—no business of theirs though!

For you, be that you are, long; and your misery increase with
age! I say to you, as I was said to, Away!

They are left laughing; won, nevertheless, to the verdict of

A noble fellow, I warrant him.

VOLUMNIA COMES, AND THE CONQUEROR IS CONQUERED

Coriolanus and Aufidius were, it seems, on their way to a
council of war; they are taking their places at its table now.[49]
First, formally and for all to hear, the two exchange assurances
that so far in this strange business all has been frankly done.
Aufidius is most generous in his assurance. Coriolanus then falls
to confession; and—how changed!—it is of kindly, politic trickery. "With a cracked heart" it was, then, that he stood outfacing
Menenius there; and he had offered him in the letter, to make
things easier for them both, something to carry away that he yet
knew must be rejected. It was only

A very little
I have yielded to. . . .

but it is right they know it. That is all finished now. Then

Shout within.

He asks what it may mean, knowing too well:

Shall I be tempted to infringe my vow
In the same time 'tis made? . . .

The dreaded trial has come. He steels himself:

I will not.

<hr>

[49] The Folio stage direction for the first scene is simply *Enter Coriolanus and
Aufidius.* Capell added *and others*; and pretty plainly Coriolanus is not speaking
to Aufidius alone. The council of war at a table set upon the inner stage is as
easily deduced. The curtains will be closed as the two pass across the outer stage,
finding Menenius there. They could be discovered when the curtains are drawn,
the fifteen lines or so spoken by the Watch and Menenius allowing them that
much time to take their places, or, having gone off by the side door, they can
wait and enter again upon the inner stage.

The pending struggle has been fully prepared. Cominius, Consul and General, revered as both, kneeling, repulsed, the loved Menenius dismissed—this the one aspect, completed by the sentry's admiring view of the traitor-hero as

> the rock, the oak not to be wind-shaken.

For another; he has armored himself with an oath offered to Aufidius, a vow solemnly taken. The closer our sight of him, the plainer it is that nevertheless he feels not so sure of the issue. He has a fight still to win. And the play is not over yet.

When he sees the figures of the women approaching the scene's tension rises instantly to high pitch. It is to be a long scene, of a struggle the deadlier for its quiet; even as wrestlers in a lock strain silently, motionless, until one is exhausted and as silently loosens grasp, and the match is over. The tension will hardly relax; a moment's relief, and it tightens again. The action is clearly articulated, deliberate, sparse; the speech indicates it and allows for it. Marcius is its firm and sensitive center. The argument ranges round him, widely, closely; touches him as husband, lover, father, son, Roman, uses his wife's tears, his boy's gallantly shrill defiance, Volumnia's desperate barring of the end to this road on which—it was she that set him. Silence is his ultimate answer; and the whole, with its passion, in its intimacies and simplicities, is keyed to the tenor of a great event.

Note the dramatic generalship with which Shakespeare employs his forces. First is the duel effect made by the mute, anonymous approach of the women, their speech, even for a moment their identity, held in reserve, while Marcius, describing them, at once interprets besides the effect made on him.[50] The battle begins and ends with a struggle within himself. It will end in silence; it

---

[50] The *in mourning habits* of the stage direction for this entrance is owed, apparently, to Capell. It implies veils, and is, I think, justified. The stage picture intended is not hard to reconstruct. Coriolanus will be seated at the council table on the inner stage surrounded by the contrastingly uniformed Volscian generals. The *Shout within* heralds the entry by a side door of the little group of veiled women and their attendants, who stand facing him and more or less with their backs to the audience, so that the "curtsy," and, upon Virgilia's unveiling, the "doves' eyes" and Volumnia's "bow" take effect more directly upon him than upon us. "Describing them"; I do not, of course, mean to imply to the Volscian generals, but to himself and to us, as the convention of that stage allowed.

begins articulately. Back and forth he is swayed; by the very sight, the first since his exile, of those three that he loves.[51]

> But out, affection!
> All bond and privilege of nature break!
> Let it be virtuous to be obstinate! . . .

Then, his wife's "doves' eyes" turned on him:

> I melt, and am not
> Of stronger earth than others. . . .

Lastly, to break the spell of Volumnia's grave obeisance, and against his boy's

> aspect of intercession, which
> Great nature cries, "Deny not." . . .

he violently flings away with

> Let the Volsces
> Plough Rome and harrow Italy; I'll never
> Be such a gosling to obey instinct, but stand
> As if a man were author of himself
> And knew no other kin.

But he is drawn to face Virgilia and her gentle

> My lord and husband.

to invite, with his repelling

> These eyes are not the same I wore in Rome.

her as gently keen

> The sorrow that delivers *us* thus changed
> Makes you think so.

He owns to the effect of the thrust:

> Like a dull actor now,
> I have forgot my part, and I am out,
> Even to a full disgrace. . . .

and, the next instant, she is in his arms.

---

51 "Long as my exile. . . ," he says later. Actually how long Shakespeare leaves indeterminate; but while the suggestion, when he comes to Aufidius in Antium, is that he has lost little time in doing so, here and hereabouts the implication is that, at any rate, much has changed in his absence. There is no need at either juncture to be exact, so that—open inconsistency avoided—the dramatic best can be made of each calendar.

> Best of my flesh,
> Forgive my tyranny; but do not say
> For that "Forgive our Romans." O, a kiss,
> Long as my exile, sweet as my revenge!
> Now, by the jealous queen of heaven, that kiss
> I carried from thee, dear, and my true lip
> Hath virgined it e'er since. You gods! I prate. . . .

Much of Marcius is lit up in this. In his love for his wife a quality of nature rarer than that bred of the exchange of pride between him and his mother. From it had sprung at his triumphal entry into Rome the thought of the Volscian widows left desolate; the kindling touch of her lips might free him to sudden forgiveness now. Love and hate are near akin in him, are but the two sides of the one shield; and each he justifies by what he does, and that by what he is. To spend more words on either is to "prate."

He turns to

> the most noble mother of the world . . .

and with a

> Sink, my knee, i' the earth. . . .

gives her full due. She bids him

> stand up blest!

then kneels herself, thus "unproperly," she says, to

> Show duty, as mistaken all this while,
> Between the child and parent.

She shocks him, and means to. But the irony is rather in the event; and when he raises her she unconsciously gives it voice again:

> Thou art my warrior;
> I holp to frame thee.

She did indeed! As well her teaching as his learning has brought them to this pass.[52]

~~~~~~~~~

[52] This kneeling of each to other recalls Cordelia and King Lear. Shakespeare had found that in the old play about King Lear and his daughters. It clearly makes an affecting picture. Whether it was a favorite one with other dramatists of the time I am not well enough read to say. Whether or no, ceremonial kneeling was then in habitual use, and widely by comparison with the few occasions on which it is called for now.

Valeria, dignified, beautiful, silent—

> The noble sister of Publicola,
> The moon of Rome, chaste as the icicle
> That's curded by the frost from purest snow,
> And hangs on Dian's temple . . .

—follows in her place. Is she also to find her fate in the sack of a city?[53] Lastly the boy is put forward, sturdily stubborn, even against this great man his father's thrilling exhortation, until Volumnia takes order with a stern

> Your knee, sirrah!

and Marcius, delighting in him:

> That's my brave boy!

He, who has never counted the odds at which he fought, has never had to fight, surely, at such odds as this.

Volumnia, with due dignity, opens her plea. Upon its very threshold he stops her, the more petitionary himself in his denials:

> Do not bid me
> Dismiss my soldiers. . . .
> tell me not
> Wherein I seem unnatural, desire not
> To allay my rages and revenges. . . .

But she answers with an insistence matching his own:

> O, no more, no more!
> You have said you will not grant us any thing,
> For we have nothing else to ask but that
> Which you deny already. . . .

an obstinacy too:

> Yet we will ask. . . .

So he turns back to Aufidius and the Volsces, returns to their

---

[53] To suggest this, by her mere appearance in the scene, with, for aid, the gem-like phrase describing her put into Coriolanus' mouth, seems to be her only use to it. But it is an incidental use of some little value; and since Shakespeare had her available, why not bring her on? One may even speculate whether the part itself does not chiefly owe its existence to such a fact as that the King's Men had, at this juncture, a boy in the company, who could both look and act it well. Even in these, their well-furnished days, they were unlikely to be overburdened with that sort of thing.

council table, seats himself there again, as in judgment with them.[54]

Her speech before this strange tribunal comes from a Volumnia compelled at last to see Coriolanus' valor from the standpoint of the vanquished. The exulting fierceness of her once-triumphant

> Death, that dark spirit, in 's nervy arm doth lie. . . .

has melted to the grief of

> Think with thyself
> How more unfortunate than all living women
> Are we come hither. . . .
>   the mother, wife and child to see
> The son, the husband and the father tearing
> His country's bowels out. . . .

grief highly argued:

>   thou barr'st us
> Our prayers to the gods. . . .
>   for how can we,
> Alas! how can we for our country pray,
> Whereto we are bound, together with thy victory,
> Whereto we are bound? . . .

Yet out of the deadlock and division to which pride and wrath—his fostering of it, and hers—have brought them, out of the fatal dilemma—

>   for either thou
> Must, as a foreign recreant, be led
> With manacles through our streets, or else
> Triumphantly tread on thy country's ruin. . . .

—she sees one way. But—Volumnia still!—her passion bids fair to swamp her very plea for following it

>   For myself, son . . .
>   if I cannot persuade thee
> Rather to show a noble grace to both parts
> Than seek the end of one, thou shalt no sooner
> March to assault thy country than to tread—
> Trust to 't, thou shalt not—on thy mother's womb,
> That brought thee to this world.

---

[54] Note (once more) the visual effect of this, the contrast in the dress they wear, he the single Roman among these Volsces.

Virgilia echoing her with

> Ay, and mine,
> That brought you forth this boy, to keep your name
> Living to time.

even the child, ridiculously, gallantly defiant:

> A' shall not tread on me;
> I'll run away till I am bigger, but then I'll fight.

Thus does this breed set about making peace.[55]
Marcius sits silent until the effect of the triply unanswerable
challenge has died away. Then, quietly, reflectively, to the foiled
self in him:

> Not of a woman's tenderness to be,
> Requires nor child nor woman's face to see.

And he rises and moves mechanically away, defeated and avoiding
defeat. Volumnia's pursuing arguments sound strange to him;
from her to him they well may! "Our suit is, that you reconcile
..."! The Volsces are to say,

> "This mercy we have showed"; the Romans
> "This we received"; and each in either side
> Give the all-hail to thee, and cry "Be blest
> For making up this peace!"

She to be telling him:

> The end of war's uncertain. . . .

asking him:

> Thinkst thou it honourable for a noble man
> Still to remember wrongs?

Is this Volumnia?

---

[55] Were Shakespeare a didactic dramatist how well he might from this point
build up his play to a moral and a happy ending: Marcius and his family
reunited, Romans and Volsces clasping hands, peace over all! But he has the
historic story to deal with (Plutarch is not to be lightly treated) and the tragedy
it involves—which, however, we must remark, is a tragedy, not wholly of
character, but of character and circumstance combined.

Volumnia (of all people) urges reconciliation. Coriolanus is not the man to
sponsor that; he can at best, he feels, stand aside and "make convenient peace."
But Aufidius also has to be reckoned with, and the Volscians who, for their part,
want loot. It is in the fresh circumstances of the squabble over this that
"character" once more plays Coriolanus false, and Aufidius can seize the chance to
kill him.

It is here that his silence comes to be stressed by the baffled recurrence of her

> Speak to me, son. . . .
> Why dost not speak? . . .
> yet here he lets me prate

Like one i' the stocks. . . .

> He turns away.

And the technique of the scene is in itself remarkable. Usually such a speech as this will concentrate our attention on the speaker; and, the more strongly, the less of even a side-glance from us can surrounding characters claim. But Volumnia makes Virgilia's tears, the child's high spirit, Valeria's quiet dignity a living part of the action, adding their eloquence in its kind to her own, to wield it all against the opposing silence of Marcius' last stand.

His silence counterbalances, and by a little will outbalance, her share in the encounter. For she ceases her attack, unbeaten but munition spent—

> I am husht until our city be a-fire,
> And then I'll speak a little.

—and still he has not answered.

> *Holds her by the hand, silent.*

is the stage direction, Shakespeare's own certainly. In the silence is his answer, and he spares her all other. She has won. And for him

> the heavens do ope,
> The gods look down, and this unnatural scene
> They laugh at. . . .

—unnatural, since pride and her pride in him have brought him to this, and she that helped make him is bidding him remake himself now. And that he can no longer do. Mercy and forgiveness are not for him. And it is she that has vanquished him. Only she could.

He gently warns her of what may follow:

> O, my mother, mother! O!
> You have won a happy victory to Rome;
> But for your son, believe it, O, believe it,

> Most dangerously you have with him prevailed
> If not most mortal to him. . . .

But, the great strain relaxed, she seemingly thinks but of her victory and does not heed. He braces himself again—as at the beginning of the struggle, so now to what must follow—with a

> But let it come.

next, pride abated, turns to Aufidius—out of all the world—for sympathy:

> Now, good Aufidius,
> Were you in my stead, would you have heard
> A mother less, or granted less, Aufidius?

—who, coldly observant, commits himself to no more than a

> I was moved withal.

and then comes to the decision that is to be his death:

> for my part,
> I'll not to Rome. I'll back with you; and pray you,
> Stand to me in this cause. . . .

Aufidius felt sure (we heard him say) that even those in Rome who feared Marcius most

> Will be as rash in the repeal, as hasty
> To expel him thence . . .

But if the traitor prefers conflict in Corioles, so much the worse for him—and the better for Aufidius!

It is not in Marcius to enter Rome again. For the last time—he knows to what he may be going—he lets himself be stirred to his depths:

> O, mother! wife!

After which, lest they should now catch up with his thoughts, should try, as it seems they will, to keep him there, he plays the man of affairs with them, the game loser:

> Ay, by and by;
> But we will drink together, and you shall bear
> A better witness back than words. . . .

Gallantly courteous, he addresses the whole train:

> Ladies, you deserve
> To have a temple built to you: all the swords
> In Italy, and her confederate arms,
> Could not have made this peace.

ROME DELIVERED

Rome fearfully awaits news of her fate. *We* already know it, so the suspense must not be spun out. Menenius returning meets Sicinius, while the issue is still, he supposes, in doubt, and he can avenge on him his own repulse by assurance that Volumnia will do no better. The old Tribune is in despair:

> He loved his mother dearly.

and Menenius finds satisfaction of the perverser sort in:

> So did he me; and he no more remembers his mother now
> than an eight-year-old horse. The tartness of his face sours ripe
> grapes. . . . Mark what mercy his mother shall bring from him:
> there is no more mercy in him than there is milk in a male
> tiger; that shall our poor city find. . . .

and so falls back upon

> all this is long of you.

There comes yet more for him in a messenger's tidings that the Plebeians have now seized upon the wretched Brutus,

> And hale him up and down; all swearing, if
> The Roman ladies bring not comfort home,
> They'll give him death by inches.

So when the good news arrives that

> the ladies have prevailed,
> The Volscians are dislodged, and Marcius gone. . . .

he can but be at first a trifle disappointed. Sicinius, for his part, who would not credit the bad news when it came, is wary of the good news now.

> Friend,
> Art thou certain this is true? is it most certain?

But the rejoicing sounds without are evidence enough:

> *Trumpets, hoboyes, drums beate altogether.*

Shakespeare's theater can do no more. From Menenius, then, breaks a generously happy

> This is good news:
> I will go meet the ladies. This Volumnia
> Is worth of consuls, senators, patricians,
> A city full . . .

with, for a last humorous gibe,

> of Tribunes, such as you,
> A sea and land full.

and he is away.[56]

Sicinius, so barely saved, must reassert his dignity:

> First, the gods bless you for your tidings; next,
> Accept *my* thankfulness.

The Messenger, afflicted by no such pomposity:

> Sir, we have all
> Great cause to give great thanks.

Rome's saviors near the city; at point to enter! A Tribune's benign presence is called for:

> We will meet them,
> And help the joy.

VOLUMNIA'S TRIUMPH

Enter two Senators, with Ladies, passing over the stage, with other Lords.

Thus this short stretch of the action ends, with such a procession, so acclaimed, as that which once brought Coriolanus back in triumph from his wars. And the people are to

> Unshout the noise that banished Marcius,
> Repeal him with the welcome of his mother. . . .

—but too late.

THE END

Enter Tullus Aufidius with Attendants.

—the *Attendants* an opening suggestion of authority.

---

[56] The Folio's stage directions leave him, by default, included in the general *Exeunt* a few lines later. But clearly he does not wait for Sicinius.

Aufidius gives the tone to this, the play's last scene. Its doings
are to win him success, and he promptly assumes control of them:

> Go tell the lords o' the city I am here;
> Deliver them this paper: having read it,
> Bid them repair to the market place. . . .
>   Him I accuse
> The city ports by this hath entered, and
> Intends to appear before the people, hoping
> To purge himself with words. Dispatch.

Of all men, Coriolanus, "to appear before the people" that he may
"purge himself with words"! The attendants go about the
business given them, and are replaced by

> *3 or 4 Conspirators of Aufidius' Faction.*

and he and they proceed to make the case against Coriolanus.
Aufidius is an injured man, and although

> We must proceed as we do find the people.

—as troublesome in Corioles as in Rome apparently—it should
not be hard to show him a wronged man. Such generosity as he
has shown, with such advantage taken of it! For the "witchcraft," we may note, which once made men "fly to the Roman"—
Aufidius among them!—has now become the

>   dews of flattery,
> Seducing so my friends . . .

And, above all,

> When he had carried Rome, and that we looked
> For no less spoil than glory—

for this, at least, Aufidius promises,

>   my sinews shall be stretched upon him. . . .
>   he sold the blood and labour
> Of our great action; therefore he shall die,
> And I'll renew me in his fall. . . .

—at which moment

> *Drums and trumpets sound, with great shouts of the people.*

So Marcius comes in triumph, if not back to Rome, into
Corioles. His rival stands to listen. And, were more provocation
needed, friends provide it in their low reminder that

Coriolanus 273

Your native town you entered like a post,
And had no welcomes home; but he returns
Splitting the air with noise.
                    And patient fools,
Whose children he hath slain, their base throats tear
With giving him glory.

The lords of the city, now arriving, offer their welcome, none
the less—which Aufidius, with a certain sulky modesty, disclaims.
More to the purpose, they have digested his charges against
Marcius, the last that he should

                    give away
The benefit of our levies, answering us
With our own charge: making a treaty where
There was a yielding; this admits no excuse.

and Aufidius can afford to stand aside; with an

          He approaches: you shall hear him.

    Note now the stage direction:

*Enter Coriolanus marching with drum and colours; the
Commoners being with him.*

He is in full panoply of war, an impressive, a commanding figure.
This is he to whose side Aufidius' soldiers flocked. Aufidius himself looks and will feel nothing beside him. Moreover, the
commoners are with him, to cheer or hoot him, as the Roman
commoners did. They are cheering him now. And whatever the
Volscian case against him, he means to make a good one for
himself. But it is a hardened Marcius that makes it:

          Hail, lords! I am returned your soldier,
          No more infected with my country's love
          Than when I parted hence, but still subsisting
          Under your great command. . . .

a Marcius brought to claiming that

              Our spoils we have brought home
          Doth more than counterpoise a full third part
          The charges of the action. . . .

—the man of whom it could be said in Rome that

> Our spoils he kicked at,
> And looked upon things precious as they were
> The common muck of the world. . . .

Not that a third of the cost of the war is matter of great account either! But he means to make himself a place here too. He must. He has no other left.

Aufidius sees this, and that he must strike hard, and without delay. "Traitor" is a sharp blow; and the derisive "Marcius" added—

> Ay, Marcius, Caius Marcius. Dost thou think
> I'll grace thee with that robbery, thy stolen name
> Coriolanus in Corioles?

—will draw his enemy towards tricky ground. He says no word of his own wrongs; only that:

> You lords and heads o' the state, perfidiously
> He has betrayed your business, and given up,
> For certain drops of salt, your city Rome,
> I say "your city". . . .

The commoners are listening too, the conspirators are on the watch. Aufidius drives on:

> Breaking his oath and resolution like
> A twist of rotten silk . . .
> He whined and roared away your victory. . . .

To all of which Coriolanus has reasonable answer. But the insults to his soldiership, his manhood, blot out all else:

> Hear'st thou, Mars?

Aufidius ends with a contemptuous

> Name not the god, thou boy of tears. . . .
> No more.

Marcius, incandescent with anger:

> Measureless liar, thou hast made my heart
> Too great for what contains it. . . .

yet it is the "boy" that has pricked deepest, and the more intolerably for the truth of it. Of the lies let these "grave lords" judge; but for the liar himself:

> Who wears my stripes impressed upon him, that
> Must bear my beating to his grave . . .

Here is the old exultant—that boyishly exultant—Marcius. Let his enemies take vengeance on him if they will:

> Cut me to pieces, Volsces; men and lads,
> Stain all your edges on me. . . .

for

> If you have writ your annals true, 'tis there,
> That, like an eagle in a dove-cote, I
> Fluttered your Volscians in Corioles:
> Alone I did it. Boy!

One of Shakespeare's master-moments this, in which he brings the tragic figure to the very edge of the ridiculous, but stays him there.

Even as his friends in Rome were wont to check and save him, so might the Volscian lords, would he but let them:

> The man is noble, and his fame folds in
> This orb o' the earth. His last offence to us
> Shall have judicious hearing. . . .

But Aufidius, who while he rages can still calculate, in appealing to them is appealing over their heads to the commoners, those commoners that, in Corioles as in Rome, Coriolanus will so obligingly provoke for him:

> Why, noble lords,
> Will you be put in mind of his blind fortune,
> Which was your shame, by this unholy braggart,
> 'Fore your own eyes and ears?

It is the conspirators' cue for a fomenting

> Let him die for 't.

and, as once before, the mob howls for his blood. As once before too he draws his sword, disdaining aid:

> O! that I had him,
> With six Aufidiuses, or more, his tribe,
> To use my lawful sword.

An "Insolent villain!" from Aufidius gives the conspirators their cue again; and, with vociferous "Kills" to drown the cries of "Hold!", they crowd in on him, daggers drawn. He falls, and

Aufidius stands on him.

He stands on him! Could words say more?
His first thought is to justify his deed—

> My noble masters, hear me speak.

—and not until he hears the shocked reproaches does he realize
what he is shamefully doing now.

> O, Tullus! . . .
> Tread not upon him. Masters, all be quiet.
> Put up your swords.

But it will not be so difficult to persuade moderate men that,
though it has been wrong to kill him, yet Coriolanus is better
dead. Therefore

> Bear from hence his body,
> And mourn you for him. Let him be regarded
> As the most noble corse that ever herald
> Did follow to his urn.

The Second Lord already sees clearly the other side of the matter:

> His own impatience
> Takes from Aufidius a great part of blame.
> Let's make the best of it.

and Aufidius adds in all sincerity:

> My rage is gone,
> And I am struck with sorrow.

The Verse

In listening to the play we shall be conscious of the verse as a
thing in itself only at certain intenser moments, which are thus—
by one metrical device or another—emphasized and made
memorable. For the rest it will impress us rather as powerful,
rounded speech, resonant somewhat above the ordinary, and, in
particular, borne forward by a most compelling rhythm. A
change from verse to prose, even, we may chiefly remark as a
change of temper, a lessening of emotional pressure, or merely
a timely contrast.

Not for long now—by the measure of his swift development—
has Shakespeare habitually dealt in "set pieces" of verse, "Queen
Mab" speeches, pronouncements that "All the world's a stage" or

that "The quality of mercy is not strained"; and, even when he did, they would seldom lack some direct dramatic sanction. Portia's, for instance, is legitimate forensic eloquence, and Jaques has been cast, in the Arden pastoral, for the part of moralizer-in-chief to the banished Duke. Again, the speeches of the two Henrys upon sleeplessness, ceremony and kingship may, in method, be more rhetorical than reflective, but they suit both character and occasion. A little later, Brutus' ordered soliloquies come as the due expression of an ordered mind, and Mark Antony's oratory is directed first to his Roman hearers, and only through them upon us, the audience; and let actor or audience forget this and its dramatic purpose is warped. Then, with *Hamlet*—and in Hamlet's own speech particularly—we come within reach of a seeming spontaneity. Shakespeare allows him all possible scope of expression, both in prose and verse; and in the choice between them, and in the form and color of the verse as well as in its content, his every mood, of contemplation, irony or despair, will be sensitively reflected. It is, of course, only a "seeming spontaneity." People do not naturally speak verse, be it but blank verse; and even in prose, and for the simple speech of citizen or peasant, Shakespeare never lapses into an *imitated* spontaneity, so to forfeit all the aids of form and accepted convention.[57]

It is a consonant part—this reaching towards a seeming spontaneity—of Shakespeare's general development as a dramatist, and it necessarily tends to loosen and even break down the form of the verse. To begin with he is a poet writing plays—as Marlowe was, and Lyly—and his lengths of verse, often narrative or descriptive in their bent, will readily fall into regular form. And for long enough the form, a little eased or a little fortified, accommodates the direct expression of character and emotion very well, as, for instance, in the forthright Hotspur, less well for the subtler Richard II. It is when character and emotion gain complexity and extraordinary force that—as a stream in flood eats

---

[57] An earlier instance of this "seeming spontaneity" in verse can be found in the Nurse in *Romeo and Juliet*. Really, it sometimes seems as if Shakespeare must have had all the secrets of his art stored in him from the beginning, as if he had only to enlarge upon what he already knew.

its banks away—the verse breaks bounds; then Shakespeare himself has developed from the poet writing plays into the true
dramatic poet.

This is not a quibbling distinction, it indicates a very fertile
difference. Incidentally, it overrides the question of the medium
used, prose or verse. *Macbeth* could have been written in prose
without fundamental loss; it is poetically conceived. There is as
much poetry in the prose of *As You Like It* as in its verse.[58]
Convention and convenience, both to the dramatist and his actors,
will commonly have recommended verse; but from the beginning
Shakespeare seemingly tended to use whichever, that or prose,
better suited his immediate purpose.[59] Shylock's supreme outburst
is in prose; there is dramatic value in the mere contrast with
the mellifluous verse surrounding it. *Richard II*'s exceptional
uniformity of verse remains unbroken, though we might look for
prose in the short gardeners' scene. Bottom and Weaver and his
friends demand prose, if only because they have a play to rehearse
and perform. Its medium must not be their own, and it will go
best in doggerel. But who that could write verse would not write
it for the rest of *A Midsummer Night's Dream?* Prose suits
Falstaff to perfection; and Beatrice and Benedick, Rosalind and
Orlando, leave the verse of the plays they animate sounding dull
by comparison. But, comedy yielding to tragedy, verse comes to
its own again; since it can excite emotion and sustain illusion as
prose cannot.

The verse must not, in its new-won freedom, be let flow too
freely, too slackly, or it will lose its power—as did so much of the
verse of Shakespeare's immediate successors; and when Dryden
and his school thought at last to come to the rescue the mischief
had gone too far. With Shakespeare himself there will always
be some recurrent check, in the shape of a line or a passage of
stricter meter. Not mechanically inserted; if dramatic demand
breaks the form of the verse, dramatic demand will also restore
it. Hamlet is recalled from the overflowing emotion of

---

[58] Without *fundamental* loss: for some proof of this see Maeterlinck's
translation of *Macbeth*. And Dover Wilson discovers in *As You Like It* the
fossils of a verse version, of which Shakespeare presumably thought better.

[59] "Convention and convenience": Blank verse may well, with a little practice,
prove easier to write than formal prose; it is certainly easier to learn.

Bloody, bawdy villain!
Remorseless, treacherous, lecherous, kindless villain!
O, vengeance!

to the controlled thought of

About my brain! I have heard
That guilty creatures, sitting at a play,
Have by the very cunning of the scene . . .

And the firm rhythm of Othello's

Farewell the tranquil mind! farewell content!
Farewell the plumed troop and the big wars. . . .

or of his

It is the cause, it is the cause, my soul:
Let me not name it to you, you chaste stars! . . .

—with other such counterbalancings to the succession of minor
metrical liberties lodged (inconspicuously for the most part) in
the general run of the verse—help to keep him heroically
dominant over the commoner traffic of the play. The larger the
liberties taken, the greater the need for this recurrent control.
For drama is a disciplined art, hedged in by a hundred restrictions.
It is akin to poetry and to verse in that, and the restrictions themselves are akin. And in the poetic play a loosening of the ties of
verse only leaves it to depend the more upon a more essential
order of character and idea, upon which—and not chiefly upon
form—it must in fact be built. But this will be essentially poetic
and dramatic too since it will deal with the metaphysical things
with which poetry most properly deals, and with conflicts of the
human will. Shakespeare evolves, then, for the major medium of
his maturer plays, this enfranchised verse; a rhythmic and
melodious speech, powerful and malleable at once. Of its form
we shall often be but indefinitely aware; as much is kept as will
keep the structure intact, now more, now less being needed.
Little sense of artifice is left to intervene between us and the acted
play; the medium grows transparent. Sacrificing none of them, he
molds his diversity of means into a unity of dramatic expression;
and he lifts us—we have only to surrender—to the level of it.
Not much is to be gained—in appreciation, that is to say, of its
living qualities—by carrying such verse, cold and dead, to the

dissecting table, there to demonstrate its spondees and dactyls, its overrun lines and feminine endings. Assuredly Shakespeare never planned it so; and, multiply rules as we may in trying to round his practice into some sort of system, the exceptions will outrun them. We do not think in terms of prosody at all of

> I am dying, Egypt, dying; only
> I here importune death awhile, until
> Of many thousand kisses the poor last
> I lay upon thy lips.

noting, as we speak the lines, that the first has—rather surprisingly —the orthodox ten syllables; nor do we remember Lear's

> Never, never, never, never, never!

as five successive trochees. Form and meaning are not to be separated.

But for all the freedom in the general run of the verse the later plays furnish us still with rhymed couplets enough, "sentences," lengths of octosyllabics, and such like conventional forms. There is the difference, however, that these things now owe their place to some particular dramatic use that can be made of them—to clinch an argument, stress a desperate moment or clarify a reflective one.[60] And the use is overt; the effect made will stand out like a patch of bright color, or, if the main speech-fabric hereabouts is already brightly colored, of contrasting shade. Shakespeare never abandons a well-tried dramatic device; let it still serve his purpose, that is the only test.

One freedom opens up another. Individual expression besides, the verse may now be molded to the character of particular scenes, or of the play itself. The fantastic rhyming of Edgar and the Fool, attuned to Lear's own lunacy, does much for the storm-scenes in *King Lear*. The verse of *Othello* combines energy and color and ease in a manner of its own. And contrast in color and in rhythm generally is to be added to the others between *Antony and Cleopatra* and *Coriolanus*. Imperial Rome and exotic Egypt

---

[60] And here, it may be added, at the very opening of *Coriolanus*, is a "set piece," in the story of the Belly and the Members. But it is put to direct dramatic use. The picture of Menenius cajoling the assembled citizens, to be contrasted immediately after with Marcius' swift hard way with them—the two passages together serve as a sort of opening statement of this aspect of the play.

and the searching minds and sweeping passions which inform
them—the magnificent many-faceted verse of the one reflects
these, even as concentration on a narrower strife finds fitting
voice in the closer woven, more angular, lines of *Coriolanus*.

There is little in subject or characters to carry Shakespeare off
his feet and set the verse of *Coriolanus* soaring. Egoism, rivalry,
cunning and pride (the more generous traits, making by comparison a poor show) leave the radiant passages few, incidental
usually and as likely as not to illuminate some minor figure.

> Now the fair goddess Fortune
> Fall deep in love with thee: and her great charms
> Misguide thy opposers' swords! Bold gentleman,
> Prosperity be thy page!

—the old warrior, himself outdone, but lavish in admiration of
his heroically truculent young comrade; those few lines brighten
the whole scene. And it is to an anonymous messenger that is
given the brilliant little

> 'Tis thought
> That Marcius shall be Consul.
> I've seen the dumb men throng to see him, and
> The blind to hear him speak: matrons flung gloves,
> Ladies and maids their scarfs and handkerchers,
> Upon him as he passed: the nobles bended
> As to Jove's statue, and the commons made
> A shower and thunder with their caps and shouts:
> I never saw the like.[61]

DRAMATIC VERSE INDEED

The verse in the main is vigorous, and it drives hard and
exclusively at its dramatic purpose. The rhythm is apt to be of
more import than the melody. The words are often unmusical
in themselves, and they may be crushed into the lines like fuel to
stoke a furnace. It is a cast of speech well fitting the reason-
searching strife which pervades the play; and none in the canon

[61] It is evident, I think, that for the later plays Shakespeare had actors who
could be relied upon to make good effect with these small but striking parts.
There are several others in *Coriolanus*, some in *King Lear*, and a dozen or
more in *Antony and Cleopatra*. They were doubled no doubt.

is fuller of quarrel of one sort or another from beginning to end.

But if the verse—with nothing in the matter of it to stir the imagination—does not soar, neither does it ever sag. The play in this respect has not a single weak spot. One detects, in the frequent lack of clarity, a certain effort in the writing; but at least the effort is never shirked. The most patent instance comes, perhaps, in Aufidius' summary of his rival's failings:

> Whether 'twas pride,
> Which out of daily fortune ever taints
> The happy man; whether defect of judgment,
> To fail in the disposing of those chances
> Which he was lord of; or whether nature,
> Not to be other than one thing, not moving
> From th' casque to th' cushion, but commanding peace
> Even with the same austerity and garb
> As he controlled the war; but one of these,
> As he hath spices of them all—not all,
> For I dare so far free him—made him feared,
> So hated and so banished. . . .

—and so on, until the long succession of saving clauses is tied off in a complex aphorism.[62] If Shakespeare could not render down his thought into something clearer than this he might better, surely, have omitted the passage altogether. But no; Aufidius at this point, he feels, needs rationalizing, Coriolanus too. And if the idea involved will not distill and flow freely, it must just be wrung out. It cannot be omitted, and a flaw left in the fabric of thought.

Clarity yields to intensity. Witness Sicinius' malignly prescient

> Doubt not
> The commoners for whom we stand, but they
> Upon their ancient malice will forget
> With the least cause these his new honours; which
> That he will give them, make I as little question
> As he is proud to do't.

Put on paper, the last part of this may not parse well. But in speech, if the speaker be skillful, the thoughts themselves can be

---

[62] There is corruption in the text of the closing lines. But its elucidating would still leave the passage as a whole far from clear.

related—the "which" linked to the "least cause," the "proud" given its proper prominence—and the very lack of clarity be made to suggest their urgency.

Volumnia's disingenuous arguments, which send Marcius back to the market place, are wound out smoothly:

> If it be honour in your wars to seem
> The same you are not . . .
>   now it lies on you to speak
> To the people; not by your own instruction,
> Nor by the matter which your heart prompts you,
> But with such words that are but roted in
> Your tongue, though but bastards and syllables
> Of no allowance to your bosom's truth.
> Now this no more dishonours you at all . . .

—the verse cold, sustained, regular, unmelodious, fitted to the occasion and her temper, its sense aridly clear.

The man himself, if but a worse side of him, is alive both in the matter and manner of Marcius' beginning:

> What's the matter, you dissentious rogues,
> That, rubbing the poor itch of your opinion,
> Make yourselves scabs?

with its curt "What's the matter?", its veritably physical repugnance for the "rogues" set in the ugly images which follow, these followed the next moment by

> What would you have, you curs,
> That like not peace nor war? The one affrights you,
> The other makes you proud. He that trusts to you,
> When he should find you lions, finds you hares;
> Where foxes, geese: you are no surer, no,
> Than is the coal of fire upon the ice,
> Or hailstone in the sun.

with its banging-about of contraries, like so many boxes on the ear; the scolding then carried on into the crowded, contemptuous

> Hang 'em! They say!
> They'll sit by the fire, and presume to know
> What's done i' the Capitol; who's like to rise,
> Who thrives, and who declines; side factions, and give out
> Conjectural marriages. . . .

together with such tunelessness as is in "hunger broke stone walls," "horns o' the moon," "insurrection's arguing"—suitably, not a line of clear melody or smooth rhythm.

Further than which—one may at this point note—in the shaping and attuning of his verse to the expression of *individual* character, Shakespeare, here or elsewhere, in this play or another, hardly goes. For there must be some prevailing unity of form, or a play would fall in pieces; so, whatever the liberty given to the verse, its ten-syllable, five-stress foundation is left (as we have seen already) solidly underlying it still. And characters, even at their most individual, are still only emergent from type; this is true of Hamlet, of Falstaff even, Rosalind or Beatrice. Coriolanus himself is a variation of the soldier-hero, Aufidius of a villainous rival, while Menenius fills—if overfills—the place of the worldly-wise old counsellor, and Volumnia traces a little less theatrical descent as Roman matron. And the scope and individual character of all dramatic speech, be this remembered, since it must be instantly understood, has its limits there.

Dialogue and action are made to interpret one the other with exact economy. We actually see, first the failure, then the exciting success of the attack on Corioles, the city's capture and its token sacking; and with this goes no more dialogue than is needed—a bare line or two might at a pinch be omitted—for illustration. Cominius in six lines—

> Breathe you, my friends: well fought; we are come off
> Like Romans, neither foolish in our stands,
> Nor cowardly in retire: believe me, sirs,
> We shall be charged again. Whiles we have struck,
> By interims and conveying gusts we have heard
> The charges of our friends.

—is made to tell us what we need to know of his share in the battle and its further prospects, to paint us himself as general (just such a one as Marcius is not; the contrast striking), to tell us something besides of the lie of the battlefield, even of the weather! When Corioles has been taken, and Marcius is speeding Cominius' aid and the discomfiture of Aufidius, old Titus Lartius, with him his general's drummer and trumpeter, a scout also,

distinguished by his light running gear, come from the inner to
the outer stage, an officer and some more soldiers following:

> So, let the ports be guarded: keep your duties
> As I have set them down. If I do send, dispatch
> Those centuries to our aid; the rest will serve
> For a short holding; if we lose the field,
> We cannot keep the town. . . .
> Hence, and shut your gates upon us.
> Our guider, come; to the Roman camp conduct us.

Seven lines of speech, together with the significance of the figures
and their movement—away from the city: back into it; the closing
of the gates—suffice for this taste of Roman caution and cool
judgment in warfare. The contrast is to come this time in the next
scene's furious duel between Marcius and Aufidius.

The verse in general is meaty and lean; it contains few images
and is all but free of extended metaphor. Its quality of direct
attack is a strength to the actor. As an instance:

> Officious, and not valiant; you have shamed me
> In your condemned seconds.

—for Aufidius, left standing there while Marcius triumphantly
pursues the unwelcome interlopers, the least wordiness would
seem weakness; but that one spare sentence an actor can pack with
spleen.

Marcius' magnanimity is given as direct and simple expression.
The battle over:

> I sometime lay here in Corioles
> At a poor man's house; he used me kindly.
> He cried to me; I saw him prisoner.
> But then Aufidius was within my view,
> And wrath o'erwhelmed my pity. I request you
> To give my poor host freedom.

It makes part—with the immediate weary-minded forgetting of
the man's name; has he not the right to be weary!—of the upbuilding of his character, is a counterpart to that scornful rating
of the commoners. And the verse accommodates this; as it does
his joking response to the army's acclaim of him:

> I will go wash;
> And when my face is fair you shall perceive
> Whether I blush or no.

as it will later his lovingly ironic reproof to his wife's tears of welcome:

> Wouldst thou have laughed had I come coffin'd home,
> That weeps't to see me triumph? . . .

Surely the very perfection of such simplicity!

The play contains little or no superfluous matter. With the civic struggle at full pitch, the effect to be made one of riot and confusion, each character, either chorus of Senators and plebeians, contributes exactly to the scene's need.

BRUTUS.	Aediles, seize him!
CITIZENS.	Yield, Marcius, yield!
MENENIUS.	Hear me one word;
	Beseech you, Tribunes, hear me but one word.
AEDILES.	Peace, peace!
MENENIUS.	Be that you seem, truly your country's friend,
	And temperately proceed to what you would
	Thus violently redress.
BRUTUS.	Sir, these cold ways,
	That seem like prudent helps, are very poisonous
	Where the disease is violent. Lay hands upon him,
	And bear him to the rock.
MARCIUS.	No, I'll die here.
	There's some among you have beheld me fighting:
	Come, try upon yourselves what you have seen me.
MENENIUS.	Down with that sword! Tribunes, withdraw awhile.
BRUTUS.	Lay hands upon him.
MENENIUS.	Help Marcius! Help!
	You that be noble, help him, young and old!
CITIZENS.	Down with him! Down with him!

In this mutiny, the Tribunes, the Aediles, and the People are beat in.

The passage is scored as it might be for an orchestra, each instrument given its task: Brutus' sharp order, reinforced by the plebeians' shout; Menenius' half-heard remonstrance; the Aediles' command for the silence in which Menenius and Brutus exchange their acid arguments; this sharply broken again by Brutus. And no shout follows now; since Marcius, mute and motionless so far, suddenly draws his sword and challenges combat. Circumspect old Menenius presses peace on both parties. It is Brutus who is reckless and hounds on his outnumbering mob. Then, for Menenius, if it is to come to fighting, each must stand to his own side. And the fit few prove too much for the many.

THE DYNAMIC PHRASE

Spare dialogue need not be poor dialogue. The little said can be made to suggest much left unsaid. Dramatic art matures to this. In the cruder sort of play the characters will often not be fully dramatized, the dramatist himself to be heard speaking through them too plainly. But when they are, and their speech is authentically their own, then, by planning and a close collaboration with the actor, it can be brought to the expression of the implicit too, of those confusions of thought that trouble men, of feelings that never, in life, find words. The expression must be kept seemingly lifelike, not translated into overexplicit—into explanatory—terms: this would falsify the effect of it. The art of the dramatist lies in the discovering of more covert means.

The dynamic phrase, into which the actor is to pack the effect of a cumulated mass of thought and feeling, is one means. Shakespeare early learned the use of it. When Romeo hears of Juliet's death:

Is it even so? Then I defy you, stars!

rhetoric will follow later; but nothing of such deep and suggestive feeling. Falstaff's

Master Shallow, I owe you a thousand pound.

is a line of the sort, with its comically generous divining of Master Shallow's feelings too. So, when he has watched Cressid dallying with Diomed, is Troilus' response to Ulysses' "All's done, my lord," his grim "It is."

The dynamic phrase can be used in more ways than one. And there is purer tragedy in Macduff's cold

He has no children.

than in all his throbbing grief for his loss of them. Macbeth's own response to what once his servants would hardly have dared tell him:

> The Queen, my lord, is dead.

is no more than a silence, to be followed—when that bitter emptiness, his loss of the very power to feel, has made itself felt—by the wearily impatient

> She should have died hereafter:
> There would have been a time for such a word. . . .

and some detached reflections upon the meaninglessness of life. The effect—as of spiritual impotence—is not simply in these. To gain it, the underlying tragedy has been the play's length in development.

In a play, text apart from context may lose most of its meaning. The story itself, with Shakespeare, will run directly and openly along; there is no plot (the term will be misleading) to be spun and unraveled.[63] The play's structure is built up by the interlocking of character and event, and the opposition of character to character; this gives it body, balance and strength. In *Coriolanus* the main stresses are between Marcius and the Senate on the one side, the people on the other; this beside, between Marcius and Aufidius, Marcius and Volumnia, jolly Menenius and the sour Tribunes. These are plain to be seen, and they implement the action. But there is much of auxiliary consequence as well, not set out at length or very explicitly, left latent, rather, for the actors to develop or elucidate in their acting.

The dramatist plans the essentials of this auxiliary action. Directions for it will be implicit in those passages of thrifty dialogue and their context; but only as realized and expanded will its full significance be made clear. When, for instance, in the play's first scene Marcius and Cominius and the Senators come together, their conduct to each other, the friendly yielding of precedence, Marcius' show of respect for the Consul and "our best elders," his easy acceptance otherwise of his own heroic eminence, and (pointed omission telling too) the ignoring of the

---

[63] *Othello*, among the greater plays, really the single exception, nor fully an exception even so.

new Tribunes—twenty pregnant lines and their acting suffice to picture us men and party; and not even the anonymous among them are left lay figures.

So it is with the triumphal entry after the victory at Corioles. Action and speech are knit together, the one clarifying and enhancing the other. The shouts of welcome hushed, Marcius' look is turned—ours too again—to the women modestly withdrawn there; Roman mother and wife, the harsh Volumnia shaken by emotion, Virgilia happily weeping. Then he, Rome's hero, kneels dutifully to his mother, dries his wife's tears with words of gentle, magnanimously grave irony, frees himself from that mood with a joke for Menenius, his courteous bow to Valeria. More telling too will be this second ignoring of the Tribunes (on a third occasion, Marcius, confident of his consulship, will openly voice his contempt for them). Again, it is a matter of thirty-five lines or less. Yet not only their own significance, their illustration and the interplay of the response they demand, brings every participant in the scene into helping to give it life.

Shakespeare has come to demanding more of his actors, and to giving them more—though it may be less ostensible—opportunity. He demands their imaginative collaboration, leaves much to their discretion, gives them outlines to color in lightly or heavily. How large a part, for instance, does wine-flushed stubbornness play in Aufidius' repeated refusal to recognize the unmuffled Marcius, waiting by his hearth in Antium? The actor may decide. The text leaves him latitude and discretion, Shakespeare providing neither comment nor response to clinch the matter.

When Menenius returns with Volumnia and Virgilia from parting with the banished Marcius at the city gate: the strain now relaxed, the day lost, old age in him suddenly gives way; and against their vituperatings he can only set a "Peace, peace! be not so loud," a "Come, come; peace!"; and finally, the triumphant Tribunes departing, a

> You have told them home;
> And, by my troth, you have cause. You'll sup with me?

With no more to be done, there's left at least the comfort of a meal! The mere words given their surface meaning do little

more than somewhat superfluously help the action on. But as
bits of material to be used for filling out the figure of Menenius
a skillful actor can put them to lively use. And that final con-
solatory bidding to supper then becomes also the better spring-
board for the grim, indomitable

> Anger's my meat; I sup upon myself,
> And so shall starve with feeding.

by which—its immediate effect besides—we shall be helped to
keep Volumnia vividly in mind during her coming absence from
the action.

   The actor thus potently collaborating, one scene can be made
to feed others that follow, and repeated expounding be avoided.
Aufidius' backsliding from Marcius as they march together upon
Rome is fully set out in his talk with his Lieutenant. After this
merely his watchful presence through successive scenes will be
eloquent, and the few cold phrases with which he breaks its
silence need no enlarging: for example, his dry approbation of
Marcius' rebuffing of Menenius with that

> You keep a constant temper.

his ironic sympathy for the son's breaking at last under the
mother's pleading:

> I was moved withal.

A moment later comes an aside as explicit as was the talk with the
Lieutenant:

> I am glad thou hast set thy mercy and thy honour
> At difference in thee: out of that I'll work
> Myself a former fortune.

and this keeps the trend of the action incontestably clear. But his
open share in the two scenes, those two dry sentences (and one
other) which positively do little more than emphasize his continuing presence, these an Aufidius can discreetly color, can most
effectively charge with the strange blend of hatred and admiration
that we know possesses the man. Such acting it is that adds
something of another dimension to the personified narrative of a
play, a dimension of being.

   A speech may have an auxiliary sense, to which the actor must
give value by his own particular means. When Marcius has finally

yielded Rome's fate to Volumnia's plea he knows—and we are aware—that he has also put his own in Aufidius' hands. He turns to him:

> Aufidius, though I cannot make true wars,
> I'll frame convenient peace. Now, good Aufidius,
> Were you in my stead, would you have heard
> A mother less, or granted less, Aufidius?

The expressed resolve beside, in the mere repetitions of that "Aufidius," as the actor can give them varying cadence, will sound all the pleading on his own behalf—it is little!—that Marcius' pride could ever let him make.

To hark back to his banishment: much of the preceding scene is but preparation for the promised self-control of the curt

> I am content.

with which on his return to the market place he answers the Tribunes' provocative demand:

> If you submit you to the people's voices,
> Allow their officers, and are content
> To suffer lawful censure for such faults
> As shall be proved upon you?

for the countering too, a little later, of a yet more insolently peremptory

> Answer to us.

with the measured

> Say then; 'tis true. I ought so.

Such effects of self-control can, it is obvious, only be convincingly made when the elements of something to control have already been as convincingly built into the character.

THE USE OF SILENCE

Shakespeare has learned to put silence to a variety of uses. Although, later in this same scene, intolerably stung by that "traitor to the people," Marcius finally forswears his promised temperance, yet he stands rigidly silent while Sicinius

> in the name o' the people,
> And in the power of us the Tribunes . . .

passes formal sentence of banishment upon him, while the people ratify it with a chorused

It shall be so.

Thus he multiplies many times—when anger finally does break bounds—the effect of his

You common cry of curs! whose breath I hate . . .

And there is the silence to which the unhappy Tribunes are reduced when, while Cominius and Menenius mock them, the news accumulates that this once banished Marcius is marching with the Volscians upon Rome—one meek

But is this true, sir?

from Brutus, put in to emphasize it. There is most particularly the

Holds her by the hand, silent.

—Shakespeare's own direction, that rarity! It is no more than a simple gesture, with which Marcius accepts the doom his surrender to his mother brings on him; a mere silence, yet it is the culminating moment of the play.

In the vivifying of such silences, the imaginative use of the "dynamic phrase" with its pent emotions, expressing things left latent, in the general demand now made upon the actor that he altogether assimilate himself to the character he is presenting, much is changed from the earlier illustrative declaiming of verse or prose. Yet Shakespeare's is, and remains through all changes, the drama of eloquence. And his art's chief achievement in this kind has been to turn eloquence for its own sake into a *relative* eloquence (so to call it) springing, seemingly spontaneously, from character-enlivening occasion; the poetic form not broken, set free rather to be as personal and malleable a medium of expression as may be.

DRAMATICALLY LEGITIMATE ELOQUENCE

The story of *Coriolanus* is pre-eminently one of public life; and throughout the play—from Menenius' persuasive tale of the Belly and the Members to Marcius' last desperate haranguing of his Volscian masters—scene after scene offers dramatically legitimate occasion for eloquence. There is much variety of occasion too, as

Coriolanus

of speaker and temper of speech; the mutiny of the citizens, so
differently dealt with by Menenius and Marcius; the crisis on the
battlefield, the thanks to Marcius for his great part in the victory,
later the public address to him with its carefully sought phrases;
the war of words between Marcius and the Tribunes; Volumnia's
spitfire retorting on them, to find contrast later in her stern,
measured defense of Rome; Marcius finally brought to bay,
fatally unchanged—here are many sorts of eloquence validly
provided for. But there will be—and as legitimately—more likeness than difference in the matter of it, and between the speakers.
For Menenius, Cominius and the Tribunes, Marcius and his
mother, even the Volscians and Aufidius look—if not always from
one standpoint—all towards the same horizon. There is the
difference, truly, that less bitterness goes to battling against
Volscian neighbors without the gates than against enemy kindred
within. And this likeness lends to the temper of the verse a
consistency which Marcius' own inevitable domination of it will
but confirm, since there is little to be expressed in him that
outranges the scope of the rest. And here again the close woven
pattern of event and character, the internecine in the struggle, is
an element of the tragedy.

There is nothing profound in Marcius, nor anything to set him
inwardly apart from friend or foe, and all introspection is foreign
to him. Of his two brief soliloquies, one is little more than an
outburst of febrile ill-temper, a climax to his infatuate protest
against donning the gown of humility and asking the citizens
for their votes:

> Better it is to die, better to starve,
> Than crave the hire which first we do deserve.
> Why in this woolvish gown should I stand here,
> To beg of Hob and Dick, that does appear,
> Their needless vouches? . . .

—and the exceptional succession of six rhymed couplets with
their jangling iteration goes to painting this. The second is
detached comment, hardly more. He is in Antium, the revolution
within him already accomplished.

> O world, thy slippery turns! . . .

If we hear of no doubts or misgivings or struggles of conscience it is because there will have been none. Plunged in misery,

> Longer to live most weary . . .

by a sudden "slippery turn" he has become—so he supposes— another man:

> My birth-place hate I, and my love's upon
> This enemy town.

It is as simple as that. Of the workings of a troubled mind he knows no more than does a child. He is frank and direct with mother, wife or friend, eloquent in anger. Of the inward Marcius we have passing glimpses only; in his thought for his one-time host in Corioles, for the widows his valor has left grieving there; in his respect for his mother, his chaste love for his wife; finally in the resigned realization of

> Not of a woman's tenderness to be,
> Requires nor child nor woman's face to see.

—its reflective cadence throwing it gently into relief against the stronger rhythm of the current speech.

The Question of Act-Division

THE play's action falls dramatically into three main divisions. The first, after some preliminary excursions into the citizens' discontent, covers the Volscian war; the second begins with Marcius' triumphant return from it, develops the struggle around his consulship and finishes upon his banishment; the third runs from his surrender to Aufidius, through the threats and alarms of his return, the surrender to his mother and the catastrophe of the end. This, however, being among the plays first found in the Folio, is there submitted to the formal five-act division—which, lacking more than once any dramatic warrant, one doubts to be Shakespeare's. A tricky question to answer, this of act-division; since we do not very certainly know how, at performances—and with what consistency—the act-pause was used. As a ten-minute interval during which the audience could relax? As a more formal minute's breathing-space for the actors? The punctuating power of the act-division will differ greatly.

What dramatic value can there be in the Folio's division here that parts Act II from Act III? In the action itself there is continuity. In Marcius' own tones and in his friends' attitude towards him, their deference to him as "Lord Consul," his readiness for more war with the Volscians, one may perhaps distinguish a change of key; but nothing, one would say that needs an act-division—certainly not a long pause—for its emphasis. Again, a fresh dramatic chapter in the story certainly begins with Coriolanus' appearance at Antium, *in mean apparel, disguised and muffled*. Just before this comes the "bridge scene" between the Roman and Volscian spies; and, from a dramatic standpoint, the Folio could suitably either end its third act with this or begin its fourth. It does neither. And if the practical convenience of a Marcius who must doff his Consul's insignia to make himself all but unrecognizable in his mean apparel ought also to be considered—it is not. Nor does there seem to be any very patent dramatic reason for ending a fourth act where the Folio ends this, nor for beginning the fifth act with Menenius setting forth on his errand after refusing to.

We may feel certain, surely, that Shakespeare sought, first and last, to make his plays dramatically viable, although we may not be so certain as we begin to think we are of the effects made by his stage on his stagecraft. But when we can be fairly certain of this, it is good evidence that what offends against these effects is not from his hand.

The Stage Directions

SOME of these are among the play's most notable features. Incidentally, their dramatic value apart, they stand among the items of evidence of a retirement to Stratford and the writing of the latest plays in a semi-detachment from the theater. Such evidence is, of course, inferential, no better than guesswork if you will. But *Coriolanus* at least speaks in this respect pretty plainly of a manuscript to be sent to London, and of a staging which the author did not expect to supervise himself.

The directions are always expert, devised by someone who has visualized the action very clearly. They may be such a mere memorandum as a prompter might write in, as where, in the passage covering the battle for Corioles, after the customary indicative

> *The fight is renewed. The Volsces retire into Corioles, and Marcius follows them to the gates.*

comes for Marcius the mandatory

> *Enter the gates.*

One builds nothing on that. But

> *Enter Cominius, as it were in retire, with soldiers.*

and later

> *Enter two Officers, to lay cushions, as it were, in the Capitol.*

—these "as it weres" are, so to say, "advisory"; the actors must devise their expression for themselves. On the other hand, action of dramatic importance may be underlined, though the spoken text indicate it clearly enough:

> *Enter Coriolanus, in a gown of humility . . .*

and the next words spoken are

> Here he comes, and in the gown of humility. . . .

And later—though nothing will be plainer than the sight itself—

> *Enter Coriolanus, in mean apparel, disguised and muffled.*

Here is the author, stressing these effects upon the actors, for his own satisfaction, to make sure they miss none of them; for his own great satisfaction, one feels, when it comes to

> *Draw both the Conspirators and kils Martius, who falles, Auffidius stands on him.*

And

> *Enter Menenius to the Watch or Guard.*

"*Watch or Guard*"; whichever you please, it comes to the same thing.

But the direction to be valued most of all is that given to the actor of Marcius himself. Before he yields to Volumnia he

> *Holds her by the hand, silent.*

—for an appreciable moment, it must be. Had Shakespeare had his actors at hand to direct should we now ever have had that?

Did a foolishly rash Macbeth go speeding on after the sledge-hammer blow of

> The Queen, my lord, is dead.

Not if Shakespeare was there to stop him!

Corry-ols, Corry-o-les, or Corī-o-les; Corry-o-lanus or Corī-o-lanus?

It is related of John Philip Kemble that once, when making at the end of a performance the customary announcement of the next, he told the house that the company would present Shakespeare's play of Corry-o-lanus in which he himself would undertake the part of Corī-o-lanus.[64] Such disputes would occasionally enliven the already livelier theater of those days, resembling as it could—the "Pit" of it—rather an unruly club than a mere shop in which plays are so tamely bought and sold. And while, despite three centuries of searching out—and willfully creating!—Shakespearean problems, there remain more than enough to be solved, few, whether of greater or less import, offer us such a free choice as does this. Nor is it of such little dramatic import as the pronunciation of a word will commonly be. It proclaims the hero's glory; its refusal to him is the final insult which he will not brook; at a dozen moments it is made the keynote of eloquence and emotion. The cadence of the word, and its music; those, therefore, are, dramatically, the two important things about it. Whatever Shakespeare's intention, we may be certain that he meant it to sound well.

It is not first met with precisely in that form, but coming from a Volscian Senator in his jaunty

> Let us alone to guard Cor-ī-oles. . . .

which is as simple a decasyllable as the play contains. But when, two scenes later, a messenger enters with his news, this is that

> The citizens of Corry-ols have issued,
> And given to Lartius and to Marcius battle. . . .

---

[64] I have the story from that able, and now so deeply regretted, theatrical historian Harold Child.

and the minor actor who did anything but stress the "Corry . . ." might count, surely, upon sharp correction. Yet only twenty-three lines later Marcius will be all but bound to say that Titus Lartius is

> Holding Co-ri-o-les in the name of Rome . . .

—and would possibly not be so amenable to correction. And a little later he tells Aufidius,

> Within these three hours, Tullus,
> Alone I fought in your Co-ri-o-les walls. . . .

And what other than the longest of long ī's can that Corioles contain?

But here, of course, are sources only of the "Coriolanus" of our question; and this, when it first appears a scene later, still is so much a proclamation (with an exulting echo) that it can be counted out of the verse and its demands altogether. One can only say that as it is surrounded by "Corioles" (one before and two after), with their long ī's indubitable, "Coriolanus" would seem to be the most instinctive derivative.

It comes again in the verse of a proclamation; and the Herald may have it either way he will—or both.

> Know, Rome, that all alone Marcius did fight
> Within Corioles gates, where he hath won . . .

(there is the long ī undoubtedly)

> With fame, a name to Caius Marcius: these
> In honour follows Corry-o-lanus.

with, to conclude, either a

> Welcome to Rome, renownèd Corry-o-lanus!

or a

> Welcome to Rome, renowned Cor-ī-olanus!

which you choose; Volumnia also having her choice between a poor line in

> What is it? Corry-o-lanus must I call thee?

and a better one in

> What is't? Cor-ī-olanus must I call thee?

—being sure, in rehearsal at any rate, of loud ironic protests from the rest of the company when, with a wink, she poses the problem!

Thereafter, however, and on all hands, the pronunciation "Corry-o-lanus" slides more easily into the verse, though never stimulating it. Sicinius can even squeeze a certain mockery into the tunelessness of

> Your Corry-olanus is not much missed
> But with his friends. . . .

Again, Volumnia will do the better with

> To his surname Cor-ī-olanus longs more pride
> Than pity to our prayers.

though the verse does not force it on her, and fits the word ill at best. But "Cor-ī-o-les," a minute later, it must be.

With the play's closing moments we are nearing the name's most pointedly dramatic use. Aufidius'

> Ay, Marcius, Caius Marcius. Dost thou think
> I'll grace thee with that robbery, thy stolen name
> Coriolanus in Corioles?

"Corry-o-lanus in Corry-ols" or "Corry-o-les" it certainly cannot be; "Corry-o-lanus in Cor-i-o-les" it just may be. But how much finer "Cor-ī-olanus in Cor-ī-o-les"! And what Marcius will hesitate an instant over

> "Boy"! false hound!
> If you have writ your annals true, 'tis there,
> That, like an eagle in a dove-cote, I
> Fluttered your Volscians in Cor-ī-o-les. . . .

"Corry-o-lanus," then, it would seem has the majority of voices. But let there never be one for "Corry-ols" or "Corry-o-les"!

One is tempted towards what is, doubtless, an indefensible heresy. Were the Elizabethans as inconsistent in the pronouncing of some uncommon words as in the spelling of them? Was it as possible for an actor to say "Corry-o-lanus" at one moment and "Cor-ī-olanus" at another—whichever suited the verse the better —with none of the hearers finding the change objectionable as it would be for a dramatist to sign himself "Shakespeare" at one moment and "Shaxpeer" the next? It would need, of course, a braver man than the present writer to plead this.

Romeo and Juliet

ROMEO AND JULIET is lyric tragedy, and this must be the key to its interpreting. It seems to have been Shakespeare's first unquestionable success, proof positive of his unique quality. If marred by one or two clumsy turns, its stagecraft is simple and sufficient; and the command of dramatic effect is masterly already. It is immature work still, but it is not crude. The writing shows us a Shakespeare skilled in devices that he is soon to reject or adapt to new purpose. This, which to the critic is one of the most interesting things about the play, is a stumbling block to its acting. But the passion and poignant beauty of it all, when we surrender ourselves to them, make such reservations of small enough account.

Whether we have the play as Shakespeare first wrote it may be doubted; we probably have it in the second Quarto as it last left his hands. But signs, as they may seem to be, of rewriting and retouching at one time or another, must always, in this or any of his plays, be warily viewed. They may, of course, be so obvious as to ask no proof; but when they depend on nice calculation one must remember that the critical foot-rule is poor measure for genius—and the very poorest for genius in its springtime.

The Mercutio of the Queen Mab speech is not, it can be argued, the Mercutio of

> No, 'tis not so deep as a well, nor so wide as a church-door;
> but 'tis enough, 'twill serve. . . .

Did the Juliet, one asks, of

Hath Romeo slain himself? Say thou but "I,"
And that bare vowel "I" shall poison more
Than the death-darting eye of cockatrice:
I am not I, if there be such an "I". . . .

and the rest of the fantasia, turn within a sitting or so into the
Juliet of

Ancient damnation! O most wicked fiend!
Is it more sin to wish me thus forsworn,
Or to dispraise my lord with that same tongue
Which she hath praised him with above compare
So many thousand times?

and the Romeo of

more courtship lives
In carrion flies than Romeo: they may seize
On the white wonder of dear Juliet's hand. . . .
This may flies do, when I from this must fly. . . .

into the stark figure of the scene in Mantua, meeting the news of
her death with

Is it even so? Then I defy you, stars!

—into the Romeo who pays the apothecary with

There is thy gold; worse poison to men's souls,
Doing more murder in this loathsome world
Than these poor compounds that thou mayst not sell:
I sell thee poison, thou hast sold me none.

By all the rules, no doubt, there should be two Shakespeares at
work here. But in such a ferment as we now find him (himself,
in some sort, a young Romeo on the turn from a Rosaline of
phrase-making to a deeper-welling love) he may well have been
capable of working on Tuesday in one fashion, on Wednesday in
another, capable of couplet, sonnet, word-juggling, straight sober
verse, or hard-bitten prose, often as the popular story he was
turning to account and the need of the actors for the thing they
and he were so apt at seemed to demand, at times out of the new
strength breeding in him. Our present concern, however, is with
the play as we have it, and its interpreting in the theater.

The Conduct of the Action

THE dominating merit of this is that Shakespeare takes Brooke's tale, and at once doubles its dramatic value by turning its months to days.

> These violent delights have violent ends. . . .

and a sense of swiftness belongs to them, too. A Hamlet may wait and wait for his revenge; but it accords with this love and its tragedy that four days should see its birth, consummation and end. Incidentally we can here see the "Double Time"—which has so exercised the ingenuity of commentators, who will credit him with their own—slipping naturally and easily into existence.[1] He makes dramatic use of time when he needs to.

> CAPULET. But soft, what day is this?
> PARIS.   Monday, my lord.
> CAPULET. Monday! Ha! ha! Well, Wednesday is too soon;
>   O' Thursday let it be:—o' Thursday, tell her,
>   She shall be married to this noble earl. . . .

This sense of the marriage looming but three days ahead is dramatically important; later to intensify it, he even lessens the interval by a day. But (his mind reverting now and then to Brooke's story as he read it, possibly before he saw that he must weave it closer) he will carelessly drop in phrases that are quite contradictory when we examine them. But what audience will examine them as they flash by?

> I anger her sometimes [says the Nurse to Romeo], and tell her that Paris is the properer man. . . .

(when neither Paris nor Romeo has been in the field for four and twenty hours).

> Is it more sin to wish me thus forsworn,
> Or to dispraise my lord with that same tongue
> Which she hath praised him with above compare
> So many thousand times?

(when, all allowance made for Juliet's exaggeration, the Nurse has not had twice twenty-four hours in which to praise or dis-

---

[1] In the Preface to *The Merchant of Venice* this discussion is raised again, and, of course, pursued at length in *Othello*.

praise). But notice that this suggestion of the casual slackness of normal life conveniently loosens the tension of the tragedy a little. There is, indeed, less of carelessness than a sort of instinctive artistry about it; and the method is a natural by-product of the freedom of Shakespeare's theater.

But he marshals his main action to very definite purpose. He begins it, not with the star-crossed lovers (though a prologue warns us of them), but with a clash of the two houses; and there is far more significance in this than lies in the fighting. The servants, not the masters, start the quarrel. If Tybalt is a firebrand, Benvolio is a peacemaker; and though Montague and Capulet themselves are drawn in, they have the grace to be a little ashamed after. The hate is cankered; it is an ancient quarrel set new abroach; and even the tetchy Capulet owns that it should not be so hard for men of their age to keep the peace. If it were not for the servants, then, who fight because they always have fought, and the Tybalts, who will quarrel about nothing sooner than not quarrel at all, it is a feud ripe for settling; everyone is weary of it; and no one more weary, more impatient with it than Romeo;

> O me! What fray was here?
> Yet tell me not—for I have heard it all. . . .

We are not launching, then, into a tragedy of fated disaster, but —for a more poignant if less highly heroic theme—of opportunity muddled away and marred by ill-luck. As a man of affairs, poor Friar Laurence proved deplorable; but he had imagination. Nothing was likelier than that the Montagues and Capulets, waking one morning to find Romeo and Juliet married, would have been only too thankful for the excuse to stop killing each other.

> And the continuance of their parents' rage,
> Which, but their children's end, nought could remove . . .

says the Prologue. Nought in such a world as this, surmises the young Shakespeare; in a world where

> I thought all for the best.

avails a hero little; for on the heels of it comes

> O, I am fortune's fool!

Having stated his theme, he develops it, as his habit already is (and was to remain; the method so obviously suits the continuities of the Elizabethan stage), by episodes of immediate contrast in character and treatment. Thus, after the bracing rattle of the fight and the clarion of the Prince's judgment, we have our first sight of Romeo, fantastic, rueful, self-absorbed. His coming is preluded by a long passage of word-music; and, that its relevance may be plain, the verse slips into the tune of it at the first mention of his name. Benvolio's brisk story of the quarrel, dashed with irony, is finishing—

> While we were interchanging thrusts and blows,
> Came more and more, and fought on part and part,
> Till the Prince came, who parted either part.

—when Lady Montague interposes with

> O, where is Romeo? Saw you him to-day?
> Right glad am I he was not at this fray.

and promptly, like a change from wood-wind, brass and tympani to an andante on the strings, comes Benvolio's

> Madam, an hour before the worshipped sun
> Peered forth the golden window of the east . . .

Montague echoes him; and to the wooing smoothness of

> But he, his own affections' counsellor,
> Is to himself—I will not say how true—
> But to himself so secret and so close,
> So far from sounding and discovery,
> As is the bud bit with an envious worm,
> Ere he can spread his sweet leaves to the air,
> Or dedicate his beauty to the sun.
> Could we but learn from whence his sorrows grow,
> We would as willingly give cure as know.

Romeo appears; moody, oblivious of them all three. It is a piece of technique that belongs both to Shakespeare's stage in its simplicity and to the play's own lyrical cast.

Then (for contrasts of character and subject), close upon Romeo's mordant thought-play and word-play with Benvolio come Capulet and Paris, the sugary old tyrant and the man of wax, matchmaking—and such a good match for Juliet as it is to be!

Close upon this comes Benvolio's wager that he'll show Romeo at the feast beauties to put Rosaline in the shade; and upon that, our first sight of Juliet, when she is bid take a liking to Paris at the feast if she can.

The scene of the procession of the Maskers to Capulet's house (with Romeo a spoil-sport as befits his mood) is unduly lengthened by the bravura of the Queen Mab speech, which is as much and as little to be dramatically justified as a song in an opera is.[2] But Shakespeare makes it serve to quicken the temper of the action to a pitch against which—as against the dance, too, and Tybalt's rage—Romeo's first encounter with Juliet will show with a quiet beauty all its own. Did he wonder for a moment how to make this stand out from everything else in the play? They share the speaking of a sonnet between them, and it is a charming device.

One must picture them there. The dance is over, the guests and the Maskers are in a little chattering, receding crowd, and the two find themselves alone.[3] Juliet would be for joining the others; but Romeo, his mask doffed, moves towards her, as a pilgrim towards a shrine.

If I profane with my unworthiest hand . . .

It is hard to see what better first encounter could have been devised. To have lit mutual passion in them at once would have been commonplace; the cheapest of love tragedies might begin like that. But there is something sacramental in this ceremony, something shy and grave and sweet; it is a marriage made already. And she is such a child; touched to earnestness by his trembling

---

[2] The young gentlemen are gate-crashers, we perceive; there are few novelties in the social world! But Capulet is delighted; he even, when the unlooked-for fun is over and the recalcitrant regular guests have been coaxed to dance, presses a "trifling foolish banquet" upon the strangers; cake and wine upon the sideboard, that is to say, and not, as the word now implies, a substantial sit-down affair. But etiquette, it seems, is against this. Having measured them a measure and so wound up the occasion very merrily, the "strangers" do begone. Seriously, the conduct of this scene, when it is staged, needs attention. It is generally quite misunderstood and misinterpreted.

[3] The company, that is to say, drift up towards the inner stage, from which, as from the withdrawing rooms beyond the great hall, Capulet and the guests had come to welcome the masked invasion, and as they all move away the guessing at who the strangers are dies down,

306 Prefaces to Shakespeare

earnestness, but breaking into fun at last (her defense when the granted kiss lights passion in him) as the last quatrain's meter breaks for its ending into

> You kiss by the book.

The tragedy to come will be deepened when we remember the innocence of its beginning. The encounter's ending has significance too. They are not left to live in a fool's paradise for long. Romeo hears who she is and faces his fate. An hour ago he was affecting melancholy while Mercutio and his fellows laughed round him. Now, with the sport at its best, he braces to desperate reality. Then, as the guests and Maskers depart and the laughter dies, Juliet grows fearful. She hears her fate and must face it, too.

> My only love sprung from my only hate!
> Too early seen unknown, and known too late!
> Prodigious birth of love it is to me
> That I must love a loathed enemy.

The child is no more a child.

A chorus follows. This may have some further function than to fill up time while furniture is shifted or stage fittings are adjusted; it is of no dramatic use.[4] Then Romeo appears alone.

And now, with his finest stroke yet, all prepared and pending (the love duet that is to be spoken from balcony to garden), Shakespeare pauses to do still better by it; and at the same time fits Mercutio to his true place in the character scheme.[5] To appreciate the device we must first forget the obliging editors with their *Scene i, A lane by the wall of Capulet's orchard. Enter Romeo....* *He climbs the wall and leaps down within it. . . . Scene ii,* *Capulet's orchard. Enter Romeo*—for all this has simply obliterated the effect.[6] The *Enter Romeo alone* of the Quartos and

---

[4] But for more argument about the question of act-division that is involved, see p. 323ff.

[5] The Bodleian has recently recovered its original First Folio, and the pages of the balcony-scene are the best thumbed of all.

[6] Rowe is responsible for this. A few of the later editors scented something wrong, but only half-heartedly tried to put it right. Grant White was an honorable exception; but he places Mercutio and Benvolio in the orchard too. Juliet's line
> The orchard walls are high and hard to climb. . . .
discounts that.

Folio is the only authentic stage direction concerning him. What happens when Mercutio and Benvolio arrive in pursuit? He hides somewhere about the stage. He has, they say, "leapt this orchard wall"; but no wall is there, and—more importantly—there is no break in the continuity of the scene, now or later; it should be proof enough that to make one we must cut a rhymed couplet in two. The confusion of whereabouts, such as it is, that is involved, would not trouble the Elizabethans in the least; would certainly not trouble an audience that later on was to see Juliet play half a scene on the upper stage and half on the lower, with no particular change of place implied. The effect, so carefully contrived, lies in Romeo's being well within hearing of all the bawdry now to follow, which has no other dramatic point; and that the chaff is about the chaste Rosaline makes it doubly effective.

Dominating the stage with his lusty presence, vomiting his jolly indecencies, we see the sensual man, Mercutio; while in the background lurks Romeo, a-quiver at them, youth marked for tragedy.[7] His heart's agonizing after Rosaline had been real enough. He has forgotten that! But what awaits him now, with another heart, passionate as his own, to encounter? This is the eloquence of the picture, which is summed up in Romeo's rhyming end to the whole dithyramb as he steals out, looking after the two of them:

> He jests at scars that never felt a wound.

The discord thus struck is perfect preparation for the harmony to come; and Mercutio's ribaldry has hardly died from our ears before Juliet is at her window.

Throughout the famous scene Shakespeare varies and strengthens its harmony and sustains its drama by one small device after another. We must return to more careful study of it. At its finish, the brisk couplet,

> Hence will I to my ghostly father's cell,
> His help to crave, and my dear hap to tell.

brings us to earth again; and the action speeds on, to find a new

---

[7] The effect will, of course, be intensified if he never leaves our sight, but the mere continuity of the scene, and our sense of him there, produces it.

helmsman in Friar Laurence. His importance to the play is made
manifest by the length of his first soliloquy, and Shakespeare is
looking forward already, we find, to the potion for Juliet. All
goes smoothly and happily; the Friar is sententious, the lovers are
ecstatic, Mercutio, Benvolio and the Nurse make a merry work-a-
day chorus. Only that one note of warning is struck, lightly,
casually:

> Tybalt, the kinsman of old Capulet,
> Hath sent a letter to his father's house.

The marriage-scene brings this "movement" to its close.

> FRIAR. So smile the heavens upon this holy act,
> That after-hours with sorrow chide us not!
> ROMEO. Amen, amen! But come what sorrow can,
> It cannot countervail the exchange of joy
> That one short minute gives me in her sight.
> Do thou but close our hands with holy words,
> Then love-devouring death do what he dare,
> It is enough I may but call her mine.
> FRIAR. These violent delights have violent ends,
> And in their triumph die. . . .

Youth triumphant and defiant, age sadly wise; a scene of quiet
consummation, stillness before the storm. We are just halfway
through the play.

> Come, come with me, and we will make short work;
> For, by your leaves, you shall not stay alone
> Till holy church incorporate two in one.

But upon this, in immediate, most significant contrast, there
stride along Mercutio and Benvolio, swords on hip, armed servants
following them, Mercutio with mischief enough a-bubble in him
for the prudent Benvolio to be begging:

> I pray thee, good Mercutio, let's retire;
> The day is hot, the Capulets abroad,
> And if we meet we shall not scape a brawl,
> For now, these hot days, is the mad blood stirring.

—and (with one turn of the dramatist's wrist) tragedy is in
train.[8]

---

[8] One cannot too strongly insist upon the effect Shakespeare gains by this vivid
contrast between scene and scene, swiftly succeeding each other. It is his chief
technical resource.

The scene that follows is the most strikingly effective thing in the play. It comes quickly to its crisis when Romeo enters to encounter Tybalt face to face. For this moment the whole action has been preparing. Consider the constituents of the situation. Tybalt has seen Romeo eying his cousin Juliet from behind a mask and its privilege, and to no good purpose, be sure. But in Benvolio's and Mercutio's eyes he is still the lackadaisical adorer of Rosaline, a scoffer at the famous family quarrel suddenly put to the proof of manhood by a Capulet's insult. We know—we only—that he has even now come from his marriage to Juliet, from the marriage which is to turn these

> households' rancour to pure love.

The moment is made eloquent by a silence. For what is Romeo's answer to be to an insult so complete in its sarcastic courtesy?

> Romeo, the love I bear thee can afford
> No better term than this: Thou art a villain.

Benvolio and Mercutio, Tybalt himself, have no doubt of it; but to us the silence that follows—its lengthening by one pulse-beat mere amazement to them—is all suspense. We know what is in the balance. The moment is, for Romeo, so packed with emotions that the actor may interpret it in half a dozen ways, each legitimate (and by such an endowment we may value a dramatic situation). Does he come from his "one short minute" with Juliet so rapt in happiness that the sting of the insult cannot pierce him, that he finds himself contemplating this Tybalt and his inconsequent folly unmoved? Does he flash into passion and check it, and count the cost to his pride and the scorn of his friends, and count them as nothing, all in an instant? Whatever the effect on him, we, as we watch, can interpret it, no one else guessing. And when he does answer:

> Tybalt, the reason that I have to love thee
> Does much excuse the appertaining rage
> To such a greeting: villain am I none;
> Therefore, farewell; I see thou know'st me not.

the riddle of it is plain only to us. Note that it is the old riddling Romeo that answers, but how changed! We can enjoy, too, the perplexity of those other onlookers and wonder if no one of them will jump to the meaning of the

> good Capulet, which name I tender
> As dearly as my own . . .

But they stand stupent and Romeo passes on.

Upon each character concerned the situation tells differently; yet another test of its dramatic quality. Benvolio stands mute. He is all for peace, but such forbearance who can defend?[9] For Tybalt it is an all but comic letdown. The turning of the cheek makes the smiter look not brave, but ridiculous; and this "courageous captain of compliments" takes ridicule very ill, is the readier, therefore, to recover his fire-eating dignity when Mercutio gives him the chance. And Mercutio, so doing, adds that most important ingredient to the situation, the unforeseen.

> Why the devil came you between us? [he gasps out to Romeo
> a short minute later] I was hurt under your arm.

But what the devil had he to do with a Capulet-Montague quarrel? The fact is (if one looks back) that he has been itching to read fashion-monger Tybalt a lesson; to show him that "*alla stoccata*" could not carry it away. But "*alla stoccata*" does; and, before we well know where we are, this arbitrary catastrophe gives the sharpest turn yet to the play's action, the liveliest of its figures crumples to impotence before us, the charming rhetoric of the Queen Mab speech has petered out in a savage growl.

The unexpected has its place in drama as well as the plotted and prepared. But observe that Shakespeare uses Mercutio's death to precipitate an essential change in Romeo; and it is this change, not anything extrinsic, that determines the main tragedy. After a parenthesis of scuffle and harsh prose he is left alone on the stage, and a simpler, graver, sterner emotion than any we have known in him yet begins to throb through measured verse.

> This gentleman, the Prince's near ally,
> My very friend, hath got this mortal hurt

---

[9] He had been forced to a bout himself with Tybalt the day before; and his description a little later of Romeo,

> With gentle breath, calm look, knees humbly bowed . . .

has exasperation, as well, perhaps, as some politic exaggeration in it.

In my behalf; my reputation stained
With Tybalt's slander—Tybalt, that an hour
Hath been my cousin. O sweet Juliet,
Thy beauty hath made me effeminate,
And in my temper softened valour's steel!

Then he hears that his friend is dead, accepts his destiny—

This day's black fate on more days doth depend;
This but begins the woe others must end.

—and so to astonish the blood-intoxicated Tybalt! With a hundred words, but with expression and action transcending them, Shakespeare has tied the central knot of his play and brought his hero from height to depth.

We are sped on with little relaxation; returning, though, after these close-woven excitements, to declamation with Benvolio's diplomatic apologies (to the play's normal method, that is to say), while a second massed confronting of Montagues and Capulets marks, for reminder, this apex of the action.

We are sped on; and Juliet's ecstasy of expectation, the—

Gallop apace, you fiery-footed steeds. . . .

—makes the best of contrasts, in matter and manner, to the sternness of Romeo's banishing. A yet sharper contrast follows quickly with the Nurse's coming, carrying the ladder of cords (the highway to the marriage bed, for emphasis of irony), standing mute a minute while Juliet stares, then breaking incontinently into her

he's dead, he's dead, he's dead.

From now—with hardly a lapse to quiet—one scene will compete with the next in distraction till Friar Laurence comes to still the outcry of mourning over the drugged Juliet on her bed. The lovers compete in despair and desperate hope; Capulet precipitates confusion; the Friar himself turns foolhardy. All the action is shot through with haste and violence, and with one streak at least of gratuitous savagery besides. For if the plot demands Capulet's capricious tyrannies it does not need Lady Capulet's impulse to send a man after Romeo to poison him. But the freshly kindled virus of hatred (does Shakespeare feel?) must now spend itself even to exhaustion. From this point to the play's end, indeed, the one reposeful moment is when Romeo's

> dreams presage some joyful news at hand . . .

But the next is only the more shattering; and from then to the last tragic accidents it is a tale of yet worse violence, yet more reckless haste.[10]

It is, of course, in the end a tragedy of mischance. Shakespeare was bound by his story, was doubtless content to be; and how make it otherwise? Nevertheless, we discern his deeper dramatic sense, which was to shape the maturer tragedies, already in revolt. Accidents make good incidents, but tragedy determined by them has no significance. So he sets out, we see, in the shaping of his characters, to give all likelihood to the outcome. It is by pure ill-luck that Friar John's speed to Mantua is stayed while Balthasar reaches Romeo with the news of Juliet's death; but it is Romeo's headlong recklessness that leaves Friar Laurence no time to retrieve the mistake. It is, by a more subtle turn, Juliet's overacted repentance of her "disobedient opposition," which prompts the delighted Capulet to

> have this knot knit up to-morrow morning.

And this difference of a day proves also to be the difference between life and death.

Before ever the play begins, the chorus foretells its ending. The star-crossed lovers must, we are warned,

> with their death bury their parents' strife.

But Shakespeare is not content with the plain theme of an innocent happiness foredoomed. He makes good dramatic use of it. Our memory of the Prologue, echoing through the first scenes of happy encounter, lends them a poignancy which makes their

---

[10] The slaughtering of Paris is wanton and serves little dramatic purpose. Lady Montague is dead also by the end of the play (though no one gives much heed to that) and Q1 even informs us that

> young Benvolio is deceased too.

Here, however, the slaughter is probably less arbitrary—from one point of view. The actors had other parts to play. By the time Q2 has come into being Shakespeare knows better than to call attention to Benvolio's absence. Who notices it? But his audiences—a proportion of them—no doubt loved a holocaust for its own sake, and he was not above indulging them now and then.

beauties doubly beautiful. The sacrament of the marriage, with Romeo's invocation—

> Do thou but close our hands with holy words,
> Then love-devouring death do what he dare,
> It is enough I may but call her mine.

—read into it, stands as symbol of the sacrifice that all love and happiness must make to death. But character also is fate; it is, at any rate, the more dramatic part of it, and the life of Shakespeare's art is to lie in the manifesting of this. These two lovers, then, must in themselves be prone to disaster. They are never so freed from the accidents of their story as his later touch would probably have made them. But by the time he has brought them to their full dramatic stature we cannot—accidents or no—imagine a happy ending, or a Romeo and Juliet married and settled as anything but a burlesque.

So, the turning point of Mercutio's death and Tybalt's and Romeo's banishing being past, Shakespeare brings all his powers to bear upon the molding of the two figures to inevitable tragedy; and the producer of the play must note with care how the thing is done. To begin with, over a succession of scenes—in all but one of which either Romeo or Juliet is concerned—there is no relaxing of tension, vehemence or speed; for every flagging moment in them there is some fresh spur, they reinforce each other too, the common practice of contrast between scene and scene is more or less foregone.[11] And the play's declamatory method is heightened, now into rhapsody, now into a veritable dervish-whirling of words.

Shakespeare's practical ability—while he still hesitates to discard it—to turn verbal conventions to lively account is shown to the full in the scene between Juliet and the Nurse, with which this stretch of the action begins—his success, also his failure. The passage in which Juliet's bewildered dread finds expression in a cascade of puns is almost invariably cut on the modern stage, and one may sympathize with the actress who shirks it. But it is, in fact, word-play perfectly adapted to dramatic use; and to the Elizabethans puns were not necessarily comic things.

---

11 I say deliberately "in all but one," not two, for the reason I give later.

> Hath Romeo slain himself? Say thou but "I,"
> And that bare vowel "I" shall poison more
> Than the death-dealing eye of cockatrice:
> I am not I, if there be such an "I,"
> Or those eyes shut that make thee answer "I."
> If he be slain, say "I"; or if not, no:
> Brief sounds determine of my weal or woe.

Shut our minds to its present absurdity (but it is no more absurd than any other bygone fashion), allow for the rhetorical method, and consider the emotional effect of the word-music alone—what a vivid expression of the girl's agonized mind it makes, this intoxicated confusion of words and meanings! The whole scene is written in terms of conventional rhetoric. We pass from play upon words to play upon phrase, paradox, antithesis.

> O serpent heart, hid with a flowering face!
> Did ever dragon keep so fair a cave?
> Beautiful tyrant; fiend angelical!
> Dove-feathered raven! wolfish ravening lamb!
> Despised substance of divinest show!
> Just opposite to what thou justly seem'st;
> A damned saint, an honourable villain! . . .

The boy-Juliet was here evidently expected to give a display of virtuosity comparable to the singing of a *scena* in a mid-nineteenth century opera. That there was no danger of the audience finding it ridiculous we may judge by Shakespeare's letting the Nurse burlesque the outcry with her

> There's no trust,
> No faith, no honesty in men; all perjured,
> All forsworn, all naught, all dissemblers!

For it is always a daring thing to sandwich farce with tragedy; and though Shakespeare was fond of doing it, obviously he would not if the tragedy itself were trembling on the edge of farce.

The weakness of the expedient shows later, when, after bringing us from rhetoric to pure drama with the Nurse's

> Will you speak well of him that killed your cousin?

and Juliet's flashing answer,

> Shall I speak ill of him that is my husband?

—one of those master touches that clarify and consummate a
whole situation—Shakespeare must needs take us back to another
screed of the sort which now shows meretricious by comparison.
For a finish, though, we have the fine simplicity, set in formality,
of

> JULIET. Where is my father and my mother, Nurse?
> NURSE. Weeping and wailing over Tybalt's corse:
>   Will you go to them? I will bring you thither.
> JULIET. Wash they his wounds with tears! Mine shall be
>   spent,
>   When theirs are dry, for Romeo's banishment.
>   Take up those cords. Poor ropes, you are beguiled,
>   Both you and I, for Romeo is exiled.
>   He made you for a highway to my bed,
>   But I, a maid, die maiden-widowed.

By one means and another, he has now given us a new and a
passionate and desperate Juliet, more fitted to her tragic end.

In the scene that follows, we have desperate Romeo in place of
desperate Juliet, with the Friar to lift it to dignity at the finish and
to push the story a short step forward. The maturer Shakespeare
would not, perhaps, have coupled such similar scenes so closely;
but both likeness and repetition serve his present purpose.

To appraise the value of the next effect he makes we must again
visualize the Elizabethan stage.[12] Below

> *Enter Capulet, Lady Capulet and Paris.*

With Tybalt hardly buried, Juliet weeping for him, it has been
no time for urging Paris' suit.

> 'Tis very late [says Capulet], she'll not come down to-night:
> I promise you, but for your company,
> I should have been a-bed an hour ago.

Paris takes his leave, asks Lady Capulet to commend him to her
daughter. She answers him:

> I will, and know her mind early to-morrow;
> To-night she's mewed up to her heaviness.

But *we* know that, at this very moment, Romeo and Juliet, bride
and bridegroom, are in each other's arms.

---

12 But we must do this throughout.

Paris is actually at the door, when, with a sudden impulse, Capulet recalls him.[18]

> Sir Paris, I will make a desperate tender
> Of my child's love. I think she will be ruled
> In all respects by me; nay, more, I doubt it not.
> Wife, go you to her ere you go to bed;
> Acquaint her here of my son Paris' love,
> And bid her, mark you me, on Wednesday next . . .

And by that sudden impulse, so lightly obeyed, the tragedy is precipitated. Capulet, bitten by an idea, is in a ferment.

>   Well, Wednesday is too soon;
> O' Thursday let it be:—o' Thursday, tell her,
> She shall be married to this noble earl.
> Will you be ready? Do you like this haste? . . .

(In a trice he has shaken off the mourning uncle and turned jovial, roguish father-in-law.)

> Well, get you gone! O' Thursday be it then.—
> Go you to Juliet ere you go to bed,
> Prepare her, wife, against this wedding day. . . .

(What, we are asking, will Lady Capulet find if she does go?)

> Farewell, my lord.—Light to my chamber, ho!
> Afore me, it's so very late
> That we may call it early by and by:—
> Good-night.

Now comes the well-prepared effect. Hardly have the three vanished below, bustling and happy; when with

> Wilt thou begone? It is not yet near day. . . .

Juliet and Romeo appear at the window above, clinging together, agonized in the very joy of their union, but all ignorant of this new and deadly blow which (again) *we* know is to fall on them.

Only the unlocalized stage is capable of just such an effect as this. Delay in the shifting of scenery may be overcome by the

---

[18] And we may rely on this as one of the very few authenticated pieces of Shakespearean "business." For Q1 says,

> *Paris offers to goe in and Capolet calls him againe.*

If the presumed reporter watching the performance thought it important and had the time to note this down, it must have been markedly done.

simple lifting of a front scene to discover Romeo and Juliet in her chamber behind it; but Shakespeare's audience had not even to shift their imaginations from one place to another. The lower stage was anywhere downstairs in Capulet's house. The upper stage was associated with Juliet; it had served for her balcony and had been put to no other use.[14] So while Capulet is planning the marriage with Paris not only will our thoughts have been traveling to her, but our eyes may have rested speculatively, too, on those closed curtains above.

Shakespeare speeds his action all he can. Capulet, itching with his new idea, gives invaluable help. Romeo has hardly dropped from the balcony before Lady Capulet is in her daughter's room.[15] Capulet himself comes on her heels. It is barely daybreak and he has not been to bed. (The night is given just that confused chronology such feverish nights seem to have.) With morning Juliet flies to the Friar, to find Paris already with him, the news already agitating him; she herself is the more agitated by the unlooked-for meeting with Paris. The encounter between them, with its equivoque, oddly echoes her first encounter with Romeo; but it is another Juliet that now plays a suitor with words. It is a more deeply passionate Juliet, too, that turns from Paris' formal kiss with

> Oh, shut the door, and when thou hast done so,
> Come weep with me; past hope, past cure, past help!

than so passionately greeted the news of Tybalt's death and Romeo's banishment. Child she may still be, but she is now a wife.

We should count the Friar's long speech with which he gives her the potion, in which he tells her his plan, as a sort of strong pillar of rhetoric, from which the play's action is to be swung to the next strong pillar, the speech (in some ways its counterpart) in which Juliet nerves herself to the drinking it. For, with Romeo removed for the moment, the alternating scene falls to Capulet and his bustlings; these are admirable as contrast, but

[14] The musicians at Capulet's supper would probably have sat in it; but this is hardly a dramatic use. Nor does the mere association with Juliet *localize* it. There is no such scientific precision in the matter.
[15] For the stage business involved here, see p. 327ff.

of no dramatic power, and the action at this juncture must be well braced and sustained.

We come now to another and still more important effect, that is (yet again) only to be realized in the theater for which it was designed. The curtains of the inner stage are drawn back to show us Juliet's bed. Her nurse and her mother leave her; she drinks the potion, and—says that note-taker at the performance, whose business it was, presumably, to let his employers know exactly how all the doubtful bits were done—

She falls upon the bed within the curtains.

There has been argument upon argument whether this means the curtains of the bed or of the inner stage—which would then close on her. The difference in dramatic effect will be of degree and not kind. What Shakespeare aims at in the episodes that follow is to keep us conscious of the bed and its burden; while in front of it, Capulet and the servants, Lady Capulet and the Nurse pass hither and thither, laughing and joking over the preparation for the wedding, till the bridal music is playing, till, to the very sound of this, the Nurse bustles up to draw back the curtains and disclose the girl there stark and still.[16]

This is one of the chief dramatic effects of the play; and it can only be gained by preserving the continuity of the action, with its agonies and absurdities cheek by jowl, with that bridal music sharpening the irony at the last. It is a comprehensive effect, extending from the drinking of the potion to the Nurse's parrot scream when she finds Juliet stiff and cold; and even beyond, to the coming of the bridegroom and his train, through the long-spoken threnody, to the farce of the ending—which helps to remind us that, after all, Juliet is not dead. It is one scene, one integral stretch of action; and its common mutilation by *Scene iv. Hall in Capulet's house . . . Scene v. Juliet's chamber. Enter*

16 To Shakespeare's audience it would make little matter which sort of curtains they were. A closed bed standing shadowed on the inner stage is at once to be ignored and recognized. We also, with a little practice, can ignore it, with Capulet; though to our more privileged gaze there it significantly is, in suspended animation, as it were, till the Nurse, fingering its curtains, brings it back to dramatic life, as we have known she must, as we have been waiting breathlessly for her to do. Whether they should be bed curtains or stage curtains is a matter of convention, a question of more imagination or less.

Nurse. . . , with the consequences involved, is sheer editorial murder.

Modern producers, as a rule, do even worse by it than the editors. They bring down a curtain upon a display of virtuosity in a "potion-scene," long drawn out, worried to bits, and leave us to recover till they are ready with Romeo in Mantua and the apothecary. And even faithful Shakespeareans have little good to say of that competition in mourning between Paris and Capulet, Lady Capulet and the Nurse. It has been branded as deliberate burlesque. It is assuredly no more so than was Juliet's outbreak against Romeo upon Tybalt's death; to each, we notice, the Nurse provides a comic, characteristic echo, which would have little point if it did not contrast, rather absurdly, with the rest. Burlesque, of a sort, comes later with Peter and the musicians; Shakespeare would not anticipate this effect, and so equivocally! The passage does jar a little; but we must remember that he is working here in a convention that has gone somewhat stale with him, and constrainedly; and that he can call now on no such youthful, extravagant passion as Juliet's or Romeo's to make the set phrases live. The situation is dramatically awkward, besides; in itself it mocks at the mourners, and Friar Laurence's reproof of them, which comes unhappily near to cant, hardly clarifies it. Shakespeare comes lamely out; but he went sincerely in. Nor does the farce of Peter and the musicians, conventional as it is, stray wholly beyond likelihood. Peter is comic in his grief; but many people are. Will Kempe, it may be, had to have his fling; but this part of the scene has its dramatic value, too. It develops and broadens—vulgarizes, if you will—the irony of the bridal music brought to the deathbed; and, the traditional riddle-me-ree business done with (and Will Kempe having "brought off an exit" amid cheers), there is true sting in the tail of it:

> FIRST MUSICIAN. What a pestilent knave is this same!
> SECOND MUSICIAN. Hang him, Jack! Come, we'll in here;
> tarry for the mourners, and stay dinner.

And, of course, it eases the strain before tragedy gets its final grip of us.

We find Romeo in Mantua poised upon happiness before his last sudden plunge to despair and death. Shakespeare has now achieved simplicity in his treatment of him, brought the character to maturity and his own present method to something like perfection. What can be simpler, more obvious yet more effective than the dream with its flattering presage of good news—

> I dreamt my lady came and found me dead—
> Strange dream, that gives a dead man leave to think!—
> And breathed such life with kisses in my lips,
> That I revived, and was an emperor. . . .

—followed incontinently by Balthasar's

> Her body sleeps in Capels' monument,
> And her immortal part with angels lives. . . .

So much for dreams! So much for life and its flatteries! And the buying of the poison shows us a Romeo grown out of all knowledge away from the sentimental, phrase-making adorer of Rosaline.

> There is thy gold; worse poison to men's souls,
> Doing more murder in this loathsome world
> Than these poor compounds that thou mayst not sell:
> I sell thee poison, thou hast sold me none.

This aging of Romeo is marked by more than one touch. To the contemptuous Tybalt he was a boy; now Paris to him, when they meet, is to be "good gentle youth."

Then, after one more needed link in the story has been riveted, we reach the play's last scene. Producers are accustomed to eliminate most of this, keeping the slaughtering of Paris as a prelude, concentrating upon Romeo's death and Juliet's, possibly providing a sort of symbolic picture of Montagues and Capulets reconciled at the end. This is all very well, and saves us the sweet kernel of the nut, no doubt; but it happens not to be the scene that Shakespeare devised. To appreciate that we must once more visualize the stage for which it was devised. The authorities are in dispute upon several points here, but only of detail. Juliet lies entombed in the inner stage; that is clear. The outer stage stands for the churchyard; as elastically as it stood before for the street or the courtyard of Capulet's house in which the Maskers marched about, while the serving-men coming forth with their napkins converted it, as vaguely, into the hall. Now it is as near

to the tomb or as far from it as need be, and the action on it (it
is the larger part of this that is usually cut) will be prominent
and important. The tomb itself is the inner stage, closed in,
presumably, by gates which Romeo breaks open, through the
bars of which Paris casts his flowers. Juliet herself lies like a
recumbent effigy upon a rectangular block of stone, which must
be low enough and wide enough for Romeo to lie more or less
beside her; and other such monuments, uneffigied, Tybalt's
among them, may surround her.[17]

Once more Shakespeare hurries us through a whole night of
confusion; from the coming of Paris, the cheated bridegroom,
and Romeo, the robbed husband, to this ghastly bride-bed, through
one tragic miscarrying after another, to the Prince's summing-up:

> A glooming peace this morning with it brings. . . .

All is confusion; only the regularity of the verse keeps it from
running away. Paris is fearful of disturbance,[18] and Romeo, when
he comes, is strained beyond endurance or control. It is not till
he has fleshed the edge of his desperation upon poor Paris, till
he is sobered by seeing what he has done, that, armed securely
with his poison, he can take his calm farewell. Once he is dead,
confusion is let loose. The Friar approaches with

> Saint Francis be my speed! How oft to-night
> Have my old feet stumbled at graves! . . .

Balthasar and he whisper and tremble. Then Juliet wakes; but
before he can speak to her, the watch are heard coming. He flies;

---

17 We need not comb the text for objections to this arrangement, which is
practicable, while no other is. For an explanation of

> Why I *descend* into this bed of death . . .

for instance, we have only to turn to Brooke's poem (lines 2620-2630). The
frontispiece to Rowe's edition of the play is (incidentally) worth observing. It
does not show a stage-setting, even a Restoration stage-setting, but the tomb
itself may well be the sort of thing that was used. Paris and Romeo, it can be
seen, wear semi-Roman costume. Is this, by any hazardous chance, explicable by
the fact that Otway's perversion of the play, *Caius Marius*, was then current in the
theaters (*Romeo and Juliet* itself was not, it seems, revived till 1744; and then
much altered)? Did Du Guernier begin his drawing with the Roman lovers in his
mind?

18 For no compelling reason; but Shakespeare felt the need of striking this
note at once, since a first note will tend to be the dominant one.

and she has but time to find the empty phial in Romeo's hand, bare time to find his dagger and stab herself before they appear, and the hunt is up:

> PARIS' PAGE.   This is the place; there, where the torch doth
>   burn.
> CAPTAIN OF   The ground is bloody; search about the
> THE WATCH.   churchyard:
>   Go, some of you, whoe'er you find, attach.
>   Pitiful sight! here lies the county slain,
>   And Juliet bleeding, warm and newly dead,
>   Who here hath lain this two days buried.[19]
>   Go, tell the Prince; run to the Capulets;
>   Raise up the Montagues; some others search. . . .

Cries, confusion, bustle; some of the watch bring back Balthasar, some others the Friar; the Prince arrives with his train, the Capulets surge in, the Montagues; the whole front stage is filled with the coming and going, while, in dreadful contrast, plain to our sight within the tomb, the torchlight flickering on them, Romeo and Juliet lie still.[20]

The play is not over, another hundred lines go to its finishing; and, to appease our modern impatience of talk when no more is to be done, here, if nowhere else, the producer will wield the blue pencil doughtily. Why should the Friar recount at length—after saying he'll be brief, moreover!—what we already know, with Balthasar to follow suit, and Paris' page to follow him? There are half a dozen good reasons. Shakespeare neither could nor would, of course, bring a play to a merely catastrophic end; the traditions of his stage no less than its conditions forbade this. Therefore the Prince's authoritative

> Seal up the mouth of outrage for a while,
> Till we can clear these ambiguities,
> And know their spring, their head, their true descent;
> And then I will be general of your woes,
> And lead you even to death: meantime forbear. . . .

---

[19] Another instance of Shakespeare's use of time for momentary effect—or of his carelessness. Or will someone find a subtle stroke of character in the Watchman's inaccuracy?

[20] It is of some interest to note that *Antony and Cleopatra* ends with a similar stage effect.

with which he stills a tumult that threatens otherwise to end the play, as it began, in bloody rough-and-tumble—this is the obvious first note of a formal full-close. But the Friar's story must be told, because the play's true end is less in the death of the star-crossed lovers than in the burying of their parents' strife; and as it has been primarily a play of tangled mischances, the unraveling of these, the bringing home of their meaning to the sufferers by them, is a natural part of its process. How else lead up to the Prince's

> Where be these enemies? Capulet—Montague!
> See what a scourge is laid upon your hate. . . .

and to the solution with Capulet's

> O brother Montague, give me thy hand. . . .

For us also—despite our privileged vision—it has been a play of confused, passion-distorted happenings, and the Friar's plain tale makes the simple pity of them clear, and sends us away with this foremost in our minds. Again, declamation is the norm of the play's method, and it is natural to return to that for a finish. Finally, as it is a tragedy less of character than of circumstance, upon circumstance its last emphasis naturally falls. Yet, all this admitted, one must own that the penultimate stretch of the writing, at least, is poor in quality. Shakespeare has done well by his story and peopled it with passionate life. But, his impulse flagging, his artistry is still found immature. Compare the poverty of this ending with the resourceful breadth of the effect made in the rounding of the story of *Cymbeline* to a close.

The Question of Act-Division

NEITHER Quartos nor Folio mark act-division; Rowe first supplies it, and his arrangement has commonly been accepted since. There are several questions involved. Did Shakespeare plan out the play as an indivisible whole? If he did, was it so acted; and, if not, were the pauses made mere formal pauses, or intervals, in which the emotional tension would not only relax, but lapse altogether? And, pauses or intervals, is Rowe's placing of them authentic? With the historical aspect of all this I am incompetent

to deal. But Rowe's dividing-up of the action is, clearly, neither
here nor there; and even if it is not his, but a somehow inherited
tradition, that still will not make it Shakespeare's. A play, as we
know, soon passed beyond its author's control, and Elizabethan
practice may have differed from play to play, and as between the
public theater and the private. How did Shakespeare *plan* his
play? That is what we have to divine if we can; and from that
we may pass directly to the question of our own convenience in
the acting of it.

The one internal piece of evidence of a lost scheme of act-
division is the second chorus. This, incidentally, does not appear
in the first Quarto. Is it capable of any other explanation? It has
little dramatic point, as to this Johnson's robust verdict suffices;
". . . it conduces nothing to the progress of the play, but relates
what is already known, or what the next scene will show; and
relates it without adding the improvement of any moral sentiment." It has been held very doubtfully Shakespearean. There is
one thing to note about it and the scene which precedes it. This
requires stools to be set on the outer stage for the use of Capulet
and his cousin. They are presumably the joint-stools of the text,
and the text makes provision for their setting. But we find none
for their taking-away, no dialogue to help out the business, and
they could not well be moved during the latter half of the scene,
when Romeo and Juliet are love-making. In an act-pause they
could presumably have been moved; but if there were none—was
the chorus by chance written in to cover this technical clumsiness? It is possible; but the remedy seems as clumsy as the fault.[21]

Later, Shakespeare lands himself in a more serious technical
difficulty, from which, though at some sacrifice of dramatic effect,
an act-pause would have extricated him. He wants to show us
Romeo and Juliet parting on their wedding night, Romeo
descending from the very balcony which had seen their wooing and
their brief happiness, and to follow this quickly by the bringing of
the news to Juliet that she is to marry Paris. The double blow,
no respite given, was the important thing to him dramatically,

[21] It looks as if another stool were needed on the outer stage when the Nurse
returns to Juliet with her news of Romeo. But in this case no special provision
is made either for its placing or removing.

without doubt. But would he not have saved himself, if he well could, from the present ensuing clumsiness that brings Juliet from upper stage to lower in the middle of a scene, her bedroom on her back, as it were? Though an Elizabethan audience might make light of a lapse of this sort, it is none the less clumsy, and from the beginning he was an apt if a daring craftsman.[22]

Lastly, was the scene between Peter and the musicians written for its own sake, or to please Will Kempe, or (possibly) to make more time than the two scenes which carry on the plot allow for the moving of the bed and the setting of the tomb upon the inner stage?[23] If Rowe's act-pause had intervened there would have been time enough. These are trivial matters, but not wholly negligible.

If five acts there must be, Rowe's five may serve. But one could vary the division as legitimately in half a dozen different ways; and this in itself argues against any division at all. Nor is there any scene-division in the play, where an act-division might fall, over which some immediate bridge does not seem to be thrown. Either a strong contrast is devised between the end of one scene and the beginning of the next that a pause would nullify, or the quick succession of event to event is an integral part of the dramatic effect Shakespeare is seeking. (But it is, of course, in the very nature of the play, of its precipitate passion, to forge ahead

---

[22] The scene could have been staged in no other way. *Enter Romeo and Juliet at the window*, says Q1; *Enter Romeo and Juliet aloft*, says Q2. Later Q1 tells us, *He goeth downe*; and later still we have

Enter Nurse hastily.

NURSE. Madame, beware, take heed the day is broke,
Your Mother's comming to your Chamber. Make
all sure.
She goeth downe from the window.

Whether Juliet or the Nurse, does not matter. In fact they both must go down; for there follows immediately:

Enter Juliet, Mother, Nurse.

And a second later, after her

How now, who calls?

Juliet is on the stage. By Q2 the scene has been much rewritten. The Nurse is given more time for her descent. The later stage directions are less explicit. But that the business was approximately the same is certain, if for no other reason than that the last part of the scene, containing Capulet's outburst, could have been effectively played nowhere but on the lower stage.

[23] "Or/and," as the lawyers sometimes have it, with regard to the last possibility.

without pause.) What value is there in an act-pause after Capulet's supper, between Romeo's first meeting with Juliet and the balcony-scene? There is no interval of time to account for, nor has the action reached any juncture that asks for the emphasis of a pause. An act-pause after the marriage falls with a certain effect, but it nullifies the far better effect by which Tybalt is shown striding the streets in search of Romeo at the very moment when the Friar is marrying him to Juliet; and that Romeo should seem to come straight from the marriage to face Tybalt's challenge is a vital dramatic point. The whole action surges to a crisis with the deaths of Tybalt and Mercutio and Romeo's banishing; and here, one could argue, a pause while we asked, "What next?" might have its value. But Rowe marks no act-pause here; and if he did, the fine effect by which Juliet's ecstatic

> Gallop apace, you fiery-footed steeds. . . .

follows pat upon the Prince's

> let Romeo hence in haste,
> Else, when he's found, that hour is his last.

would be destroyed. The break made between Juliet's departure to the Friar's cell for counsel how to escape the marriage with Paris and her arrival there and the encounter with him relates to no pause, nor check, nor turn in the action. Rowe's Act IV, we may say, then begins with the new interest of the giving of the potion, as it ends upon an echo of its taking. And a pause—a breathing-space before the great plunge into tragedy—before we find Romeo in Mantua waiting for news (before Rowe's Act V, that is to say) may have dramatic value. But the comic scene with the musicians provides just such a breathing-space. And if we remove it (and there may have been, as I suggest, merely incidental reasons for putting it in) a continuity of action is restored which gives us a most dramatic contrast between the mourning over Juliet and Romeo's buoyant hopes.

What we should look for, surely, in act-division, is some definite advantage to the play's acting. Where, in this play, do we find that? But the gains are patent if we act it without check or pause. Whatever the Elizabethan practice may have been, and whatever concessions are to be made to pure convenience, everything seems to point to Shakespeare having *planned* the play as a thing indivisible. It can be so acted without much outrunning the two hours' traffic.[24] If this will overtax the weakness of the flesh—the audience's; for actors will profit by the unchecked flow of action and emotion—some sacrifice of effect must be made. The less then, the better. A single pause after the banishing of Romeo would be my own solution.

Staging, Costume, Music, Text

THE producer wishing to enscene the play must devise such scenery as will not deform, obscure or prejudice its craftsmanship or its art. That is all. But it is not easy to do.

There are no signs in the text that Shakespeare saw Italian touches added to the players' normal costumes. Italian costumes will serve, as long as rapier and dagger go with them, and may add something to the effect of the play upon us; but Elizabethan doublet and hose will take next to nothing of it away.

The text tells us pretty plainly what music is needed. It is a consort of recorders that Paris brings with him to the wedding; and the musicians either enter with him, playing, to be stopped incontinently by the sight of the tragic group round the bed; or (this is, I think, more likely) they stay playing the bridal music without, a tragically ironical accompaniment to the lamenting over Juliet, till they are stopped and come clustering—scared, incongruous figures—into the doorway.[25]

> Faith, we may put up our pipes and be gone.

says the leader, when the mourners depart (all but the Nurse,

---

[24] A casual phrase, surely, which means nearer two hours than either one or three.

[25] According to Q1 they were fiddlers, *i.e.* a consort of viols, so they could not enter playing. Also, viols would not be well heard through dialogue except from the musicians' gallery, so their entrance was perhaps delayed by the time it took them to finish there and descend. Q2 has the first reference to "pipes." (Had the Globe acquired another quartet in the meantime?) These could easily be heard playing "off." Q2, however, marks no entrance for them. They are there when the mourners depart; that is all. The entrance with Paris and the Friar belongs to the undated Quarto, which is of doubtful authority.

who needs a line or two to speak while she draws the inner-stage curtains), leaving them alone.

The recorders could play for the dance at Capulet's too. But a consort of viols is perhaps likelier here, for there is dialogue throughout the music, and one does not speak through wood-wind with impunity. The musicians probably sat in their gallery.

The text itself raises many minor questions that need not be dealt with here. But no one should omit to read the first Quarto. For all its corruptions, it gives us now and then a vivid picture of a performance Shakespeare himself must presumably have supervised. It may not be much to know that Juliet entered *somewhat fast* and embraced Romeo[26]; that when Romeo *offers to stab himself* the Nurse *snatches the dagger away*; that (but this point we have remarked as important) at one juncture *Paris offers to goe in and Capolet calls him againe*; that they cast rosemary on the Juliet they think dead; and that Paris comes with his page to the tomb bringing flowers and *sweete water* with him too. But Shakespeare's stage directions are rareties indeed; and these and other such small touches give life to the rudimentary text, and an actuality to the play that scrupulous editing seems, somehow, to reform altogether.

Not but that the text has needed editing enough; and there are puzzles, such as the notorious "runaway's eyes" (twenty-eight pages devoted to it in the Furness Variorum!), yet unsolved. But few, if any, of them are of dramatic moment; and there is amply varied authority to bow to. The producer has his own few problems to face. There is the minor one of indecency. One or two of Mercutio's jokes are too outrageous for modern public usage; they will create discomfort among a mixed audience instead of laughter. But this full-blooded sensuality is (as we have seen) set very purposefully against Romeo's romantic idealism, and the balance and contrast must not be destroyed. A Mercutio who lets his mouth be stopped by a prim Benvolio each time he launches on a smutty joke will be a cowed, a "calm, dishonourable, vile" Mercutio indeed.

---

[26] But this scene was badly muddled, either by the reporter of these performances, or the actors, or by somebody. For further discussion of the point, see p. 347, note 37.

But a producer is tempted to far more cutting than this, and most producers fall. The play as commonly presented to us starts fairly true to Shakespeare, a troublesome passage suppressed here and there; but, as it advances, more and more of the text disappears, till the going becomes hop-skip-and-jump, and "Selections from the tragedy of Romeo and Juliet" would be a truer title for it. This will not do. The construction, very naturally, does not show the skill of Shakespeare's maturity, nor does every character stand consistent and foursquare; the writing runs to extravagant rhetoric and often to redundancy. But his chosen method of close consecutive narrative will be lamed by mutilation; and rhetoric and redundancy, the violence, the absurdities even, are the medium in which the characters are quite intentionally painted. To omit the final scurry of Montagues and Capulets and citizens of Verona to the tomb and the Friar's redundant story for the sake of finishing upon the more poignant note of Juliet's death is, as we have seen, to falsify Shakespeare's whole intention; and to omit the sequel to the drinking of the potion is as bad and worse! Restoring the play to its own sort of stage will serve to curb these follies, at least.

The verbiage and its eccentricities—as they sound to our modern incurious ears—seem, at first blush, harder to compass. No producer need be pedantic; it is his business to gain an effect, not to prejudice it. But much that strikes one as strange in print, that may jar under the repetition and cold-blooded analysis of rehearsals, will pass and make its own effect in the rush of performance. The cutting of a speech or two from a scene is like the removal of a few bricks from a wall; it may be a harmless operation and it may not. The structure may stand up as strongly with the hole in it, or it may sag, or come tumbling altogether. The antiphonal mourning over Juliet is crude, doubtless, and one is tempted to get rid of it, or at least to modify it. Do so, and what becomes of the calming effect of Friar Laurence's long speeches? There will be nothing for him to calm. Cut this too, and Capulet will have to turn without rhyme or reason from distracted grief to dignified resignation, while the others, the Friar included, stand like foolish lay figures.

To protest against the omission of the—to us—incongruous pun which bisects Romeo's passionate outburst, his

This may flies do, when I from this must fly. . . .

would be pedantry. The play will not be the worse for its loss; the only question is whether it is worth omitting. But to shirk Juliet's delirium of puns upon "Ay" and "I" and "eye" is to lower the scene's temperature and flatten it out when Shakespeare has planned to lift it, by these very means, to a sudden height of intoxicated excitement, giving us a first and memorable taste of the Juliet of quick despair, who later, in a flash of resolution, will sheath Romeo's dagger in her heart.

There is no more dangerous weapon than the blue pencil.

The Characters

THIS is a tragedy of youth, as youth sees it, and age is not let play a very distinguished part. Friar Laurence is sympathetic, but he is compact of maxims, of pedagogic kindness; he is just such a picture of an old man as a young man draws, all unavailing wisdom. There is no more life in the character than the story asks and gives; but Shakespeare palliates this dramatic weakness by keeping him shadowed in his cell, a ghostly confessor, a refuge for Romeo, Paris and Juliet alike, existing—as in their youthful egoism we may be sure they thought—in their interests alone.

It is noteworthy what an arbitrary line is drawn between youth and age; arbitrary, but at times uncertain. Capulet and Montague are conventionally "old," though their children are young enough for them not to have passed forty. Capulet gives some excuse for this by saying of Juliet that

The earth hath swallowed all my hopes but she. . . .

So we may surmise, if we will, a cluster of sons killed in the vendetta, or that sad little Elizabethan procession of infant effigies to be carved in time on his tomb. But Lady Capulet passes from saying that she was but fourteen herself at Juliet's birth fourteen years ago to telling us in the end that

This sight of death is as a bell
That warns my old age to a sepulchre.[27]

---

[27] In her speech to Juliet "a" mother has been read for "your" mother; but without any warrant.

And the Nurse is old, though not fourteen years ago she had a child of her own and was suckling Juliet. It is futile trying to resolve these anomalies. Shakespeare wants a sharp conflict set between youth and age; he emphasizes every aspect of it, and treats time of life much as he treats time of day—for effect.

THE NURSE

The Nurse, whatever her age, is a triumphant and complete achievement. She stands foursquare, and lives and breathes in her own right from the moment she appears, from that very first

> Now, by my maidenhead at twelve year old,
> I bade her come.

Shakespeare has had her pent up in his imagination; and out she gushes. He will give us nothing completer till he gives us Falstaff. We mark his confident, delighted knowledge of her by the prompt digression into which he lets her launch; the story may wait. It is not a set piece of fireworks such as Mercutio will touch off in honor of Queen Mab. The matter of it flows spontaneously into verse, the phrases are hers and hers alone, character unfolds with each phrase. You may, indeed, take any sentence the Nurse speaks throughout the play, and only she could speak it. Moreover, it will have no trace of the convention to which Shakespeare himself is still tied (into which he forces, to some extent, every other character), unless we find her burlesquing it. But the good Angelica—which we at last discover to be her perfect name—needs no critical expanding, she expounds herself on all occasions; nor explanation, for she is plain as daylight; nor analysis, lest it lead to excuse; and she stays blissfully unregenerate. No one can fail to act her well that can speak her lines. Yet they are so supercharged with life that they will accommodate the larger acting—which is the revelation of a personality in terms of a part—and to the full; and it may be as rich a personality as can be found. She is in everything inevitable; from her

> My fan, Peter.

when she means to play the discreet lady with those gay young sparks, to that all unexpected

> Faith, here 'tis; Romeo
> Is banished; and all the world to nothing,
> That he dares ne'er come back to challenge you;
> Or if he do, it needs must be by stealth.
> Then, since the case so stands as now it doth,
> I think it best you married with the county.

—horrifyingly unexpected to Juliet; but to us, the moment she has said it, the inevitable thing for her to say.

This last turn, that seems so casually made, is the stroke that completes the character. Till now we have taken her—the "good, sweet Nurse"—just as casually, amused by each comicality as it came; for so we do take the folk that amuse us. But with this everything about her falls into perspective, her funniments, her endearments, her grossness, her good nature; upon the instant, they all find their places in the finished picture. And for a last enrichment, candidly welling from the lewd soul of her, comes

> O, he's a lovely gentleman;
> Romeo's a dishclout to him; an eagle, Madam,
> Hath not so green, so quick, so fair an eye
> As Paris hath. Beshrew my very heart,
> I think you are happy in this second match,
> For it excels your first; or if it did not,
> Your first is dead, or 'twere as good he were
> As living hence and you no use of him.

Weigh the effect made upon Juliet, fresh from the sacrament of love and the bitterness of parting, by the last fifteen words of that.

> Speak'st thou from thy heart?
>   And from my soul too,
> Or else beshrew them both.
>   Amen!

It is gathered into the full-fraught "Amen." But best of all, perhaps, is the old bawd's utter unconsciousness of having said anything out of the way. And when she finds her lamb, her ladybird, returning from shrift with merry look—too merry!— how should she suppose she has not given her the wholesomest advice in the world?

We see her obliviously bustling through the night's preparations for this new wedding. We hear her—incredibly!—start to stir

Juliet from her sleep with the same coarse wit that had served to deepen the girl's blushes for Romeo's coming near. We leave her blubbering grotesquely over the body she had been happy to deliver to a baser martyrdom. Shakespeare lets her pass from the play without comment. Is any needed?[28]

CAPULET

Capulet, again, is a young man's old man. But he is more opulently done than the Friar, if he has not the flesh, blood, bones and all of the good Angelica. He suffers more than any other character in the play by its customary mutilations; for these leave him a mere domestic tyrant, and Shakespeare does not. With his benevolent airs, self-conscious hilarity, childish ill-temper, he is that yet commoner type, the petted and spoiled husband and father and head of the house; and the study of him might be more effective if it were not strung out through the play, and so intermittently touched in. But he is planned consistently—with all his inconsistencies—from the beginning.

The flavor of gratified vanity in

> But Montagu is bound as well as I
> In penalty alike . . .

puts us at once upon easy terms with him. And Shakespeare hardly wrote,

> But woo her, gentle Paris, get her heart,
> My will to her consent is but a part. . . .

without having

> An you be mine, I'll give you to my friend;
> An you be not, hang, beg, starve, die in the streets. . . .

in his mind already. Our next sight of him gives us the breeze with Tybalt, the chop and change of

> Well said, my hearts! You are a princox; go:
> Be·quiet, or—More light, more light!—For shame!
> I'll make you quiet.—What, cheerly, my hearts!

---

[28] Unless it be for Juliet's youthful, ruthless
Ancient damnation! O most wicked fiend! . . .

This is Capulet at home, a familiar figure in many a home; the complete gentleman, the genial host, the kindliest of men—as long as no one crosses him.

Old as he is, he was ready enough to take part in the earlier brawl; but we note that he stands silent before Tybalt's body, and Lady Capulet is left to cry out for revenge. He did not the less love Tybalt dearly because he can turn promptly from the thought of him to Juliet's marriage to Paris, and change his decorous resolve to

> keep no great ado; a friend or two;
> For, hark you, Tybalt being slain so late,
> It may be thought we held him carelessly,
> Being our kinsman, if we revel much.

into

> Sirrah, go hire me twenty cunning cooks.

He is incorrigibly hospitable, that is one thing. For another, it is obviously a wise move, Capulets and Montagues both being now in worse odor than ever in Verona, to marry Juliet as soon as may be to this kinsman of the Prince. And except for the haste of it (nor would even that greatly astonish them) his

> Sir Paris, I will make a desperate tender
> Of my child's love. I think she will be ruled
> In all respects by me; nay, more, I doubt it not.

would not seem to an Elizabethan audience very unusual. His vituperative raging against the obstinate girl does bring his wife and the Nurse to her rescue.

> Out, you green-sickness carrion! out, you baggage!
> You tallow face!

—moves even Lady Capulet to protest. But he is merely raging; and parents of the day, finding their fingers itch to chastise young ladies of riper years than Juliet, did not always let them itch in vain. For a thrashing then and there ample precedent could be cited. And an hour or two later he is quite good-tempered again.

> How now, my headstrong! where have you been gadding?

he hails her.

He is not insincere, as he is not undignified, in his heartbroken outcry at her supposed death, if we may divine Shakespeare's intention through a crudely written scene. And he stands, dignified and magnanimous in his sorrow, at the last. It is a partial picture of a man, no doubt, ill-emphasized at times, and at times crippled by convention; but of a most recognizable man, and never untrue. Note lastly that it is the portrait of a very English old gentleman.[29] When did the phlegmatic Englishman— or the legend of him—come into fashion as the type of his kind?

THE MINOR CHARACTERS; AND MERCUTIO

The play has its full share of merely conventional figures, from the Prince to Peter, Abram and his fellows, to Balthasar and Paris' page; and they must be treated for what they are. Lady Capulet is sketchily uncertain. Benvolio is negative enough, confidant to Romeo, foil to Mercutio. But there are such men; and Shakespeare endows him with a kindly patience, sharpens his wit every now and again to a mild irony, gives him a steady consistency that rounds him to something more than a shadow.

Tybalt we must see somewhat through Mercutio's eyes. Pretty obviously we are meant to; and the actor must take the hint, nor make him a mere blusterer, but something at least of a

> courageous captain of compliments . . . the very butcher of a silk button, a duellist, a duellist; a gentleman of the very first house, of the first and second cause.

He need not, however, place him irretrievably among the

> antic, lisping, affecting fantasticoes, these new tuners of accents . . . these fashion-mongers, these *pardonnez-mois* . . .

He may reasonably discount a little Mercutio's John Bull prejudices.

For Mercutio, when Shakespeare finally makes up his mind about him, is in temperament very much the young John Bull of his time; and as different from the stocky, stolid John Bull of our later picturing as Capulet from the conventional heavy father. There can be, of course, no epitomizing of a race in any one figure. But the dominant qualities of an age are apt to be set in a

---

[29] But *not* (to compare his position to Capulet's in Verona) of an English nobleman; of a prosperous English merchant, rather. See Miss St. Clare Byrne's chapter on "The Social Background" in *A Companion to Shakespearean Studies*.

pattern, which will last in literature, though outmoded, till another replaces it.

We learn little about Mercutio as he goes racketing to Capulet's supper, except that John Bull is often a poetic sort of fellow, or as he returns, unless it be that a man may like smut and fairy tales too. But he is still in the toils of conventional versifying, and a victim besides, probably, to his author's uncertainty about him. The authentic Mercutio only springs into life with

> Where the devil should this Romeo be? Came he not home to-night?

when he springs to life indeed. From now on he abounds in his own sense, and we can put him to the test the Nurse abides by; not a thing that he says could anyone else say. He asks as little exposition, he is what he is with perfect clarity; the more so probably because he is wholly Shakespeare's creation, his namesake in Brooke's poem giving no hint of him. And (as with the Nurse) we could transport this authentic Mercutio into the maturest of the plays and he would fall into place there, nor would he be out of place on any stage, in any fiction.

A wholesome self-sufficiency is his cardinal quality; so he suitably finds place among neither Capulets nor Montagues. Shakespeare endows him, we saw, with a jolly sensuality for a setoff to Romeo's romancings; and, by a later, significant touch, adds to the contrast. When their battle of wits is ending—a breathless bandying of words that is like a sharp set at tennis— suddenly, it would seem, he throws an affectionate arm round the younger man's shoulder.[30]

> Why, is not this better now than groaning for love? Now art thou sociable, now art thou Romeo, now art thou what thou art. . . .

Mercutio's creed in a careless sentence! At all costs be the thing you are. The more his—and the more John Bullish—that we find it dropped casually amid a whirl of chaff and never touched on again! Here is the man. No wistful ideals for him; but life as it

---

[30] We are not definitely told so, but certainly Mercutio seems a little the older of the two; and here again he is exempt from that other party-division into young and old.

comes and death when it comes. A man of soundest common sense
surely; the complete realist, the egoist justified. But by the day's
end he has gone to his death in a cause not his own, upon pure
impulse and something very like principle. There is no inconsistency in this; such vital natures must range between extremes.

> Rightly to be great
> Is not to stir without great argument,
> But greatly to find quarrel in a straw,
> When honour's at the stake.

That is a later voice, troublously questioning. Mercutio pretends
neither to greatness nor philosophy. When the moment comes,
it is not his own honor that is at stake; but such calm, dishonorable, vile submission is more than flesh and blood can bear. That
the Mercutios of the world quarrel on principle they would hate
to be told. Quarrel with a man for cracking nuts, having no
other reason but because one has hazel eyes; quarrel, with your
life in your hand, for quarreling's sake, since quarreling and
fighting are a part of life, and the appetite for them human
nature. Mercutio fights Tybalt because he feels he must, because
he cannot stand the fellow's airs a moment longer. He'll put him
in his place, if no one else will. He fights without malice, not
in anger even, and for no advantage. He fights because he is
what he is, to testify to this simple unconscious faith, and goes
in with good honest cut and thrust. But *alla stoccata* carries it
away; and he, the perfect realist, the egoist complete, dies for an
ideal. Extremes have met.

No regrets though; nor any hypocrisy of resignation for him!
He has been beaten by the thing he despised, and is as robustly
angry about it as if he had years to live in which to get his own
back.

> Zounds! a dog, a rat, a mouse, a cat, to scratch a man to death!
> A braggart, a rogue, a villain, that fights by the book of
> arithmetic!

He is brutally downright with Romeo:

> Why the devil came you between us? I was hurt under your
> arm.[31]

---

[31] All the technical talk of swordplay must, of course, have been a dozen
times livelier to the Elizabethans than it ever can be to us.

and, after that, says no more to him, ignores the pitifully futile
I thought all for the best.
dies with his teeth set, impenitently himself to the last.

ROMEO

We have Romeo and Juliet themselves left to consider; the
boy and girl—they are no more—caught with their love as in a
vice between the hatreds of their houses, to be crushed to death
there.

Romeo has been called an early study for Hamlet. It is true
enough to be misleading. The many ideas that go to make up
Hamlet will have seeded themselves from time to time in Shakespeare's imagination, sprouting a little, their full fruition delayed
till the dominant idea ripened. We can find traits of Hamlet in
Romeo, in Richard II, in Jaques, in less likely habitations. But
Romeo is not a younger Hamlet in love, though Hamlet in love
may seem a disillusioned Romeo. The very likeness, moreover,
is largely superficial, is a common likeness to many young
men, who take life desperately seriously, some with reason,
some without. The study of him is not plain sailing. If Hamlet's
melancholy is of the soul, Romeo's was something of a pose; and
there is Shakespeare's own present convention to account for, of
word-spinning and thought-spinning, in which he cast much of
the play, through which he broke more and more while he wrote
it; there are, besides, the abundant remains of Brooke's Romeus.
Romeo is in the making till the end; and he is made by fits and
starts. Significant moments reveal him; but, looking back, one
perceives screeds of the inessential, more heat than light in them.
The actor's first task will be to distinguish between the significant
and the passingly effective, and his last, as he plays the part, to
adjust and reconcile the two.

Decorative method allowed for, the Romeo of

> Why then, O brawling love! O loving hate!
> O anything, of nothing first create!
> O heavy lightness! serious vanity!
> Misshapen chaos of well-seeming forms!
> Feather of lead, bright smoke, cold fire, sick health!
> Still-waking sleep, that is not what it is! . . .

pictures an actual Romeo truly enough; and, if it seems to over-color him, why, this Romeo was busy at the moment over-coloring himself. Yet amid all the phrase-mongering we may detect a phrase or two telling of a deeper misprision than the obduracy of Rosaline accounts for. The inconsequent

> Show me a mistress that is passing fair,
> What doth her beauty serve but as a note
> Where I may read who passed that passing fair?

is very boyish cynicism, but it marks the unhappy nature. And Rosaline herself was a Capulet, it seems (in that camp, at any rate); so, had she smiled on him, his stars would still have been crossed. He is posing to himself certainly, more in love with love than with Rosaline, posing to his family and friends, and not at all displeased by their concern. But beneath all this, the mind that, as he passes with the Maskers and their festive drum to Capulet's feast,

> misgives
> Some consequence, yet hanging in the stars . . .

shows the peculiar clarity which gives quality to a man, marks him off from the happy-go-lucky crowd, and will at a crisis compel him to face his fate. By a few touches, then, and in a melody of speech that is all his own, he is set before us, a tragic figure from the first.

He sees Juliet. Shakespeare insists on the youth of the two, and more than once on their innocence, their purity—his as well as hers. It is not purposelessly that he is given the Dian-like Rosaline for a first love; nor that his first words to Juliet, as he touches her finger tips, are

> If I profane with my unworthiest hand
> This holy shrine . . .

nor that their first exchange is in the pretty formality of a sonnet, the kiss with which it ends half jest, half sacrament.[32] But their fate is sealed by it, there and then. They cannot speak again, for

---

[32] Elizabethan kisses were given and taken with greater freedom and publicity and less significance than Victorian kisses, at any rate, were. But was not the kiss of greeting (which Erasmus found so pleasant) oftenest a kiss on the cheek? Romeo kisses Juliet on the lips.

Lady Capulet calls Juliet away; and Benvolio, ever cautious, urges Romeo out of danger before there may be question of unmasking and discovery. Not before he has accepted his fate, though, and she hers—for better, for worse, without doubt, question, or hesitation! He (if we are to note niceties) accepts it even more unquestioningly than she. But her cry when she first hears his name gives us early promise of the rebellious Juliet, the more reckless and desperate of the two.

They look into the abyss and then give no more heed to it. Virginal passion sweeps them aloft and away, and to its natural goal. What should hinder? Nothing in themselves, none of the misgiving that experience brings; and for counselors they have Nurse and Friar, she conscienceless, he as little worldly as they. Juliet is no questioner, and Romeo's self-scrutinies are over. The balcony-scene is like the singing of two birds; and its technical achievement lies in the sustaining at such length—with no story to tell, nor enlivening clash of character—of those simple antiphonies of joy.

Rosaline's adorer, aping disillusioned age, is hardly to be recognized in the boyishly, childishly happy Romeo that rushes to the Friar's cell. From there he goes to encounter Mercutio, still overflowing with spirits, apt for a bout of nonsense, victorious in it, too. From this and the meeting with the Nurse, back to the cell, to Juliet and the joining of their hands!

Note that the marriage and its consummation are quite simply thought of as one, by them and by the Friar. And fate accepts Romeo's challenge betimes.

> Do thou but close our hands with holy words,
> Then love devouring death do what he dare,
> It is enough I may but call her mine.

It is of the essence of the tragedy that, for all their passionate haste, the blow should fall upon their happiness before it is complete, that they must consummate their marriage in sorrow. And, in a sense, it is Romeo's ecstatic happiness that helps precipitate the blow. It lets him ignore Tybalt's insult:

> O sweet Juliet,
> Thy beauty hath made me effeminate,
> And in my temper softened valour's steel.

But, for all that, it has fired him to such manliness that he cannot
endure the shame put upon him by Mercutio's death. Nothing is
left now of the young Romeo, lovesick for Rosaline, and so
disdainful of the family feud. His sudden hardihood is the
complement to his chaffing high spirits of a few hours earlier;
even as the grim

> This day's black fate on more days doth depend;
> This but begins the woe others must end.

makes a counterpart to his confident challenge to fate to give him
Juliet and do its worst after. He must seem of a higher stature as
he stands over Tybalt's body, stern, fated and passive to the next
Capulet sword that offers, did not Benvolio force him away.

The hysterics of the next scene with the Friar, when he hears
of his banishment, may seem as retrograde in character as they
certainly are in dramatic method; but Shakespeare has taken the
episode almost intact—and at one point all but word for word—
from Brooke. And it does attune us, as we noted, to the fortuitous
disasters of the story. Then the tragic parting of the two echoes
the happy wooing of the first balcony-scene; and later in Mantua
we find Shakespeare's Romeo, come to his full height.

Euphuism has all but vanished from the writing now. We have
instead the dynamic phrase that can convey so much more than
its plain meaning, can sum up in simplicity a ferment of emotion
and thought.

> Is it even so? Then I defy you, stars!

is his stark comment on the news of Juliet's death; but what
could be more eloquent of the spirit struck dead by it? He knows
in a flash what he means to do. We are not told; Balthasar is to
hire horses, that is all. Then, when he is alone:

> Well, Juliet, I will lie with thee to-night.

And what better epitome of the love in death, which is all that is
left them![33]

There follows the scene with the apothecary; its skeleton

---

[33] This whole passage is also notable in that it calls for sheer acting, for the
expression of emotion without the aid of rhetoric. This demand was a compara-
tively new thing when the play was written. Its fulfillment will have been one of
the factors in the great success won.

Brooke's, its clothing Shakespeare's, who employs it, not so much for the story's sake, as to give us, in repose, a picture of the Romeo his imagination has matured.

> How oft, when men are at the point of death,
> Have they been merry! which their keepers call
> A lightning before death. . . .

he lets him say later. He does not make him merry; but he gives him here that strange sharp clarity of eye and mind which comes to a doomed man, a regard for little things when his own end means little to him. He brings him to a view of life far removed from that first boyish, selfish petulance, to a scornful contemplation of what men come to, who will not dare to throw with fate for happiness, and be content to lose rather than be denied. As he watches the apothecary fumble for the forbidden poison:

> Art thou so bare, and full of wretchedness,
> And fearest to die? . . .

But for him it is:

> Come, cordial and not poison, go with me
> To Juliet's grave, for there must I use thee.

Life has broken him, and he in turn breaks all compact with life. If Balthasar dares to spy into the tomb his blood be on his head. He knows that he sins in killing himself: very well, he will sin. He implores Paris not to provoke him; but, provoked, he slaughters him savagely. At last he is alone with his dead.

At this juncture we lose much by our illegitimate knowledge of the story's end, and the actor of Romeo, presuming on it, usually makes matters worse. He apostrophizes Paris and Tybalt and Juliet at his leisure. But the dramatic effect here lies in the chance that at any minute, as we legitimately know, Juliet may wake or Friar Laurence come; and it is Romeo's haste—of a piece with the rest of his rashness—which precipitates the final tragedy. Shakespeare has provided, in the speech to the dead Juliet, just enough delay to stimulate suspense, but it must appear only as the last convulsive checking of a headlong purpose. He has added a last touch of bitter irony in letting Romeo guess at the truth that would have saved him, and her, and never guess that he guesses it.

O my love! my wife!
Death, that hath sucked the honey of thy breath,
Hath had no power yet upon thy beauty:
Thou art not conquered; beauty's ensign yet
Is crimson in thy lips and in thy cheeks,
And death's pale flag is not advanced there. . . .

After his glance at the dead Tybalt he turns to her again, obscurely marveling:

Ah, dear Juliet,
Why art thou yet so fair? . . .

And it is upon a sardonic echo of the eloquence to which his love's first happiness lifted him that he ends. Then it was

I am no pilot, yet, wert thou as far
As that far shore washed by the farthest sea,
I would adventure for such merchandise.

Now, the phial in his hand, it is

Thou desperate pilot, now at once run on
The dashing rocks thy sea-sick weary bark!
Here's to my love! . . .

With that he drinks and dies.

From the beginning so clearly imagined, passionately realized in the writing, deeply felt at the end; this Romeo, when he had achieved him, must have stood to Shakespeare as an assurance that he could now mold a tragic figure strong enough to carry a whole play whenever he might want to.

JULIET

The first thing to mark about Juliet, for everything else depends on it, is that she is, to our thinking, a child. Whether she is Shakespeare's fourteen or Brooke's sixteen makes little difference; she is meant to be just about as young as she can be; and her actual age is trebly stressed.[34] Her tragedy is a child's

---

[34] It has been held that Shakespeare may have taken her age from a later edition of Brooke's poem in which the XVI had perhaps been transformed by the printer into XIV; also that he may have reduced her age to suit the very youthful appearance of some boy-actress. This is at any rate unlikely; fourteen is not distinguishable from sixteen on the stage. Moreover, he has other almost as youthful heroines: Miranda is fifteen, Perdita sixteen.

tragedy; half its poignancy would be gone otherwise. Her bold innocence is a child's, her simple trust in her nurse; her passionate rage at the news of Tybalt's death is easily pardonable in a child, her terrors when she takes the potion are doubly dreadful as childish terrors. The cant saying that no actress can play Juliet till she is too old to look her should therefore go the way of all parroted nonsense. A Juliet must have both the look and the spirit of a girl of from fourteen to sixteen, and any further sophistication—or, worse, a mature assumption of innocence—will be the part's ruin. One must not compare her, either, to the modern girl approaching independence, knowing enough to think she knows more, ready to disbelieve half she is told. Life to Juliet, as she glimpsed it around her, was half jungle in its savagery, half fairy tale; and its rarer gifts were fever to the blood. A most precocious young woman from our point of view, no doubt; but the narrower and intenser life of her time ripened emotion early.

Not that there is anything of the budding sensualist in her; for to be sensual is to be sluggish, not fevered. Her passion for Romeo is ruled by imagination. And were this not the true reading of it, Shakespeare would have been all but compelled, one may say, to make it so; doubly compelled. Of what avail else would be his poetry, and through what other medium could a boy-actress realize the part? The beauty of the girl's story, and its agonies too, have imagination for their fount. The height of her joy (anticipated, never realized) is reached in the imaginative ecstasy of

> Gallop apace, you fiery-footed steeds. . . .

And she suffers to the full, even in thinking of them, all the shame of the marriage to Paris and the terrors of the vault.

Her quick florescence into womanhood is the more vivid for its quiet prelude; for the obedient

> Madam, I am here.
> What is your will?

when she first appears, for the listening to the Nurse's chatter, the borrowed dignity with which she caps her mother's snub that ends it, the simple

> It is an honour that I dream not of.

with which she responds to the hint of the great match awaiting
her, the listening to her mother's talk of it and the

> I'll look to like, if looking liking move;
> But no more deep will I endart mine eye
> Than your consent gives strength to make it fly.

that seal our first impression of her. Where could one find a more
biddable young lady?

What could one guess, either, from her first meeting with
Romeo, from the demure game of equivoque she plays; though
something shows, perhaps, in the little thrust of wit—

> You kiss by the book.

—by which she evades the confession of a kiss returned.[35] One
moment later, though, there comes the first flash of the true
Juliet; a revelation to herself, is it, as to us?

> My only love sprung from my only hate! . . .

And she stands, lost in amazement at this miracle that has been
worked in her (even as Romeo will stand later lost in the horror
of Tybalt's slaying), till the puzzled Nurse coaxes her away.

We next see her at her window. Yet again Shakespeare holds
her silent a little, but for that one "Ay me!" to tell us that now the
still depths in her are brimming; when they brim over, again it is
to herself she speaks.[36] The scene is conventionalized to a degree,
with its overheard soliloquies, its conceits, its lyric flow. It turns
every exigency of stage and acting to account, and its very setting,
which keeps the lovers apart, stimulates passionate expression and
helps sustain it. It left the boy-actress in imaginative freedom;
nothing asked of him that his skill could not give. But the
conceits come to life and blend insensibly with the simplicities.
The fanciful

> Thou know'st the mask of night is on my face,
> Else would a maiden blush bepaint my cheek. . . .

flows into the frank coquetry of

---

[35] And how admirably suited to the effective resources of the boy-actress the
pretty formality of this passage is!

[36] Not a sigh, this! There is nothing sentimental about Juliet.

> O gentle Romeo,
> If thou dost love, pronounce it faithfully;
> Or if thou think'st I am too quickly won,
> I'll frown and be perverse and say thee nay,
> So thou wilt woo; but else, not for the world.

and

> My bounty is as boundless as the sea,
> My love as deep; the more I give to thee,
> The more I have, for both are infinite.

comes from her as naturally as the very practical

> Three words, dear Romeo, and good-night indeed.
> If that thy bent of love be honourable,
> Thy purpose marriage, send me word to-morrow. . . .

And the scene's finest moment comes with

> JULIET.   Romeo!
> ROMEO.   My dear?
> JULIET.   At what o'clock to-morrow
> Shall I send to thee?
> ROMEO.   By the hour of nine.
> JULIET.   I will not fail. 'Tis twenty years till then.
> I have forgot why I did call thee back.
> ROMEO.   Let me stand here till thou remember it.
> JULIET.   I shall forget, to have thee still stand there,
> Remembering how I love thy company.
> ROMEO.   And I'll still stay, to have thee still forget,
> Forgetting any other home but this.

This is the commonplace made marvelous. What is it, indeed, but the well-worn comic theme of the lovers that cannot once for all say good-by and part turned to pure beauty by the alchemy of the poet? Modesty, boldness, shyness, passion, chase their way through the girl's speech; and Romeo, himself all surrender, sings to her tune. Together, but still apart, this is their one hour of happiness, and she is enskied in it, even as he sees her there.

We find her next, two scenes later, impatient for the Nurse's return with news of him; and in reckless delight and quick imagery for its expression she rivals Romeo now—the Juliet that could stand so mute! Then comes the quiet moment of the marriage. Making her reverence to the Friar, she may seem still to

be the self-contained young lady we first saw; but even in the
few lines of formal speech we hear a stronger pulse-beat and a
deeper tone. She stands, not timidly at all, but just a little awed
upon the threshold of her womanhood.[37]

After the tragic interval that sees Mercutio and Tybalt killed
we find her alone again, and again her newly franchised self,
expectant of happiness, the blow that is to kill it pending. To the
modern Juliet, as we have noted, this scene probably presents
more difficulties than any other in the play. Victorian Juliets
customarily had theirs drastically eased by the eliminating of

> Gallop apace, you fiery-footed steeds. . . .

(some of the finest verse in the play) on the ground—God save the
mark!—of its immodesty. One hopes that the last has been heard
of such nonsense. But few performances since Shakespeare's
time can have given the rest of the scene, with its elaborately
embroidered rhetoric intact.[38] It will all of it, needless to say, be
out of place upon a realistic stage; acted by a mature, ultra-
feminine Juliet it will be intolerable. But we can hardly blame
Shakespeare for that. He took here full advantage of his theater's
convention. The epithalamium has no more realism about it than
a song or a sonnet would have; and the verbal embroideries which
follow, meant to be taken at a high pitch of emotion and at a
surprising pace, owe their existence in great part to the bravura
skill of the boy-actresses who could compass such things with
credit. The actress of today need not lack the skill, though the
audiences may (and no great harm done) less consciously admire
it; they probably will not break into applause as audiences at an
opera do, as do French audiences at the declaiming of a fine
passage of verse. She must think of the scene largely in terms

---

[37] I make no attempt to say how and why this scene as it is in Q1 is so
completely changed in Q2. But it is worth while remarking that we have far
more than a rewriting of the words.

> *Enter Juliet somewhat fast and embraceth Romeo.*

says Q1; and her first word is "Romeo." In Q2, on the contrary, it is

> Good even to my ghostly confessor.

and there is no sure sign that she embraces Romeo at all. I think myself that
she does not, that the short scene was kept formal and dignified, the lovers
standing on either side the Friar as if they were already before the altar.

[38] For whatever reason, much of this is missing from Q1.

of virtuosity; but there is far more in it, of course. It brings us
the first clash of Montague and Capulet in other and sharper
terms than swordplay, in the heart agonies of this child, as she
is torn, now one way, now the other:

NURSE. Will you speak well of him that kill'd your cousin?
JULIET. Shall I speak ill of him that is my husband?

The tragedy is summed up for the first time in that.

Till now, we have seen Juliet at intervals; but with Romeo's
farewell to her and his passing to Mantua she becomes for a
space the sole center of the play, while misfortune batters at her.
In her helpless courage is the pathos, in her resolve from the first
to kill herself sooner than yield—she is fourteen!—is the high
heroism of the struggle. She is a child in the world's ways still.
But she faces her mother when the marriage to Paris is broached,
dignified and determined—and takes that good lady very much
aback. The next moment, though, she has broken into a storm of
impotent tears, which puzzle her father, but move him not at all,
except to match and outdo her in storming. Her mother repulses
her, her nurse betrays her; the trap is closing on her. She flies to
the Friar. There is Paris himself; and for appearance' sake she
must stop and parley with him while he claims her with calm
assurance as his wife, must let him kiss her, even! Back she flies
again from the shaken old man, armed with the only aid he can
give her, one little less desperate than the dagger that never leaves
her. The time is so short; and, in her distraction—playing the
hypocrite as she must, and overplaying it—she even contrives
to make it shorter. It escapes her quite that she will now—and
fatally—not be following the Friar's directions.[39] She easily hood-
winks her mother and her nurse; then, left alone, outfacing
terror, she drinks the potion.

She wakes in the vault, hopefully, happily:

O comfortable friar, where is my lord?
I do remember well where I should be,
And there I am. Where is my Romeo?

---

[39] "Tomorrow night" she was to take the potion; but the wedding is
suddenly put forward by a day. Juliet does not seem to notice what this may
involve, and we may not either. Quite possibly Shakespeare didn't. At any rate
he makes no use of the mistake, but brings in Friar John's mishap instead. The
immediate effect of the extra haste was all he cared about.

to have for all answer,

> Thy husband in thy bosom there lies dead.

and to see Friar Laurence—even he!—turn and desert her. Should we wonder at the scorn sounded in that

> Go, get thee hence, for I will not away.

Romeo's dagger is all she has left.

The simplest reason for Juliet's leave-taking of life being short is that Romeo's has been long. But, theatrical effect apart, the sudden brutal blow by which her childish faith in the "comfortable Friar" is shattered, and her unquestioning choice of death, make a fitting end to the desperate confidence of her rush to escape from what is worse than death to her. In the unreflecting haste of it all lies her peculiar tragedy. One day a child, and the next a woman! But she has not grown older as Romeo has, nor risen to an impersonal dignity of sorrow. Shakespeare's women do not, for obvious reasons, so develop. They are vehicles of life, not of philosophy. Here is a life cut short in its brightness; and it is a cruel business, this slaughter of a child betrayed.

Julius Caesar

JULIUS CÆSAR is the gateway through which Shakespeare passed to the writing of his five great tragedies. He had *Henry V* close behind him, *Hamlet* was not far ahead; between times he writes the three mature comedies, *Much Ado About Nothing, As You Like It* and *Twelfth Night.* In the themes, emphasis and methods of the work of this year or two we may watch the consummating development of his art.

Henry V gives the last touch to a hero of happy destiny. We might call it the latest play in which rhetoric for rhetoric's sake prevails. Shakespeare makes it occasion for a complaint of the inadequacy of his theater to his theme. And it is, as one says, altogether a man's play. Woman's interest rules the three comedies; further, they contain much prose and make no extraordinary demands upon staging or acting. *Julius Cæsar*, again, is the manliest of plays. For the first time, too, Shakespeare fully submits his imagination to the great idea of Rome; new horizons seem to open to him, and there is to be no return to the comparative parochialism of the Histories. Nor, with this far mightier theme to develop, do we have any hint of discontent with the means to his hand. No Chorus bows apology for the bringing of the foremost man of all the world upon such an unworthy scaffold.[1] And for Philippi, not only must a few ragged foils suffice, we are back to the simple convention by which whole armies face each other across the stage. His playwright's mind is

---

[1] It may well be, however, that with *Henry V* Shakespeare had surmised a patriot audience's instinct to demand for their hero trappings that a legendary foreigner like Cæsar could do well enough without.

clearly not troubled by such things now. What chiefly occupies
it in the planning and writing of *Julius Cæsar*? He is searching,
I think we may answer, for a hero, for a new sort of hero. The
story offers him more than one, and does not force him to a choice.
He chooses, in the event, but haltingly. Very significantly, however.

From the beginning Shakespeare's dramatic development has
lain in the discovering and proving of the strange truth that in
the theater, where external show seems everything, the most
effective show is the heart of a man. No need to suppose it was
lack of resource in stage furnishings drove him to the drama of
inward struggle, triumph and defeat. That choice was inner-
mostly made, and no playwright worth calling one but will make
it on demand, whatever the theater he writes for. Henry V is
not weakened as a character by lack of a pawing charger, but
neither would he be more of a hero set astride one. In himself
he is by no means all rhetoric; witness the scene with his father
and the soliloquy before Agincourt. But his career has the power
and the glory for an end; and the parade of this, at its best, only
cumbers your hero—at its worst may make him ridiculous.
Henry finishes a fine figure of a man; but long enough before
Shakespeare has done all he can with him, and our retrospect is
rather of the youthful junketings with Falstaff. For his next
hero it is in quite another direction he turns. The next true hero
is Hamlet: and Hamlet, foreshadowed in Rosaline's Romeo, in
Richard II, in Jaques, is imminent in Brutus. A hero, let us be
clear, is the character of which a dramatist, not morally, but
artistically, most approves. Macbeth is a hero. Shakespeare's sympathy with Brutus does not imply approval of the murder of
Cæsar; it only means that he ultimately finds the spiritual problem
of the virtuous murderer the most interesting thing in the story.
Brutus best interprets the play's theme: Do evil that good may
come, and see what does come!

He is more interested, as he always has been, in character than
in plot. He pays, goodness knows, small respect to the plots of the
three contemporary comedies; they live by character alone. This,
however, is history again, and plot must count. But it is not the
homespun of Holinshed, nor the crude stuff of the *Famous
Victories*. Plutarch gives him, not only the story he must abide

by, but characters already charged with life. His task now is less to elaborate or invent than to capture and transmit as much of such events and such men as his little London theater will hold. It is a feat of stagecraft to show us so many significant facets of this more than personal tragedy, a finer one to share out the best of the play's action among three chief characters and yet hardly lessen the strength of any of them.

But Shakespeare will never be too sure that he understands these Romans. He does not instinctively know their minds, as he knew Henry's or Hotspur's or Falstaff's. He is even capable of transcribing a fine-sounding passage from Plutarch and making something very like nonsense of it. He never gets to grips with Cæsar himself; whether from shrewd judgment that he could not maneuver such greatness in the space he had to spare, or, as looks more likely, from a sort of superstitious respect for it. In which case—well, idols, as we know, are apt to be wooden. Casca, raw from Plutarch, has mettle enough to ride off with a scene or two. Decius Brutus, Ligarius, Lucilius are lifted whole from his pages. And the story itself and its power, once Shakespeare is in its grip, can breed from him moment after moment of pure drama. In no earlier play do the very messengers and servants partake as they do in this. But Brutus, Cassius and Antony, though he has found them alive, he must set out to recreate in his own terms. He does it by trial and error, with a slip here and there, not disdaining a ready-made patch that comes handy; the transformation is never, perhaps, complete. But he seems to be giving them their fling, tempting them to discover themselves, passionate himself to know the truth of them, whatever it may be, and ready to face it. From no other play, probably, does he learn so much in the writing. Collaborating with Plutarch he can be interpreter and creator too. He finds what is to him a new world of men, which he tests for dramatic worth by setting it on this stage of his. *Julius Cæsar* is an occasion to which he rises, his greatest so far; it is a point of advance, from which he never falls back.

The Characters

BRUTUS

Тнат the development of Brutus should be slow is proper enough; such characters do not too readily reveal themselves. Shakespeare builds the man up for us trait by trait; economically, each stroke of value, seldom an effect made merely for its own sake. With his usual care that the first things we learn shall be essential things, that very first sentence—measured, dispassionate, tinged with disdain—by which Brutus transmits to Cæsar the cry in the crowd:

> A soothsayer bids you beware the Ides of March.

gives us so much of the man in perfection; and its ominous weight is doubled in his mouth, its effect trebled by the innocent irony. Brutus draws aside from the procession to the games, withdrawn into himself.

> I am not gamesome: I do lack some part
> Of that quick spirit that is in Antony.
> Let me not hinder, Cassius, your desires;
> I'll leave you.

The strain of self-consciousness, that flaw in moral strength! A suspicion of pose! But self-consciousness can be self-knowledge; Shakespeare holds the scales even.

> Into what dangers would you lead me, Cassius,
> That you would have me seek into myself
> For that which is not in me?

Wisdom itself could give no apter warning. But is this next passage, in Brutus, something of a flourish, or in Shakespeare a touch of an earlier quality?

> What is it that you would impart to me?
> If it be aught toward the general good,
> Set honour in one eye and death i' the other,
> And I will look on both indifferently;
> For let the gods so speed me as I love
> The name of honour more than I fear death.

It will be captious to call it so. The lines come hard upon the first of those shouts which are perhaps the acclaiming of Cæsar as king. Brutus is not a passionless man, though he may both despise passion and dread it. A minute later he is saying:

> I would not, so with love I might entreat you,
> Be any further mov'd.

Let the actor be wary, however, with that moment of rhetoric; and let him see that his Brutus does not compete here with Cassius. For the jealous, passionate Cassius, to whom and to whose mood eloquence and rhetoric are natural, must indisputably dominate this scene.

Brutus, if we are to learn more of him, needs a different setting. It is soon found. We see him in the calm of night. He is kindly to his sleepy page, gracious to his guests. We see him alone with his wife, left all alone in the quiet with his thoughts. Much comment has been spent upon the first soliloquy in this scene:

> It must be by his death: and, for my part,
> I know no personal cause to spurn at him. . . .

Wise editors have found this inconsistent, some with their own ideal of Brutus, some, rather more reasonably, with the fully drawn figure of Shakespeare's play. But, at this stage of its development, why should we be puzzled? If the argument is supersubtle and unconvincing, why should it not be? It may be that Shakespeare himself is still fumbling to discover how this right-minded man can commit his conscience to murder, and why should his Brutus not be fumbling too? This is how it will seem to an audience, surely.

The scene's marrow is the working of Brutus' mind, alone, in company. He is working it to some purpose now. But because it is, by disposition, a solitary mind, unused to interplay, and because the thoughts are not yet fused with emotion, that commoner currency between man and man, the scene may seem to move a little stiffly and Brutus himself to be stiff. Is not this, again, dramatically right? Would he not speak his thoughts starkly, while the rest only listen and acquiesce?—though Cassius does interpose one broken sentence of protest. They respect him, this upright, calm, self-contained man. He can command, but he cannot stir them; he is not a born leader. If the scene lacks suppleness and ease, one thought not prompting another revealingly, if it burns bright and hard, with never a flash into flame, so it would have been. But see how Shakespeare finally turns this very stiffness and suppression to a greater emotional account, when, after the silence Brutus keeps in the scene with Portia, the cry is wrung from him at last:

> You are my true and honourable wife,
> As dear to me as are the ruddy drops
> That visit my sad heart.

For let no one imagine that the overwhelming effect of this lies in the lines themselves. It has been won by his long impassiveness; by his listening, as we listen to Portia, till he and we too are overwrought. It is won by the courage with which Shakespeare holds his dramatic course.

Our sympathy with Brutus has next to weather the murder, through the planning and doing of which he stalks so nobly and disinterestedly and with such admirable self-control, and our interest in him to survive the emotional storm raised and ridden by Antony. This last might, one would think, sweep him forever from his place in the play. The contriving of his recovery is, indeed, a most remarkable technical achievement. It depends upon several things. For one, upon Shakespeare's honest but ruthless treatment of Antony and his appeal to the mob; we too may be carried away by his eloquence, but the worth of it and of the emotions it rouses is kept clear to us all the time. For another: had he, as playwright, not been faithful to Brutus and his stern consistency, Brutus would fail him now; but now, the emotional debauch over, the stoic's chance is due. And the fourth act opens, it will be remembered, with a most unpleasant glimpse of Antony, the plain blunt man, triumphant, coolly dealing out death sentences—

> These many then shall die; their names are pricked.

—and, as coolly, preparing to leave his colleague Lepidus in the lurch. After that the stage is reset for Brutus and his tragedy.

In the clash with Cassius, Shakespeare, intent upon the truth about the man, shows him, we may protest, no undue favor.

> Cassius. Most noble brother, you have done me wrong.
> Brutus. Judge me, you gods! wrong I mine enemies?
> And, if not so, how should I wrong a brother?

CASSIUS. Brutus, this sober form of yours hides wrongs;
          And when you do them——
BRUTUS.   Cassius, be content;
          Speak your griefs softly. . . .

By the stoic's moral code it is Cassius himself, of course, who is in the wrong. But which of us might not side with him against this comrade, who, with war declared, will be just to his enemies; and, with things going desperately for his side, must needs stiffen his stiff conscience against some petty case of bribery? Is this a time for pride in one's principles? Cæsar is dead—what matter now why or how?—and the spoils must be scrambled for, and the devil will take the hindmost. Cassius is no mere opportunist; yet so weary and distracted is he, that it almost comes to this with him. And he is answered:

> What! shall one of us
> That struck the foremost man of all this world
> But for supporting robbers, shall we now
> Contaminate our fingers with base bribes,
> And sell the mighty space of our large honours
> For so much trash as may be grasped thus?

Noble sentiments doubtless! But to depreciate and dispirit your best friends, to refuse their apologies for having lost patience with you, to refuse even to lose your own in return? Brutus tries many of us as high as he tries Cassius. And what is so quelling to the impulsive, imperfect human being as the cold realism of the idealist?

CASSIUS. When Cæsar liv'd, he durst not thus have mov'd
          me.
BRUTUS. Peace, peace! you durst not so have tempted him.
CASSIUS. I durst not?
BRUTUS. No.
CASSIUS. What? durst not tempt him?
BRUTUS.   For your life you durst not.

Supercilious, unforgiving—and in the right! And when anger does rise in him, it is such a cold, deadly anger that poor passionate Cassius only breaks himself against it. Yet there is a compelling power in the man, in his integrity of mind, his truth to himself, in his perfect simplicity. Even the detached, impersonal,

CASSIUS. You love me not.
BRUTUS.   I do not like your faults.
CASSIUS. A friendly eye could never see such faults.
BRUTUS. A flatterer's would not. . . .

though we may palate it no better than its immediate hearer
does, is and sounds the simple truth. Cassius cannot, somehow, be
simple. The dagger and the naked breast—who would be more
surprised than he, we feel, were he taken at his word? But when
Brutus relents his moral guard goes down so utterly; there
sweeps over him such a sense of the pitifulness, not of Cassius
and his self-conscious passion only, but of all these petty quarrels
of human nature itself, of his own:

> When I spoke that I was ill-tempered too.

It is a child making friends again with his fellow-child.

Shakespeare has now all but prepared us for the scene's great
stroke; for the winning stroke in Brutus' own cause with us.
The quarrel is over and the "jigging fool" has been dismissed.
Cassius took his turn as mentor when Brutus snapped at the
wretched poet.

> Bear with him, Brutus, 'tis his fashion.[2]

They set themselves to their business and call for a bowl of
wine; we are in the vein of workaday. The one confesses to his
"many griefs"; the other responds with kindly platitude. And
to this comes the simple answer, three naked words completing it:

BRUTUS. No man bears sorrow better: Portia is dead.
CASSIUS. Ha! Portia!
BRUTUS. She is dead.
CASSIUS. How 'scaped I killing when I crossed you so!

The seal is set upon Brutus' pre-eminence in the play, which from
now to its end is to be, in its main current, the story of the doom
towards which he goes unregretful and clear-eyed.

Hamlet, we have said, originating in Richard and Romeo, is
imminent in Brutus; but the line of descent is broken. Shakespeare, we may add, fails in Brutus just where he will succeed in
Hamlet; he is instinctively searching, perhaps, to express some-

---

[2] Cf. p. 377 also.

thing which the poet in Hamlet will accommodate, which the philosopher in Brutus does not. Having lifted his heroic Roman to this height, he leaves him, we must own, to stand rather stockishly upon it. There is more than one difficulty in the matter; and they were bound to come to a head. Brutus reasons his way through life, and prides himself upon suppressing his emotions. But the Elizabethan conventions of drama—and most others— are better suited to the interpreting of emotion than thought. The soliloquy, certainly, can be made a vehicle for any sort of intimate disclosure. Shakespeare has converted it already from a direct telling of the story or a length of sheer rhetoric, but not to turn it into a length of mere reasoning. His actors could, indeed, better hope to hold their audiences by fine sounds than by mental process alone. Brutus' soliloquies in Act II are all but pure thought, and in their place in the play, and at this stage of his development, are well enough, are very well. But—does Shakespeare feel?—you cannot conduct a tragedy to its crisis so frigidly. Had Brutus been the play's true and sole hero a way might have been found (by circling him, for instance, with episodes of passion) to sustain the emotional tension in very opposition to his stoic calm. The murder of Cæsar and its sequel sweeps the play up to a passionate height. The quarrel with the passionate Cassius, and the fine device of the withheld news of Portia's death, lift Brutus to an heroic height without any betrayal of the consistent nature of the man. But now we are at a standstill. Now, when we expect nemesis approaching, some deeper revelation, some glimpse of the hero's very soul, this hero stays inarticulate, or, worse, turns oracular. The picturing of him is kept to the end at a high pitch of simple beauty; but when—so we feel—the final and intimate tragic issue should open out, somehow it will not open. When Cæsar's ghost appears:

> BRUTUS.   Speak to me what thou art.
> GHOST.   Thy evil spirit, Brutus.
> BRUTUS.   Why com'st thou?
> GHOST.   To tell thee thou shalt see me at Philippi.
> BRUTUS.   Well: then I shall see thee again.
> GHOST.   Ay, at Philippi.
> BRUTUS.   Why, I will see thee at Philippi, then.

That may be true Brutus, but it comes short of what we demand from the tragic hero of this caliber. And before Philippi, a step nearer to the end of this work the Ides of March began, we have from the philosopher so confused a reflection on his fate that we may well wonder whether Shakespeare himself, transcribing it from a mistranslated Plutarch, is quite certain what it means.[3]

We are left with

> O! that a man might know
> The end of this day's business ere it come;
> But it sufficeth that the day will end,
> And then the end is known.

That is the voice, they are all but the very words of Hamlet. Shakespeare is to run the gamut of the mood of helpless doubt—the mood which has kept Hamlet our close kin through three disintegrating centuries—to more if not to better purpose. With Brutus it but masks the avoiding of the spiritual issue. And he is sent to his death, a figure of gracious dignity, the noblest Roman of them all, but with eyes averted from the issue still.

> Countrymen,
> My heart doth joy that yet in all my life
> I found no man but he was true to me. . . .
> Night hangs upon mine eyes; my bones would rest,
> That have but labour'd to attain this hour.

The plain fact is, one fears, that Shakespeare, even if he can say he understands Brutus, can in this last analysis *make* nothing of him; and no phrase better fits a playwright's particular sort of failure. He has let him go his own reasoning way, has faithfully abetted him in it, has hoped that from beneath this crust of thought the fires will finally blaze. He can conjure up a flare or two, and the love and grief for Portia might promise a fusing of the man's whole nature in a tragic passion outpassing anything yet. But the essential tragedy centered in Brutus' own soul, the tragedy of the man who, not from hate, envy nor weakness, but

---

3   Even by the rule of that philosophy
          By which I did blame Cato . . .

Furness collects four full pages of notes endeavoring to discover exactly what Brutus does mean.

> only, in a general honest thought
> And common good to all . . .

made one with the conspirators and murdered his friend; this,
which Shakespeare rightly saw as the supremely interesting issue,
comes to no more revelation than is in the last weary

> Cæsar, now be still:
> I killed not thee with half so good a will.

Shakespeare's own artistic disposition is not sufficiently attuned
to this tragedy of intellectual integrity, of principles too firmly
held. He can appreciate the nature of the man, but not, in the
end, assimilate it imaginatively to his own. He is searching for
the hero in whom thought and emotion will combine and contend
on more equal terms; and when the end of Brutus baffles him,
here is Hamlet, so to speak, waiting to begin. For the rest, he at
least reaps the reward, a better than Brutus did, of integrity and
consistency. He never falsifies the character, and, in its limited
achievement, it endures and sustains the play to the end. He had
preserved, we may say, for use at need, his actor's gift of making
effective things he did not fully understand; and the Brutus of the
play will make call enough upon any actor, even should he know
a little more about the historic Brutus—whom, after all, he is not
here called on to understand—than Shakespeare did.

CASSIUS

Cassius, the man of passion, is set in strong contrast to Brutus,
the philosopher; and to stress the first impression he himself will
make on us, we have Cæsar's own grimly humorous assessment
of him:

> Yond Cassius has a lean and hungry look;
> He thinks too much: such men are dangerous. . . .
> I fear him not;
> Yet if my name were liable to fear,
> I do not know the man I should avoid
> So soon as that spare Cassius. He reads much;
> He is a great observer, and he looks
> Quite through the deeds of men; he loves no plays,
> As thou dost, Antony; he hears no music;

> Seldom he smiles, and smiles in such a sort
> As if he mocked himself, and scorned his spirit
> That could be moved to smile at any thing.
> Such men as he be never at heart's ease
> Whiles they behold a greater than themselves,
> And therefore are they very dangerous. . . .

—a Puritan, that is to say, something of an ascetic, and with the makings of a fanatic in him too. Already it will not be, to Shakespeare's audience, a wholly unfamiliar figure. A dangerous man, doubtless; and as much so sometimes to his friends, they will feel, as to his enemies.

> Into what dangers would you lead me, Cassius,
> That you would have me seek into myself
> For that which is not in me?

the besought Brutus protests. At the best a man difficult to deal with; jealous and thin-skinned; demanding much of his friends, and quick to resent even a fancied slight. His very first approach to Brutus:

> I do observe you now of late:
> I have not from your eyes that gentleness
> And show of love as I was wont to have. . . .

And in their later quarrel the burden of his grievance is

> You love me not.

An egoist certainly; yet not ignobly so, seeking only his own advantage. Convinced in a cause—as we find him convinced; that Cæsar's rule in Rome must be free Rome's perdition—he will fling himself into it and make no further question, argue its incidental rights and wrongs no more, as Brutus may to weariness. For argument will have now become a kind of treason. There lie doubt and the divided mind, which he detests in others, and would dread in himself, since there lies weakness too, while passion will carry him through, and give him power to goad others on besides. Egoist he is, yet not intellectually arrogant. He sees in Brutus the nobler nature and a finer mind, and yields to his judgment even when he strongly feels that it is leading them astray. These principles! It would have been practical good sense to add Antony's death to Cæsar's; it was foolish to a degree—

rapidly it proved so—to let him speak in the market place later; that was a petty business, after all, about Lucius Pella and his bribes; and to what does Brutus' insistence on his strategy lead them but to Philippi? It is as if he felt that in some such yielding fashion he must atone for those outbursts of rage that he will not control. And yet, despite exasperating failings, the man is lovable, as those which are spendthrift of themselves can be, and as—for all his virtues—Brutus is not.

Cassius is by no means all of a piece, and makes the more lifelike a character for that. He ruthlessly demands Antony's death (the cause demands it), but in a desperate crisis, with danger threatening, he can take sudden thought for Publius' age and weakness. He has marked respect for Brutus; but he does not scruple to play tricks on him, with the letter laid in the Prætor's chair, the placard pinned to the statue. And, despite his outbursts of passion, he can calculate at times pretty coolly. Why does he not go with the rest on that fatal morning to conduct Cæsar to the Senate House? He has said he will go—

> Nay, we will all of us be there to fetch him.

—and it will not be sudden timidity, certainly, that sways him. Do second thoughts suggest that since Cæsar, as he knows, mistrusts him, his presence may rouse suspicion? Shakespeare leaves this to be implied—or not, since we may not remark his absence. Yet he has been so prominent a figure in the earlier scenes, that we can hardly help remarking it.[4]

He is cynical, and can be brutally downright. While Brutus is appealing to Antony's higher nature (Cæsar dead there between them) he comes out plump with a

> Your voice shall be as strong as any man's
> In the disposing of new dignities.

But his deep affection for Brutus rings true; even in the midst of their quarrel, when he hears of Portia's death, as they mutually say farewell.

---

[4] The omission of his name among the entrants may, of course, be a mere slip. In that case it is his silence throughout the scene which will be remarkable—which the actors of Cæsar and Cassius, at any rate, could hardly help making so.

BRUTUS. For ever, and for ever, farewell, Cassius!
If we do meet again, why, we shall smile;
If not, why then this parting was well made.
CASSIUS. For ever, and for ever, farewell, Brutus!
If we do meet again, we'll smile indeed;
If not, 'tis true this parting was well made.

—there is harmony in the echoing exchange itself; and they do not meet again.

The cynical Cassius shows in the soliloquy:

Well, Brutus, thou art noble; yet, I see,
Thy honourable metal may be wrought
From that it is disposed: therefore 'tis meet
That noble minds keep ever with their likes;
For who so firm that cannot be seduced? . . .

—it is at this very moment that he is scheming to seduce his much-admired friend by the papers thrown in at his window and other such devices. Beneath his enthusiasms and rash humors there is a certain coldness of passion, which gives him tenacity, lets him consider and plan, the tension of his temper never slackening; and it is in this combination of opposites that the man is most dangerous. He will put his very faults to use, do things for his cause that he never would for himself, yet not, as with Brutus, studiously justifying them. His hatred for Cæsar the tyrant may well be rooted in jealousy of Cæsar the man; if so, he is at no pains to disguise it. But he is incapable of protesting his love for him at one moment, while—on principle—he will strike him down the next.

So forthcoming a man, so self-revealing as he naturally is, what character could better animate the play's opening, and get the action under way? But there must soon come a check. No play can continue at such a strain, to the fatiguing of actors and audience both. It comes with this very soliloquy,

Well, Brutus, thou art noble. . . .

and here, if Shakespeare meant to dig deeper into Cassius' nature, would be the chance. But he avoids it. Brutus is to be the introspective character, the play's spiritual hero, so to speak; and there will not be room for two. Nor (as we said) is Cassius the man to spend time in self-searching, though he urges Brutus to. So the soliloquy—the only one allotted him—matched against the extraordinary vitality of the earlier dialogue, falls a little flat, runs somewhat mechanically, rather too closely resembles one of those conventional plot-forwarding discourses to the audience, to which Shakespeare has long learned to give richer use; and it demands the final whip-up of that rhymed couplet. At this juncture, then, and for a while longer we learn little more about Cassius. In the scene of the storm that follows he is eloquent and passionate still. But it is the same gamut that he runs. And in the scenes which follow this he strikes the same notes, of a rather arid desperation. Not until the later quarrel with Brutus is he fully and strikingly reanimated; but then indeed the intimacy opens up, of which we shall have felt deprived before. We have no deliberate and explanatory self-confession (that, again, belongs to Brutus), simply an illustrative picture of Cassius in word and action, companion to that earlier one.

He has not changed, yet circumstances have changed him. In that paradox lies the tragedy of such natures. He was jealous of Cæsar then, and he has turned jealous of Brutus now; of his friend as he was of his enemy. So Cæsar read him aright:

> Such men as he be never at heart's ease
> Whiles they behold a greater than themselves. . . .

He slights Brutus' generalship as he once contemned Cæsar's courage. He is as quick and as shrewd and as shrewish as ever. But then it was:

> Well, honour is the subject of my story. . . .

and now he is prudently excusing a rogue, with his own honor in question. The one-time eloquent candor has turned to blustering and scolding. Yet, even while he rages, he knows he is in the wrong. His pride is little more than a mask. And the lofty Brutus has but to soften towards him—one touch of simple humanity suffices—and he breaks down like a child. He is pleading now:

> O, Brutus!
>   What's the matter?
> Have you not love enough to bear with me,
> When that rash humour which my mother gave me
> Makes me forgetful?

And from now on, as if—so we noted—in atonement, he will
follow the younger man's mistaken lead, convinced as he is that
it is mistaken. He only craves affection:

> O, my dear brother,
> This was an ill beginning of the night:
> Never come such division 'tween our souls!
> Let it not, Brutus.

abases himself—he, the elder soldier—with that

> Good night, my lord.

the now indulgent Brutus quickly preventing him with a

> Good night, good brother.

But thus it is with these catastrophic natures. They spend themselves freely, but demand half the world in exchange. They
behave intolerably, try their friends' patience beyond all bounds,
confidently expecting, for the sake of their love for them, to be
forgiven. They know and confess to their faults, but with no
intention of amendment; you must take them, they say, "as they
are."

> Old Cassius still!

mocks Antony, when the two meet again, parleying before the
battle. And certainly the sharp tongue is by then as sharp as ever.
At which point we remark too that the quarrel with Brutus and
the reconciliation after have proved to Cassius both relief and
comfort. For despite ill-omens, and his unchanged distrust in
Brutus' soldiership, he proclaims himself

> fresh of spirit and resolved
> To meet all perils very constantly.

But, the battle joined, in the fury of fancied defeat he will kill
his own standard-bearer, and himself, in his impatient despair.
Old Cassius still!

ANTONY

> There is a tide in the affairs of men,
> Which, taken at the flood, leads on to fortune. . . .

Mark Antony cannot always talk so wisely, but he takes the
tide that Brutus loses. He is a born opportunist, and we see him

best in the light of his great opportunity. He stands contrasted with both Cassius and Brutus, with the man whom his fellows respect the more for his aloofness, and with such a rasping colleague as Cassius must be. Antony is, above all things, a good sort.

Shakespeare keeps him in ambush throughout the first part of the play. Up to the time when he faces the triumphant conspirators he speaks just thirty-three words. But there have already been no less than seven separate references to him, all significant. And this careful preparation culminates as significantly in the pregnant message he sends by his servant from the house to which it seems he has fled, bewildered by the catastrophe of Cæsar's death. Yet, as we listen, it is not the message of a very bewildered man. Antony, so far, is certainly—in what we might fancy would be his own lingo—a dark horse. And, though we may father him on Plutarch, to English eyes there can be no more typically English figure than the sportsman turned statesman, but a sportsman still. Such men range up and down our history. Antony is something besides, however, that we used to flatter ourselves was not quite so English. He can be, when occasion serves, the perfect demagogue. Nor has Shakespeare any illusions as to what the harsher needs of politics may convert your sportsman once he is out to kill. The conspirators are fair game doubtless. But Lepidus, a little later, will be the carted stag.

> A barren-spirited fellow; one that feeds
> On abject orts and imitations,
> Which, out of use and staled by other men,
> Begin his fashion: do not talk of him
> But as a property . . .

to serve the jovial Antony's turn! This is your good sort, your sportsman, your popular orator, stripped very bare.

The servant's entrance with Antony's message, checking the conspirators' triumph, significant in its insignificance, is the turning point of the play.[5] But Shakespeare plucks further advantage from it. It allows him to bring Antony out of ambush completely effective and in double guise; the message fore-

---

[5] As Moulton demonstrates in an admirable passage.

shadows him as politician, a minute later we see him grieving deeply for his friend's death. There is, of course, nothing incompatible in the two aspects of the man, but the double impression is all-important. He must impress us as uncalculatingly abandoned to his feelings, risking his very life to vent them. For a part of his strength lies in impulse; he can abandon himself to his feelings, as Brutus the philosopher cannot. Moreover, this bold simplicity is his safe-conduct now. Were the conspirators not impressed by it, did it not seem to obliterate his politic side, they might well and wisely take him at his word and finish with him then and there. And at the back of his mind Antony has this registered clearly enough. It must be with something of the sportsman's— and the artist's—happy recklessness that he flings the temptation at them:

> Live a thousand years,
> I shall not find myself so apt to die:
> No place will please me so, no mean of death,
> As here by Cæsar, and by you cut off,
> The choice and master spirits of this age.

He means it; but he knows, as he says it, that there is no better way of turning the sword of a so flattered choice and master spirit aside. It is this politic, shadowed aspect of Antony that is to be their undoing; so Shakespeare is concerned to keep it clear at the back of our minds too. Therefore he impresses it on us first by the servant's speech, and Antony himself is free a little later to win us and the conspirators both.

Not that the politician does not begin to peep pretty soon. He tactfully ignores the cynicism of Cassius,

> Your voice shall be as strong as any man's
> In the disposing of new dignities.

But by Brutus' reiterated protest that Cæsar was killed in wise kindness what realist, what ironist—and Antony is both—would not be tempted?

> I doubt not of your wisdom.
> Let each man render me his bloody hand. . . .

And, in bitter irony, he caps their ritual with his own. It is the ritual of friendship, but of such a friendship as the blood of Cæsar, murdered by his friends, may best cement. To Brutus the

place of honor in the compact; to each red-handed devotee his
due; and last, but by no means least, in Antony's love shall be
Trebonius who drew him away while the deed was done. And
so to the final, most fitting apostrophe:

Gentlemen all!

Emotion subsided, the politician plays a good game. They shall
never be able to say he approved their deed; but he is waiting,
please, for those convincing reasons that Cæsar was dangerous.
He even lets slip a friendly warning to Cassius that the prospect
is not quite clear. Then, with yet more disarming frankness,
comes the challenging request to Brutus to let him speak in the
market place. As he makes it, a well-calculated request! For how
can Brutus refuse, how admit a doubt that the Roman people will
not approve this hard service done them? Still, that there may
be no doubt at all, Brutus will first explain everything to his
fellow-citizens himself, lucidly and calmly. When reason has
made sure of her sway, the emotional, the "gamesome," Antony
may do homage to his friend.

                                        Be it so;
I do desire no more.

responds Antony, all docility and humility, all gravity—though
if ever a smile could sharpen words, it could give a grim edge to
these. So they leave him with dead Cæsar.

    In this contest thus opened between the man of high argument
and the instinctive politician, between principle (mistaken or
not) and opportunism, we must remember that Antony can be
by no means confident of success. He foresees chaos. He knows, if
these bemused patriots do not, that it takes more than correct
republican doctrines to replace a great man. But as to this Roman
mob—this citizenry, save the mark!—whoever knows which way
it will turn? The odds are on the whole against him. Still he'll
try his luck; Octavius, though, had better keep safely out of the
way meanwhile. All his senses are sharpened by emergency.
Before ever Octavius' servant can speak he has recognized the
fellow and guessed the errand. Shakespeare shows us his mind at
its swift work, its purposes shaping.

Passion, I see, is catching, for mine eyes,
Seeing those beads of sorrow stand in thine,
Began to water.

—from which it follows that if the sight of Cæsar's body can so
move the man and the man's tears so move him, why, his own
passion may move his hearers in the market place presently to
some purpose! His imagination, once it takes fire, flashes its way
along, not by reason's slow process though in reason's terms.[6]

To what he is to move his hearers we know: and it will be
worth while later to analyze the famous speech, that triumph of
histrionics.[7] For though the actor of Antony must move us with it
also—and he can scarcely fail to—Shakespeare has set him the
further, harder and far more important task of showing us an
Antony the mob never see, of making him clear to us, moreover,
even while we are stirred by his eloquence, of making clear to us
just by what it is we are stirred. It would, after all, be pretty poor
playwriting and acting which could achieve no more than a plain
piece of mob oratory, however gorgeous; a pretty poor compliment
to an audience to ask of it no subtler response than the mob's.
But to show us, and never for a moment to let slip from our
sight, the complete and complex Antony, impulsive and calcu-
lating, warm-hearted and callous, aristocrat, sportsman and
demagogue, that will be for the actor an achievement indeed; and
the playwright has given him all the material for it.

Shakespeare himself knows, no one better, what mere histrionics
may amount to. He has been accused of showing in a later play

---

[6] How many modern actors upon their picture stage, with its curtain to close
a scene for them pat upon some triumphant top note, have brought this one to
its end twenty lines earlier upon the familiar, tremendous, breathless apostrophe
(did Shakespeare ever pen such another sentence?) that begins,

Woe to the hand that shed this costly blood!
Over thy wounds now do I prophesy . . .

But to how untimely an end! The mechanism of Shakespeare's theater forbade
such effects. Cæsar's body is lying on the main stage, and must be removed,
and it will take at least two people to carry it. Here is one reason for the arrival
of Octavius' servant. But as ever with Shakespeare, and with any artist worth his
salt, limitation is turned to advantage. If dead Cæsar is to be the mainspring
of the play's further action, what more forceful way could be found of making
this plain than, for a finish to the scene, to state the new theme of Octavius'
coming, Cæsar's kin and successor?

[7] See p. 392.

(but unjustly, I hold) his too great contempt for the mob; he might then have felt something deeper than contempt for the man who could move the mob by such means; he may even have thought Brutus made the better speech. Antony, to be sure, is more than an actor; for one thing he writes his own part as he goes along. But he gathers the ideas for it as he goes too, with no greater care for their worth than the actor need have so long as they are effective at the moment. He lives abundantly in the present, his response to its call is unerring. He risks the future. How does the great oration end?

> Mischief, thou are afoot;
> Take thou what course thou wilt!

A wicked child, one would say, that has whipped up his fellow-children to a riot of folly and violence. That is one side of him. But the moment after he is off, brisk, cool and businesslike, to play the next move in the game with that very cool customer, Octavius.

He has had no tiresome principles to consult or to expound.

> I only speak right on. . . .

he boasts;

> I tell you that which you yourselves do know. . . .

An admirable maxim for popular orators and popular writers too! There is nothing aloof, nothing superior about Antony. He may show a savage contempt for this man or that; he has a sort of liking for men in the mass. He is, in fact, the common man made perfect in his commonness; yet he is perceptive of himself as of his fellows, and, even so, content.

What follows upon his eloquent mourning for Cæsar? When the chaos in Rome has subsided he ropes his "merry fortune" into harness. It is not a very pleasant colloquy with which the fourth act opens.

ANTONY.   These many then shall die; their names are
           pricked.
OCTAVIUS. Your brother too must die; consent you, Lepidus?
LEPIDUS.   I do consent.
OCTAVIUS.   Prick him down, Antony.

LEPIDUS.   Upon condition Publius shall not live,
            Who is your sister's son, Mark Antony.
ANTONY.   He shall not live; look, with a spot I damn him.

The conspirators have, of course, little right to complain. But four lines later we learn that Lepidus himself, when his two friends have had their use of him, is to fare not much better than his brother—than the brother he has himself just given so callously to death! Can he complain either, then? This is the sort of beneficence the benevolent Brutus has let loose on the world.

But Antony finishes the play in fine form; victorious in battle, politicly magnanimous to a prisoner or two, and ready with a resounding tribute to Brutus, now that he lies dead. Not in quite such fine form, though; for the shadow of that most unsportsman-like young man Octavius is already moving visibly to his eclipse.

These, then are the three men among whom Shakespeare divides this dramatic realm; the idealist, the egoist, the opportunist. The contrast between them must be kept clear in the acting by all that the actors do and are, for upon its tension the living structure of the play depends. And, it goes without saying, they must be shown to us as fellow-creatures, not as abstractions from a dead past. For so Shakespeare saw them; and, if he missed something of the mind of the Roman, yet these three stand with sufficient truth for the sum of the human forces, which in any age, and in ours as in his, hold the world in dispute.

OCTAVIUS CÆSAR

He tags to the three another figure; and perhaps nothing in the play is better done, within its limits, than is the outline of Octavius Cæsar, the man who in patience will reap when all this bitter seed has been sown. He appears three times, speaks some thirty lines, and not one of them is wasted. We see him first with Antony and Lepidus. He watches them trade away the lives of their friends and kinsmen. And when Antony, left alone with him, proposes to "double-cross" Lepidus, he only answers,

                            You may do your will;
        But he's a tried and valiant soldier.

It is the opening of a window into this young man's well-ordered mind. Lepidus is a good soldier, he approves of Lepidus. But Antony is powerful for the moment, it won't do to oppose Antony. Lepidus must suffer then. Still, should things turn out differently, let Antony remember that this was his own proposal, and that Octavius never approved of it.[8]

By the next scene, however, this quiet youth has grown surer— not of himself, that he has no need to be, but of his place amid the shifting of events.

> ANTONY.   Octavius, lead your battle softly on,
> Upon the left hand of the even field.
> OCTAVIUS. Upon the right hand, I; keep thou the left.
> ANTONY.   Why do you cross me in this exigent?
> OCTAVIUS. I do not cross you; but I will do so.

He is quite civil about it; but he means to have his way, his chosen place in the battle and chief credit for the victory. And Antony does not argue the point. When the opponents in the coming battle are face to face, Cassius and Antony and even Brutus may outscold each the other for past offenses. The practical Octavius, with a mind to the present and to his own future, is impatient of such childishness.

> Come, come, the cause: if arguing make us sweat,
> The proof of it will turn to redder drops.
> Look, I draw sword against conspirators;
> When think you that the sword goes up again?
> Never, till Cæsar's three-and-thirty wounds
> Be well aveng'd; or till another Cæsar
> Have added slaughter to the sword of traitors.

This is the first time he has spoken out, and he speaks to some purpose. Nor does he give place to Antony again. When we see them together for the last time in victorious procession, Octavius has the lead.

> All that serv'd Brutus, I will entertain them.

"I," not "we." And Shakespeare gives him the play's last word.

---

[8] *Julius Cæsar* begins the cycle of Shakespeare's greater plays, and *Antony and Cleopatra* ends it. The later relations of Octavius and Antony are implicit in this little scene. The realist, losing grip, will find himself "out-realized" by his pupil.

CÆSAR

What now of the great shadow of Cæsar which looms over the whole? Let us admit that, even while he lives and speaks, it is more shadow than substance. Is it too harsh a comment that Cæsar is in the play merely to be assassinated? But to have done better by him would have meant, would it not, doing worse by the play as it is planned? Certainly to center every effort—and it could hardly be done with less—upon presenting to us

the foremost man of all this world . . .

and then to remove him at the beginning of Act III would leave a gap which no new interest could fill. But there are innate difficulties in the putting of any great historical figure upon the stage: and these, as it happens, would have pressed hard upon Shakespeare just at this stage of his development. He had left behind him the writing of that formal rhetoric which was the accepted dramatic full dress for the great man. He was molding his verse to the expressing of individual emotion, fitting his whole method to the showing of intimate human conflict. Now a great man's greatness seldom exists in his personal relations. To depict it, then, the dramatist will be thrown back on description, or narrative, or on the effect of the greatness upon the characters around. The last expedient may shift our interest to the surrounding characters themselves. Narrative soon becomes tiresome. And as to description; the great man himself, in the person of his actor, is too apt to belie it. Keep him immobile and taciturn, and the play will halt. But if he talks of his own achievements he will seem a boaster. And if he is always seen in action we can have no picture of the inner man. The convention of Greek drama offers some escape from these dilemmas; for there the man is, so to speak, made in his greatness a symbol of himself, and in a symbol one may sum up a truth. Shakespeare had, certainly, the refuge of soliloquy. Show us the heart of a Cæsar, though, by that means, and where will our interest in the self-revealings of a Brutus be? And it is, we have argued, upon Brutus' spiritual tragedy that Shakespeare's best thoughts are fixed. He comes, therefore, to showing us a Cæsar seen somewhat from Brutus' point of view; a noble figure and eloquent, but our knowledge of him stays skin-deep. It is historically possible, of course, that the virtue had gone out of Cæsar, that no more was left now than this façade of a great man. But we need not credit Shakespeare with the theory. Quite certainly he wishes to show us the accepted Cæsar of history. The innate difficulty of doing so may defeat him; the limitations of the play, as he has planned it, must. And if he has to choose, and it becomes a question of his play's safety, Cæsar will count no more with him than any other character.

But it follows that, as he cannot attempt to do Cæsar dramatic justice, the more we see of him the worse it is. For the devices by which his supremacy can be made effective are soon exhausted and do not bear repetition. The start is excellent. What could be more impressive than that first procession across the stage? Here Shakespeare tries the taciturn-immobile method, and couples it with a strict simplicity of speech; all one can call a trick is the repetition of the name, and Cæsar's own use of it, and even this is legitimate enough. While, for a finish, the confronting of the Soothsayer:

CASSIUS.   Fellow, come from the throng; look upon
              Cæsar.
CÆSAR.   What say'st thou to me now? Speak once
              again.
SOOTHSAYER.   Beware the Ides of March.
CÆSAR.   He is a dreamer; let us leave him: pass.

Here is the great man; assuming no attitude, explaining nothing, indifferent to seeming trifles. What could be better? The last line is pure gold.

The episode of the returning procession is as good. That side-long perceptive survey of Cassius with its deep-biting humor:

Let me have men about me that are fat,
Sleek-headed men, and such as sleep a-nights.
Yond Cassius has a lean and hungry look;
He thinks too much: such men are dangerous.

The yet deeper-bitten realism of

He reads much;
He is a great observer, and he looks
Quite through the deeds of men; he loves no plays,

As thou dost, Antony; he hears no music;
Seldom he smiles, and smiles in such a sort
As if he mock'd himself, and scorn'd his spirit
That could be mov'd to smile at any thing.
Such men as he be never at heart's ease
Whiles they behold a greater than themselves,
And therefore are they very dangerous.

The precise simplicity of thought and language mark the man raised above his fellows. Do we need, then,

> I rather tell thee what is to be fear'd
> Than what I fear, for always I am Cæsar.

But it is from this very moment that the direct picturing of Cæsar turns to talk about Cæsar by Cæsar. Fine talk; but the living man is lost in it. For a line or two he may emerge, only to be lost again in some such operatic sonority as

> Cæsar should be a beast without a heart
> If he should stay at home to-day for fear.
> No, Cæsar shall not; danger knows full well
> That Cæsar is more dangerous than he:
> We are two lions littered in one day,
> And I the elder and more terrible;
> And Cæsar shall go forth.

—while the Olympian speech in the Senate House leaves one a little surprised that a moment later blood can be supposed to flow from him. Shakespeare, in fact, has now slipped not merely into this queer *oratio obliqua* but back to the discarded rhetoric for its own sake, though the writing of the characters round Cæsar stays directly dramatic enough. The actor must effect what sort of reconciliation he can between this simulacrum of greatness and the dramatic life around. To think of Cæsar as now no more than an empty shell, reverberating hollowly, the life and virtue gone out of him, is one way. It must weaken the play a little; for will it be so desperate an enterprise to conspire against such a Cæsar? Or is such a frigid tyranny the more dangerous of the two? But the supersubtlety of that interpretation is worse.

CASCA AND THE REST

Among the men no other characters reach primary importance. Casca is effective rather than important, and the only question about him is of the break from prose to verse (as between Act I, Scenes ii and iii), which points a kindred but hardly warrantable break in the composition of the character itself. It is all very well to say with Dowden that Casca appears in the storm with his "superficial garb of cynicism dropt," and that, while dramatic consistency may be a virtue, Shakespeare here gives us an instance of "a piece of higher art, the dramatic inconsistency of his characters." If it were so the thing would still be very clumsily done. What means is the actor given of showing that this is a dramatic inconsistency? We never see one flutter of that superficial garb of cynicism again. Casca remains hereafter the commonplace Casca of the storm-scene; the humorous blunt fellow seems forgotten quite. Certainly we have had Cassius' apology for him, that he

puts on this tardy form . . .

But the passage in which that occurs is itself weak and mechanical, and it might arguably have been written in to excuse the clumsiness of the change. The actor must do what he can to weld the two halves of the man together; but it is doubtful whether he can make this "piece of higher art" very valid.

The producer must remember that nine-tenths of the play is, so to speak, orchestrated for men only; the greater the need in the casting of the parts to set them in due contrast with each other. The sort of acting a part needs is usually made plain enough; if not by some reference, acting itself will test this. For instance, if nothing definitely directs us to make the Flavius and Marullus of the first scene a mild man and a masterfully noisy one, yet in the acting they will be found to answer effectively to that difference. For the casting of Cicero, on the other hand, we have definite, if mainly *ex post facto*, direction; his elderly dry irony is set, when the two meet, in strong contrast with the new ebullient Casca. It is to be noted, by the way, that Shakespeare, history apart, thinks of the conspirators as fairly young men. By theatrical tradition Caius Ligarius is made old as well as ill, but there is nothing to warrant this (for an ague does not warrant it), nor any dramatic gain in it.

Cinna the poet is specified plainly enough in the dandification of

> What is my name? Whither am I going? Where do I dwell? Am I a married man or a bachelor? Then, to answer every man directly and briefly, wisely and truly; wisely I say, I am a bachelor.

The nameless poet of Act IV must be even more eccentric if his flying visit is to be made effective. Cassius calls him a cynic. He is, one supposes, a shabby, ballad-mongering fellow; his modern instance shuffles through the *cafés* of Montmartre today. Shakespeare, rapt in this world of great doings, is a little hard on poets—as some poets are apt to be.

The soldiers that belong to the play's last phase, Messala, Lucilius, Titinius, young Cato, Pindarus, Volumnius, Strato and the rest, can all be known for what they are by considering what they do. In no play, I think, does Shakespeare provide, in such a necessarily small space, for such a vivid array. As parts of a battle-piece, the unity of the subject harmonizes them, but within that harmony each is very definitely and effectively himself.

CALPURNIA AND PORTIA

The boy Lucius has sometimes been played by a woman. This is an abomination. Let us not forget, on the other hand, that Calpurnia was written to be played by a boy. Producers are inclined to make a fine figure of her, to give her (there being but two women in the play) weight and importance, to fix on some well-proportioned lady, who will wear the purple with an air. But Shakespeare's intention is as plain as daylight; and in a part of twenty-six lines there can be no compromise, it must be hit or miss. Calpurnia is a nervous, fear-haunted creature. Nor does she, like Portia, make any attempt to conceal her fears. She is desperate and helpless. Portia, with her watchful constancy, can win Brutus' secret from him. Cæsar treats Calpurnia like a child. Her pleading with him is a frightened child's pleading. Her silence when Decius and the rest come to fetch him to the Senate House is as pathetic in its helplessness. She stands isolated and tremulous, watching him go in to taste some wine with these good friends. Failing the right sort of Calpurnia, the dramatic value of her share in the scene will be lost.

A quiet beauty is the note of Portia, and Shakespeare sounds it at once. Her appearance is admirably contrived. The conspirators have gone, Brutus is alone again, and the night's deep stillness is recalled.

> Boy! Lucius! Fast asleep? It is no matter;
> Enjoy the honey-heavy dew of slumber:
> Thou hast no figures nor no fantasies
> Which busy care draws in the brains of men;
> Therefore thou sleep'st so sound.

But so softly she comes, that for all the stillness he is unaware of her, until the soft voice, barely breaking it, says,

> Brutus, my lord!

Portia is a portrait in miniature. But how suited the character itself is to such treatment, and how Shakespeare subdues his power to its delicacy! The whole play is remarkable for simplicity and directness of speech; nothing could exemplify her better. For she is seen not as a clever woman, nor is she witty, and she speaks without coquetry of her "once-commended beauty." She is home-keeping and content; she is yielding, but from good sense, which she does not fear will seem weakness. She has dignity and perfect courage.

Note how everything in the scene—not the words and their meaning only—contributes to build up this Portia. The quiet entrance, the collected thought and sustained rhythm of her unchecked speech, the homely talk of supper-time and of the impatient Brutus scratching his head and stamping, and of the risk he is running now of catching cold; nothing more wonderful than this is the foundation for the appeal to

> that great vow
> Which did incorporate and make us one . . .

Nor does the appeal at its very height disturb the even music of the verse. For with her such feelings do not ebb and flow; they lie deep down, they are a faith. She is, as we should say, all of a

piece; and her very gentleness, her very reasonableness is her
strength. Even her pride has its modesty.

> I grant I am a woman, but, withal,
> A woman that Lord Brutus took to wife;
> I grant I am a woman; but, withal,
> A woman well-reputed, Cato's daughter;
> Think you I am no stronger than my sex,
> Being so father'd and so husbanded?

The repeated phrase and the stressed consonants give the verse
a sudden vigor; they contrast with the drop back to simplicity of

> Tell me your counsels, I will not disclose 'em.
> I have made strong proof of my constancy,
> Giving myself a voluntary wound
> Here, in the thigh: can I bear that with patience
> And not my husband's secrets?

To this, with imperceptibly accumulating force, with that one
flash of pride for warning, the whole scene has led. A single stroke,
powerful in its reticence, as fine in itself as it is true to Portia.

Then, lest she should seem too good to be true, Shakespeare
adds a scene of anticlimax; of a Portia confessing to weakness, all
nerves, miserably conscious that her page's sharp young eyes are
fixed on her; outfacing, though, the old Soothsayer, and, with a
final effort, spiritedly herself again. While, for one more touch of
truth, he gives us,

> O Brutus!
> The heavens speed thee in thine enterprise.

Murder is the enterprise, and Cato's daughter knows it. But he is
her Brutus, so may the heavens speed him even in this.

The Play's Structure

THERE is a powerful ease in the construction of *Julius Cæsar*
which shows us a Shakespeare master of his means, and it is the
play in which the boundaries of his art begin so markedly to
widen. We find in it, therefore, a stagecraft, not of a too
accustomed perfection, but bold and free. The theme calls forth
all his resources and inspires their fresh and vigorous use; yet it
does not strain them, as some later and, if greater, less accommo-

dating themes are to do. We may here study Elizabethan stagecraft, as such, almost if not quite at its best; and a close analysis
of the play's action, the effects in it and the way they are gained—
a task for the producer in any case—will have this further interest.

Plutarch was a godsend to Shakespeare. Rome, Cæsar and high
heroic verse, one knows what such a mixture may amount to in
the theater; though we may suppose that, with his lively mind,
he would never have touched the subject had he not found that
admirable historian, who, with happy familiarity, tucks an arm in
ours, so to speak, and leads us his observant, anecdotic way,
humanizing history, yet never diminishing its magnificence.
Plutarch's genius, in fact, is closely allied to Shakespeare's own,
with its power to make, by a touch or so of nature, great men
and simple, present and past, the real and the mimic world, one
kin. And this particular power was in the ascendant with Shakespeare now.

He redraws the outline of the story more simply, but he cannot
resist crowding characters in. What wonder, when they are all so
striking, and he knows he can make a living man out of a dozen
lines of dialogue? The fifth act is a galaxy of such creations. And
if, on the other hand, Artemidorus and the Soothsayer have little
or no life of their own, while the poet of Act IV is a mere
irruption into the play, a species of human ordnance shot off,
their momentarily important part in the action lends them
reflected life enough. But much of the play's virtue lies in the
continual invention and abundant vitality of these incidental
figures by which the rarer life, so to call it, of the chief characters
is at intervals nourished. And as there is no formal mechanism of
plot, it is largely with their aid that the action moves forward
with such a varied rhythm, upon an ebb and flow of minor event
that is most lifelike. The whole play is alive; it is alive in every
line.

Elizabethan stagecraft, with its time-freedom and space-
freedom, gives the playwright great scope for maneuvering minor
character and incident. He may conjure a character into sudden
prominence, and be done with it as suddenly. He has not, as in
the modern "realistic" theater, to relate it to the likelihoods of
hard-and-fast time and place. The modern dramatist plans his
play by large divisions, even as the Greek dramatist did. Time

and place must suit the need of his chief characters; if minor ones can't be accommodating they can't be accommodated, that's all. The Elizabethan dramatist has his story to tell, and the fate of the chief figures in it to determine. But, as long as the march of the story is not stayed, he may do pretty well what he likes by the way. The modern dramatist thinks of his play constructively in acts; and the scenes must accommodate themselves to the act, as the acts to the play as a whole. The Elizabethan would instinctively do the contrary. This is not to say that a play did not commonly move to some larger rhythm than the incidental. Every playwright, every sort of artist indeed, feels for the form which will best accommodate his idea, and will come to prefer the comprehensive form. But whether this rhythm with Shakespeare resolved itself into acts is another matter; and that it would resolve itself into the five acts of the editors is more than doubtful.

The larger rhythm of *Julius Cæsar* can be variously interpreted. The action moves by one impetus, in a barely checked crescendo, to the end of Act III. Cæsar's murder is the theme; the mob provides a recurrent chorus of confusion, and ends, as it has begun, this part of the story. Acts IV and V are given to the murder's retribution; this unifies them. They are martial, more ordered, and, for all the fighting at the end, consistently pitched in a lower key. The five-act division can, however, be defended dramatically; and, if it is valid, it shows us some interesting points of Elizabethan stagecraft. Act I is preparatory and leads up to the conspirators' winning of Brutus, though this itself is kept for the start of Act II. Modern practice would dictate a division after Act I, Sc. ii; for here is a time interval and a change from day to night. But to Shakespeare—or his editor—it would be more important to begin a new act upon a new note, and with the dominant figure of Brutus to impress us. And this we find: each act of the five has a significant and striking beginning, while the ends of the first four all tail away. Act III begins with the ominous

> CÆSAR.   The Ides of March are come.
> SOOTHSAYER.   Ay, Cæsar, but not gone.

Act IV with the sinister

> ANTONY.   These many then shall die; their names are
>   pricked.

Act V with the triumphant

> Octavius. Now, Antony, our hopes are answered. . . .

It is easy to see why the beginning of an Elizabethan "act" had
to be striking.[9] There was no lowering of the lights, no music, no
warning raps, while eyes "in front" concentrated upon an enigmatic curtain. The actors had to walk on and command the
unprepared attention of a probably restless audience, and they
needed appropriate material. Equally, to whatever crisis of
emotion a scene might mount, they would have to walk off again.
Therefore neither acts nor scenes, as a rule, end upon a crisis.

The play is too strenuous, if not too long, to be acted without
at least one pause. It must occur, of course, at the end of Act III.
This one should, I personally think, be enough; if pauses are to
mean long intervals of talk and distraction, it certainly would be.
But if a producer thinks more relief from the strain upon the
audience is advisable (his actors do not need it), there is the
breathing-space at the end of Act II—better not make more of it—
and, if that will not suffice, he can pause at the end of Act I. He
will be unwise, though, to divide Acts IV and V.

But the form of the play should first be studied in relation to
its minor rhythms, for it is in these, in the setting of them one
against the other, in their adjustment to the larger rhythm of the
main theme, that the liveliness of Shakespeare's stagecraft is to be
seen.

The action begins with the entry of the two Tribunes . . . *and
certain commoners over the stage.* The Roman populace is to play
an important part; we have now but a minute's glimpse of it,
and in harmless holiday mood.

> Hence! home, you idle creatures, get you home:
> Is this a holiday?

The first lines spoken are a stage direction for the temper of the
scene. It may be that the Globe Theatre "crowd" was not much
of a crowd, was liable to be unrehearsed and inexact. Line after
line scattered through the scene is contrived to describe indirectly
how they should look and what they should be expressing. No
audience but will accept the suggestion, though the crowd itself

---

[9] But this might often be as true, if in another degree, of the individual scene.

be a bit behindhand. Nor need a producer, here or elsewhere, strive to provide a realistically howling mob. The fugleman convention is a part of the convention of the play; reason enough for abiding in it.

Note before we leave this scene how its first full-bodied speech has Pompey for a theme, and what emphasis is given to the first sound of his name. After the chattering prose of the cobbler comes Marullus'

> Wherefore rejoice? What conquest brings he home?
> What tributaries follow him to Rome
> To grace in captive bonds his chariot wheels?
> You blocks, you stones, you worse than senseless things!
> O you hard hearts, you cruel men of Rome,
> Knew you not Pompey?

For Pompey dead is to Cæsar something of what Cæsar dead is to be to Brutus and the rest. And—though Shakespeare naturally does not prejudice an important effect by anticipating it and elaborating its parallel—the name's reiteration throughout the first part of the play has purpose.

A unity is given to these first three acts by the populace; by keeping them constantly in our minds. They are easily persuaded now, controlled and brought to silence:

> They vanish tongue-tied in their guiltiness.

The devastation of the third act's end has this mild beginning.

Against the disorder and inconsequence, Cæsar's processional entrance tells with doubled effect. We are given but a short sight of him, our impression is that he barely pauses on his way. His dominance is affirmed by the simplest means. We hear the name sounded—sounded rather than spoken—seven times in twenty-four lines. The very name is to dominate. It is the cue for Cassius' later outburst:

> Brutus and Cæsar: what should be in that "Cæsar"?
> Why should that name be sounded more than yours?
> Write them together, yours is as fair a name;
> Sound them, it doth become the mouth as well;
> Weigh them, it is as heavy; conjure with 'em,
> "Brutus" will start a spirit as soon as "Cæsar."

The procession passes. And now that these opposites, the many-

headed and the one, the mob and its moment's idol, have been
set in clear contrast before us, the main action may begin.

It is Cassius' passion that chiefly gives tone and color to the
ensuing long duologue. He sets it a swift pace too, which is only
checked by Brutus' slow responses; Brutus, lending one ear to his
vehement friend, the other keen for the meaning of the distant
shouts. Yet, in a sense, it is Cæsar who still holds the stage; in
Cassius' rhetoric, in the shouting, in Brutus' strained attention.
With his re-entrance, then, there need be no impression given of
a fresh beginning, for the tension created by that first passage
across the stage should hardly have been relaxed. It now increases,
that is all. Cæsar pauses a little longer on his way, and with
purpose. It is like the passing of a thundercloud; presage, in
another sort, of the storm by which Nature is to mark his end.
To the stately words and trumpet music the procession moves on;
and we are left, with the proper shock of contrast, to Casca's
acrid and irreverent prose. Now the tension does relax. Then
Casca goes, and Brutus and Cassius part with but brief comment
on him, without attempting to restore the broken harmony of
their thoughts; and Cassius' closing soliloquy, as we have seen,
is little more than a perfunctory forwarding of the story.

Thunder and lightning . . .

This, the stage empty, would emphasize well enough for the
Elizabethans some break of time and place, and a few claps and
flashes more might suffice to put a whole storm on record. It does
not now suffice Shakespeare. He sets out upon a hundred and
sixty-five lines of elaborate verbal scene-painting; in the economy
of the plot they really stand for little more. It is not, of course,
merely a passing pictorial effect that he is branding on his
audience's imagination. Consider this passage in connection with
those appeals of the Chorus in *Henry V*:

> Think when we talk of horses that you see them
> Printing their proud hoofs i' the receiving earth;
> For 'tis your thoughts that now must deck our kings . . .

> O! do but think
> You stand upon the rivage and behold
> A city on the inconstant billows dancing;

For so appears this fleet majestical,
Holding due course to Harfleur.

All that the listeners were to do for themselves, since the
dramatist could not even attempt to do it for them. Here Shakespeare is certainly concerned to picture Rome under the portentous
storm, but it is upon the personal episodes he fixes—upon the
slave with his burning hand, the

> hundred ghastly women,
> Transformed with their fear, who swore they saw
> Men all in fire walk up and down the streets . . .

upon the marvel of the lion that "glar'd upon" Casca and "went
surly by." And their value to him lies chiefly in their effect upon
the emotions of his characters; this is his path to an effect upon
ours. He has discovered, in fact, the one dramatic use to which
the picturesque can be put in his theater, and the one and only
way of using it. It was not, of course, a discovery sought and
made all complete for the occasion. But this is, I think, the first
time he brings Nature under such serious contribution. Make
another comparison, with the storm-scenes in *King Lear*. Set this
scene beside those, with their perfect fusion of character and
surroundings and their use to the play, and its method seems
arbitrary and crude enough. It takes the plot little further. And
Cicero is a walking shadow, Cinna a mere convenience; Casca,
unnerved and eloquent, is unrecognizable as the Casca of the
previous scene, is turned to a convenience for picturing the storm;
while Cassius only repeats himself, and his rhetoric, dramatically
justified before, grows rodomontade. By the end of the hundred
and sixty-five lines we have learned that Cicero is cautious, Casca
ripe, that things are moving fast with Cinna and the rest, that
Brutus must be won. At his best Shakespeare could have achieved
this in fifty lines or less and given us the storm into the bargain.

The contrasting calm of the next act's beginning is an appropriate setting for Brutus, the stoic, the man of conscience and
gentle mind. The play's scheme now opens out and grows clear,
for Brutus takes his allotted and fatal place among his fellows
as moral dictator. To his dominance is due the scene's coldness
and rigidity, though the unity of tone gives it dignity and its
circumstance alone would make effective drama. Incidental

things give it vitality and such color as it needs; the coming and
going of the sleepy boy, the knocking without, the striking of the
clock followed by those three short echoing speeches. It all stays
to the end rather static than dynamic; for high-mindedly as
Brutus may harangue his "gentle friends," fervently as they may
admire him, there is never, now or later, the spontaneous sympathy between them that alone gives life to a cause. The ultimate
as well as the immediate tragedy is in the making.

The scene with Portia is the due sequel. Even from her he
holds aloof. He loves her; but the more he loves her the less he
can confide in her. Even the avowal of his love is wrung from
him in a sort of agony. And Portia's own tragedy is in the
making here. In her spent patience with his silence we might
well divine the impatience at his absence which was to be her
death. We may question why, after a vibrant climax, Shakespeare
so lowers the tension for the scene's end. Caius Ligarius' coming
will surely thrust Portia and this more intimate Brutus to the
background of our remembrance. There are two answers at least.
The play's main action must not only be carried on, but it must
seem now to be hurried on, and Brutus, his philosophic reserve
once broken, must be shown precipitate.[10] For another answer;
the Caius Ligarius episode keeps the scenes between Brutus and
Portia, Cæsar and Calpurnia apart. It would discount the second
to bring it on the heels of the first.

Thunder and lightning herald the next scene's beginning; the
purpose of its repetition is plain enough. The mood wrought in
us by the storm must be restored; and in a moment comes
Calpurnia's speech, which is a very echo of Casca's description of
the signs and portents. Cæsar, rocklike at first against the pleadings
of his wife, wavers from his love for her and yields to Decius'
friendliness and flattery, reinforced by the thronging-in of the

---

[10] Here, incidentally, is an instance of an effect made for its own sake and in
the confidence that no awkward questions will be asked. The immediate suggestion
is that Brutus and Ligarius go straight to the conspirators, thence with them to
Cæsar and the Senate House. It is left mere suggestion and not further defined,
for Portia has to be told of the conspiracy "by and by," and, when we next see
her, the suggestion—still mere suggestion—is that she has been told. But
Shakespeare knows that no questions will be asked as long as the effects are
spaced out, if distractions intervene and positive contradiction is avoided.

rest, looking, as Brutus bid them look, so "fresh and merrily." It is good preparation for the catastrophe, the sudden livening of the scene with this group of resolute, cheerful men. Besides, might not the slim Decius have overreached himself but for their coming? Cæsar was no fool, and Calpurnia would be apt to every sort of suspicion. But the friendly faces disperse the last clouds of the ominous night. Cassius is not here. It is Brutus, the irreproachable Brutus, who gives tone to the proceeding. Does he, even at this moment, feel himself

> arm'd so strong in honesty . . .

that he can meet Cæsar's magnanimity without flinching? Is it only ague that makes Caius Ligarius shake as Cæsar presses his hand? And that nothing of tragic irony may be wanting—

> Good friends, go in, and taste some wine with me,
> And we, like friends, will straightway go together.

The sacrament of hospitality and trust! It is a supreme effect, economized in words, fully effective only in action. And for an instance of Shakespeare's dramatic judgment, of his sense of balance between an immediate effect and the play's continuing purpose, of his power, in striking one note, to strike the ruthlessly right one, take the two lines with which Brutus, lagging back, ends the scene:

> That every like is not the same, O Cæsar!
> The heart of Brutus yearns to think upon.

Not that a pun or a quibble upon words necessarily struck an Elizabethan as a trifling thing. But it takes a Brutus to find refuge in a quibbling thought at such a moment, and in his own grief for his victim.

Cæsar is now ringed by the conspirators, the daggers are ready, and the two scenes that follow are to hold and prolong the suspense till they strike.[11] Artemidorus, with his paper and its comment, may seem unduly dry and detached. But the solitary anonymous figure comes as a relief and contrast to that significant group, and against that wrought emotion his very detachment

---

[11] Unless every clearance of the stage is to mark a division of scenes, they are, of course, but one. No particular change of location is implied. Upon the question of the act-division here, see also page 381.

tells. It contrasts too with Portia's tremulous intimate concern. The act's end here—if it is to mean a short empty pause while the audience stay seated and expectant, not an interval of talk and movement—will have value. The blow is about to fall, and in silence suspense is greatest. We draw breath for the two long scenes that form the center section of the play.

Trumpets sound, the stage fills. Cæsar comes again as we saw him go, still circled by these friends, confident, outwardly serene. The trumpets silent, we hear another prelude, of two voices, the one ringing clear, the other pallidly echoing:

> CÆSAR.   The Ides of March are come.
> SOOTHSAYER. Ay, Cæsar, but not gone.

Then follows a little scuffle of voices, a quick shifting and elbowing in the group round Cæsar as the petitions are thrust forward and aside, and once again that fivefold iteration of the potent name. Despite the ceremony, nerves are on edge. Cæsar goes forward to be greeted by the Senators and to mount his state. Now comes a passage of eighteen lines. Toneless it has to be, that the speakers betray not their feelings. In the group of them there is hardly a movement; they must measure even their glances. Popilius Lena's threading his way through them is startling in itself. Yet on this monotone the whole gamut of the conspiracy's doubts, fears and desperation is run. Its midway sentence is the steely

> Cassius, be constant. . . .

with which Brutus marks his mastery of the rest. Cæsar is seated. His

> Are we all ready?

turns the whole concourse to him. Some few of them are ready indeed. And now, in terms of deliberate rhetoric, Shakespeare once more erects before us the Colossus that is to be overthrown. Then in a flash the blow falls. Butchered by Casca, sacrificed by Brutus—these two doings of the same deed are marked and kept apart—Cæsar lies dead.

Remark that we are now only a quarter of the way through the scene; further, that the play's whole action so far has been a preparation for this crisis. Yet, with dead Cæsar lying there,

Shakespeare will contrive to give us such fresh interest in the living that, with no belittling of the catastrophe, no damping-down nor desecration of our emotions, our minds will be turned forward still. This is a great technical achievement. He might well have shirked the full attempt and have wound up the scene with its next seventy lines or so. But then could the play ever have recovered strength and impetus? As it is, by the long scene's end our concern for Cæsar is lost in our expectations of the Forum. The producer must note carefully how this is brought about, lest even the minor means to it miscarry.

The mainspring of the renewed action will lie, of course, in the creation of Antony. We may call it so; for, as we saw, he has been cunningly kept, in person and by reference, an ineffectual figure so far. But now both in person and by reference, by preparation, by contrast, Shakespeare brings him to a sudden overwhelming importance.

We have the helter-skelter of the moment after Cæsar's fall; Brutus is the only figure of authority and calm. Old Publius stands trembling and dumb; Antony, that slight man, has fled, and the conspirators seem confounded by their very success. Before, then, they face the Rome they have saved from tyranny, let them make themselves one again, not in false courage—if Rome is ungrateful they must die—but in high principle that fears not death. Let them sign themselves ritual brothers—and in whose blood but Cæsar's?

> Stoop, Romans, stoop,
> And let us bathe our hands in Cæsar's blood
> Up to the elbows, and besmear our swords:
> Then walk we forth, even to the market place,
> And, waving our red weapons o'er our heads,
> Let's all cry, "Peace, freedom, and liberty!"

We need not doubt Brutus' deep sincerity for a moment.

> Fates, we will know your pleasures.
> That we shall die, we know; 'tis but the time
> And drawing days out, that men stand upon.

This is the man of principle at his noblest. But what else than savage mockery is Casca's

> Why, he that cuts off twenty years of life
> Cuts off so many years of fearing death.

And does Brutus, the rapt ideologue, perceive it? Into the sophistical trap he walks:

> Grant that, and then is death a benefit:
> So are we Cæsar's friends, that have abridg'd
> His time of fearing death.

And he anoints himself devotedly. Then Cassius, febrile, infatuate:

> Stoop, then, and wash. How many ages hence
> Shall this our lofty scene be acted o'er,
> In states unborn and accents yet unknown!

Brutus echoes him as well. And by this last daring and doubly dramatic stroke, Shakespeare reminds us that we are ideal spectators of these men and the event, having vision and prevision too. Comment is forbidden the playwright, but here is the effect of it contrived. For as we look and listen we hear the verdict of the ages echoing. In this imperfect world, it would seem, one can be too high-minded, too patriotic, too virtuous altogether. And then the commonest thing, if it be rooted firm, may trip a man to his ruin. So these exalted gentlemen, led by their philosophic patriot, are stopped on their way—by the arrival of a servant.[12]

This is the play's turning point. And, if but pictorially, could a better be contrived? On the one side the group of triumphant and powerful men; on the other, suddenly appearing, a humble, anonymous messenger.

> Thus, Brutus, did my master bid me kneel;
> Thus did Mark Antony bid me fall down;
> And, being prostrate, thus he bade me say . . .

And so aptly and literally does he represent his master that Brutus, with this chance to test the smooth words apart from their deviser, might, we should suppose, take warning. But it is Brutus who is infatuate now. It is not, as with Cassius, passions that blind him, but principles. He has done murder for an ideal. Not to credit his adversaries, in turn, with the highest motives

---

[12] For an excellent analysis of this passage see MacCullum's *Shakespeare's Roman Plays*, quoted by Furness. And for the effect of the servant's entrance see, as before noted, R. G. Moulton's *Shakespeare as Dramatic Artist*.

would be unworthy, would seem sheer hypocrisy. And Antony's
message is baited with an uncanny knowledge of the man.

> Brutus is noble, wise, valiant, and honest;
> Cæsar was mighty, bold, royal, and loving:
> Say I love Brutus, and I honour him;
> Say I fear'd Cæsar, honour'd him, and lov'd him.

Wisdom and honesty, valor and love, honor and again honor;
Brutus will harp on the very words in his own apology. It is
Cassius, with his vengeance fulfilled and his passions gratified,
who now sees clear, knowing his Antony as truly as Antony
knows his Brutus. His

>   misgiving still
> Falls shrewdly to the purpose.

But he lacks authority to lead.

Then follows the revelation of Antony, in his verbal duel with
the conspirators; his devoted rhapsody over Cæsar's body; and the
swift foresight of the passage with Octavius' servant. It is to be
noted that the beginning of the scene in the Forum tags dramatically not to the end of this but to the earlier departure of Brutus
and the others. Hence, perhaps, the short opening in verse and
Brutus' echoing of his last spoken line,

> Prepare the body, then, and follow us.

with

> Then follow me, and give me audience, friends.

Once he is in the pulpit we have a sharp change to prose.

Editor after editor has condemned Brutus' speech as poor and
ineffective, and most of them have then proceeded to justify
Shakespeare for making it so. It is certainly not meant to be
ineffective, for it attains its end in convincing the crowd. Whether
it is poor oratory must be to some extent a matter of taste.
Personally, accepting its form as one accepts the musical convention of a fugue, I find that it stirs me deeply. I prefer it to
Antony's. It wears better. It is very noble prose. But we must, of
course, consider it first as a part of the setting-out of Brutus'
character. Nothing—if the speech itself does not—suggests him to
us as a poor speaker; nor, at this moment of all others, would he
fail himself. But we know the sort of appeal he would, deliberately

if not temperamentally, avoid. Shakespeare has been accused, too, of bias against the populace. But is it so? He had no illusions about them. As a popular dramatist he faced their inconstant verdict day by day, and came to write for a better audience than he had. He allows Brutus no illusions, certainly.

> Only be patient till we have appeas'd
> The multitude, beside themselves with fear. . . .

This is the authentic voice of your republican aristocrat, who is at no pains, either, to disguise his disdain.

> Be patient till the last.
> Romans, countrymen and lovers! hear me for my cause; and be silent, that you may hear. . . .

For the tone belies the words; nor is such a rapping on the desk for "Quiet, please" the obvious way into the affections of the heady crowd. He concedes nothing to their simplicity.

> Censure me in your wisdom, and awake your senses, that you may be the better judge.

But the compliment, one fears, is paid less to them than to his own intellectual pride. It is wasted in any case, if we may judge by the Third and Fourth Citizens:

> Let him be Cæsar.
>   Cæsar's better parts
> Shall be crown'd in Brutus.

He has won them; not by what he has said, in spite of it, rather; but by what he is. The dramatic intention, and the part the crowd plays in it, is surely plain. Men in the mass do not think, they feel. They are as biddable as children, and as sensitive to suggestion. Mark Antony is to make it plainer.

Antony has entered, and stands all friendless by Cæsar's bier. Brutus descends, the dialogue shifting from prose to easy verse as he shakes free of the enthusiasm, and departs alone. His austere renouncing of advantage should show us how truly alone.

Antony makes no glib beginning; he protests, indeed, that he has nothing to say. He tries this opening and that, is deprecatory, apologetic.

> The noble Brutus
> Hath told you Cæsar was ambitious;
> If it were so, it was a grievous fault,
> And grievously hath Cæsar answered it.

But he is deftly feeling his way by help of a few platitudes to his true opening, and alert for a first response. He senses one, possibly, upon his

> He was my friend, faithful and just to me. . . .

—for that was a human appeal. But he knows better than to presume on a success; he returns to his praise of the well-bepraised Brutus. He embellishes his tune with two grace notes, one appealing to sentiment, the other to greed. More praise of Brutus, and yet more! But the irony of this will out, and he checks himself. Irony is a tricky weapon with an audience uncertain still. Nor will too much nice talk about honor serve him; that sort of thing leaves men cold. A quick turn gives us

> I speak not to disprove what Brutus spoke,
> But here I am to speak what I do know.

and, to judge by the hammering monosyllables of the last line, he is warming to his work, and feels his hearers warming to him.

One may so analyze the speech throughout and find it a triumph of effective cleverness. The cheapening of the truth, the appeals to passion, the perfect carillon of flattery, cajolery, mockery and pathos, swinging to a magnificent tune, all serve to make it a model of what popular oratory should be. In a school for demagogues its critical analysis might well be an item in every examination paper. That is one view of it. By another, there is nothing in it calculated or false. Antony feels like this; and, on these occasions, he never lets his thoughts belie his feelings, that is all. And he knows, without stopping to think, what the common thought and feeling will be, where reason and sentiment will touch bottom—and if it be a muddy bottom, what matter!—because he is himself, as we said, the common man raised to the highest power. So, once in touch with his audience, he can hardly go wrong.

How easy he makes things for them! No abstract arguments:

> But here's a parchment with the seal of Cæsar;
> I found it in his closet, 'tis his will.[13]

---

13 And later, he will propose to his colleagues Octavius and Lepidus that they all three consider
> How to cut off some charge in legacies.

We pass now, however, to a less ingenuous, more ingenious, phase of the achievement. Those—it is strange there should be any —who range themselves with the mob and will see in Antony no more than the plain blunt man of his own painting, have still to account for this slim manipulator of Cæsar's will that Shakespeare paints. It is tempting, no doubt, to make men dance to your tune when the thing is done so easily. When they stand, open-eared and open-mouthed, how resist stuffing them with any folly that comes handy? And as there is no limit, it would seem, to their folly and credulity, greed and baseness, why not turn it all to good account—one's own account? Antony is not the man, at any rate, to turn aside from such temptation. Is he less of a demagogue that Cæsar's murder is his theme, and vengeance for it his cause? Does poetic eloquence make demagogy less vicious—or, by chance, more? Shakespeare's Antony would not be complete without this juggling with Cæsar's will.

What so impresses the unlearned as the sight of some document? He does not mean to read it. They are Cæsar's heirs. There, he never meant to let that slip! Trick after trick of the oratorical trade follows. The provocative appeal to the seething crowd's self-control tagged to the flattery of their generous hearts, the play with the mantle, which they "all do know," that soft touch of the "summer's evening" when Cæsar first put it on! Self-interest well salted with sentiment, what better bait can there be? Much may be done with a blood-stained bit of cloth!

> Through this the well-beloved Brutus stabbed;
> And as he pluck'd his cursèd steel away,
> Mark how the blood of Cæsar followed it,
> As rushing out of doors, to be resolved
> If Brutus so unkindly knocked, or no. . . .

If our blood were still cold the simile might sound ridiculous, but it thrills us now.

> This was the most unkindest cut of all;
> For when the noble Cæsar saw him stab,
> Ingratitude, more strong than traitors' arms,
> Quite vanquished him: then burst his mighty heart;
> And, in his mantle muffling up his face,
> Even at the base of Pompey's statua,
> Which all the while ran blood, great Cæsar fell.

How fine it sounds! How true, therefore, by the standards of popular oratory, it is! There is poetic truth, certainly, in that ingratitude; and as for Pompey's statue, if it did not actually run blood, it might well have done.

> O! what a fall was there, my countrymen;
> Then I, and you, and all of us fell down,
> Whilst bloody treason flourished over us.
> O! now you weep, and I perceive you feel
> The dint of pity. . . .

What were Brutus' tributes to their wisdom compared to this? Antony has won their tears, and has but to seal his success by showing them the very body of Cæsar, and to endorse it with

> Good friends, sweet friends, let me not stir you up
> To such a sudden flood of mutiny.
> They that have done this deed are honourable. . . .

for irony is a potent weapon now; and to forbid mutiny is only to encourage it, the word of itself will do so.

The peroration is masterly, a compendium of excitement. We have again the false restraint from passion, the now triumphant mockery of those honorable men, of their wisdom, their good reasons and their private grief; again, the plain blunt man's warning against such oratorical snares as the subtle Brutus set; and it is all rounded off with magnificent rhythm, the recurrent thought and word flung like a stone from a sling.

> but were I Brutus,
> And Brutus Antony, there were an Antony
> Would ruffle up your spirits, and put a tongue
> In every wound of Cæsar that should move
> The stones of Rome to rise and mutiny.

And to what end? To the routing of the conspirators from Rome, truly. A good counterstroke. But the first victim of Antony's eloquence, as Shakespeare takes care to show us, is the wretched Cinna the poet, who has had nothing to do with Cæsar's murder at all.[14] The mob tear him limb from limb, as children tear a rag doll. Nor does knowledge of his innocence hinder them.

~~~~~~~~~

[14] A scene which the average modern producer takes great care to cut.

> Truly, my name is Cinna.
> Tear him to pieces, he's a conspirator.
> I am Cinna, the poet, I am Cinna the poet.
> Tear him for his bad verses, tear him for his bad verses.
> I am not Cinna the conspirator.
> It is no matter, his name's Cinna; pluck but his name out of
> his heart, and turn him going.

Well, we have had Antony's fine oratory; and we may have
been, and should have been, stirred by it. But if we have not at the
same time watched him, and ourselves, with a discerning eye,
and listened as well with a keener ear, the fault is none of
Shakespeare's. He draws no moral, does not wordily balance the
merits of this cause against that. He is content to compose for the
core of his play, with an artist's enjoyment, with an artist's
conscience, in getting the balance true, this ironic picture; and,
finally, to set against the high tragedy of the murder of Cæsar a
poor poetaster's wanton slaughter.

The beginning of the fourth act sets against the calculations of
the conspirators the arithmetic of the new masters of Rome.

> These many then shall die; their names are pricked.

It is an admirably done scene, of but fifty lines all told, giving
an actor, with just twenty-two words, material for Lepidus (the
feat would seem impossible, but Shakespeare manages it; and so
can an actor, rightly chosen and given scope), giving us Octavius,
showing us yet another Antony, and outlining the complete
gospel of political success. Brutus and Cassius, its finish informs
us, are levying powers. We are shown them straightway at the
next scene's beginning, and from now to the play's end its action
runs a straight road.

> Drum. Enter Brutus. . . .

The philosopher has turned general. He is graver, more austere
than ever.

> Your master, Pindarus,
> In his own change, or by ill officers,
> Hath given me some worthy cause to wish
> Things done undone. . . .

But he says it as one who would say that nothing, be it big or little, can ever be undone. We hear a *Low march within*, congruous accompaniment to the somber voice. It heralds Cassius.

> *Enter Cassius and his Powers.*
>
> | CASSIUS. | Stand, ho! |
> |---|---|
> | BRUTUS. | Stand, ho! |
> | 1ST SOLDIER. | Stand! |
> | 2ND SOLDIER. | Stand! |
> | 3RD SOLDIER. | Stand! |

The voices echo back, the drumbeats cease, the armed men face each other, silent a moment.[15]

This long scene—the play's longest—thus begun, is dominated by Brutus and attuned in the main to his mood. Now the mood of the good man in adversity may well make for monotony and gloom; but Shakespeare is alert to avoid this, and so must producer and actors be. We have the emotional elaboration of the quarrel, the eccentric interlude of the poet as preparation for the sudden drop to the deep still note struck by the revelation of Portia's death; next comes the steady talk of fighting plans (note the smooth verse), then the little stir with which the council breaks up and the simple preparations for the night. Varro and Claudius are brought in, so that their sleep, as well as the boy's, may throw the calm, wakeful figure of Brutus into relief. The tune and its lapsing brings a hush, we can almost hear the leaves of the book rustle as they are turned. Then the ghost appears; the tense few moments of its presence have been well prepared. The scene's swift ending is good stagecraft too. Lucius' protesting treble, the deeper voices of the soldiers all confused with sleep, the dissonance and sharp interchange break and disperse the ominous spell for Brutus and for us. And the last words look forward.[16]

---

15 The Chorus in *Henry V* could not apologize enough for the theater's failure to show armies in being. But by a little music, this cunning of speech and action, and a bold acceptance of convention, these "ciphers to this great account" can be made to work well enough upon the "imaginary forces" of the audience.

16 "Sleep again, Lucius," would point, if nothing else did, to the drawing-together of the curtains of the inner stage upon the scene. Where Varro and Claudius have been lying is a question. They enter, of course, upon the main stage. Brutus apparently points to the inner stage with "Lie in my tent and sleep." They offer to keep watch where they are, *i.e.* by the door. I am inclined

The last act of *Julius Cæsar* has been most inconsiderately depreciated. Nothing, certainly, will make it effective upon the modern "realistic" stage, but we can hardly blame Shakespeare for that. He writes within the conventions of his own theater, and he here takes the fullest advantage of them. He begins by bringing the rival armies, led by their generals, face to face.

> *Enter Octavius, Antony and their army. . . .*
> *Drum. Enter Brutus, Cassius and their army.*

BRUTUS.	They stand, and would have parley.
CASSIUS.	Stand fast, Titinius; we must out and talk.
OCTAVIUS.	Mark Antony, shall we give sign of battle?
ANTONY.	No, Cæsar, we will answer on their charge.
	Make forth; the generals would have some words.

This to the Elizabethans was a commonplace of stagecraft. Before scenery which paints realistically some defined locality, it must needs look absurd. But, the simpler convention accepted, Shakespeare sets for his audience a wider and more significant scene than any the scenic theater can compass. And, confronting the fighters, he states the theme, so to speak, of the play's last event, and gives it value, importance and dignity.

The whole act is constructed with great skill, each detail has its purpose and effect. But we must dismiss, even from our memories if possible, the *Scene ii, The same, the Field of Battle*; and *Scene iii, Another Part of the Field*, of the editors. What happens to begin with is this. Antony, Octavius and their powers departed, the talk between Brutus and Cassius over—it is (for us) their third and last, and a chill quiet talk; they feel they are under the shadow of defeat—the stage is left empty. Then the silence is broken by the clattering *Alarum*, the symbol of a battle begun. Then back comes Brutus, but a very different Brutus.

> Ride, ride, Messala, ride, and give these bills
> Unto the legions on the other side.

Now a *Loud alarum*, which his voice must drown.

---

to think that they lie down there, too. This would not only make the business with the ghost better, but it would bring the scene's final piece of action upon the center stage and give it breadth and importance.

Let them set on at once, for I perceive
But cold demeanour in Octavius' wing,
And sudden push gives them the overthrow.
Ride, ride, Messala: let them all come down.

And he is gone as he came. In its sharp contrast it is a stirring passage, which restores to Brutus whatever dominance he may have lost. But it cannot be achieved if tension is relaxed and attention dissipated by the shifting of scenery, or by any superfluous embroidering of the action.

Remark further that to follow the course of the battle an audience must listen keenly, and they must be able to concentrate their minds on the speakers. When the defeat of Cassius is imminent, when Titinius tells him:

O Cassius! Brutus gave the word too early;
Who, having some advantage on Octavius,
Took it too eagerly: his soldiers fell to spoil,
Whilst we by Antony are all enclos'd.

the situation is made clear enough. But if we do not master it at this moment, the rest of the scene and its drama will go for next to nothing.

Now we have Cassius grasping the ensign he has seized from the coward who was running away with it (and, being Cassius, not content with that, he has killed the man), the very ensign the birds of ill omen had hovered over; and he makes as if to plant it defiantly, conspicuously in the ground.

This hill is far enough.

His death is of a piece with his whole reckless life. He kills himself because he will not wait another minute to verify the tale his bondman tells him of Titinius' capture. He ends passionately and desperately—but still grasping his standard. Even at this moment he is as harsh to Pindarus as Brutus is gentle to his boy Lucius and the bondman who serves him:

Come hither, sirrah:
In Parthia did I take thee prisoner;
And then I swore thee, saving of thy life,
That whatsoever I did bid thee do,
Thou shouldst attempt it.

His last words are as bare and ruthless.

> Cæsar, thou art reveng'd,
> Even with the sword that kill'd thee.

Pindarus' four lines that follow may seem frigid and formal. But we need a breathing-space before we face the tragically ironic return of Titinius radiant with good news. The stagecraft of this entrance, as of others like it, belongs, we must (yet again) remember, to the Elizabethan theater, with its doors at the back, and its distance for an actor to advance, attention full on him. Entrance from the wing of a conventional scenic stage will be quite another matter.

MESSALA.   It is but change, Titinius; for Octavius
                    Is overthrown by noble Brutus' power,
                    As Cassius' legions are by Antony.
TITINIUS.   These tidings will well comfort Cassius.
MESSALA.   Where did you leave him?
TITINIUS.   All disconsolate,
                    With Pindarus his bondman, on this hill.
MESSALA.   Is that not he that lies along the ground?
TITINIUS.   He lies not like the living. O my heart!
MESSALA.   Is not that he?
TITINIUS.   No, this was he, Messala,
                    But Cassius is no more.

Stage direction is embodied in dialogue. We have the decelerated arrival telling of relief from strain, the glance around the seemingly empty place; then the sudden swift single-syllabled line and its repetition, Titinius' dart forward, Messala's graver question, the dire finality of the answer.

We come to Titinius' death; and it is a legitimate query why, with two suicides to provide for, Shakespeare burdened himself with this third. The episode itself may have attracted him; the soldier crowning his dead chief with the garland of victory; then, as the innocent cause of his death, set not to survive it.[17] The death speech is fine, and the questioning sentences that begin it whip it to great poignancy. But neither here nor anywhere, we must admit, does Shakespeare show full understanding of the "Roman's part" and the strange faith that let him play it. His

[17] Shakespeare finds this more clearly put in Plutarch than he leaves it in the play.

Romans go to their deaths stoically enough, but a little stockily too. Hamlet, later, will find the question arguable, and Macbeth will think a man a fool not to die fighting. Brutus and Cassius and Titinius, it is true, could hardly be made to argue the point here. But there is an abruptness and a sameness, and a certain emptiness, in the manner of these endings.

Another and technically a stronger reason for adding Titinius to the suicides, is that it is above all important Brutus' death should not come as an anticlimax to Cassius'. This episode helps provide against that danger, and the next scene makes escape from it sure.

The bodies are carried out in procession with due dignity, and again the effect of the empty stage keys us to expectancy. Then

> *Alarum. Enter Brutus, Messala, Cato, Lucilius and Flavius.*
> *Enter soldiers and fight.*

It is a noisy melee; so confused that, though we hear the voices of the leaders from its midst, Brutus disappears unnoticed. The scene has its touch of romance in young Cato's death, its dash of intrigue in Lucilius' trick. If these things are given value in performance, they knot up effectively the weakening continuity of theme, which, by its slacking, would leave the death of Brutus and the play's end a fag end instead of a full close.

Yet the effects of the last scene are in themselves most carefully elaborated. Hard upon the clattering excitement of the fight, and the flattering magnanimity of the triumphant Antony, comes into sight this little group of beaten and exhausted men, the torchlight flickering on their faces.[18]

> BRUTUS. Come, poor remains of friends, rest on this rock.
> CLITUS. Statilius show'd the torch-light; but, my lord,
> He came not back: he is or ta'en or slain.
> BRUTUS. Sit thee down, Clitus: slaying is the word;
> It is a deed in fashion. . . .

They throw themselves down hopelessly; to wait—for what!— and to brood in a silence which Brutus hardly breaks by his whisper, first to Clitus, next to Dardanius. Then he paces apart

---

18 It has been held (I do not stress the point) that Elizabethan outdoor performances were timed to end near twilight. In that case the torchlight would prove doubly effective here.

while the two watch him and themselves whisper of the dreadful demand he made. He calls on Volumnius next, to find in him, not hope, only the instinctive human reluctance to admit an end. But his own end—and he knows and desires it—is here. Threatening low alarums vibrate beneath his calm, colorless speech. His followers cry to him to save himself, and a like cry from far off pierces that still insistent alarum, and they echo it again. Well, these men have life and purpose left in them; let them go. He praises and humors their loyalty. But, at his command, they leave him. The end is very near.

But Shakespeare himself is not yet at the end of his resources, nor of his constant care to weave the action in a living texture, to give the least of its figures life. What, till this moment, do we know about Strato? He makes his first appearance in the battle; he is Brutus' body-servant, it seems. A thick-skinned sort of fellow; while the others counted the cost of their ruin, he had fallen asleep. Twelve lines or so (he himself speaks just seven) not only make a living figure of him but keep Brutus self-enlightening to the last. For the very last note struck out of this stoic, whose high principles could not stop short of murder, is one of gentleness.

> BRUTUS. I prithee, Strato, stay thou by thy lord:
> Thou art a fellow of a good respect;
> Thy life hath had some smatch of honour in it:
> Hold then my sword, and turn away thy face,
> While I do run upon it. Wilt thou, Strato?
> STRATO. Give me your hand first: fare you well, my lord.
> BRUTUS. Farewell, good Strato. . . .

The man's demand for a handshake, the master's response to it; —how much of Shakespeare's greatness lies in these little things, and in the love of his art that never found them too little for his care! Then Brutus closes his account.

> Cæsar, now be still:
> I kill'd not thee with half so good a will.

In silence on both sides the thing is done. Nor does Strato stir while the loud alarum and retreat are sounded; he does not even turn at the conquerors' approach—Antony, Octavius and the already reconciled Messala and Lucilius, who only see by the light of the torches this solitary figure standing there.

Nor have we even yet reached the play's formal close, the ceremonial lifting of the body, the apostrophe to the dead, and that turning towards the living future which the conditions of the Elizabethan stage inevitably and happily prescribed. Chief place is given here, as we have noted, to Octavius, Cæsar's heir and—if Shakespeare may have had it in mind—the conqueror-to-be of his fellow-conqueror. But we have first a bitter-sweet exchange between Strato and Messala. They—and they know it—are commoner clay than their master who lies here; no vain heroism for them. Next Antony speaks, and makes sportsmanlike amends to his dead enemy.

The play is a masterpiece of Elizabethan stagecraft, and the last act, from this point of view, especially remarkable; but only by close analysis can its technical virtues be made plain. Within the powerful ease of its larger rhythm, the constant, varied ebb and flow and interplay of purpose, character and event give it richness of dramatic life, and us the sense of its lifelikeness.

Staging and Costume

No difficulties arise—why should they?—in fitting the play to such a stage as we suppose Shakespeare's at the Globe to have been; at most a few questions must be answered as to the use of the inner stage for this scene or that. Further, the resources of this stage, its adapting of space and time to the playwright's convenience, are so fully exploited that the producer who means to use another had better be very careful he does not lose more than he gains.

Act I can be played wholly on the main stage.

Act II. *Enter Brutus in his Orchard*, says the Folio. This looks like a discovery upon the inner stage. There will certainly be the dramatic effect of contrast, after the feverish excursions through the night of storm, in our seeing Brutus, a chief subject of them, sitting in the contained quiet of his garden. The opening speech, by which, as a rule, Shakespeare paints us the aspect of his scene if he wants to, gives it its tone and in its interspersed silences both the solitary man and the stillness after the storm:

What, Lucius! ho!
I cannot, by the progress of the stars,
Give guess how near to day. Lucius, I say!
I would it were my fault to sleep so soundly.
When, Lucius, when! Awake, I say! what, Lucius!

Lucius may enter directly upon the inner stage. Brutus might speak his first soliloquy still sitting there. It is possible that at the Globe he did not, the actor there may have needed a better point of vantage for such an intimately reflective passage.[19] The knocking would almost certainly be heard beyond one of the main-stage doors, through which the conspirators would come, for the scene's general action must be upon the main stage without a doubt. For the scene which follows the traverse must, one would suppose, be closed, to hide whatever properties suggested Brutus' garden. But *Enter Cæsar in his nightgown*, even though he enter upon the main stage, will sufficiently suggest an interior. And the main stage will serve for the rest of the second act.

We should note the space-freedom Shakespeare assumes. "Here will I stand," says Artemidorus, "till Cæsar pass along"; but, speaking five lines more, he goes off, to reappear with the crowd that follows Cæsar. And Act III begins with a most significant instance of it. The inner stage is disclosed and Cæsar's "state" is set there. Cæsar, the conspirators, the Senators and the populace enter upon the main stage. Cassius speaks to Artemidorus:

> What! urge you your petitions in the street?
> Come to the Capitol.

Eighteen lines later we have

CÆSAR.   Are we all ready? what is now amiss
          That Cæsar and his Senate must redress?
METELLUS. Most high, most mighty, and most puissant
          Cæsar,
          Metellus Cimber throws before thy seat
          An humble heart—

Nothing more complicated has occurred than Cæsar and the Senators taking their places, while the crowd disperses and the

---

[19] I write this very much under correction. But I believe that only experiment will tell us what could and could not be made effective upon the inner and upper stages at the Globe.

conspirators regroup themselves, so that the "state" becomes the center of attraction—and we are in the Senate House. Later, Cæsar must fall and lie dead in a most conspicuous position upon the main stage; still later provision must be made—as it is—for removing the body.

For the following scene the traverse is closed and the upper stage is used for the pulpit. Moreover, the dialogue tells us, to a second or so, the time it takes to ascend and come down.

The first scene of Act IV might, but need not, be played in relation to the inner stage.[20] The second and third scenes, which are not divided in the Folio—which are indeed conspicuously left undivided there—present us with another significant instance of space-freedom, and of Shakespeare's ready use of the conventions which belong to it.[21] We have

> *Enter Brutus, Lucilius and the Army.* . . .

The editors cannot leave this alone. "*The Army*" becomes "*and soldiers.*"[22] This falsifies Shakespeare's intention. By "*the Army*"

---

[20] I think that scenes were more often played "in relation to" the inner stage than consistently within its boundaries; that is to say, the actors, having gained the effect of a discovery, would be apt to advance upon the main stage, where their movements would be less cramped, where they would be in closer touch with the audience and certainly in a better position to hold an unruly audience. I see this happening in the scene in Brutus' garden, and possibly in this scene. There are signs of such a treatment, too, of the scene in Brutus' tent. When he asks Lucius, "Where is thy instrument?" "Here in the tent" is the answer, not a simple "I have it here." When he calls in Varro and Claudius, he says, "I pray you, sirs, lie in my tent and sleep." It sounds very much like people upon the main stage indicating the inner stage with a gesture. Certain things, the study of the map, the playing of the lute, the reading by the taper's light, show, of course, the use of furniture. This would probably be set and left upon the inner stage, though it would be advantageous to have it placed as near the traverse-line as possible, and actors, using it, would be constantly passing the line. And, speaking generally, one need not suppose that the Elizabethan actor ever saw the division between inner stage and main stage as a fixed boundary, nor that the Elizabethan audience had cultivated such a sense of locality that they questioned its crossing and recrossing or even asked themselves at certain ambiguous moments where exactly the characters were meant to be. The main effect and its dramatic purpose were reckoned with; whatever assisted this was allowed.

[21] The play in the Folio (and there are no Quartos) is one of those which start bravely with *Actus Primus, Scæna Prima* and then pay no further attention to scene-division at all. I refer in my enumeration of scenes to the current modern editions, which are, however, in this particular most misleading to the student of the Elizabethan stage and of Shakespeare the dramatist.

[22] Capel did no worse than change it to "*Forces.*"

406 Prefaces to Shakespeare

he does not mean a few casual soldiers, he means the integral group of followers, in some uniform possibly, and with banner, drum and trumpet, which in Elizabethan stage convention personified and symbolized an army entire. Later, after a *Low march within* comes

Enter Cassius and his Powers.

And much the same thing is meant. The effect to be gained is of the spaciousness and order of armies in the field in contrast with that chaos of the market place; and it is as important as an explanatory scene would be.

And what really occurs where modern editors mark a change of scene?

> BRUTUS. Let us not wrangle: bid them move away;
> Then in my tent, Cassius, enlarge your griefs,
> And I will give you audience.
> CASSIUS. Pindarus,
> Bid our commanders lead their charges off
> A little from this ground.
> BRUTUS. Lucius, do you the like; and let no man
> Come to our tent till we have done our conference.
> *Exeunt. Manet Brutus and Cassius.*

Then, without more ado, with no slackening of tension nor waste of this excellently ominous preparation, the intimate wrangle begins. The stagecraft is plain enough. The symbolized armies, with their banners and drums, go off; and either the traverse is now drawn, disclosing the tent furniture, in which case Brutus and Cassius have but to place themselves in relation to it for the scene to be effectively changed; or it is as possible that the traverse has been open from the beginning and that the removal of the "armies" and the reorientation of the chief actors were felt to be change enough. This would repeat the mechanics of the Senate House scene (but it would, of course, forbid an immediately previous use of the inner stage for Antony and Octavius).

We come to Act V, which must be envisaged as a whole. The locality is a battlefield. We have still the symbolical armies. The scenes are divided by alarums. The conventions, in fact, are all accepted. The upper stage is used, for a moment, as the high point of a hill.

> Go, Pindarus, get higher on that hill,

says Cassius, and six lines later the direction reads:

> *Pindarus above.*

The only sign of use of the inner stage is for the scene beginning,

BRUTUS. Come, poor remains of friends, rest on this rock.

Brutus and his friends may need something better to sit upon than the floor. It need be no realistic rock, for a while back when Cassius said,

> This hill is far enough.

there certainly was no hill. On the other hand, if you require some things to sit on it is as easy to make them look like rocks as anything else. The rock or rocks, in that case, would have to be set upon the inner stage. A further indication of its use is the mention of torches, for these would show up better in its comparative shade.

The question of costume raises difficulties. Shakespeare, by convention, dressed his Romans more or less in Elizabethan clothes. To those of the chief characters (for whom this could be afforded) some definitely exotic touches have been added.[23] Nationality, we know, was, at times, pointed by costume. So, possibly, was period; but not, one suspects, with any consistency, not, for a certainty, with any historical accuracy. In this text, at any rate, while there are no direct indications of "Roman habitings," there are a round dozen of references to the Elizabethan. Therefore we cannot simply ignore Shakespeare's convention in favor of our own, which pictures the ancient Roman, bare-headed, clean-shaven and wrapped in a toga.[24] But then, neither can we very easily and altogether ignore our own. The questions of costume and scenery differ in this: whatever the background, if one is kept conscious of it once the play's acting is under way, it is a bad background; but the look of the actors is of

---

[23] See the Henry Peacham illustration to *Titus Andronicus,* reproduced in Chambers' *Shakespearean Gleanings* and elsewhere.

[24] Whether our picture is a true one is beside the point. Quite possibly the Roman Senate assembled did *not* look like the cooling-room of a Turkish bath.

constant importance. We are in this dilemma, then. Cæsar, we hear, plucks ope his doublet; the conspirators' hats are plucked about their ears; Brutus walks unbraced and turns down the leaf of a book which he keeps in the pocket of his gown. Do these seem trivial things? Nothing in a play is trivial which bears upon the immediate credibility of the action. The theater is a game of make-believe, and the rules of any game may be varied by use and acceptance, but mere contrariness is tiresome. An actor may point into vacancy and fill it by description, and we shall be at one with him; but to wear a toga, and call it a doublet, will be distracting. And, apart from direct verbal contradictions, there are passages enough whose full effect must remain one with the picture Shakespeare made of them. The boy Lucius asleep over his lute; who ever can have realized that episode in its exact and delicate detail and want to transform and botch it? Yet it must be confessed that a Cæsar in doublet and hose may offend and will undoubtedly distract us.

The difficulty must, I suggest, be met by compromise, in which we can find some positive advantage too. We are not concerned with the accuracy of our own picturing of Rome, but to reconcile two dramatic conventions. It goes without saying that the nearer we can in general come to Shakespeare's point of view the better. But for a particular gain, has not the vulgar modern conception of Rome, nourished on Latin lessons and the classic school of painting, become rather frigid? Are not our noble Romans, flinging their togas gracefully about them, slow-moving, consciously dignified, speaking with studied oratory and all past middle age, rather too like a schoolboy's vision of a congress of headmasters? Compare them with the high-mettled, quick-tongued crew of politicians and fighters that Shakespeare imagines; and if it comes to accuracy, has he not more the right of it than we, even though his Cæsar be dressed in doublet and hose? So let the designer at least provide an escape from this cold classicism, which belongs neither to the true Rome nor to the play he has to interpret. His way can be the way of all compromise. What need each side insist on? The figure of Brutus must not make a modern audience think all the time of Shakespeare himself, but where the gain to Shakespeare that it should? On the other hand, whatever has been woven, even casually, into the fabric of the play, we must somehow manage to respect. If we change, we must not falsify.

The methods of the Masque and the way of Renaissance painters with classical subjects give us the hint we need. Whether from taste or lack of information, when it came to picturing Greeks and Romans they were for fancy dress; a mixture, as a rule, of helmet, cuirass, trunk hose, stockings and sandals, like nothing that ever was worn, but very wearable and delightful to look at. Women's dresses seem to have been manipulated less easily; perhaps the wearers were not so amenable, or so tolerant of the outrage upon fashion.[25] But even here something of the sort is managed. And something of the sort, with emphasis upon this period or that, according to his judgment, will get our designer out of his difficulty. Shakespeare's own consent, so to speak, to such a compromise can be determined, for the tests are all to hand before ever the play is acted. Upon the tacit consent of an audience one can only speculate. But the problem with an audience in this as in other things is less to satisfy their opinion, if they have one, than to release them from its burden for the fuller, the unself-conscious, enjoyment of the play. *Julius Cæsar!* They may come expecting the familiarized figures set against some popular picture-book background of Rome. For good reasons given they cannot have this. The designer must over-reach them. He must appeal, that is to say, past expectation and opinion, to their readiness to be pleased and convinced; and there are no rules by which that can be forecast. But this much law can be laid down. He must first be sure that his work will fuse with Shakespeare's. What Shakespeare's purposes will not accept, he must reject. For the rest, he may be bold or cautious as it suits him. He had better be simple. If he can so picture the play to himself that nothing in the picture raises any thought but of the play, he will probably not go far wrong.

The Music

ONLY one difficulty presents itself; we are given no text for the *Music and a Song* of Act IV, Scene iii. Custom prescribes the use of

---

[25] Women appeared in the Masques, though not in the publicly given plays.

Orpheus with his lute made trees. . . .

from *Henry VIII*, and this may well be allowed. Mr. Richmond
Noble in his *Shakespeare's Use of Song* suggests that the stage
direction in the Folio may be a later interpolation and that no
song is called for, only the playing of an air. This he would
presumably justify by Brutus'

> Canst thou hold up thy heavy eyes awhile,
> And touch thy instrument a strain or two?

But a song would be more usual, a lute solo not very audible in a
public theater, and the evidence of the Folio is not negligible.[26]
This apart, we have only to give careful attention to the sennets,
flourishes, drums, and marches, alarums, low alarums and
retreats, which find place throughout the play, for they have each
a particular purpose.

A Stumbling Block in the Text

THE text, as the first Folio gives it us, is an exceptionally clean
one and I do not examine its few minor difficulties here. There is,
however, one serious stumbling block in Act IV. What are we to
make of the duplicate revelation of Portia's death? The question
has, of course, been argued high and low and round about, and
weighty opinion will be found set out in the Furness Variorum.
The weightier the worse, one is driven to complain. For surely
it is clear that a mere corruption of text is involved, not the
degeneracy of Brutus' character. Shakespeare may have fumbled
a little at this point. But that his final intention was to give us a
Brutus wantonly "showing off" to Messala or indulging at this
moment in a supersubtle defense of his grief, I would take leave
to dispute against the weightiest opinion in the world. One must,
however, suggest some explanation; and here is mine. It is not
provably correct, but I suggest that corrections of text are not
provable. The vagaries of a playwright's mind may be guessed

---

26 Mr. Richmond Noble also says that he has recommended the use of "Weep
ye no more, sad fountains," from Dowland's *Third Book of Airs*. It is difficult
not to recommend such an entirely beautiful song when any opportunity occurs.
But the words of "Orpheus with his lute" are very appropriate; they could,
indeed, be made a pertinent enough illustration of Shakespeare's use of song.

at, they can never be brought within the four corners of a system and so tested.

My guess is that Shakespeare originally wrote this, or something like it:

> BRUTUS. Lucius, a bowl of wine.
> CASSIUS. I did not think you could have been so angry.[27]
>
> *Enter boy with wine, and tapers.*
>
> BRUTUS. In this I bury all unkindness, Cassius. . . .

And so on as the text now stands, omitting, however, both

> CASSIUS. Portia, art thou gone?
> BRUTUS. No more, I pray you.

and (possibly)

> CASSIUS. Cicero one?
> MESSALA. Cicero is dead, and by that order of proscription.

These have something the air of additions, designed to keep Cassius active in the scene; and the first, of course, involves his knowledge of Portia's death. By this text Brutus first hears the news from Messala, and he exhibits a correct stoicism.[28] Then Shakespeare found that this made his hero not so much stoical as wooden, so he threw the disclosure back into closer conjunction with the quarrel and made it an immediate, and sharply contrasted, sequel to the eccentric-comic interruption by the poet. The passage here has all the air of a thing done at a breath, and by a man who had taken a fresh breath for it too. Whether or no thereafter he cut Messala's disclosure I do not feel positive.[29] He may have thought there was now a double effect to be gained (the original one had not been perhaps so bad, it had only not been good enough); and, in performance, there is an arbitrary sort of effect in the passage as it stands. It is quite likely that, patching at the thing, he did not see to what subtle reflections upon Brutus' character the new combination would give rise (so seldom apparently did he consider the troubles of his future editors!). I

---

[27] This line of Cassius might be a later addition.
[28] Cassius' "I have as much of this in art as you" does not tell against this, for "art" does not of course mean anything like "artfulness."
[29] I now feel positive that he did (1945).

hope that he made the cut. I think on the whole that he did. I am sure that he should have done; and I recommend the producer of today to make it, and by no means to involve his Brutus in that incidental lie, nor his character in the even more objectionable subtleties of an escape from it.

Love's Labour's Lost

Here is a fashionable play; now, by three hundred years, out of fashion. Nor did it ever, one supposes, make a very wide appeal. It abounds in jokes for the elect. Were you not numbered among them you laughed, for safety, in the likeliest places. A year or two later the elect themselves might be hard put to it to remember what the joke was.

The Producer's Problem

Were this all one could say of *Love's Labour's Lost*, the question of its staging today—with which we are first and last concerned—would be quickly answered, and Lose No Labour here be the soundest advice. For spontaneous enjoyment is the life of the theater. If a performance must be accompanied by a lecture, if, for instance, when Holofernes is at the point of

> Bone, bone for benè: Priscian a little scratched. 'Twill serve.

we need his modern exemplar in cap and gown, standing on one side of the proscenium, to interrupt with "One moment, please! The allusion here, if you wish to appreciate its humor, is to . . ."; or if he must warn us, "In the next scene, ladies and gentlemen, you will notice a reference to the charge-house on the top of the mountain. This is thought by the best authorities to denote . . ." not much fun will survive. For a glossary in the program something might be said, even for a preliminary lecture. No; this last, one fears, would leave the actors with too hard a task turning classroom back to theater. Half-digested information lies a little heavily on one's sense of humor.

It is true that with no play three hundred years old can we press our "spontaneous" too hard. For the full appreciation of anything in Shakespeare some knowledge is asked of its why and wherefore. Hamlet and Falstaff however, Rosalind and Imogen, are compact of qualities which fashion cannot change; the barriers of dramatic convention, strange habits, tricks of speech are of small enough account with them. But what is back of these word-gymnastics of Rosaline and Berowne, Holofernes' jargon, Armado's antics? The play is a satire, a comedy of affectations. The gymnastics, the jargon and the antics are the fun. Yet a play hardly lives by such brilliancies alone. While the humor of them is fresh and holds our attention, actors may lend it a semblance of life; for there at least *they* are, alive in their kind! No play, certainly, can count on survival if it strikes no deeper root nor bears more perennial flowers. If its topical brilliance were all, Shakespeare's name tagged to this one would keep it a place on the scholar's dissecting table; in the theater *Love's Labour's Lost* would be dead, past all question. But there is life in it. The satire beside, Shakespeare the poet had his fling. It abounds in beauties of fancy and phrase, as beautiful today as ever. We find in it Shakespeare the dramatist learning his art. To students the most interesting thing about the play is the evidence of this; of the trial and error, his discovery of fruitful soil and fruitless. The producer, pledged to present an audience with a complete something, cannot, of course, be content with promise and experiment. Measuring this early Shakespeare by the later, we may as well own there is not much more. But the root of the matter is already in him; he is the dramatist born, and all, or nearly all, is at least instinct with dramatic life. It is oftenest his calculations and his cleverness that betray him.

For satire and no more is too apt to prove dramatically fruitless. A play's values are human values, and a playwright's first task is to give his creatures being. Imaginative love for them may help him to; even hate may; but a mocking detachment cannot. If he is to shoot at their follies he must yet build up the target first; and if it is not a convincing one there will be little credit in the shooting. He cannot, of course, in a play, take direct aim himself, unless he use the method of the Moralities or its like. There is the less direct method of twisting a set of familiar heroic figures awry.

Shakespeare made this experiment, not too successfully, in *Troilus and Cressida*. But his obvious plan will be to turn one or more of his creatures satirists themselves, and under their cover plant his own shafts. Even so, he must give the victims their chance, or the play will be lopsided and come tumbling down.

The Shakespeare who sets out to write *Love's Labour's Lost* is a very clever young man, a wit, a sonneteer. He is "in the movement." He flatters his admirers by excelling in the things they admire; he will flatter his rivals hardly less by this attention he means to pay them. But your clever young man is usually more than a little impressed by the things he mocks at; he mocks at them in self-defense, it may be, lest they impress him too much. Mockery is apt, indeed, to capitulate to the thing mocked, to be absorbed by it. And these academic follies of Navarre, the fantastic folly of Armado, the pedantic folly of schoolmaster and parson—sometimes the satire is so fine that the folly seems the clever young man's own. Yet this weakness of the would-be satirist is the budding dramatist's strength. Shakespeare cannot resist his creatures; he never quite learned to. He cannot make mere targets of them. He cannot resist his own genius, poetic or dramatic; all through the play we find the leaven of it working.

He has not written ten lines before the poet in him breaks bounds. Is this the voice of that frigid wiseacre Navarre; does this suggest the "little academe"?

> Therefore, brave conquerors—for so you are,
> That war against your own affections
> And the huge army of the world's desires . . .

But the clever young man recollects himself; and here, soon enough, is the sort of thing he has set out to write.

KING.	How well he's read, to reason against reading!
DUMAIN.	Proceeded well, to stop all good proceeding!
LONGAVILLE.	He weeds the corn, and still lets grow the weeding.
BEROWNE.	The spring is near, when green geese are a-breeding.
DUMAIN.	How follows that?
BEROWNE.	Fit in his place and time.
DUMAIN.	In reason nothing.
BEROWNE.	Something then in rhyme.

Pretty tricksy stuff! Well enough done to show that he quite enjoyed doing it, but the sort of thing that almost anyone could learn to do. No signpost on the road to *Hamlet*, certainly.

But mark the dramatist in his provision at the outset of the conflict and balance that every play needs, in the setting of Berowne against his companions, one man's common sense against the crowding affectations (a sporting conflict), an ounce of reality for counterweight to a ton of shams (an instructive balance). Here also, for the moralist-critic, is the play's moral issue defined at the outset; but let us not suppose Shakespeare to have been oppressed by this. Despite his present-day idolaters he was probably not high-purposed from his cradle; moreover, he is likely to have gained most of his knowledge of life by writing plays about it. That is not a provocative paradox, but a key to the mind and method of the artist. Time and again Shakespeare tells us that he sees the world as a stage. He would not think that a belittling comparison; he takes his art too seriously. Not portentously, but as simply seriously as any man will take his purpose in life when he is lucky enough to be sure of it. We all need some center of experience to argue from, if the world beyond our experience is to have any meaning for us. The artist transforms and multiplies experience by imagination, and may even come to think that what is true of his art will be true of the world it mirrors. This sounds absurd. But life does seem to be governed by surprisingly simple laws; and human beings, wherever and whatever they may be, do not greatly differ in essentials. That is the working hypothesis upon which art and religion, with imaginative genius to vitalize them, proceed. And let it be said of the theater that a very short time in it will teach one how little fine clothes and fine manners may amount to. The theater was for Shakespeare a laboratory where he worked—if but in a mimic sense—with human material. His method, his means to enlightenment, was to take a story and put the worth of it, its truth to nature, to the test of personal expression. The story might suffer; if it was not true to nature, it generally would. But Shakespeare was, on the whole, a most unconscientious story-teller, except when history bound him. Sometimes he would make a sacrifice to symmetry, as when, in *Measure for Measure*, he marries Isabella to the Duke; but he may have felt this to be poetic justice upon such a morally consistent lady. The story may be burked, neglected or finished off anyhow, as in *Much Ado About Nothing*, *Twelfth Night* and *As You Like It*. It may hang at the heels of the chief character, as in *Hamlet*. What men are, in fact, comes to concern him far more than what they do. Already in this pretty play of *Love's Labour's Lost* it instinctively concerns him, though not even doing but mere clever talk is his ostensible concern. And when he passes to the giant theme of *King Lear*, to the sweep of historic vision that is in *Antony and Cleopatra*, stretching his medium of expression till it seems to crack and break, he concerns himself, even then, with little which cannot be rendered into human passion, human pity—which cannot, in fact, be put to this laboratory test. He—literally—has no use for theories and abstract ideas. He is neither philosopher nor moralist, except as he must seem to be making his creatures one or the other. He is a playwright; he projects character in action, and with the truth of the one to the other his power and responsibility end. If this is the playwright's limitation, it is also his strength; for to this test of human response—not mimic, truly, but real; yet the mimic but reflects the real—all philosophy and morality must finally be put.

In this earliest essay, then, we may divine the dramatist to be; and we find dramatist putting wit and poet to the proof. Shakespeare will have set out to do his best by his creatures one and all; but while Berowne grows under his hand into a figure, finally, of some dramatic stature, while the Princess, simple, straightforward, shrewd, is made flesh and blood, in the speaking of seven lines, Navarre, though a natural focus of attention and discussing himself unsparingly, remains a bundle of phrases, and Dumain and Longaville have about the substance of echoes. Of the humbler folk; Costard for three-quarters of the play is the stage Fool, but suddenly, when he comes to the acting of his Worthy, we have:

COSTARD. I Pompey am, Pompey surnam'd the Big—
DUMAIN. The Great.
COSTARD. It is "Great," sir; Pompey surnam'd the Great;
    That oft in field, with targe and shield, did make
      my foe to sweat;
    And travelling along this coast, I here am come
      by chance,

> And lay my arms before the legs of this sweet lass
> of France.
> If your ladyship would say, "Thanks, Pompey,"
> I had done.
> PRINCESS. Great thanks, great Pompey.
> COSTARD. 'Tis not so much worth; but I hope I was perfect:
> I made a little fault in "Great."

And these two last lines have, mysteriously and unexpectedly, given us the man beneath the jester. Then, with another thirty words or so, Costard (and Costard's creator) settles Sir Nathaniel the Curate, till now little but a figure of fun, snugly in our affections.

> There, an't shall please you; a foolish mild man; an honest man, look you, and soon dashed! He is a marvellous good neighbour, in sooth; and a very good bowler: but, for Alisander,—alas, you see how 'tis;—a little o'erparted.

And settles himself there yet more snugly in the doing it! Throughout the play, but especially towards the end, we find such outcroppings of pure dramatic gold.

Drama, as Shakespeare will come to write it, is, first and last, the projection of character in action; and devices for doing this, simple and complex, must make up three-quarters of its artistry. We can watch his early discovery that dialogue is waste matter unless it works to this end; that wit, epigram, sentiment are like paper and sticks in a fireplace, the flaring and crackling counting for nothing if the fire itself won't light, if these creatures in whose mouths the wit is sounded won't "come alive." To the last he kept his youthful delight in a pun; and he would write an occasional passage of word-music with a minimum of meaning to it (but of maximum emotional value, it will be found, to the character that has to speak it). His development of verse to dramatic use is a study in itself. He never ceased to develop it, but for a while the dramatist had a hard time with the lyric poet. The early plays abound, besides, in elaborate embroidery of language done for its own sake. This was a fashionable literary exercise and Shakespeare was an adept at it. To many young poets of the time their language was a new-found wonder; its very handling gave them pleasure. The amazing things it could be made to do! He had to discover that they were not much to his purpose; but it is not easy to stop doing what you do so well. Yet even in this play we may note the difference between the Berowne of

> Light seeking light doth light of light beguile;
> So ere you find where light in darkness lies
> Your light grows dark by losing of your eyes!

and of the soliloquy beginning

> And I forsooth in love . . .[1]

Turn also from one of the many sets of wit to Katharine's haunting answer when Rosaline twits her with rebellion against Cupid:

ROSALINE.   You'll ne'er be friends with him: he kill'd your
             sister.
KATHARINE.   He made her melancholy, sad, and heavy;
             And so she died: had she been light, like you,
             Of such a merry, nimble, stirring spirit,
             She might have been a grandam ere she died;
             And so may you, for a light heart lives long.

Compare it with the set of wit that follows:

ROSALINE.   What's your dark meaning, mouse, of this light
             word?
KATHARINE.   A light condition in a beauty dark.
ROSALINE.   We need more light to find your meaning out.
KATHARINE.   You'll mar the light, by taking it in snuff;
             Therefore I'll darkly end the argument.

But Rosaline won't let her, and they manage to get five more rather spicier exchanges. It is all very charming; the mere sound is charming, and a "set of wit" describes it well. Get a knowledge of the game and it may be as attractive to watch for a little as are a few sets of tennis. But pages on pages of such smart repartee will not tell us as much of the speakers as those few simple lines of Katharine's tell us—of herself and her love of her sister, and of Rosaline too.

The play sets out, as we said, to be a flattering satire upon such humors, and the playwright must set up before he pulls down,

---

[1] Which, says Dr. Dover Wilson, belongs to the play's revising. But this does not invalidate my point; rather the contrary.

break before he satirizes; and the two processes do, doubtless, get mixed. Can we detect a Shakespeare impatient, for a moment, with his pleasant task? He has punned and joked his best.

> BEROWNE. White-handed mistress, one sweet word with thee.
> PRINCESS. Honey, and milk and sugar; there is three.
> BEROWNE. Nay then, two treys, an if you grow so nice,
>   Metheglin, wort and malmsey:—well run, dice!

Nor will he neglect the ever-satisfying humors of cuckoldry.

> KATHARINE.   Veal, quoth the Dutchman:—is not veal a
>   calf?
> LONGAVILLE. A calf, fair lady?
> KATHARINE.   No, a fair lord calf.
> LONGAVILLE. Let's part the word.
> KATHARINE.   No, I'll not be your half;
>   Take all and wean it; it may prove an ox.
> LONGAVILLE. Look, how you butt yourself in these sharp
>   mocks!
>   Will you give horns, chaste lady? do not so.
> KATHARINE.   Then die a calf, before your horns do grow.

It amused him, no doubt, as it amused his audience; it is just too well done to have been done mechanically. But when, of a sudden, the Princess breaks out with

> Are these the breed of wits so wondered at?

may we not hear for the moment his voice sounding through hers? For it is a barren business finally, and his fecund spirit could not long be subdued to it. With but little violence we could twist the play into a parable of his own dramatic progress. Even as Berowne at its end forswears

> Taffeta phrases, silken terms precise,
> Three-piled hyperboles, spruce affectation,
> Figures pedantical . . .

so might Shakespeare be swearing to pass from them himself on towards the prose of *As You Like It* and the strong verse of *Julius Cæsar*. A notion not to be taken too seriously, perhaps. But a few years hence he is to let Hamlet record a taste for plays set down with as much modesty as cunning, with

> no sallets in the lines to make the matter savoury, nor no matter

in the phrase that might indict the author of affectation; but . . .
an honest method, as wholesome as sweet and by very much more
handsome than fine.

And certainly there are signs that, whether he knew it or not, the
leaven was already working beneath this bright wit, this delight
in words and their rhythm and melody, that was soon to turn a
pretty speechifying Mercutio into the stark man of

> A plague of both your houses!
> They have made worms' meat of me: I have it,
> And soundly too. . . .

and the word-spinning Romeo into that doomed figure of

> It is even so? Then I defy you, stars!

The dramatist was in the making who was to fashion a Falstaff
out of the old pickpurse of Gadshill, who was to pitch on the
preposterous tale of *The Merchant of Venice*, and charge it
(triumphantly, yet all but disastrously) with the passion of
Shylock.[2]

But the producer must consider carefully just what the
carrying-power of this embryonic drama is, and how he can effectively interpret to a modern audience the larger rest of the play.
What life can his actors give to this fribble of talk and nice
fantasy of behavior? As satire it means nothing to us now. Where,
then, are the prototypes of these cavaliers and ladies—of Armado
and Holofernes, Moth and Nathaniel the Curate? We can at best
cultivate an historical sense of them. There remains the verse,
and the pretty moving picture of the action. Our spontaneous
enjoyment will hang upon pleasant sounds and sights alone, sense
and purpose apart. Really, it almost amounts to this! Better face
the difficulty at its worst. Is there any surmounting it?

The Method of the Acting

IF only the last act were in question we should not need, I think,
to qualify our Yes; for this is throughout as much Masque as

---

[2] He pitched, we may say, upon two preposterous tales, and redeemed the
second by the romantic beauty of Portia.

play, it is meant to charm us as much by sight and sound as by story and character. To take one passage:

ROSALINE. What would these strangers? Know their minds, Boyet.
           If they do speak our language, 'tis our will
           That some plain man recount their purposes:
           Know what they would.
BOYET.   What would you with the princess?
BIRON.   Nothing but peace and gentle visitation.
ROSALINE. What would they, say they?
BOYET.   Nothing but peace and gentle visitation.
ROSALINE. Why, that they have, and bid them so be gone.
BOYET.   She says, you have it, and you may be gone.
KING.   Say to her we have measured many miles
           To tread a measure with you on the grass.
BOYET.   They say that they have measured many a mile
           To tread a measure with you on this grass.
ROSALINE. It is not so. Ask them how many inches
           Is in one mile: if they have measured many,
           The measure then of one is easily told.
BOYET.   If to come hither you have measured miles,
           And many miles, the princess bids you tell
           How many inches do fill up one mile.
BEROWNE.   Tell her we measure them by weary steps.
BOYET.   She hears herself.

The action is implicit. Boyet must move, to the rhythm of the verse, between one group and the other. He bids fair to tread out a mile himself if the game last much longer. But the two groups draw together after this, and then break into couples. In a moment the music starts. Instead of dancing, however, we have a dance of dialogue. The couples circle the stage to the sound of the music, speaking their lines as they pass through the arc the audience commands. Finally, Boyet, who can have held his place in the center, steps forward as chorus; and for comment, full to the audience:

          The tongues of mocking wenches are as keen
          As is the razor's edge invisible,
          Cutting a smaller hair than may be seen;
          Above the sense of sense; so sensible
          Seemeth their conference; their conceits have wings
          Fleeter than arrows, wind, thought, swifter things.

The music stops. Four lines more, and the scene is over.

Now this has no dramatic value, properly so-called. It hardly furthers such plot as the play has; unless to make a tangle to be disentangled a scene later without more consequence can be called the furthering of a plot. It does not develop character. The dialogue is mere mischief. There is, of course, the satire; its edge is blunted by time. But if the music is clear and fine, as Elizabethan music was, if the costumes strike their note of fantastic beauty, if, above all, the speech and movements of the actors are fine and rhythmical too, then this quaint medley of Masque and play can still be made delightful. But it asks for style in the acting. The whole play, first and last, demands style. A vexingly indefinable thing, a hackneyed abracadabra of a word! One should apologize for bringing it into such a practical discussion as this pretends to be. Nor will the play as a whole, perhaps, be so entirely susceptible to its magic. But the theater must deal in magic sometimes.

The conjecture that *Love's Labour's Lost* was first written for the delectation of a coterie of magnificent young men has been capped by the conjecture that some of them may have acted in it at the time. As custodians of the culture of the age, sponsors to this reborn mirroring art of the drama, they might well have recognized that they, in their own persons, apparel and conversation, mirrored and witnessed to that culture supremely. And they might, just for once, have condescended! They would have been cast, of course, for Navarre, Berowne, Dumain and Longaville. Some senior-junior might have been found to fit Boyet, and someone who would modestly prefer himself to Monsieur Marcade. Whether there is much historical likelihood in the suggestion I do not know. If so, the other parts would be played, we may suppose, by professionals. There are the Masque and the antic (the anti-Masque) in the last act; and we know that in the great Court shows the lords and ladies did the graceful dancing and left the grotesque to trained tumblers and dancers. One would like to complete the picture by imagining the Princess and her ladies played by some of those Maids of Honor, who used on occasion to "friske and hey about." Would not that Mistress Fitton who— most historically—tucked up her skirts and, cloaked like a man, marched out of Whitehall to meet her lover, have been ready for once to play the boy and act the woman? It could further be argued that the dialogue for Navarre and his lords is of just such stuff as those young bloods of culture delighted to try their wits and tongues at; and that there is not much more in it, nothing emotional (except for Berowne; and his most emotional outburst is counted a later addition, when the play was perhaps being revised for the public stage), no impersonation, nothing that demands the professional actor with his greater comic or rhetorical force. Navarre and his lords are, in modern stage slang, "walking gentlemen"; but they need to walk magnificently and to talk with a fine assurance. The historical question is not pertinent to our present discussion, but these implications of it are. Whoever acted the play, it must have been in these respects exquisitely done, or it could not have endured its two hours' traffic, though its every joke made a topical hit. Happy-go-lucky, with the hope of a few guffaws for punctuation, could never have been a method for this sort of thing. The audience, too, must have been attuned to its fantasies, to its exquisite passions. How passionate the Elizabethans were! They were capable—those that were articulate and responsive at all—of intellectual passion, as Englishmen have hardly been since. And when poetry and rhetoric display it in the charged atmosphere of the theater, the effect—even the distant echo of it—is intense. Navarre and his

> little academe,
> Still and contemplative in living art.

are oath-bound fanatics; Berowne's gibing is but at the futility and hypocrisy of their professions.

> Warble, child: make passionate my sense of hearing.

says Armado, who is their caricature. Holofernes, that passionate latinist, Sir Nathaniel ridiculously emulating him, little Moth, with his piping and strutting, an incarnate mockery of them all, Costard reflecting their features in grimaces, their fine phrases in nonsense, the most reverberate things sounding hollow under the thwack of his bauble—all these, then, in accent and motion must be keyed to a sort of ecstasy, to a strange surpassing of this modern workaday world, if the play is to be anything at all but a sonata thumped out on a dumb piano, a picture painted by the color-blind. A hard task for the actor; doubly hard, in that he must key up his audience too. For by time and subject it is all three hundred years' strange to us. We need an interpretation of absolute value; and that comes near to being a contradiction in terms. We must have a beauty of speech that will leave us a little indifferent to the sense of the thing spoken. Navarre and his friends and their ladies must show such distinction and grace that we ask no more pleasure in their company than that. Armado and the rest must command us by the very skill with which they remake mankind. It must indeed all be (to quote Berowne), if it is to exist at all,

> as the style shall give us cause to climb in the merriness.

The Staging, Costume and Casting

THE play will profit little by any departure from Shakespeare's own staging; nor is this, in its simplicity, hard to deduce. A designer may shift the period of costume fifty years or so back— or forward, for that matter—if his taste dictate, and no great harm done. A certain grace may be added to Navarre and his friends by dressing them French fashion, or Italian. The Englishman was not famous for his taste in dress; though, if Portia may be trusted, he only made matters worse when he picked up notions abroad, his doublet in Italy, his round hose in France, his bonnet in Germany and his behavior everywhere. But these scrupulous young men would be purists in tailoring too. And a comedy of affectations, of nice phrases, asks that its characters should be ex-pressive to their boot-toes, significant in the very curl of a feather. None of the others are hard to picture. Shakespeare sets Armado before us clearly, the refined traveler from tawny Spain, dignified and mock-melancholy, carrying his rapier as might a conqueror of kingdoms, though for "remuneration" to his messengers he cannot exceed three farthings, and must go shirtless, woolward for penance; he is black-suited, of course. Figure of fun as he is, though, his pride is not pinchbeck, nor must he look merely ridiculous. He sponges on no one, and hides his poverty all he can. When Costard infamonizes him among potentates—and the potentates, we may be sure, die with laughing—Shakespeare gives him great dignity in humiliation. We can picture Moth, that well-educated infant. Navarre, we may suppose, has made him page to the tall angular Spaniard for the fun of the contrast in the looks of them. Moth knows this well enough, be sure; and just how to make the best of his own share in the composition. He should not dress like Armado, that would coarsen the joke. He might still be wearing the King's livery. So might Costard, who makes a third in this conjunction, and has a flavor of Sancho Panza about him, even as Armado every now and then sets one thinking of that greater Don, yet in the womb of imagination. To complete this group we have the harsh, drab aspect of Holofernes; Sir Nathaniel, sober-suited but well-liking; and Dull, who is dull of countenance and clothing too. These will stand in somber contrast to the choice-garmented Court and the rainbow beauty of the Princess and her ladies; till, for their show of the Nine Worthies, they too burst into flower, and into most wondrous and gaudy flowering.

The pictorial values in the pageantry of this last scene have their dramatic value too. The Russian maskings have been laid aside, cumbrously fantastic things, convenient cloakings. Yesterday Navarre and his friends were recluse philosophers; splendid even so, no doubt, but with a pallid splendor. Today they are in love and glowingly appareled, in which symbolism their ladies can match them; and against this delicately blended coloring the village pageant tells crude and loud. Into the midst there suddenly steps Marcade, in black from head to foot. He hardly needs to speak.

> The king your father—
> Dead, for my life!
> Even so, my tale is told.

Berowne takes order.

> Worthies, away! The scene begins to cloud.

And it must seem to cloud; the gay colors fading out, the finery folding about its wearers like wings. But this is not the end, for the end must not be melancholy. The countryfolk have yet to sing and dance their antic; a little crowd of them, dressed to match the

> daisies pied and violets blue,
> And lady-smocks all silver white,
> And cuckoo-buds of yellow hue . . .

The comedy of affectations comes to its full close upon notes of pastoral freshness and simplicity.

As with costume, so with scene; we shall gain nothing, we shall indeed be the worse for surrendering the freedoms of Shakespeare's stage. If we insist on placing and picturing the play's action now definitely here, now exactly there, we shall only be making complex what he has left simple, and find ourselves set to answer riddles which he never asked. The convention of place involved is "about Navarre's Court"; outdoors, it seems to be, nothing more definite. The recluse King and his courtiers may walk there, the Princess may be met there, and no vows be broken; a pricket may be driven near for shooting, a pageant be shown there, a measure trod on the grass. Armado and his page walk there; so do the parson and the schoolmaster, unquestioned. Closer definition than this will be troublesome. The place, in fact, is not a place at all, within the modern scenic meaning. If we needs must paint the picture, it will need to be generalized, atmospheric, symbolic; the problem for a designer is quite a pretty one. Shakespeare, we may notice, hardly makes full practical demand upon the resources of the public theater of the time. No use is made of the inner stage, though this might have served well for the Princess' pavilion. But the line:

Whip to our tents as roes run o'er the land . . .

suggests a further flight. Except for one episode the play asks no more than a bare stage with a couple of openings to it, just such a provision as would be found in that great hall where we may suspect it was first acted. The scene of the philosophers' mutual discovery that they are, all four of them, forsworn and in love calls, however, for three hiding-places, of which one must be aloft; for Bérowne says:

Like a demi-god here sit I in the sky. . . .

But no harder mechanical problem faces the producer.[3]

~~~~~~~~~

[3] And at this point in the play, also at this particular point in the scene, Dr. Dover Wilson scents revision. It may well be that Berowne, like the King and Longaville, originally hid on the stage level. But the stagecraft as we have it is worth examination. When Berowne is aloft Dumain does not come into his view

This convention of place, and a similar freedom with time, encourages a very different method of construction from that proper to the theater we know today, in which place, and even time, are positive and definite things. The dramatist, so set free, thinks more of his characters and less of their surroundings; he can maneuver them, absolved from such conformity, in the varied world of their own humors and passions. Elizabethan dramatic form has greater flexibility than ours; this, with its vehicle of verse (a further, more potent enfranchisement), gives it an emotional range which the modern dramatist must seek to compass by quite other means, by thrift of expression and tension sustained, by many hard economies. The scenic articulation of Shakespeare's later plays is masterly. They may seem loose-jointed, they are really supple and strong, delicate occasionally, never to be hacked at with impunity. *Love's Labour's Lost* is put together very simply; a little clumsily here and there, but alongside simplicity a little clumsiness will pass muster. The main device—an obvious escape from monotony—is the alternating of one group of characters with the other, and of verse scenes with prose. The blending of the two groups at the last is as obvious a conclusion. But in the contriving of the changes we find him

till some minutes after Longaville espies him. This suggests that, if and when the play was revised for a public theater, the tree (of some editors) to be climbed was no more than the gallery at the back of the stage, though a property tree might have been set against it, so that he would appear to be in its branches. Isolated property trees that can be climbed must be very solid affairs indeed. Berowne knows of Longaville's approach, for the King names him. But Longaville's only warning of Dumain's is "Company! Stay!" Then he bolts to hiding, not having himself seen, perhaps, who the intruder is. This is likely, for Shakespeare was from the beginning too good a dramatist to duplicate an effect. It would seem as if the stage stayed apparently empty for a moment, while Berowne said:

All hid, all hid; an old infant play.

Next that Dumain entered, walking slowly down to the accompaniment of

Like a demi-god here sit I in the sky.
And wretched fool's secrets heedfully o'er-eye.

At which point Berowne sees his back:

More sacks to the mill!

Then identifies him:

O heavens, I have my wish!
Dumain transform'd: four woodcocks in a dish!

With all the emphasis on *four*, a climax well worked up!

feeling his way—now missing it, now forcing it, truly—to incidental dramatic advantage. Elasticity of form was always to suit him best; it gave full play to his power of developing character.

We come quickly to a petty crudity of construction, of which a later Shakespeare might not have been guilty; it is amusing to note how conventional editing, covering the fault, makes it worse. Berowne, at the King's behest, departs, with Costard in charge, to seek Armado. But close upon his heels Armado appears. The editors mark a change of scene. Some shift the locality; some are for *Scene ii, the same.* The shift of locality supposes, of course, a regard for its realities which Shakespeare never had; but *Scene ii, the same* suggests an interval of time which is the last thing a swift-moving comedy requires at its outset. Let us see how Shakespeare himself gets over the difficulty he creates. He wants to divide two scenes of comedy by a scene of caricature. He does not think of localities. Berowne and Costard are to leave the stage in search of Armado. Armado is to appear a second later upon that same stage. This is clumsy, it will seem resourceless; it will affect his audience as a false note in music would, or a trip in a dance. Therefore he has Berowne leave the stage first, lets Costard lag behind for a little solitary funniment, and then bolt after Berowne. If the funniment raises a laugh, that breaks contact, as it were, and continuity. The bolting breaks the rhythm of movement: it also brisks up the end of the scene[4] and provides a contrast to the slow, stately entrance of Armado. All of which, together with the curiosity the newcomer to the play arouses, will make us forget the incongruity and will compensate for the clumsiness. Shakespeare, of course, did not need to reason this out. His dramatic instinct served him; so would anyone's. Act the little passage as it is set down and its effect will be automatic. A pity to comment upon it! But these innocencies of drama must be protected against reasoning men; the more innocent they are the more protection they seem to need.

The rest of the play's comings and goings, by which its action

---

[4] One cannot be always defining the sense in which one is using this word; the context, one hopes, will make it plain. Here, of course, it implies a division of dialogue.

is spaced and divided, look likely enough, if we do not insist upon looking at them through distorting spectacles. They have not much other dramatic value. If we want to make main divisions the play can be made to fall well enough into three parts. The Quarto (as usual) runs it through at a stretch; the Folio (as usual) divides it into five acts. If four pauses are to mean four intervals of distraction, this is a large allowance for so slight a play. I should myself prefer the two, which would leave Acts I and II of the Folio as a unit of exposition; Acts III and IV for the uninterrupted working-out of the simple plot; and Act V (which is longer than either of the other two put together) for pageantry. This arrangement happens to exhibit some consistency in time. The first part will mark the occasion—to all intent the day —of the Princess' arrival; the second fills the following morning; the third—Holofernes and Sir Nathaniel having dined presumably at midday—the afternoon following this.[5] But a producer might do well to abide by the Quarto. It would at least compel him to keep the acting brisk. The whole play could be put through in less than two hours.

The Folio's Act IV does show, perhaps, a more complex significance of structure; there is what looks like a deliberate use of the hunting subject as a link between scene and scene. It is as if Shakespeare wanted to lead on—despite the variety and incongruity of the action here—without a marked break to the dominatingly important scene of the sonnet-reading and the four woodcocks in a dish. No disturbing climax, at any rate, intervenes between Berowne's soliloquy (which closes the third act) and this scene, which is the crisis properly evolved from it and the crisis of the play besides. How far this is deliberate, how far instinctive, may be profitless speculation; the producer should undoubtedly observe the effect.[6]

~~~~~~~~~

[5] There are some signs of confusion in Act III, Scene i. Berowne (and possibly at the moment Shakespeare) seems to think the Princess is coming to hunt in the afternoon. As it happens, she comes in the morning, only a minute or two after Berowne himself has started for his ride.

[6] Hence he should not tolerate an interval, even if he allow a pause, after the Folio's Act III.

The scene following the soliloquy, after recording Berowne's distracted spurring of his horse uphill (the audience can easily tell that it was he, if he has just been before them, booted and spurred, whip in hand), goes practically

But the best of the play's craft is lodged in the dialogue; in its twists and turns, in the shifts of time and key, which are stage directions of the clearest sort. We have the brisking of a scene's end by such a piece of cross-fire as

BOYET.	Do you hear, my mad wenches?
MARGARET.	No.
BOYET.	What then, do you see?
ROSALINE.	Ay, our way to be gone.
BOYET.	You are too hard for me.

The author of *Twelfth Night* might have thought this a little crude; but it serves its purpose.

We find another hint to the actors to "work up an exit," as the cant phrase has it, at the end of the scene of preparation for the pageant of the Nine Worthies. Dull, having spoken not a word nor understood one either, yet offers to make one in a dance and to play the tabor. Holofernes—no dancer, we presume!—turns down the offer with contempt. He departs. Armado has taken precedence of him and bidden him follow, so he departs pretty testily. But if Dull, left last, does not show us in a dozen steps what a chance they are missing—Shakespeare did not know the comedian's craft! And Shakespeare, both to his joy and sorrow, did!

Half the dramatic meaning of a passage may lie in the action it suggests.

ARMADO.	Is not lead a metal heavy, dull and slow?
MOTH.	Minime, honest master, or rather, master, no.
ARMADO.	I say lead is slow.

straight to the hunting subject. This is returned to for a finish by means of a shout within (which, I believe, should rather be "shoot" within) and Costard's running out with a halloo. The next scene begins,

Very reverend sport, truly . . .

and ends with

Away! the gentles are at their game. . . .

while Berowne begins the scene following with

The king he is hunting the deer. . . .

Conventionalized time is used, of course, throughout the four scenes. This, moreover, is all we hear of the day's hunting. But it is enough for Shakespeare. A hunt is toward; and no more excuse is needed in an English countryside or an English theater—nor would be in the most categorical of plays—for anyone and everyone to turn up incontinently.

> MOTH.   You are too swift to say so:
> Is that lead slow which is fired from a gun?
> ARMADO. Sweet smoke of rhetoric!
> He reputes me a cannon; and the bullet, that's he;
> I shoot thee at the swain.
> MOTH.   Thump, then, and I flee.

We must picture the long black barrel of a man, slow-gaited even in talk, and the little page, daintily at fence with him, and then off the stage at a bound. The art of it is akin to the artifice of a ballet.

The actor, in fine, must think of the dialogue in terms of music; of the tune and rhythm of it as at one with the sense—sometimes outbidding the sense—in telling him what to do and how to do it, in telling him, indeed, what to *be*. By the sense and sound together of the very first words spoken, Shakespeare is apt to make a character clear to actor and audience both.

> Boy, what sign is it when a man of great spirit grows melancholy?

Who, after the ample measure and high tone of that, could mistake Armado? See, again, his taciturn, self-conscious, amorous condescension and the wench Jaquenetta's mumchance allurement—the comic likeness and contrast of the two—hit out for us in a duet just forty-five words long.

> Maid.
> Man.
> I will visit thee at the lodge.
> That's hereby.
> I know where it is situate.
> Lord, how wise you are!
> I will tell thee wonders.
> With that face?
> I love thee.
> So I heard you say.
> And so, farewell.
> Fair weather after you.

—though, alas, Jaquenetta's country phrases have lost half their flavor for us now.

Shakespeare seems in the main content with the obvious

contrast which the two groups and the shifts from verse to prose and back to verse again afford him. Prose is first brought into the play naturally enough by Costard and Dull and the reading of Armado's letter. The constricted pedantry of Armado's soliloquy ending the first act is followed pat—if no interval is allowed—by the strongest, simplest blank verse we have had yet. This effect is definitely dramatic, as of a sudden breeze of common sense blowing in. Berowne, it is true, has been preaching to us from this pulpit, but all tangled up himself in pun and antithesis. Even with the Princess and the ladies, however, we are back thirty lines later at

> The only soil of his fair virtue's gloss,
> If virtue's gloss will stain with any soil,
> Is a sharp wit match'd with too blunt a will. . . .

at

> The young Dumain, a well-accomplish'd youth,
> Of all that virtue love for virtue lov'd . . .

and the like. Shakespeare's dramatic instinct has prompted the change; his art does not sustain it. He is still too occupied with the actual writing of the play, with himself, in fact, and his own achievements, to spare to his characters that superabundant strength which can let them seem to develop a life of their own. He relapses, therefore, to the thing he has learned how to do; as a man may find every new tune he whistles turning, despite him, into that one old tune he knows. He is still a little tangled—to make the point again—as his own Berowne is, in the affectations he is out to satirize.

But Berowne is the play's truly dynamic figure, and he and Shakespeare struggle out of the toils together. His

> And I forsooth in love . . .

lifts the play into living comedy. It is his comic ecstasy that gives life to the scene planned as the play's crisis, when all four men discover that they are all four in love. The rest of it is mere liveliness of wit and humor, and as arbitrary as a practical joke. The King, Longaville and Dumain are as much frigid phrase-makers in love as ever they were out of it. Shakespeare has still a last act to write, it may be argued. He must not anticipate the promise to woo

In russet yeas and honest kersey noes . . .

But we shall not find him in the flush of his genius missing one chance because another must be waited for and hanging up a character's development. If characters are only to be moved by a series of jerks from one rigidity to the next, they will be more suitably played by marionettes than men. Man as marionette will be amusing for one scene, for a second less so; we shall find as much interest in a third look at him as in a look at any other stage furniture. And when we do reach the last act, Shakespeare, it seems, can make no more of his King, Longaville and Dumain in the end than he could at the beginning. There is no life in the fellows, and that's all about it. This lack of dramatic life, then, from which, let us own, the larger part of the play, and its more purposed part, suffers, its producer must face. It is, five-sixths of it, more decorative exercise than drama. It must therefore be given, as near as may be, what we have called an absolute value in sight and sound.

In yet one more respect the play may suffer by its transference from the Elizabethan stage. The acting of women by boys was in itself a contribution to these absolute values. Further, if we do not allow for the effect of this stringency upon Shakespeare's stage-craft even at its most mature, we shall be constantly at fault. Not that he seems to have felt it a drawback; among all his side-glances at actors and acting we find, I think, no hint that it irks him. It did not impoverish his imagination nor lead, on the whole, to any undue suppression of the womanly side in his plays.[7] It may influence his choice of subject; he does not trouble with domestic drama. Without doubt it determines what he will and will not ask woman characters and boy actors to do. Their love scenes are never embarrassing. They do not nurse babies. They seldom weep. He puts them, in fact, whenever he can, upon terms of equality with men; and women have been critically quick ever since to appreciate the compliment, not well aware, perhaps, how it comes to be paid them. For those conflicts of character which are the very life of drama he appoints weapons that each sex can wield with equal address; insight and humor,

[7] Except in the actual fewness of women's parts, for which the fewness of the boy apprentices allowed may be accountable.

a quick wit and a shrewd tongue—the woman's the shrewder, indeed; in compensation, is it, for the softer advantages, the appealing charm, that his celibate theater denied them? Out of a loss he plucks a gain. Release from such reality drew him to set the relation of his men and women upon the plane of the imagination. It asked from the boy actors a skill, and a quite impersonal beauty of speech and conduct; those absolute qualities, in fact, of which we speak. The Elizabethan theater lacked many refinements, but at least its work was not clogged nor its artistry obscured by the crude appeal of sex, from which the theater today is perhaps not wholly free. No one wants to banish women from the stage; and it might not be an easy thing to do. But actresses may well be asked to remember what their predecessors achieved, and by what means.

In *Love's Labour's Lost*, however, the Princess and the ladies are not, and cannot be made, much more than mouthpieces for wit and good sense. As to love-making, the Princess gives us the cue with

> We have received your letters, full of love;
> Your favours, the ambassadors of love;
> And, in our maiden council, rated them
> At courtship, pleasant jest, and courtesy,
> As bombast, and as lining to the time:
> But more devout than this, in our respects,
> Have we not been; and therefore met your loves
> In their own fashion, like a merriment.

It is all to be gallant, open and aboveboard.

> Saint Cupid, then! and, soldiers, to the field.

They are to be leagued encounters; and no two of the lovers are ever alone. But how few of Shakespeare's love scenes now or later need it embarrass anyone to overhear! In more than one sense he habitually wrote for daylight effect upon an open stage. Passion and tragedy and high romance he has still to deal with; he has still to find out how to write Juliet and Isabella, Desdemona, Cleopatra. But already the problem of Portia and Beatrice is solved, and Rosalind can be heard telling Orlando:

> You shall never take her without her answer unless you take her without her tongue.

The Text, and the Question of Cutting It

THE text presents practical difficulties, and one is fortunate to have Dr. Dover Wilson's fresh work upon it in the new *Cambridge Shakespeare*. A flaw or so in method or result there may be; to set about correcting them with his own tools one would need uncommon skill. But it will be worth while to test his conclusions by their effect—as far as we can divine it—upon the play's staging, for good or ill. This is, in fact, the ultimate test to which many of these bibliographical subtleties must submit.

The pronouncement upon two imperfectly canceled passages in Act IV, Scene iii, and Act V, Scene ii, answers to this test well. Some repetition in the first passage is patent; and, given a blue pencil and told to consider the dramatic upbuilding of the speech, who could make any other cut than that between lines 292 and 315? The textual muddle in the second is as obvious; and if Dr. Dover Wilson's solution of it (though here, certainly, he but follows other editors) needs a stage-manager's support, it can be had for the sake of Berowne's

> Studies my lady? mistress, look on me.

For the dramatic intention is unmistakable. The King and Princess have made their exchanges, important and effective ones. If Berowne's and Rosaline's follow close, the importance of theirs must be lessened, unless some violent contrast is achieved, boisterous and quite out of key. But by the simple device of keeping these two chief characters still and silent while Dumain and Katharine, Margaret and Longaville, say their say—it must not be too long a say, nor important enough to demand our entire attention—we are put on the alert, held in suspense, brought to be wondering whatever will occur when the silence between them is broken. And an actual silence, a pause—no actor could help making one—must occur before

> Studies my lady? . . .

Thereafter, without effort or undue emphasis, or any illiberal self-assertion, Rosaline and Berowne, as they are meant to, top the scene.

This passage surely shows redrafting, and evidence of Shakespeare's more practised hand. But do the alterations run quite on Dr. Dover Wilson's lines? Would Dumain begin, *"But* what to me . . ."* unless a previous speech had begun, *"And* what to me, my love?" It is unlikely that Shakespeare would ever have let the love-affairs even of two less important couples lapse in silence. May not Berowne's

> A twelvemonth! Well, befall what will befall. . . .

originally have followed upon Margaret's

> The liker you; few taller are so young.

And why, here and elsewhere, does Dr. Dover Wilson bring in evidence the possible size of Shakespeare's writing-paper and the number of lines he could write on it? It was a scarcer substance with him, no doubt, than it is with his commentators. To suppose, though, that having taken a piece on which to write a new passage he could not stop till he had filled it. . . ! But Dr. Dover Wilson *cannot* suppose this.

Another point of consequence is the Rosaline-Katharine confusion in Act II, Scene i. The suggested elucidation is best studied in the new *Cambridge Shakespeare* itself. It is as good as a detective story. Really, Scotland Yard should turn sometimes to our scientific bibliographers! Is one graceless to make any question of a verdict reached by such ingenuity? By the practical, dramatic test it stands, in the main. It is only that these nice investigations have the defects of their qualities; they tend to prove too much.

The case for this transference of the masks and the mistaken identity motive from Act II, Scene i, to Act V is, of course, strong upon several grounds. But to conclude from this, as Dr. Dover Wilson does, that Shakespeare, making the alteration, meant to leave the earlier scene practically naked of everything but a dialogue between the King and the Princess, and a little questioning of Boyet by the young men and a little chaff for the young ladies, is to brand him as a very slack craftsman indeed. First, it is well-nigh inconceivable that he can let this scene pass, Rosaline and Berowne both present, and deny them an encounter. (Besides, without the first of the two passages between them, or something in its place, how is the King to read his letter?) The dialogue was originally written for Rosaline to play masked, no doubt. Later, Shakespeare did not care to change it; there was no compelling reason he should. She could just as well hold up her traveling-mask at Berowne's approach to tantalize him and fog him in his patronizing recognition of her. We must remember the space convention of the Elizabethan stage; the distance across it was anything in reason. Cannot we see him stalking the lady? And a mask in those days was a woman's accustomed protection in more senses than one.

The scene's second encounter between the two, however, is redundant in itself, and of no constructional use; it is, indeed, an impediment to the action. Berowne and his fellows would not hang long behind when the King had departed; the Elizabethans appreciated ceremony in the theater and out of it. But the stage, with its doors at the back, allowed for a many-paced exit. The three courtiers could follow with due observance if the questions to Boyet began promptly; hardly otherwise. The redundancy, a certain clumsiness of construction, and, not least, the extreme artificiality of this "set of wit" suggest it as part of an earlier growth, which, for some reason, was not clearly cut away. In its continuance, too, the dialogue shows every sign of having been hacked about. For instance,

> Good sir, be not offended:
> She is an heir of Falconbridge.

is halt, if not maimed.

So much, then, for the test of stage effect. But (before we pass on) among Dr. Dover Wilson's own tests, are speech-headings such a safe guide to revision as he makes out? These are not, for the dramatist, a part of his play. Shakespeare, let us say, has a character in his head called Ferdinand, King of Navarre. If he wrote the play containing it at a sitting he might—though it is by no means inevitable—begin with one speech-heading and go on using it till the end. But it is likely enough that having made it "Ferd:" on Monday and spent Tuesday at work upon Armado, on Wednesday he may be putting "King" and on Friday "Nav:" and even by the Monday following be using "King" "Nav:" "Ferd:", whichever comes first from his pen. He does not give a thought—why should he?—to such an entirely irrelevant matter.

It will be the same with stage directions. While he is waiting for a scene to take fire in his mind, he may write with careful elaboration: *Enter the Princess of France with three attending ladies and three lords,* even as a schoolboy hopefully heads his paper with a copperplate "Composition." But when he sits down to it all-fired, *Enter the ladies* is good enough. Then he can get to work.

No doubt there are clues to be picked from these confusions that will not prove loose-ended. But when the critical editor begins, "A natural and reasonable way of explaining . . . ," one's concurrence is apt to be checked, even unfairly, by the over-riding thought that what is reasonable to a critic is not therefore natural to a playwright.

We now come to the question of the permissible cutting of the text for modern performance, and no play in the canon presents greater difficulties. The principle is plain. A producer must take his stand with the first Cambridge editors and Garrick (Garrick! he may well exclaim) and resolve to "lose no drop of the immortal man." Still, no one need let his principles befool him. We need hardly hold sacred all that the printer has left us. The redundant passages in Act IV, Scene iii, and Act V, Scene ii, may go; Shakespeare's final intention is plain as a pikestaff.[8] There are besides a few sentences that are hopelessly corrupt; these we need not make a fuss about. But there are far more than a few that are nowadays almost, if not quite, incomprehensible, that require, at any rate, a professor and a blackboard as first aid. And over these principle and common sense come to loggerheads. For common sense does seem to urge: the average man in an audience will either understand these things or he won't; if he won't, cut them. The problem, however, is not quite so simple as this. If there is life in a play we cannot cut even ounces of flesh from it with impunity. If it is an articulated whole we cannot remove a joint and a sinew or two and not risk laming it. Thirty lines may be thirty lines and no more; but they may be—and they should be—an organic part of a scene.

For instance: Moth and Costard enter to Armado.

---

[8] It is the present redundancy, of course, that we keep.

MOTH.   A wonder, master; here's a Costard broken in a shin.

ARMADO.   Some enigma, some riddle: come,—thy *l'envoy*; begin.

COSTARD.   No egma, no riddle, no *l'envoy*; no salve in the mail, sir. O, sir, plantain, a plain plantain! no *l'envoy*, no *l'envoy*: no salve, sir, but a plantain!

ARMADO.   By virtue, thou enforcest laughter; thy silly thought, my spleen; the heaving of my lungs provokes me to ridiculous smiling: O, pardon me, my stars! Doth the inconsiderate take salve for *l'envoy*, and the word *l'envoy* for a salve?

MOTH.   Do the wise think them other? Is not *l'envoy* a salve?

ARMADO.   No, page: it is an epilogue or discourse, to make plain. Some obscure precedence that hath tofore been sain.

I will example it:
> The fox, the ape, and the humble-bee,
> Were still at odds, being but three.

There's the moral: Now, the *l'envoy*.

MOTH.   I will add the *l'envoy*; say the moral again.

ARMADO.   The fox, the ape, and the humble-bee,
> Were still at odds, being but three.

MOTH.   Until the goose came out of the door,
> And stay'd the odds by adding four.

Now will I begin your moral, and do you follow with my *l'envoy*.
> The fox, the ape, and the humble-bee,
> Were still at odds, being but three:

ARMADO.   Until the goose came out of door,
> Staying the odds by adding four.

MOTH.   A good *l'envoy*, ending in the goose; would you desire more?

COSTARD.   The boy hath sold him a bargain, a goose, that's flat:—
> Sir, your pennyworth is good, an your goose be fat.
> To sell a bargain well is as cunning as fast and loose:
> Let me see a fat *l'envoy*; ay, that's a fat goose.

ARMADO.   Come hither, come hither: How did this argument begin?

MOTH.   By saying that a costard was broken in a shin.
Then call'd you for the *l'envoy*.
COSTARD. True, and I for a plantain; thus came your
          argument in:
          Then the boy's fat *l'envoy*, the goose that you
          bought.
And he ended the market.
ARMADO.   But tell me; how was there a costard broken in
a shin?
MOTH.   I will tell you sensibly.
COSTARD. Thou hast no feeling of it, Moth: I will speak that
l'envoy:
          I, Costard, running out, that was safely within,
          Fell over the threshold, and broke my shin.
ARMADO.   We will talk no more of this matter.

Which last line alone we might expect an audience to appreciate!
What is a producer to do? How much of the stuff can any
modern audience be brought to understand—even to understand,
enjoyment apart? A glossary in the program could give us first
aid towards Moth's not very brilliant joke about Costard and
shin, remind us that talk of a plantain leaf made the Elizabethans
merry, even as a cry for brown paper and vinegar could once
raise a laugh in Victorian farce—and a glossary will be needed
for this very soon. But what can be done to recover such foundered
word-play as

No egma, no riddle, no *l'envoy*, no salve in the mail, sir.

or to give life and sense to Moth's

Is not *l'envoy* a salve?

When we come to

The fox, the ape, and the humble-bee . . .

we can, grown desperate, find Folio authority for a cut. The
new *Cambridge* editors insist that it is an obviously topical joke,
its application long lost; we might get rid of it upon that ground.[9]

⁹ But is this so? I can imagine an American editor three hundred years hence
testing the verse which begins,
          I never saw a purple cow. . . .
for an allusion to President Wilson. Was not Roosevelt called a bull-moose?
But the mere truth is that sixty million people or so once thought that funny in
itself.

But—worse and worse!—we next come to elaborate jesting about a goose and a market.

Should a producer expunge the whole thing and bring Costard on to hear at once of his enfranchisement? This may well be the lesser evil. But one cannot thus eviscerate a scene and expect to see no wound. Here is an effect gained by the resolving of the long Armado-Moth duet into a trio, by rounding off the sententious folly and nimble mockery with the crude humor of the clown. The dialogue passes from prose to rhymed couplets; then becomes gay with jingle, which Costard jollily burlesques in that long lolloping meter. We must think of it all in terms of music, of contrasts in tone and tune, rhythm and breaking of rhythm. There is the value of the picture too, set before us and held for its minute or two; of the egregious dignity of Armado, Moth delicately poised, and Costard square-toed and cunning, not such a fool as he looks. All this has histrionic value, the sheer sense of the dialogue apart. All plays exist, plots and character-schemes beside, as schemes of sound, as shifting pictures, in decoration of thought and phrase, and the less their dependence on plot or conflict of character the more must they depend upon such means to beauty and charm. These "set pieces" may be loosely and easily contrived, so that they still give an illusion of life; and we must never be made overconscious of them, or the charm may vanish, even though the beauty remain. But in this play, as we have seen, much depends on them. We are, indeed, never very far from the formalities of song and dance. The long last act is half Masque and half play; and in song and dance the play ends.

Therefore, it being understood that pretty picture and pleasant sound alone will never suffice, before sentence is passed on a difficult passage it might well be put upon probation. Let the actors see what they can make of it by adroit movement and the nice turning of a phrase. There is danger here. Released from that troublesome obligation to make current sense of his goings-on, the actor too readily turns acrobat; and the audience, come to do their duty by Shakespeare, hardly expect to make much sense of the stuff anyhow. Better cut half the play than act any of it on these terms; but better, then, not act it at all. There are passages, however (though the one we have just quoted is not in its entirety one of them), which do yield something to such treatment. Who, with an ear for the music and rhythm of fine prose, will not take pleasure, for instance, in the very sound of

> ARMADO. Go, tenderness of years! take this key, give enlargement to the swain, bring him festinately hither; I must employ him in a letter to my love.
>
> MOTH. Will you win your love with a French brawl?
>
> ARMADO. How meanest thou? brawling in French?
>
> MOTH. No, my complete master; but to jig off a tune at the tongue's end, canary to it with your feet, humour it with turning up your eyes; and sigh a note and sing a note as if you swallowed love with singing love, sometimes through the nose, as if you snuffed up love by smelling love; with your hat penthouse-like over the shop of your eyes; with your arms crossed on your thin belly-doublet like a rabbit on a spit: or your hands in your pockets, like a man after the old painting; and keep not too long in one tune, but a snip and away. These are complements, these are humours, these betray nice wenches that would be betrayed without these, and make them men of note—do you note me?—that are most affected to these.
>
> ARMADO. How hast thou purchased this experience?
>
> MOTH. By my penny of observation.
>
> ARMADO. But O—but O,—
>
> MOTH. The hobby-horse is forgot.
>
> ARMADO. Call'st thou my love hobby-horse?
>
> MOTH. No, master; the hobby-horse is but a colt—and your love perhaps a hackney. But have you forgot your love?
>
> ARMADO. Almost I had.
>
> MOTH. Negligent student! learn her by heart.
>
> ARMADO. By heart, and in heart, boy.
>
> MOTH. And out of heart, master: all those three I will prove.
>
> ARMADO. What wilt thou prove?
>
> MOTH. A man, if I live: and this—by, in, and without, upon the instant. By heart you love her, because your heart cannot come by her; in heart you love her, because your heart is in love with her; and out of heart you love her, being out of heart that you cannot enjoy her.

It is pure *bravura*; it hangs up the action, it hardly develops character; Shakespeare the full-fledged dramatist would not have written it. We may indeed compare it to an *aria* in an opera. It calls for a comparable execution, an audience should get the same sort of pleasure from it. And if the musical value is not quite as great—well, we mostly miss the words of the *aria* as a rule.

To make a tentative list of the passages with which nothing can be done, of the bits of dead wood, one may call them:

ARMADO.   I love not to be crossed.
MOTH.   He speaks the mere contrary, crosses love not him.

Moth's line at least might come out. The joke can't be conveyed, nor is it worth the conveying.

The dancing horse is dead past resurrection. If a ruthless pencil does away with the lines that lead up to the point and the two that drop away from it, can the most fervid Shakespearean—more royalist than his king—complain?

The reference to the ballad of the King and the Beggar might go too. On the other hand, anyone who would mangle the discourse upon the four complexions, if it were only that he might so deprive us of Armado's

Define, define, well-educated infant.

is a butcher and botcher of texts.

The whole passage between Boyet, the ladies and Costard in Act IV, Scene i, which begins with the now cryptogrammatic pun,

Who is the suitor? who is the suitor?

—if one pronounces it "sewtor" the joke is lost, so it is to a modern audience if one calls it "shooter"—asks at first sight for drastic treatment. Say we surmount this first obstacle, eke out the everlasting jokes about cuckoldry that follow with a wink or two and a nod, we shall still be utterly lost in the tangle of talk—yet more equivocal in every sense—about archery and bowling. Nevertheless, if one is not to truncate the whole scene and end it with the Princess' departure—and this is structural alteration and inadmissible—it may be better to go through with the gibberish, to let it seem so if it must. For again, consider the action, the lively picture; Boyet surrounded by the teasing girls, Costard ecstatic at the encounter! And are we to miss the little singing dance with which Rosaline takes leave? Apart from the charm of it—the girl and the gay old courtier answering and counter-stepping each other—and apart from the value of this little turmoil of rhythmic gaiety before we drop to our first experience of Holofernes and his pedantry, Shakespeare is bringing Rosaline by degrees to her due place of importance in the play, and no item of the process should be omitted.

As to Holofernes and Sir Nathaniel, it is a good part of the fun of them that neither the innocent Dull, nor we, can make out half the time what they are talking about. No need then, after all, to be troubled by

> Priscian a little scratched . . .

or even by the mystery of the charge-house on the top of the mountain. But what can—what ever *can*!—be made of Moth's pleasantries about the five vowels and the horn-book (yet once again a cuckold's horn-book!) in the first scene of the last act? If ever a passage could serve in a competition with a prize given to the set of actors that extracted some legitimate effect from it, this could! Nor is it of any constructive consequence, nor does it add one stroke of character. Why not pass boldly then, from Costard's achievement of

> honorificabilitudinitatibus: thou are easier swallowed than a flap-dragon.

to

> Arts-man, preambulate . . .

and so to the play's business?

But really there is nothing more, save a line or two of obvious indecency easily left out, that the producer need wish to conjure away. There remains but to question one apparent corruption of text, which does obscure the action at an important point, then to point out one or two possible pitfalls in the casting of the parts, and this prefacing, grown longer than the play itself, may end.

The King, that noble gentleman and Armado's very good friend, having set on his butt to provide the entertainment of the Nine Worthies, encourages his guests in the doubtless far better entertainment of making outrageous fun of him. By the standards of the time this may not have seemed to be such very caddish behavior. We recall the practical jokes played by the Duke and Duchess on Don Quixote. Cervantes could have commented, as Shakespeare cannot; but he let the business speak for itself. Still, it is possible that Shakespeare, though flattered, no doubt, by the approval of his own play's very select audience, had his private opinion upon this aspect of their gentility. Certainly, when the final trick is played on Armado, it is he, fantastic fool as he is, who shines out as the best gentleman amongst them, even as Don Quixote shone. The manner of the trick itself, however, is all confused in the text as we have it, and its matter is somewhat obscure. Berowne incites Costard to bring Armado's play-acting to utter grief by rushing on distraught with the sudden news that the wench Jaquenetta is cast away, is two months gone, Armado the culprit. The stage directions that make this clear Dr. Dover Wilson has most justly restored. And as justly he restores to Armado the line that he must speak to give point to the interruption:

> The party is gone.
> Fellow Hector, she *is* gone. . . .

exclaims Costard. But the effect is still incomplete. The first line must surely be a part of Hector the Worthy's speech (this Dr. Dover Wilson does not hold). Where is the comic incongruity of Costard's twist of the phrase otherwise? It is such an obvious trick; neither Costard, nor Shakespeare at this moment, could neglect it. One suspects a pun in "party." It can mean an antagonist, Achilles against Hector. An intermediate line may be missing; it cannot be restored unless someone should discover a colorable original of the pageant. But at least the incident and its business can be rightly outlined in action.

Further, it is surely clear—though to many editors it does not seem to be—that in the accusation poor Armado *is* most scandalously "infamonized." Where would be the joke else? The King and Princess, the courtiers and ladies, must, most of them, know by this time of his ridiculous adoration of this country wench; and we have seen how she treats him. Armado a hypocrite! The whole character is destroyed at a blow. If there were a guilty party, we might rather suspect Costard, who did "confess the wench." But it may all be a joke. Armado, at least, is convinced so, for back he comes before the play's end, quite his magnificently absurd self again. And he, faithful among the faithless, will be a votary still; but to philosophy no longer, to the plough, to rusticity. We can imagine him, though hardly a great success in the furrows behind a team, sitting like Don Quixote beneath a tree—again the comparison is irresistible—and piping to the virginal Jaquenetta. Though, if Moth's estimate of the young lady's character should, after all, be the right one, Shakespeare is a finished ironist already.

As to the casting of the comic parts; only with Costard is it not plain sailing. Holofernes is pendant incarnate, and Sir Nathaniel simple parson. Jaquenetta is a country wench and Dull is the village constable. But Costard, swain though he is,[10] smacks both of Court-jester and stage clown. Shakespeare had often to make use of these chartered comedians. Sometimes, as in *Twelfth Night, As You Like It* and *King Lear*, he can fit them to the play. Sometimes, as there is evidence, they were a sore trial to its integrity. Costard is the conventional figure thinly disguised, and he may quite rightly be played so. In his very first scene, though he is Armado's man brought by the constable for correction, he takes all the jester's liberties with the King.

KING.   Peace!
COSTARD. Be to me and every man that dares not fight.
KING.   No words!
COSTARD. Of other men's secrets, I beseech you.

His attitude towards the Princess is the same. The actor, then, is given a character to assume for the play's consistency's sake; he must keep within it about as much as a low comedian did in Victorian farce or in Edwardian musical comedy. But no more. The play does not need another slow-spoken countryman. For that we have Dull, sparse of words, and heavy of gait. Costard's is a nimble wit; we must feel that for diversion he makes himself out to be more of a fool than he is. And the actor himself must be skillful of speech and light of touch, as good jesters and stage clowns were.

10 And this need imply nothing rustic about him. He is Armado's body-servant merely.

The Music

THE indications of music and of the one dance are plain enough. Moth's "Concolinel" of Act III, Scene i, stands for a song, which no research has yet tracked. How anyone can doubt this it is hard to see. In the earlier scene Moth is asked to sing. There is no point whatever in his here disappointing Armado and the audience too with a comic catch-phrase. And why should Armado's comment upon it be

Sweet air!

Moreover, the stage direction in the Folio definitely says, *A song*. If what Shakespeare wrote or chose cannot be found, the producer must do the next best thing and make such a choice for himself as Shakespeare might have made. Many of the sources from which he picked ballads when he wanted them are open to us. A pity to have to do it, but obviously better than to leave a gap in the scene. The recurrent lightening of the play with lyrics sung or said is a part of its artistic economy.

The dance the blackamoors play, that Rosaline and the ladies will not respond to, may well be a "French brawl." A pity to miss the canarying with the feet; but the music probably lasts, as we have noted—the players in the background—till the finish of Boyet's apostrophe to the ladies' jigging tongues.

For the end we have song and dance both. *Enter all*, say Quarto and Folio too. The play finishes, as a play of merry-making should, with everyone ranged for our last look at them. The simplest sort of a thing will serve best. Pedantry, cleverness, set poses, nice speaking, are all dropped. Armado, the incorrigible, the votary still, will have it, of course, that we are to hear a dialogue by the two learned men. The two learned men are to be found but a moment later dancing a hay with the best. Moth may sing the Spring song and Jaquenetta Winter's. Dull, it turns out, can do marvels on the pipe and tabor. Costard too, no doubt.

In fact, as there is no curtain to descend, no other-world of illusion to hide, the actors are already putting off the characters so lightly worn, and telling us that, after all, it is only a play. No, Armado does not dance. It is as if, the revels over, he stalked forward to speak an epilogue:

The words of Mercury are harsh after the songs of Apollo. . . .

and could get no further. Are they ready to mock him again?
Then he bows to the quality:

You, that way; we, this way.

shepherds his motley flock and stalks after them.

1926

THE HEADBAND USED ON THE TITLE PAGE

AND AT VARIOUS OTHER PLACES IN THIS BOOK

WAS TAKEN FROM THE FIRST FOLIO

OF SHAKESPEARE

PRINTED IN LONDON BY ISAAC JAGGARD

AND ED. BLOUNT, IN 1623

THIS EDITION OF GRANVILLE-BARKER'S

PREFACES TO SHAKESPEARE

HAS BEEN COMPOSED IN 11 POINT GRANJON TYPE

TYPOGRAPHY BY P. J. CONKWRIGHT